Adapting Henry James to the Screen

Gender, Fiction, and Film

Laurence Raw

The Scarecrow Press, Inc.
Lanham, Maryland • Toronto • Oxford
2006

SCARECROW PRESS, INC.

Published in the United States of America
by Scarecrow Press, Inc.
A wholly owned subsidiary of
The Rowman & Littlefield Publishing Group, Inc.
4501 Forbes Boulevard, Suite 200, Lanham, Maryland 20706
www.scarecrowpress.com

PO Box 317
Oxford
OX2 9RU, UK

British Library Cataloguing in Publication Information Available

Library of Congress Cataloging-in-Publication Data

Raw, Laurence.
   Adapting Henry James to the screen : gender, fiction, and film / Laurence Raw.
    p. cm.
   Includes bibliographical references and index.
   ISBN-13: 978-0-8108-5707-0 (pbk. : alk. paper)
   ISBN-10: 0-8108-5707-3 (pbk. : alk. paper)
   1. James, Henry, 1843–1916–Film and video adaptations.   2. Film adaptations–
History and criticism.   I. Title.
   PS2127.F55A65   2007
   813'.4–dc22
                                              2006017710

∞ ™ The paper used in this publication meets the minimum requirements of
American National Standard for Information Sciences—Permanence of
Paper for Printed Library Materials, ANSI/NISO Z39.48-1992.
Manufactured in the United States of America.

~

Contents

Acknowledgments

The inspiration for this book came one afternoon at the Ege Conference in Literature and Cultural Studies in Izmir, Turkey. I would like to thank my two dear friends there, Günseli Sönmez İşçi and Ayşe Lahur Kırtunç, both for giving me the idea for this book and for their continued support since then.

I would like to thank the staffs of the following libraries for their continual support and response to my many queries: the British Film Institute Library, the British Library, the Margaret Herrick Library of the Academy of Motion Picture Sciences, the University of Sussex Library, the Bilkent University Library, Ankara, and the Bapkent University Library.

To the many conference organizers who allowed me to deliver papers that formed the basis for this book, much thanks. Many of the chapters started off as conference papers. In particular, I would like to thank David Kranz and Nancy Mellerski of Dickenson College, Isıl Bas and Aslı Tekinay of Boğaziçi University, Bilge Mutluay, and Meldan Tanrısal. I would also like to thank members of the Literature/Film Association, particularly Thomas Leitch and Don Whaley, who have invited me regularly to their conferences and who have been a consistent source of stimulation; Susan M. Griffin of the *Henry James Review*; and the anonymous readers of the editorial board for their encouraging comments, which helped clarify my thinking on at least two of the chapters. To Elsie Walker and David Johnson of *Literature Film Quarterly* (*LFQ*), much thanks.

My own university department has been a continual source of support, given the length of time it took for this project to come to fruition. I would like to pay special tribute to Özlem Uzundemir, Özkan Cakýrlar, Defne Ersin Tutan, Berkem Gürenci, Pürnur Uçar, and Saniye Cancı, all of whom either listened to some of the material being read or who attended some of my classes on the subject. I would like to give special thanks to Esin Ağaoğlu, our departmental secretary, who has endured my incessant requests with fortitude.

Extracts from my articles "Horrific Henry James: Michael Winner's *The Nightcomers*" (*LFQ* 31, 3 [2001]); "Reconstructing Henry James: *The Heiress*" (*LFQ* 30, 4 [2002]), and "Making Meaning: Publicizing Iain Softley's *The Wings of the Dove* (*LFQ* 32, 3 [2004]), are reprinted with permission of *Literature Film Quarterly* and Salisbury University, Salisbury, Maryland 21001. The chapter on *Somewhere in Time* and *On a Clear Day You Can See Forever* incorporates material originally published in *Interactions* 13, 1 (2004) and is reprinted by permission of the editors and Ege University Press.

The chapters on *The Innocents* and *Washington Square*—"Sexual Release: *The Innocents* (1961)" and "A New Beginning: *Washington Square* (1997)"— are based on material originally appearing in the *Henry James Review*, published by the Johns Hopkins University Press (originally titled "Hollywoodizing Henry James: Jack Clayton's *The Innocents* (1961)" and "Rethinking the Costume Drama: Agnieszka Holland's *Washington Square*" respectively). The chapters on *Daisy Miller*, *The Europeans*, and *The Bostonians* are based on articles originally published in the *Henry James E-Journal*, nos. 3 (2001) and 7 (2005).

I would like to acknowledge the following for permission to reproduce copyrighted material: Samuel French Ltd. for the nonexclusive rights for the British Empire (excluding Canada) for extracts from *Berkeley Square*; the Robert A. Freedman Dramatic Agency, Inc. for the U.S. and Canadian rights for *Berkeley Square*; Elizabeth Way for permission to reproduce extracts from William Archibald's *The Innocents*; Judy Goetz Singer for permission to reproduce extracts from *The Heiress*; Johnson & Alcock Ltd., agents for Michael Hastings, for permission to reprint extracts from the novelization of *The Nightcomers* and the screenplay for *The American*; Paramount Motion Pictures for permission to reproduce material from the press book for *Daisy Miller*; the British Broadcasting Corporation for permission to reproduce material from Jack Pulman's scripts for *The Portrait of a Lady* (1968) and *The Golden Bowl* (1972); Granada Drama and Media for permission to reproduce material from Nick Dear's script for *The Turn of the Screw* (1999); David Rosemont for permission to reproduce material from Hugh Whitemore's script for *The Haunting of Hell House* (1994); Liberation Entertainment for permission to reproduce material from the script of *Presence of Mind* (1999); and Robert Geller of Learning in Focus for permission to reprint material from *The Jolly Corner*. All still photos are reproduced by kind permission of Photofest, Inc.

I would also like to thank Andrew Yoder and the production staff at Scarecrow Press for editing and preparing this book for publication.

Lastly, I would like to pay special tribute to three people. Jim and Anne Welsh, sometime editors of *Literature Film Quarterly*, have not only helped bring this project to fruition, but they have consistently convinced me of the validity of this kind of adaptation studies. But my greatest debt is to my companion, wife, and amanuensis, Meltem, without whom . . .

INTRODUCTION

Why Film Henry James Anyway?

Beyond Formalism

It has become a commonplace of James criticism to claim that his novels are in some ways "unfilmable," and that regardless of their own merits, any adaptations will automatically be inferior to the original text. Neil Sinyard observed in 1986 that "what cannot be duplicated [in an adaptation] is his [James's] style, tone and voice, and what one might call his aesthetic idealism."[1] John Orr, in the introduction to a collection *Film and Fiction* published six years later, claimed that no adaptation can ever hope to recapture "the fluid interchangeability of the point of view which is a feature of the classic [James] novel."[2] In a 1998 article talking specifically about James, Susie Gibson observes that "adaptations of James' novels are rarely a success"—chiefly because most film directors have failed to realize that cinema is "a medium which can regulate vision. And by regulating what can and cannot be seen, film has the facility to evoke the sense of terror and anxiety underpinning his [James's] fiction."[3] Even flattering criticisms of James adaptations judge their success by the extent to which they recapture the spirit of the original text; Heidi Kaye and Imelda Whelehan suggest that films such as Jane Campion's *Portrait of a Lady* (1996) and Paul Unwin's adaptation of *The American* (1998) successfully addressed current issues "without losing a sense of the original's influence."[4]

This book seeks to depart from this exclusively formalist approach to adaptation on the basis that, as Edward Said once observed in *Culture and Imperialism*, it seems to be like "describing a road without its setting in the landscape."[5] By concentrating on the history of Henry James adaptations, from the first known adaptation (Frank Lloyd's *Berkeley Square* [1933]) to the

1

most recent works such as Merchant-Ivory's *Golden Bowl* (2001), this book focuses on questions of context—those elements that might be assumed to go "with" or "alongside" the text. However, "context" is misleading, as text and context are ultimately inseparable. With this in mind, I proceed on the assumption that the term "context" can have several meanings, all of which have an important bearing on the way James's novels have been adapted for the cinema. One context is temporal: Many adaptations have appeared several decades, even a century, after the novels were originally published, which may encourage directors to reinvent or update them for contemporary audiences—particularly in the case of James, who has acquired the reputation of being a "difficult" author. Examples of this include *The Nightcomers* (1971), Michael Winner's imaginative prequel to *The Turn of the Screw*, which imagines what would have happened to Miss Jessel and the children at Quint's hands prior to the governess's arrival. Two decades later, Rusty Lemorande's version of the same text (1992) updated it to the 1960s in an attempt to criticize the so-called permissive society that was characteristic of the period. Many revisionist adaptations of James's novels "de-repress" them in sexual and political terms, and thereby release their latent feminist spirit. This is particularly true of Campion's *Portrait of a Lady* with its scenes of Isabel Archer being punished by Gilbert Osmond but appearing to enjoy it nonetheless; a costume drama becomes a masochistic drama.

The term "context" also invokes issues of censorship, whether internal or external, conscious or unconscious. In the studio period, many Hollywood films had to be made according to the dictates of the Production Code, which regulated morality and/or ideology from the mid-1930s to the mid-1960s. While the code imposed limits on the "woman's films" (which were mostly designed to promote marriage and motherhood), it was equally clear that, in order to achieve this, the films themselves had to bring to life the opposite of their own morality. Alison Butler describes the results: "In asking the question, what should a woman do with her life? they [women's films] created the possibility of an answer different from the one they intended to provide at the end."[6] This is precisely what happens at the end of Martin Gabel's version of *The Aspern Papers*, retitled *The Lost Moment* (1947), when Tina Bordereau (Susan Hayward) apparently accepts marriage to Jeffrey Ashton (Robert Cummings), while the use of close-up and lighting (shining full on her face) suggest that she will be the dominant partner in this relationship—if it survives at all. By contrast, *The Nightcomers* appeared three years after the Production Code had been repealed, giving directors the opportunity to experiment with more "adult" material.[7] This perhaps helps to explain why the film includes scenes of sadomasochism between Quint and Miss Jessel, and subsequently shows Miles and Flora reenacting those scenes for themselves.

The term "context" also requires us to understand the conditions of production that affect any James adaptation. Contemporary Anglo-American films frequently "improve" novels by removing difficult material (for example, the interior reflections of *The Golden Bowl*) or "uncinematic" scenes (the meditational passages of *The Wings of the Dove*) in the interests of simplicity. Other directors might create new scenes in the interests of narrative clarity but also to provide opportunities for their leading actors to show off. This is especially true of material produced in the studio period, such as *The Lost Moment* and *I'll Never Forget You* (1951)—a version of *The Sense of the Past* specifically designed as a vehicle for Tyrone Power. By contrast, an adaptation produced for BBC-TV or PBS in the United States—particularly in the 1960s and 1970s, when concepts such as ratings or commercial potential seemed less important than they do now—preserved as much of the so-called difficult material as possible. Most directors and/or adapters believed it was their responsibility to inform, educate, and entertain their viewers—and thus sought to retain as much of the Jamesian text as might be dramatically possible, so that the novel's "greatness" might be readily appreciated. Such adaptations might have boasted stellar casts, but they were there to serve the text rather than vice versa.

Many television or cinematic adaptations also perform what Robert Stam describes as aesthetic mainstreaming.[8] Put simply, this means that the text has been adapted along the lines of the dominant mode of storytelling, with the emphasis placed on principal conflicts, coherent characters, and final catharsis or ending. Stam observes that "the goal [of this process] seems to be to 'de-literalize' the text, as the novel is put through an adaptation machine which removes all . . . moral ambiguity, narrative interruption, and reflexive meditation."[9] This type of adaptation is often dictated by financial concerns, with directors and producers seeking to render their material accessible to the widest possible audience—as, for example, in *Somewhere in Time* (1980), Jeannot Szwarc's version of *The Sense of the Past*, where the Jamesian text has been reshaped into a romantic vehicle for Christopher Reeve about the power of love to transcend time.

Adaptations of novels from another period also involve questions of design: Does a director opt for elaborate period recreation or choose alternative methods of design? Sometimes this choice may be dictated by artistic concerns (as the adaptation seeks to situate James's work in the era when it was originally written), but there may be other influences that have more to do with marketing and/or increasing a film's commercial potential. In *The Heiress*, William Wyler's version of *Washington Square* (1949), Harry Horner's period costumes were employed in a marketing campaign to promote "The Heiress" look in fashion magazines and department stores. Similarly, in Vincente Minnelli's musical *On a Clear Day You Can See Forever* (1970) based on *The Sense of the Past*, theater managers were encouraged to organize competitions, offering prizes for those who turned up to the film wearing the best eighteenth-century costumes. James Ivory's three James adaptations—*The Europeans* (1979), *The Bostonians* (1984), and *The Golden Bowl* (2001)—take such care with recreating historically accurate sets and costumes that they have often been thought to offer alternative lifestyles to filmgoers, appealing to their wish-fulfilling fantasies. The same is also true of recent television adaptations (for example, Ben Bolt's Anglo-American version of *The Turn of the Screw* [1999]), which have specifically set out to ensure that the money spent on each production appeared on screen, in the hope of attracting sizable ratings and/or potential overseas buyers.

All the adaptations covered in this book serve as a barometer of the ideological, social, political, and cinematic contexts of the times in which they were produced. Each re-creation of a James novel for the cinema or for television not only uncovers aspects of the novel and its period of origin but also tells us a lot about the time and culture of the adaptation. Robert Stam expresses it thus:

> Adaptation is . . . a work of reaccentuation, whereby a source work is reinterpreted through new grids and discourses. Each grid, in revealing aspects of the source text in question, also reveals something about the ambient discourses in the moment of reaccentuation. By revealing the prisms and grids and discourses through which the novel has been reimagined, adaptations grant a kind of objective materiality to the discourses themselves, giving them visible, audible and perceptible form.[10]

The elaboration of these "prisms and grids and discourses" that govern adaptations of James over the last seven decades forms the basis for this work.

Why James?

Throughout this book, I suggest that one of the principal reasons that filmmakers have chosen to film James is because of his concern with exposing, critiquing, and perpetuating gender ideologies in bourgeois turn-of-the-century Anglo-American society. His novels and short stories can be seen as both producers and critics of gender representations that self-consciously question the role that artistic and literary productions play in construing and circulating gender images. The same also applies to his views of sexuality; he was someone who questioned and yet reinforced the cultural codes and institutions that disciplined social and private behavior.[11] In many ways, he can be seen as someone who meditates on the relationship between gender, sexuality, culture, and narrative—a quality that brings him closer to contemporary theorists like Judith Butler than to his early twentieth-century peers.

Filmmakers have exploited this preoccupation with gender in different ways. In Frank Lloyd's Berkeley Square—produced a year before the Production Code came into force in 1934—Peter Standish (Leslie Howard) challenges familiar stereotypes of manhood; he is not afraid to acknowledge the emotional side of his nature and repudiates bourgeois society's expectations that he should marry and start a family. Standish only wants to be himself, buoyed up by the memories of his encounter in the past with Helen Pettigrew (Heather Angel). The point is reinforced in Roy Baker's 1951 remake I'll Never Forget You. In the post–Production Code era, films such as The Lost Moment and The Heiress were specifically conceived as women's films, characterized by the presence of a central female protagonist and a concern with specifically feminine problems and experiences. Both adaptations appear to propound a conservative view of gender in which (as Janine Basinger observes) the woman is forced to make a choice between marriage and a life of perpetual torment, "and once the choice is made, they must live with the consequences . . . the movies are frequently defining a no-win situation."[12] Despite her strength of character, Tina Bordereau (Susan Hayward) only achieves satisfaction in The Lost Moment once she is brought together with Jeffrey Ashton (Robert Cummings). In The Heiress, Catherine Sloper (Olivia de Havilland) rejects her lover, Morris Townsend (Montgomery Clift), and opts instead for a spinster's life, alone in her father's house. However, as with many women's films of the period, both The Lost Moment and The Heiress are marked by contradiction and complexity; by casting actresses with an "independent" star image in the leading roles, both directors offered new role models for women who rejected the idea of male protection—something that was hitherto considered fundamental to the domestic ideology of the period (especially in the United States).

The post-studio period witnessed a gradual fragmentation of film production. Whereas films were once targeted to a wide-ranging audience, the studios became gradually conscious of divisions within the film-going public and marketed films accordingly. This exerted a powerful influence over the way in which gender issues were approached in Jamesian adaptations. Big-budget mainstream productions tended to resonate in various ways with dominant and familiar social attitudes, so as not to alienate potentially significant audience groups. *On a Clear Day* offers a good example. Barbra Streisand plays two roles in the film; one of the characters she plays—Melinda Tentrees—is a strong eighteenth-century Englishwoman who refuses to conform to what society expects of her. She not only rejects her first husband in favor of a wastrel and a gambler but freely admits in court that she will stay with the younger man, even if found guilty of high treason. Yet the film suggests that Melinda is nothing more than an illusion conjured up in psychiatrist Marc Chabot's (Yves Montand's) imagination. The only "real" woman he encounters is his patient Daisy Gamble (also played by Streisand), whose aspirations only extend to being a good wife, as she learns how to bake a cake in domestic science classes. The same emphasis on dominant ideologies also pervades films produced during the so-called Hollywood Renaissance of the early 1970s, when the studios appeared to make a gesture towards the more liberal or radical forces in American society. Peter Bogdanovich's *Daisy Miller* (1974) portrays the eponymous central character (Cybill Shepherd) as an independent-minded woman who repudiates Winterbourne's patriarchal protection and chooses to pursue her own life instead. However, this is shown to be nothing more than a dream; not only is she destroyed at the end (as a result of her own stubbornness), but her version of femininity is regulated by Winterbourne in the sense that she remains the object of his gaze. It is Winterbourne not Daisy who, in Laura Mulvey's words, "controls events . . . [commanding] the stage of spatial illusion in which he articulates the look and creates the action."[13]

Geoff King remarks that ever since the 1980s, "the independent sector has gained increased prominence . . . [as] a valuable source of new, fresh and original material."[14] This perhaps helps to explain why many of the major studios have either developed subsidiaries of their own to make or distribute upmarket features, or acquired some of the most influential independent producer/distributors (in 1993 Miramax was bought by Disney). Yet still some of these so-called independent productions have reinforced dominant attitudes: The scenario of Iain Softley's *Wings of the Dove* (1997) resembles that of *Daisy Miller*, as Kate Croy (Helena Bonham Carter) seeks to dominate those around her but ends up with nothing, trapped by her conviction that people are there to be exploited either socially or sexually. Compared to the women's films of the 1940s, Softley's film offers a more pessimistic view of female potential, especially for those who pursue an independent life rather than opting for marriage and/or a long-term relationship.

On the other hand, many independent films have opted for a more radical treatment of Jamesian texts. In the early 1960s, Jack Clayton's *The Innocents* (1962)—another "independent" production produced under the Hollywood studios' auspices—rewrote *The Turn of the Screw* to show how the governess, Miss Giddens (Deborah Kerr), gradually acknowledges the presence of powerful sexual desires within herself. This had particular resonance at a time when the women's movement was beginning to gather momentum. Merchant-Ivory's *The Europeans* (1979) and *The Bostonians* (1984) focus in detail on issues of masculinity and femininity. In the earlier film, the Empress Eugenia (Lee Remick) plays the part of another strong woman, but Ivory shows how she attempts to feminize her suitors by casting them in a subordinate role. Rather than trying to discover new forms of self-expression, she simply reproduces the kind of dominant discourses that, as Judith Butler remarks, help to determine "what a person feels, how a person acts, and how a person expresses herself sexually."[15] In *The Bostonians*, Olive Chancellor (Vanessa Redgrave) goes some way towards behaving differently. She raises no objection to Verena Tarrant's departure for New York with Basil (even though she has been passionately attracted to the younger woman), and when the time comes for her to deliver a speech advocating women's rights, she speaks in a soft voice—in the belief, no doubt, that persuasion can be more effectively achieved by argument than by a show of strength. Another independent film to offer new constructions of femininity is Meg Richman's *Under Heaven* (1997)—another adaptation of *The Wings of the Dove*—which ends with Cynthia (the Kate Croy character of the novel) setting up home with her mother and three sisters in an environment based on mutual trust rather than domination, where everyone can experience freedom of expression without having to seek male approval.

Television adaptations of James have generally followed a similar pattern as their cinematic counterparts. Those designed for U.S. network television—for example, Dan Curtis's *Turn of the Screw* (1974)—have sought to reinforce dominant ideologies in the hope of attracting large audiences. Conversely, public service broadcasters such as the BBC or PBS have offered more radical interpretations—for example, James Cellan Jones's productions of *The Portrait of a Lady* (1968) and *The Golden Bowl* (1972), where the respective central characters Isabel Archer (Suzanne Neve) and Charlotte Stant (Gayle Hunnicutt) appear to subject themselves to patriarchal authority but refuse to explain their behavior in logical (i.e., masculine) terms, which suggests some kind of repudiation of existing values. This represents a considerable advance on *The Innocents*, for example, where Miss Giddens remains a frustrated spinster, even though she understands that her frustrations may be attributed to powerful sexual desire. Arthur Barron's PBS adaptation of *The Jolly Corner* (1975) not only focuses on the construction of masculinity but also allows a strong single woman, Alice Staverton (Salome Jens), to assume the dominant role in the story. Although the distinction between commercial and public service productions no longer appears so clear-cut (as organizations such as the BBC have become more preoccupied with ratings and overseas marketing), a critical perspective on gender issues is still evident in adaptations such as Unwin's *American*. Like Daisy Miller in Bogdanovich's film, Claire de Cintré (Aisling O'Sullivan) remains subject to the controlling power of the male gaze until the final sequence when she opts for life in a nunnery. Although confining herself voluntarily to the margins of society, she discovers her own form of self-expression.

In a medium in which the conditions of production have been so fundamental in determining an adaptation's treatment of gender issues, it is inevitable that directors also focused on issues of power. This operates at many levels—in terms of content (for example, through the tyranny one person can exert over another by inserting and trapping him or her in certain roles) as well as form (film spectatorship is never innocent, but always a mode of intruding into another person's life).[16] Graeme Clifford's cable television version of *The Turn of the Screw* (1989) transforms the novella into a surprisingly critical analysis of male sexual desire and the accompanying objectification of women. The governess (Amy Irving) is viewed as little more than a sex object by the uncle (David Hemmings), who feels that it would be "so much more pleasant having you here on my arm every evening," rather than sending her to Bly. Clifford links this kind of visual objectification to acts of violence and sexual abuse against those least able to defend themselves. Another version of *The Turn of the Screw*, Antonio Aloy's *Presence of Mind* (1999), suggests that such behavior is accepted as the norm in most societies where supposedly religious organizations such as the Catholic Church permit male sexual abuse to go unpunished—even if that means reducing women to mere sex objects in the process. Perhaps the only solution is to develop a gender identity of one's own that repudiates patriarchal authority and enables an individual to determine his or her own relationship to God and his or her fellow human beings.

The issue of power and spectatorship is convincingly explored in Bogdanovich's *Daisy Miller*, where the audience continually views the action from

Winterbourne's (Barry Brown's) perspective. This is achieved, for example, through the use of intercut close-ups of Daisy's face in profile and shots of Winterbourne staring at her. Unwin employs a similar technique in The American, where Christopher Newman (Matthew Modine) stares at Claire de Cintré as she arrives at a ball. His look represents a form of possession, as he seeks to add Claire to his collection of treasures. By contrast, Campion's Portrait incorporates anachronistic elements or fantasy sequences in the narrative in an attempt to "construct and contradict simultaneously. Startle the viewer with the juxtaposition of seeming opposites."[17] Although there are other James adaptations that make use of fantasy sequences—for example, Chabot's dream of Melinda Tentrees in On a Clear Day—Campion seeks to deny viewers the chance to control the female characters through the gaze; they should be more preoccupied with trying to make sense of a series of apparently disparate images.

Critics of the 1970s and 1980s heritage film or the costume drama, such as Andrew Higson, have suggested that many adaptations (for example, Merchant-Ivory's films) have reinforced existing power structures through their preoccupation with display—the deliberate foregrounding of sets, costumes, and historically accurate locations that recreate the imperialist, upper-class world of the late nineteenth and early twentieth centuries.[18] In a later book, Higson proposed that "post-heritage" adaptations such as The Wings of the Dove have been more critical in the sense that they depict "transgressive sexuality and/or sexual activity . . . against a backdrop of luxurious aristocratic or Bohemian lifestyles and living spaces."[19] I would argue that this critical tendency is characteristic of any James adaptation—whether it reinforces or critiques dominant ideologies—and can be clearly identified in any film irrespective of the period in which it was produced.

In the preface to The Portrait of a Lady, Henry James famously evokes "the house of fiction," a metaphor highlighting the spatial figures in his writing.

The house of fiction has in short not one window but a million. . . . These apertures, of dissimilar shape and size, hang so, all together, over the human scene. . . . They are but windows at the best, mere holes in a dead wall, disconnected, perched aloft, they are not hinged doors opening straight upon life. But they have this mark of their own that at each of them stands a figure with a pair of eyes, or at least with a field-glass.[20]

I suggest that what renders his work popular with filmmakers is the fact that directors have become aware that his house of fiction has "not one window but a million"—particularly where the topic of gender is concerned. Familiar tales such as the drama of confinement and lingering desire (*The Aspern Papers, Washington Square*) or the melodrama (*The Wings of the Dove*) or the drama of the domestic tainted with illicit sexuality (*The Bostonians*) can be reinscribed and renovated to convey specific connotations and narrative dilemmas to audiences across disparate historical and geographical locations.[21]

Stylistic Techniques

In a recent book, Lyn Thomas has suggested (following Richard Dyer) that period adaptations are often "feminine" in orientation, in the sense that they sacrifice narrative thrust to visual pleasures, placing emphasis on fashion and interior decoration, qualities traditionally associated with women and gay men. Through a survey conducted among respondents of various social backgrounds in Britain, Thomas also discovered that many men were more than willing to enter this "feminine territory" of the period adaptation, "suggesting that the cultural devalorisation of the feminine is less prevalent than it once was."[22] I contend that many directors of James adaptations have employed certain stylistic devices that invest their films with this "feminine" quality, as well as focusing our attention directly on issues of gender. One such technique has already been referred to above—the use of the fantasy sequence to disrupt the flow of the narrative. Judith Mayne has defined fantasy as "the *staging* of desire . . . a form of mise-en-scène,"[23] and this description could equally well apply to Marc Chabot's dream of Melinda Tentrees in *On a Clear Day* and Isabel Archer's fantasy of being ravished by Warburton, Ralph Touchett, and Caspar Goodwood in Campion's *Portrait*. The one reveals Chabot's desire to create an ideal woman for himself, and the other shows how Isabel possesses very strong sexual yearnings—she wants to be loved, not just regarded as a suitable prospect for a financially advantageous marriage.

Other fantasy sequences—most notably in Curtis's and Lemorande's versions of *The Turn of the Screw*—are used to suggest that female desire is somehow unnatural, especially for those denied the benefits of a "normal" (i.e., nuclear) family life. In the earlier film, Jane Cubberly (Lynn Redgrave) is shown lying in bed waiting for Quint to make love to her. This is followed by a dissolve of the two of them engaged in passionate sex: Jane's moans can be heard on the soundtrack. The sequence ends with her waking up to see Miles standing at the edge of the bed wondering whether he might be able to "aid" her. In Lemorande's film, Jenny Gooding (Patsy Kensit) experiences several dreams made up of a series of recurring images: Miles disguised as a satyr, an exposed nipple, a corpse emerging from the water, her father staring into space.

Another stylistic technique used to "feminize" a James adaptation is the deliberate alternation between historical periods within a single narrative, giving audiences the visual pleasure of focusing on the differences in costume, setting, and location. All versions of *The Sense of the Past*—*Berkeley Square, I'll Never Forget You, On a Clear Day,* and *Somewhere in Time*—employ this strategy, which also provides a means of examining contemporary attitudes towards masculinity and femininity: Is the present really that much better than the past? Peter Standish's experiences of the past in *Berkeley Square* help him acquire a "refined consciousness" of the present that rejects the dominant ideology of marriage and family in favor of a life of solitude, sustained by the memory of his love for Helen—something that "crossed the great darkness [of time] between us." Lucio Fulci's *House by the Cemetery* (1981)—another version of *The Turn of the Screw*—casts a little girl, Mae Freudstein (Silvia Collatina), as the time traveler who comes back from the dead to warn Bob Boyle (Giovanni Frezza) about the dangers lurking in the haunted house. She might be nothing more than a figment of Bob's imagination, but her role within the film suggests that children—particularly females—can operate in a world wherein everything is possible, unfettered by the social and/or gender conventions determining adult behavior.

Julianne Pidduck remarks that one of the characteristics of "feminine" genres such as the costume dramas is the use of recurrent "movement images," such as the woman at the window, that emphasize "limited character mobility or social, physical or corporeal constraint."[24] This image is frequently to be found in James adaptations. In Wyler's *Heiress,* Catherine looks out of the open window on the night of her intended elopement with Morris (Montgomery Clift) and observes that she might "never stand in the window again . . . may never see Washington Square again on a windy April night." Clearly, she has become accustomed to observing life in the square rather than participating in it. Olive Chancellor looks out of the window at Verena Tarrant (Madeleine Potter) in Ivory's *Bostonians*; this may be read as an example of female imprisonment or, more positively, as an expression of Olive's desire to challenge the conventions of heterosexual society and discover new possibilities for her life. In Agnieszka Holland's version of *Washington Square* (1997), Catherine Sloper (Jennifer Jason Leigh) throws a window open and leans out, letting her long blonde hair blow in the wind. Holland cuts to a shot of the curtains fluttering in her bedroom before focusing on Catherine, in close-up, calling to Morris (Ben Chaplin) in full view of the square. If her father had known about it, he would certainly have forbidden her to see Morris anymore. Clearly, love has persuaded Catherine to defy convention and act according to her instincts.

Whereas most James adaptations emphasize visual pleasures as much as dramatic action, it is also clear that such pleasures have a thematic as well as a decorative function. Gilbert Osmond's (James Maxwell's) sitting room in Cellan Jones's *Portrait* is stuffed full of vases and bronze figures; as Isabel sits uncomfortably on the sofa among them, it is evident that Osmond regards her as nothing more than another curio to add to his collection. Holland's *Washington Square* creates a new scene in the New York harbor, where Catherine returns from her European trip and informs her Aunt Penniman (Maggie Smith) that she wishes to marry Morris. The two of them thread their way through a crowd of tradespeople and their customers—clearly suggesting that personal feelings count for nothing in bourgeois New York. Everyone is far more interested in profit—whether personal or financial—Aunt Penniman included. Such techniques help to demonstrate that the costume drama (including every adaptation of James) is "engaged with the past insofar as the texts of culture are embedded with *past relations of power*" (emphasis added).[25] These social relations are rearticulated and perpetually redefined in every single adaptation, whether produced in the 1930s or in the present time.

By considering the sheer variety of James adaptations to appear over the last seven decades, this book hopes to fulfill two purposes. First, it seeks to demonstrate that, contrary to received opinion about his status as a "difficult" author, his novels have provided filmmakers with a rich source of material to comment on the present through the past. Secondly, the book hopefully suggests that James himself was not solely concerned with satisfying an elite readership (even after the failure of his career as a popular playwright). Even if, by 1902, he could only dream of popular acceptance, the imagery and meaning of the dream never left him. When the novelist William Dean Howells congratulated him on the beauty of *The Wings of the Dove* and remarked on its success with the periodical press, James responded in familiar terms:

> I haven't known anything about the American "notices," heaven save the mark! any more than about those here (which I am told, however, have been remarkably

genial;) so that I have *not* had the sense of confrontation with a public more than usually childish—I mean had it in any special way. I confess, however, that that is my chronic sense—the more than usual childish-ness of publics: and it is (has been,) in my mind, long since discounted, and my work definitely insists upon being independent of such phantasms and on unfolding itself wholly from its own "innards." Of course, in our conditions, doing anything decent is pure disinterested, unsupported, unrewarded heroism; but that's in the day's work.[26]

Even while professing his indifference to the market, James returned to the archetype of his dream adventure: "confrontation"—"public"—"phantasms"—"heroism." Perhaps it was the cinema that enabled his dream to be fulfilled—even if he did not live to see it happen.[27]

Notes

1. Neil Sinyard, "Historian of Fine Consciousness: Henry James and the Cinema," in *Filming Literature: The Art of Screen Adaptation* (London: Croom Helm, 1986), 32.

2. John Orr, "Introduction: Proust, the Movie," in *Cinema and Fiction 1950–90: New Modes of Adapting*, ed. John Orr and Colin Nicholson (Edinburgh: Edinburgh University Press, 1992), 3.

3. Susie Gibson, "The Terror of Representation: The Difficulty of Filming the Novels of Henry James," *Metro Magazine* 117 (1998): 49.

4. Heidi Kaye and Imelda Whelehan, "Introduction: Classics across the Film-Literature Divide," in *Classics in Film and Fiction*, ed. Heidi Kaye and Imelda Whelehan (London: Pluto Press, 2000), 5.

5. Edward Said, *Culture and Imperialism* (New York: Alfred A. Knopf, 1994), 51.

6. Alison Butler, *Women's Cinema: The Contested Screen* (London: Wallflower Press, 2002), 28.

7. "Extending the limits of what could be represented in the mainstream also enabled the studios [in the U.S. and Britain] to compete with the sex film industry." Geoff King, *New Hollywood Cinema: An Introduction* (London: I. B. Tauris, 2002), 31.

8. Robert Stam, "Introduction: The Theory and Practice of Adaptation," in *Literature and Film: A Guide to the Theory and Practice of Adaptation*, ed. Robert Stam and Alessandra Raengo (Malden, MA: Blackwell, 2005), 43.

9. Stam, "Introduction: The Theory and Practice," 43.

10. Stam, "Introduction: The Theory and Practice," 45.

11. Some of the most recent publications on the topic include Wendy Graham, *Henry James' Thwarted Love* (Stanford, CA: Stanford University Press, 1999); Donatella Izzo, *Portraying the Lady: Technologies of Gender in the Short Stories of Henry James* (Lincoln: University of Nebraska Press, 2001); Eric Haralson, *Henry James and Queer Modernity* (Cambridge: Cambridge University Press, 2003), and Leland S. Person, *Henry James and the Suspense of Masculinity* (Philadelphia: University of Pennsylvania Press, 2003).

12. Jeanine Basinger, *A Woman's View: How Hollywood Spoke to Women 1930–1960* (New York: Alfred A. Knopf, 1993), 19.

13. Laura Mulvey, "Visual Pleasure and Narrative Cinema," in *Visual and Other Pleasures* (London: Macmillan Press, 1989), 20.

14. King, *New Hollywood Cinema*, 83–84.

15. Quoted in Kathryn Woodward, ed., *Identity and Difference* (London: Sage, 1997), 215.

16. This is also true of Henry James's novels—as Winfried Fluck remarks, one of the achievements of recent critics has been to make readers aware of "the constant power plays in language as well as in social relations . . . [for example, in] the way in which [the] sympathy and care gap can function as impositions, forms and modes of disciplining through intimacy." Winfried Fluck, "Power Relations in the Novels of James: The 'Liberal' and the 'Radical' Version," in *Enacting History in Henry James: Narrative, Power and Ethics*, ed. Gert Buelens (Cambridge: Cambridge University Press, 1997), 22.

17. Mary C. Gentile, *Film Feminisms: Theory and Practice* (Westport, CT: Greenwood Press, 1985), 72.

18. Andrew Higson, "Re-presenting the National Past: Nostalgia and Pastiche in the Heritage Film," in *Fires Were Started*, ed. Lester Friedman (Minneapolis: University of Minnesota Press, 1993), 110.

19. Andrew Higson, *English Heritage, English Cinema: Costume Drama since 1980* (Oxford: Oxford University Press, 2003), 197–98.

20. Henry James, *The Portrait of a Lady* (Harmondsworth: Penguin Books, 1979), ix.

21. Julianne Pidduck, *Contemporary Costume Film* (London: BFI Publishing, 2004), 44.

22. Lyn Thomas, *Fans, Feminisms and "Quality" Media* (London: Routledge, 2002), 175.

23. Judith Mayne, *Cinema and Spectatorship* (London: Routledge, 1993), 88.

24. Pidduck, *Contemporary Costume Film*, 16.

25. Pidduck, *Contemporary Costume Film*, 177.

26. Quoted in Michael Anesko, *Henry James and the Profession of Authorship* (Oxford: Oxford University Press, 1986), 20.

27. James himself was interested in cinematic techniques. Philip Horne ("The James Gang," *Sight and Sound* [January 1998], 17) remarks that the 1909 story "Crapy Cornelia" has a hero

> gazing out of a window when the middle-aged heroine attracts his attention: her looming head "grew and grew . . . came nearer and nearer, while it met his eyes, after the manner of images in the cinematograph." The psychological impact of altering image size had clearly registered. The hero has just been indulging a phantasmagoric vision, of a bright modern future with a *nouveau riche* wife. When he recognises Cornelia from his past, James has his imagined scene dissolve under the looming face: "everything had altered, dropped, darkened, disappeared." Conjured to evoke an internal reality, this suggests that cinema, with its "thousand ways of emphasising . . . the privileged moments" *can* take on James' world.

CHAPTER ONE

~

Berkeley Square (1933)

Frank Lloyd's *Berkeley Square*, based on John L. Balderston's play of the same name, which was itself inspired by *The Sense of the Past*, was the first adaptation based on a James text to be brought to the screen. In a recent article, Craig Frischkorn argues that producer Jesse Lasky deliberately omitted any reference to the Jamesian source in the film's credits, as his reputation was "too highbrow" for most filmgoers: "Lasky needed to sell movie tickets, not send the audience to the library for James's sixteen-year-old novel, which was, after all, unfinished."[1] Instead, director Lloyd sought to popularize the story by emphasizing its romantic elements as well as focusing on eighteenth-century customs and manners. Evidently he succeeded in his task. The critic Rob Wagner wrote soon after the film's opening in November 1933 that "The preview audience at Long Beach got *every* subtlety!"[2] While *Berkeley Square* did not apparently make much money at the box office, it "did at least appeal to the romantic tastes of the depression-era class audience—with or without anyone appreciating the source."[3]

This chapter develops Frischkorn's argument by suggesting that there were two inspirations behind Jesse Lasky's decision to film *Berkeley Square*. The subject matter seemed particularly appropriate for Hollywood in the early 1930s—a time when, as Colin Shindler has remarked, all the major studios produced "wide-eyed films" offering romance as the solution to all ills, "economic or spiritual, national or personal. . . . If the characters in the movie[s] can solve their problems, there is no reason why the audience should not find equally simple solutions."[4] Secondly, *Berkeley Square* was released at a time when the studios continually looked to Broadway and/or the West End of London for bankable theatrical properties, preferably with their original casts. Other successes included Clemence Dane's *A Bill of Divorcement* starring Katharine Hepburn (1932), George S. Kaufman and Edna Ferber's *Dinner at Eight* (1933), and Noel Coward's *Cavalcade* (also produced by Lasky) (1933). Bearing this in mind, I suggest that the question of whether James's name should have been included on the credits of *Berkeley Square* was of little importance; Balderston received due recognition as the screenwriter as well as the original playwright.[5]

Yet despite this omission, I believe that the film of *Berkeley Square* was inspired by *The Sense of the Past*, as both works employ the time-traveler plot to create imaginative worlds that offer alternative conceptions of gender. In James's novel, Ralph Pendrel gradually becomes aware that he must reinterpret the relation of past and present, taking into account the "unimaginable accident" of his presence. And as he does so, he must also reinterpret himself—especially his view of masculinity. *Berkeley Square* alters the plot of the novel somewhat to make the central character (renamed Peter Standish) an American, an outsider from the early twentieth century trying to play an eighteenth-century British gentleman but discovering that this only restricts his freedom of self-expression. As Standish observes at one point—both in the play and the film—it is only when he is "muddling everything up," as a consequence of having fallen in love (in other words, forced to rethink his identity) that he discovers his true nature.[6] The emphasis on rethinking the construction of gender is reinforced through the casting of Leslie Howard in the leading role. Not only was he an "outsider" himself (born of Hungarian parents in Forest Hill, a suburb of London), but his screen persona projected an alternative version of masculinity—the urbane, intuitive, introspective, soft-spoken man-about-town—as opposed to the all-American heroes like Gable, Power, Cooper, or similar stars who could be found under contract to the major studios. *Berkeley Square* is most certainly not radical in terms of content; as Shindler remarks, the proliferation of romantic films emanating from Hollywood in the early 1930s represented an essentially conservative strategy on the studios' part, designed to defuse the "potentially revolutionary situation" caused by the Depression.[7] The crisis even affected the studios themselves; by March 1933 (some six months before the release of *Berkeley Square*), box-office receipts hit rock bottom—they were 40 percent of what they had been in January 1931. Consequently, producers were far more inclined to stick to tried-and-trusted formulae in the hope of attracting audiences back to theaters. Despite this, *Berkeley Square* seeks to suggest that every individual—especially men—should be given the freedom to determine his or her own identity in a society buffeted by political incompetence and lack of foresight.

This kind of optimistic message was characteristic of studio products of this period. As Paramount Pictures told *Saturday Evening Post* readers in 1932, "See it [this kind of film] and you'll be out of yourself, living someone else's life. . . . You'll find a new viewpoint. And tomorrow you'll work . . . not merely worry."[8] Such views made sound commercial sense; as the screenwriter and author Donald Ogden Stewart recalled, most filmgoers at that time welcomed the opportunity to "get away from the problems and the hunger" of the outside world and enjoy the kind of fare that "would take them away from their worries and cares and give them a good time for a couple of hours."[9] *Berkeley Square* more than fulfilled such requirements. Publicized by Fox as "the most beautiful love story the screen has ever told" and as a "Romance—Tender . . . Haunting! Among all the world's lovers these two alone live everyone's dream—love that lasts forever," the film concentrates on the love affair between Standish and Helen Pettigrew (Heather Angel).[10] It begins with a shot/reverse-shot sequence in which Standish pauses for a moment and asks Helen, "Why do you look at me that that?"[11] Clearly, he is affected by her presence as he stammers, "I'm an American, you know," his left hand shaking nervously as he speaks. The scene ends with a long two-shot in which the two of them stare into each other's eyes as if transfixed. Later on, Lloyd includes a spectacular montage sequence combining close-ups of Helen's face with terrifying images of the modern world—skyscrapers, machines, automobiles, airplanes, ships, guns, battles, and explosions. Helen subsequently exclaims that such visions were the work of "Devils! [And] demons!" which prompts Standish to observe somewhat mournfully that, as he originates from that world of the future, he must be in league with the devil. Helen exclaims, "You've not sold your soul to—if the Fiend comes for you, he can have me too," and falls into his arms, observing as she does so that "I loved you before I ever saw you. In my first dream of you, coming from somewhere far away, to meet me."[12] Moments like these had a particular resonance for filmgoers in the Depression period, suggesting that love is not only eternal but can offer a cure for all ills. As Lionel Collier observed in his review for the British fan magazine *Picturegoer*, Lloyd had created "a beautiful film . . . with an intelligence that fully interprets the spirit of a love which is immortal and knows not time nor space."[13]

Apart from the romantic plot, *Berkeley Square* proved particularly suitable for filming on account of its cultural prestige. The play had already been a success in London and on Broadway with Leslie Howard as leading actor and coproducer (with Gilbert Miller). In collaboration with Balderston, Howard had rewritten the text to suit his particular capabilities; when the play first appeared in London in 1928, with sets designed by Sir Edwin Lutyens, Howard had received considerable acclaim for his performance, which, according to one critic, "struck not one false note."[14] The New York first night was on November 4, 1929—only a few days after the stock market had taken a sickening lurch and slipped into what seemed a bottomless decline. It was a grim moment to try to fill a theater, yet the play was a hit. There were twenty-five curtain calls before Howard stepped forward to make his curtain speech. The critic Burns Mantle wrote, "Something of beauty breaks through even the stock-market news. . . . How pleasant a theatre adventure it is to feel that it is not necessary actually to believe anything or anybody. . . . What is reality? Only a seeming."[15] The play ran for over 220 performances and subsequently toured all over America, beginning in Boston and culminating in an extended run at the Belasco Theater in Los Angeles in the spring of 1931.

Berkeley Square was just the kind of property that producer Jesse Lasky wanted to film. Ever since the early 1920s, when he had announced on the New York dockside that he had "arranged for contributions to Paramount Pictures by James Barrie, Henry Arthur Jones, Arnold Bennett, H. G. Wells" and a host of other famous authors, he had looked to Broadway and the West End of London to provide suitable properties for filming. This became even more important for him a decade later, when he left Paramount and became an independent producer at Fox. Lasky's belief was simple: Hollywood had to learn from the theater about "how to write directly for the screen" and "develop its [the cinema's] possibilities."[16] Ever since the early 1920s, Lasky, in collaboration with the theater producer Gilbert Miller, had financed a steady stream of plays and comedies by major authors or adapted from literary sources—several of which were subsequently transferred to the screen.[17] His version of Noel Coward's *Cavalcade* (1933) won three Oscars, including Best Director for Frank Lloyd. Clearly, Lasky hoped to repeat this success with *Berkeley Square* (another product of his successful theatrical partnership with Miller). The publicity emphasized the film's prestige elements: "a great play" had become "the year's finest picture!" wherein Leslie Howard gave "the most distinguished performance of his career." The press book encouraged theater managers to persuade "teachers of English in local high schools and colleges" to attend the film—"also their pupils. . . . The same holds true for literary societies, drama clubs, reading clubs and similar organizations."[18]

Lloyd's film was clearly conceived as a prestige production, with an all-British cast including Howard and Valerie Taylor (as Kate Pettigrew) from the original New York stage production, supported by Beryl Mercer and Irene Browne, both of whom had previously appeared in *Cavalcade*. The story was deliberately rewritten to incorporate scenes of local color, which had little to contribute to the development of the narrative but were visually pleasing, giving some idea of the costumes, manners, and mores of eighteenth-century Britain (as Hollywood viewed them).[19] The opening sequence—which does not exist in the original play—has Standish arriving at the Blue Boar inn, quaffing a draft of ale with Major Castell (Alan Mowbray), and referring in passing to the recently concluded American War of Independence and the dawn of a new age of enlightenment. In another newly created scene, Standish encounters Sir Joshua Reynolds (Olaf Hytten) in his studio and renders the painter speechless with his knowledge of the Mrs. Siddons portrait— even though it is not yet finished and has not hitherto been shown to anyone.[20] As Frischkorn suggests, however, a Hollywood prestige production also had to have mass appeal; thus, Henry James's name did not appear anywhere, neither in the script nor in the publicity.[21] John L. Balderston received a double credit both as the author of the original play and as coscreenwriter (with Sonya Levien).

So far it would seem that *Berkeley Square*—in both its stage and film versions—had little in common with the novel that allegedly inspired it. *The Sense of the Past* contains very little external description; like other late James novels, it is more concerned with the convoluted speculations, questions, and judgments of the central character, Ralph Pendrel, as he endeavors to make sense of his travels back in time to the world of 1823. Only when he encounters Nan Midmore (Helen Pettigrew in *Berkeley Square*) does he discover a kindred spirit—someone who has "things in her world of imagination . . . which might verily have matched with some of those, the shyer, the stranger, the as yet least embodied, that confusedly peopled his own."[22] Her expression contains "some intelligence than he had yet touched among them all [the characters of the past]" that "determined in him the strangest inward cry. 'Why she's modern, *modern!*' he felt he was thinking—and it seemed to launch him with one push on an extraordinary sea."[23] Unlike Standish, Ralph has not fallen in love but discovered someone who—like himself— feels alienated from the world: "the light that hung during these moments . . . appeared rather that of an intelligence rather at sea, or guessing free application to have been so perversely denied it."[24] Perhaps the two of them were destined to meet one another: "how any such verification of identities, felicities, sublimities, or whatever they might be, could make her 'modern' without by the same stroke making *him* so, he naturally as yet failed of attention to discern."[25] James ends the unfinished novel on an optimistic note by having Ralph express the belief that Nan will be "drawn to him just exactly by certain features of the play of freedom that he had felt warn the others off. . . . There was nothing to light the anomaly to any degree in his impression that he should be able to make her conceive him better simply by looking at her even, as if she naturally would."[26] The final sentence suggests he will not be disappointed: "He clung to his gravity, which somehow steadied him—so odd it was that the sense of her understanding wouldn't be abated which even a particular lapse, he could see."[27]

Yet perhaps there are more resemblances between *The Sense of the Past* and *Berkeley Square* than might first be assumed. As long ago as 1952, the critic Marius Bewley suggested that James had been significantly influenced by Hawthorne's work in the sense that both authors sought to create an imaginative world of romance in which past and present become one, permitting the central characters to develop "a refined consciousness" of themselves and their place in the world. This process of psychological development was not an easy one, but it "was and is a problem of such importance that even today one hardly dare plot limits to what it may eventually mean in terms of a future English-speaking civilization."[28] This "refined consciousness" can be more precisely defined as a different way of looking at things—a commitment to "restless activity and the expansion of a sensibility that is moving on," that can discover a different order of truth and experience.[29] If the novel deals with the probable, the actual, and the present, the romance deals with the possible, the marvelous, and the past.[30] In his "Notes for *The Sense of the Past*," dictated after the 1914 revision of the text, James describes the climax of the novel, in which Ralph "gives himself away, testifies supremely to his alienism, abnormalism, the nature of his identity in fine."[31] This becomes a moment of supreme self-discovery as Ralph understands that he has been " 'sold,' horribly sold" by the contemporary world—in other words, forced to conform to certain behavioral standards (which might be termed "masculine") to maintain his social and political position.[32] While the experience of the past may make him "feel . . . lost," it also encourages "a change of attitude, a change of sensibility, as I must call it, or at least may, for want of a better word" as Ralph develops a "refined consciousness" of what it is to be male—whether in the present or the past.[33] This can be more precisely defined as listening to his instincts, as he "makes a clean breast to her [Nan] of what he feels and understands, of what his intelligence must helps him to, of what, in a word, it is necessary that she shall know—know in order to assist and relieve him . . . and so bring the whole situation to the point of its dénouement."[34] From then on Ralph "is, for the whole situation, supreme master and controller. He is 'all right' at least, and he *re-connects*, on the spot, with all the lucidity and authority we can desire of him."[35] The important word is "re-connect": Ralph's newly acquired sensibility enables him to reconnect with the present in more meaningful ways.

The film of *Berkeley Square* focuses on the same question; if we were fortunate enough to travel back into the past, would we likewise benefit from our experiences? An opening title sequence expresses the point thus:

> How many of us have wished that we might escape from the dull reality of the present into the glamor and romance of yesterday?
>
> But if we could journey back into the mystery of the past, should we find contentment—or unhappiness?
>
> This is the story of PETER STANDISH of Berkeley Square.

As the action unfolds, it would appear that the answer is no; despite Throstle's (Ferdinand Gottschalk's) complacent observation that "we are living in the eighteenth century, the age of reason,"[36] Standish's experiences of the past seem hellish rather than glamorous and romantic: "A new fire of London, that's what needed here. Yes, and a new plague, too. Dirt, disease, cruelty, smells—Lord, how the eighteenth century stinks!" This scene is preceded by a short exterior sequence taking place in the street with the bells of Big Ben chiming in the background. An uncredited town crier walks towards the camera, looking from side to side as he bangs his stick on the ground and announces "One o'clock! A fine morning! All's well!" This not only provides the kind of local color that was characteristic of a prestige adaptation of the mid-1930s but also refers ironically to Standish's state of mind—all is certainly not well with him at this present moment.

However, director Frank Lloyd emphasizes the romantic elements of the story, in which past and present become one, enabling the characters to look at the world in different ways. Standish observes to the American ambassador (Samuel Hinds) that the time traveler can view the past, present, and future simultaneously: "I'm up in the sky above you, in a plane. I'm looking down on it all. I can see it all at once; so the past, present and future of the man in the boat are all one, to the man in the plane. Doesn't that prove that all Time must really be one?"[37] However, Standish only understands the significance of this statement once he has encountered Helen, and realized that being a man has little or nothing to do with conforming to what society expects of him; instead, he must rely on his instincts—something that assumes as much importance in the present as in the past: "I'm myself, you see. I'm myself! This isn't possible; it isn't my life or yours [Helen's], it isn't my world or yours." He takes Helen in his arms and embraces her, observing that "there's never been a kiss like that . . . since the world began," while violins play a romantic melody on the soundtrack. Standish's "refined consciousness" of himself resurfaces in the film's climax, as he admits that he will love Helen "in my own time, and in whatever other times may come."[38] She crosses to the bureau and takes out a *crux ansata*, "the symbol of life and of eternity," which she gives to Standish as a perpetual reminder of their love affair: "This little thing—has crossed the great darkness between us. Mine while I live, yours in that world which I shall never see."[39]

Just like Ralph Pendrel, Standish has been transformed by the experience of the past. When he returns to the world of 1928 he cannot entertain the prospect of marriage to his fiancée, Marjorie (Betty Lawford). Standish seems oblivious to her presence as he picks up a piece of paper containing Helen's epitaph and bursts into tears before beginning to read it aloud. As he does so, Helen's voice can be heard on the soundtrack: "We shall be together, Peter. Not in my time, not in yours, but in God's." This sequence suggests that Standish has not only opted for a life of solitude, sustained only by his memories of Helen, but also that his encounter with the past has helped him discover a new form of masculinity—one that attaches no shame to an open display of emotion. Whereas the ambassador and Mrs. Barwick, his housekeeper (Hylda Tyson), might consider him "unwell,"[40] we know precisely the opposite— Standish has completed the process of acquiring a "refined consciousness."

The film's emphasis on alternative forms of male self-expression has been greatly enhanced by the casting of Leslie Howard in the title role. Ever since he had first come to Hollywood from Broadway in the late 1920s (making his first film in 1930), he had created a screen persona of an intellectual, sensitive, emotional man. The producer David O. Selznick once described him as an "intelligent" rather than a physically imposing actor.[41] Lionel Collier's review of *Berkeley Square* for *Picturegoer* succinctly defines Howard as a performer relying on his "carefully modulated voice, his restrained gestures and poise [that] bring to the character [Standish] a personality that proves irresistibly attractive."[42] In another review, Collier recognized Howard's achievement in communicating the emotional side of Standish's character to filmgoers, in a performance that was "a triumph of restrained, natural acting both in the modern and past periods."[43]

To the contemporary viewer, *Berkeley Square* might appear a period piece—a filmed record of the kind of three-act Broadway or West End play that has long gone out of fashion. The pace is slow, almost stately, as the action unfolds in a series of shot/reverse-shot sequences that may seem irritating to the contemporary viewer. One reviewer observed in 2002 that "it is only in the last third of the movie that it [the plot] really seems to take shape, but my patience had worn a bit thin by that time."[44] Many of the characterizations reflect the gender preoccupations characteristic of mainstream Hollywood films of that period, with women represented as either femmes fatales or as people for whom marriage represents the ultimate aim of their existence. Helen Pettigrew is well aware of her mortality ("Don't be sad there about a girl who's been dead so long. . . . You will come, won't you, young as I see you now, to my grave in St. Mark's churchyard."[45] By contrast, Marjorie Frant appears to want no life of her own, other than to care for Standish as his wife.[46] Nonetheless, *Berkeley Square* remained enduringly popular throughout the 1930s and 1940s, with four radio versions appearing between 1934 and 1944, including one (broadcast on December 9, 1934, where Howard reprised his screen role).[47] The play was refilmed in 1951, in an updated version by Ranald MacDougall with Tyrone Power and Ann Blyth, while two further films—*On a Clear Day You Can See Forever* (1970) and *Somewhere in Time* (1980)—owed their inspiration to Balderston's (and James's) basic plot. All of these films are analyzed in detail in later chapters.

Clearly, the romantic origins of the story—with the emphasis on the relationship between past and present through the figure of the time traveler— have appealed to filmmakers throughout the decades. Moreover, the film's representation of masculinity—both in the screenplay and through Howard's performance—remains one that seems as important now as it might have been in 1933. Standish might have been "a man apart"—someone who offered a pleasurable alternative to beleaguered audiences of the Depression era, but his commitment to a different way of thinking and behaving emphasizes the importance of rethinking gender constructions, whether in the past or the present.

Notes

1. Craig Frischkorn, "Frank Lloyd's *Berkeley Square* (1933): Re-adapting Henry James's *The Sense of the Past*," *Literature Film Quarterly* 28, no. 1 (2000): 9.

2. Rob Wagner, "The Movies: *Berkeley Square*," *Rob Wagner's Script* (November 25, 1933), 8.

3. Frischkorn, "Frank Lloyd's *Berkeley Square*," 11.

4. Colin Shindler, *Hollywood in Crisis: Cinema and American Society 1929–1939* (London: Routledge, 1996), 74.

5. John L. Balderston (1889–1954) was the London correspondent of the *New York*

World, a journalist and historian who spent seven years in England during the 1920s. He had begun to write *Berkeley Square* in the early 1920s, and by the beginning of the next decade had established himself in Hollywood as the screenwriter of horror classics such as *Dracula* (1931), James Whale's *Frankenstein* (also 1931), and Karl Freund's *The Mummy* (1932). His later credits included adaptations of *The Mystery of Edwin Drood* (1935), *The Last of the Mohicans* (1936), and MGM's classic *Prisoner of Zenda* (1937), as well as more monster epics such as *The Bride of Frankenstein* (1935).

6. John L. Balderston, *Berkeley Square: A Play in Three Acts* (New York: Macmillan, 1929), 91.

7. Shindler, *Hollywood in Crisis*, 73.

8. Quoted in Andrew Bergman, *We're in the Money: Depression America and Its Films* (New York: Harper Colophon Books, 1971), xxi.

9. Quoted in John Kobal, *Gotta Sing Gotta Dance: A Pictorial History of Film Musicals* (London: Hamlyn, 1971), 114.

10. The part was originally played on Broadway by Margalo Gillmore. Heather Angel had already been in Hollywood for two years, playing in B movies such as *The Hound of the Baskervilles* with Robert Rendel as Sherlock Holmes.

11. Balderston, *Berkeley Square*, 51.

12. Balderston, *Berkeley Square*, 91.

13. Lionel Collier, "The Greatest Romance of the Year," *Picturegoer* (November 11, 1933), 14.

14. The story of the stage production of *Berkeley Square*, from the time the critic Alexander Woollcott suggested to Howard that he should play Standish to the final performance in Los Angeles, has been well told by Howard's daughter in her biography. Leslie Ruth Howard, *A Quite Remarkable Father* (London: Longmans Green, 1959), 146–53.

15. Quoted in Howard, *A Quite Remarkable Father*, 155.

16. John Baxter, *The Hollywood Exiles* (London: Macdonald and Jane's, 1976), 92–93.

17. Lasky recalled in his autobiography of one trip to Europe in the early 1920s with Miller, where the two of them acquired the rights to Molnar's *The Swan*, plus a block of ten plays by J. M. Barrie. Lasky also talked to such luminaries as H. G. Wells, Henry Arthur Jones, Arnold Bennett, and Somerset Maugham. Jesse Lasky, *I Blow My Own Horn* (London: Victor Gollancz, 1957), 139.

18. Press book: *Berkeley Square* (Los Angeles: Fox Film, 1933), 2.

19. Baxter remarks somewhat cynically that "films [like *Berkeley Square*] succeeded because they created a fantasy . . . an amalgam of stereotypes . . . characters imperfectly recalled from history or fiction" (*The Hollywood Exiles*, 106). I suggest that this strategy was characteristic of Hollywood "prestige" pictures of the 1930s, especially those based on literary classics such as *David Copperfield* (1935).

20. Balderston's play has the Reynolds scene in reported speech, as Tom reports that the painter will paint the time traveler no more, on account of the fact that "some fault in the portrait has displeased the artist" (Balderston, *Berkeley Square*, 75).

21. Frischkorn, "Frank Lloyd's *Berkeley Square*," 7. He quotes from screenwriter

DeWitt Bodeen who recalls that at that time, "Producers didn't know who he [James] was, and those who did were apt to say 'Oh yes, that American highbrow who's trying so hard to be a British playwright" (8–9).

22. Henry James, *The Sense of the Past* (London: W. Collins, n.d), 277.

23. James, *Sense of the Past*, 275.

24. James, *Sense of the Past*, 277.

25. James, *Sense of the Past*, 277.

26. James, *Sense of the Past*, 280.

27. James, *Sense of the Past*, 281.

28. Marius Bewley, *The Complex Fate: Hawthorne, Henry James and Some Other American Writers* (New York: Gordian Press, 1967), 73–74. Original edition published in 1952.

29. Bewley, *The Complex Fate*, 8.

30. Nathaniel Hawthorne suggests that the romance should create an atmosphere of strange enchantment—a world peopled by illusive guests whose unusual gleams and shadows endow the small and trifling with dignity—with a new significance and depth, intellectual or spiritual. Nathaniel Hawthorne, "The Custom House: Introductory Sketch," in *The Scarlet Letter* (Harmondsworth: Penguin Books, 1994), 30–31.

31. James, *Sense of the Past*, 304.

32. James, *Sense of the Past*, 304.

33. James, *Sense of the Past*, 306–7.

34. James, *Sense of the Past*, 325.

35. James, *Sense of the Past*, 347.

36. Balderston, *Berkeley Square*, 77.

37. Balderston, *Berkeley Square*, 26. The text was slightly adapted for the film.

38. Balderston, *Berkeley Square*, 114.

39. Balderston, *Berkeley Square*, 115.

40. Balderston, *Berkeley Square*, 118.

41. David O. Selznick, *Memo from David O. Selznick*, ed. Rudy Behlmer (New York: Modern Library, 2000), 184.

42. Collier, "The Greatest Romance," 14.

43. Lionel Collier, "On the Screens Now," *Picturegoer* (April 7, 1934), 26. Such comments were echoed in the British fanzine *Picture Show*, which described *Berkeley Square* as containing a standard of "acting beyond reproach." "This Week's General Releases," *Picture Show* 30, no. 780 (April 14, 1934): 21.

44. Dave Sindelar, "Berkeley Square" (1933), *Scifilm Musings*, October 3, 2002, at www.scifilm.org/musings2/musing421.html (accessed September 7, 2005).

45. Balderston, *Berkeley Square*, 113–14.

46. Balderston, *Berkeley Square*, 122.

47. The other three productions—all broadcast in the United States—were on October 14, 1938, with Herbert Marshall as Standish and Heather Angel playing Helen once again; on November 29, 1939, with Maurice Evans and Sylvia Field, and on December 18, 1944, with Ronald Colman and Maureen O'Sullivan. A television version appeared on November 4, 1949, with David Niven in the title role.

CHAPTER TWO

~

The Lost Moment (1947)

The Lost Moment, Martin Gabel's adaptation of *The Aspern Papers*, has enjoyed a checkered critical career since its original theatrical release. Costing $1.3 million to make, it made no more than $700,000 at the U.S. box office, and failed to secure a British release until February 1949, owing to import restrictions. One preview patron, asked to comment on the film, wrote "104. Ha-ha"—a mocking reference to Agnes Moorehead's portrayal of the aged aunt, Juliana Bordereau.[1] The reviews were mixed, to say the least. One of the more enthusiastic opinions appeared in the British journal *Monthly Film Bulletin*, which suggested that while "the film hovers perilously between something approaching true romance and the ridiculous," it was redeemed by "impressive acting . . . and the lovely Venetian backgrounds and settings."[2] Since the 1970s, *The Lost Moment*'s reputation has steadily improved. It became a cult film from 1970 onwards; this was chiefly due to the fact that a clip from it was included in Michael Sarne's notorious adaptation of Gore Vidal's *Myra Breckinridge* (1970). Ten years later, the London listings magazine *Time Out* observed that Gabel's "ghostly web of shifting identities and sexual tensions is superbly spun."[3] Tom Milne wrote in the *Monthly Film Bulletin* in 1983 that "One reason why the film works so brilliantly is that its psychiatric basis is richly embroidered with Gothic resonances."[4]

This chapter is divided into three parts. In the first, I set *The Lost Moment* in context by surveying some of the literature of the time that focused specifically on gender roles and their relationship to the nuclear family. Secondly, I look at how James's text was transformed into a woman's film, a genre that apparently sought to emphasize the importance of marriage, home, and family to its (overwhelmingly female) audience. Thirdly, I also show how *The Lost Moment*—like many films of the period—communicated a deliberately contradictory message, as it not only puts forward new possibilities for women, but it also shows a strong female central character achieving emotional and personal success. This can be chiefly attributed to Susan Hayward's stellar performance as Tina Bordereau. Fourteen years previously, *Berkeley Square* had offered the enticing prospect of alternative role models for men; *The Lost Moment* tries to do the same for women.

This question of gender roles (particularly where women were concerned) and their importance to the family dominated much of the literature on femaleness and female sexuality that appeared at this time. Helene Deutsch's two-volume *Psychology of Women* (1944–1945) suggested that such roles were predetermined from early childhood, when "the little male's activity is directed outward; forward aspiring moment," while "the little female builds houses in order always to put something inside them. . . . Her games have the character of nest-building activity, of putting things in order and keeping them together."[5] In the best-selling *Modern Woman: The Lost Sex* (1947), the authors suggested that honorary degrees should be awarded "to women who have successfully raised well-balanced families; they would be merited more than most of those awarded to industrialists, businessmen, brokers and bankers."[6] By 1956, one quarter of all urban white college women married while completing their education. To do otherwise represented a considerable risk—as another manual suggested, women's "chances for marriage are greatly reduced if they do not make a permanent attachment during the college years." Once a woman had found a suitable husband, the question of her college education no longer seemed important: "Nothing is to be gained by women's trying to imitate men."[7] She should preoccupy herself more with fulfilling his sexual needs, as well as accepting the responsibility for child-rearing and professionalized homemaking. As a loving, erotic mate, she would prevent her husband from looking for other women; as a good mother, she would raise children to become good, healthy citizens, with a clear idea of the differences between right and wrong.

Any woman who thought otherwise was perceived as deviant. Single or divorced women were thought to be "neurotic," on account of the fact they had either failed to find a male partner or had been discarded by one. According to Helene Deutsch, "in their love life these women usually suffer great disappointments," chiefly because of their refusal to accept the appointed female role: "Their relationships . . . always end in conflicts, in which both partners are filled with hate and aggression."[8] Any woman who exhibited feminist leanings mounted a challenge to "biologic and psychologic laws. Those who regard it as an expression of a social-illusionary development are the victims of an illusion."[9] The authors of *Modern Woman: The Lost Sex* likened feminists to communists—"the political agents of the Kremlin abroad" who "continue to beat the feminist drums in full awareness of its disruptive influence among the potential enemies of the Soviet Union." The agents' objective was simple—"the achievement of maleness by the female," something that "spelled only vast individual suffering for men as well as women, and much public disorder."[10]

Despite such fears, many Hollywood films chose to focus on the issue of female identity—prompted, no doubt, by the awareness that women constituted a massive share of its audience. Alison Butler remarks that the woman's film of the 1930s and 1940s was not only marked by the presence of strong female characters but also contained "stylistic and narrative distortions which result[ed] from the irreconcilability of Hollywood's ostensible moral values and aesthetic conventions with the provision of escapist entertainment."[11] On the one hand, producers were obliged to observe the dictates of the Production Code of 1934, which explicitly forbade scenes of adultery and emphasized the fact that films must respect "the sanctity of marriage and the home."[12] On the other hand, they sought to provide women with a dream of potency and freedom. The contradiction was often resolved thus: While seeking to convince women that marriage and motherhood were the right paths to follow, films also showed them making the "mistake" of doing something else. In asking the question "What should a woman do with her life?" they suggested the possibility of an answer different from the one given at the end of the film. This is certainly the case in films like King Vidor's *Stella Dallas* (1937), whose eponymous central character (Barbara Stanwyck) rises up the social scale, in the belief that money and power will bring her happiness. She soon learns otherwise but gradually learns to build a better life through self-sacrifice and love for her daughter (Anne Shirley). Nonetheless, we are also made aware of the woman's capability to move up the social scale and compete with men on equal terms. This helps to explain why such films were as popular with the actresses who performed them as with filmgoers of the period.

The producer Walter Wanger was certainly well aware of this when he purchased Leonardo Bercovici's script for the film of *The Aspern Papers* (retitled *The Lost Moment*) as a vehicle for Susan Hayward, who was under personal contract to him at that time.[13] Wanger not only hoped to repeat the success he had enjoyed with the women's film *Smash-Up: The Story of a Woman* (1947), in which Hayward's performance as an alcoholic wife had been nominated for a Best Actress Oscar,[14] but he also sought critical recognition as the producer of a sophisticated psychological romance, reminiscent of other successful films of the time (e.g., Curtis Bernhardt's *A Stolen Life* [1946]). The press book for *The Lost Moment* expressed his intentions very clearly, as he referred to the fact that as he suggested that the main reason for going ahead with the James adaptation was that he believed there was a genuine demand for this type of film.[15]

Unlike *Berkeley Square*, fourteen years earlier, which had been based on Broadway and West End successes, *The Lost Moment* was an entirely new creation. Yet the idea of adapting a James novel for the screen was not as outlandish for Hollywood as it might seem. As early as 1941, the producer David O. Selznick had considered transforming *Wings of the Dove* into a vehicle for his wife, Jennifer Jones; a year later, the *New York Times* reported that filming would begin in early summer under the new title "She Walks in Beauty." Two years later, the same newspaper announced that Selznick had finally purchased screen rights to the novel, and was going to produce a woman's film for three of his contract players—Dorothy McGuire, Ingrid Bergman, and (possibly) Joseph Cotten.[16] Nothing ever came of the idea, nor did anything come of the (potentially interesting) prospect of Hitchcock directing *The Turn of the Screw*, which Selznick apparently offered to him following his success with *Notorious* (1946).[17] By contrast, Wanger agreed to film Bercovici's script for *The Aspern Papers* under the new title *The Lost Moment*, with Robert Cummings and Agnes Moorehead to support Susan Hayward.

Unlike James's original novella, Bercovici's script gives the narrator a name—Louis Venable—but it seems that he is obsessed by the desire to procure the mysterious papers—Aspern (renamed Ashton) papers—from the Bordereau family. The script has him observing in a voice-over that

> The glory of the world is its gathered beauty, its tragedy, the beauty that has been lost. In that empty space, there might have been a book of the greatest love letters ever written, letters of unsurpassed charm and passion, written in the last century by this man, the great poet Jeffrey Ashton to the beautiful Juliana Bordereau. Over thirty years ago I, Louis Venable, then an ambitious young publisher, read those letters. For a few tormented hours I held them in my hand, literary treasures that publishers from Europe and America had sought long and desperately.

However, Bercovici departs from James's novella by suggesting that both Juliana and Tina are equally obsessive: Juliana jealously protects her beautiful memories of Ashton, while Tina repeatedly tries to imagine a moment of beauty to liven up her life. James's novella has the narrator remarking somewhat patronizingly that Tina "evidently was of the impression that she had had a dashing youth."[18] Bercovici omits that passage entirely, and invents completely new scenes where Tina assumes the identity of Juliana as a young woman, enjoying her romance with Ashton. She mistakes Venable for her lover and embraces him, exclaiming as she does so that nothing will matter after he has kissed her.

Tina's existence is well expressed in a newly written scene where Venable, startled by a bird trapped in Tina's room as he is about to steal Ashton's letters, tenderly helps it to freedom. At first it perches on the mantelpiece, but as Venable moves towards it the bird flies away and stuns itself on a wall, falling to the ground with a loud plop. This moment suggests that if Tina were not imprisoned by her fantasies, she might experience a similar fate, as someone shut up in a cage without any opportunity to fly properly. Nonetheless, it soon becomes evident that Venable seeks to find a cure for her. Bercovici creates a new character, Father Renaldo, who advises him to love her deeply. Venable acts on this advice and asks her out to dinner, whereupon her face loses its hard edge and her voice becomes softer as she nods her head in assent. After returning home in a gondola, she says goodnight to him, admitting as she does so that she will always remember this evening. As she shuts her front door, she slowly loosens a lock of hair beneath her lace shawl. The message is obvious; and entirely coherent in terms of late 1940s domestic ideology. Having found the right man, she can now look forward to a life of security in marriage, which will successfully "cure" her of her fantasies.

Venable seems equally affected by Tina's presence; in a voice-over, he admits to himself that the memory of her sitting opposite him in the gondola now seems more important to him than the recovery of Ashton's letters. Bercovici's adaptation ends with the two of them locked in an embrace, while the camera cuts to a fragment of one of the letters bearing the legend "Forever Jeffrey." Evidently this is the outcome Ashton would have wanted, had he been alive. The ending departs from James's novella in two ways; firstly, it shows the narrator/Venable divesting himself of his obsession, as he falls for Tina. Secondly, Bercovici does not have Tina destroying the letters in a final act of resistance. Instead, they are burnt to a cinder in a fire accidentally started by Juliana as she falls to the ground, upsetting an oil lamp as she does so. In the ensuing blaze, both Juliana and the entire house are destroyed. The symbolic significance of the dénouement, as a means of releasing Tina from her fantasies, is emphasized by Venable's observation in voice-over that she had never lived, so long as she remained shut up with her aunt in that house.

Unlike academic critics of the time such as F. R. Leavis, who considered James an "intellectual poet-novelist of 'high civilization,'"[19] Bercovici rendered *The Aspern Papers* accessible to a wider audience by focusing on current concerns about gender roles. Single women such as Tina were perceived as "deviant" in the sense that they could only discover an alternative to their isolation in fantasy. Such fantasies, according to Freud's essay "A Child Is Being Beaten" (1919)—a principal source for manuals such as *Modern Woman: The Lost Sex*—were little more than an attempt to reject the erotic side of life altogether. The woman "is no longer anything but a spectator of the event which takes the place of a sexual act."[20] In another successful woman's film, *A Stolen Life*, the spinster-heroine Kate (Bette Davis) is criticized at one point for perpetually retreating into the world of the imagination. The only way she can dispel her fantasies, and thereby end her suffering, is to find a suitable marriage partner. In the final sequence, she achieves her wishes as she is hugged by Bill Emerson (Glenn Ford), who admits as he does so that as she has already suffered so much, she should be spared any further agony.

The publicity for *The Lost Moment* stressed the significance of Tina's and Venable's love affair. While the two of them lived shut up in a castle where no love had lived for over a century, watched over by Juliana Bordereau (Agnes Moorehead)—"a deathless secret of the past!"—they nonetheless managed to come together "for the most fascinating love ever known!" Another tagline described "the wild and wondrous rapture" Tina experiences at the end of the film as she finds the man of her dreams. This was appended to a poster designed for the original theatrical release that shows Venable planting a kiss on Tina's right cheek, while Tina's eyes look dreamily skywards.

On the face of it, *The Lost Moment* appears to endorse the orthodox view of marriage as women's ultimate aim. But perhaps the film's message is not as straightforward as might first appear—on account of Susan Hayward's central performance as Tina Bordereau. She is first seen in medium close-up, dressed in a long black gown with padded shoulders, her face and hands illuminated in bright light.[21] Her face remains impassive as Venable (Robert Cummings) introduces himself as William Burton; eschewing all pleasantries, she scowls at him before leaving the room, telling him that she has no choice in deciding whether he should stay with them or not—it's up to her aunt. Venable is obviously shocked by her indifference; later on, he asks her why she seems so determined to seal him off from the rest of the house. Tina's face is shown in close-up, her nostrils flaring as she responds to his question by asking why Venable should want to pay such an extravagant rent for staying with them. Whereas James describes Tina as "the oddest mixture of shyness and straightness,"[22] in *The Lost Moment* she is shown to be more than a match for the diffident Venable.

Tina's personality conforms very closely to Hayward's star persona, as constructed in newspapers and fanzines of the time. She was characterized as someone from a modest background, achieving success through sheer strength of will. A Paramount press release of 1943 described her as a "red-haired beauty who has scrapped her way to the top . . . after starting in Hollywood without a moment's acting experience."[23] As Hayward's career reached its peak in the early 1950s, the fanzines focused even more attention on her ability to overcome adversity. She was thought to possess "the instinctive reflexes of a born fighter; she is always ready to square up to anyone who stands in her way."[24] Anyone wanting to marry her would have to accept her on her own terms and not try to dominate her. Her first marriage to actor Jess Barker failed, which prompted Hayward to announce in a 1956 interview that following her divorce she was "going to enjoy [her] freedom. Marriage should be made much more difficult and divorce much easier."[25]

In *The Lost Moment*, Hayward's Tina suspects her potential suitor's intentions. Venable encounters her on the morning after he has first witnessed her playing the role of Juliana as a young woman and observes that he would have liked to have seen the real Juliana with her beauty that (according to Ashton) was beyond words. As he speaks, the camera cuts to Tina's face, which remains impassive until the phrase "her beauty is beyond words" when her eyes open wide and her lip begins to tremble. This momentary flicker of emotion soon passes, as she derisively calls Venable a writer of romantic stories. While she may be affected by his remarks, she does not feel it appropriate to show her emotions, lest Venable should take advantage of her.

But even the toughest personality can apparently change. In a later scene, Tina is discovered in the palazzo garden dressed in Juliana's white ball gown, the moonlight shining on her face. As Venable walks slowly towards her, she murmurs "Jeffrey?" and holds out her arms towards him in anticipation. The two of them embrace; Tina subsequently moves away, observing that she could never live without him. She turns slowly towards Venable, a tear slowly trickling down her right cheek, and asks, "You do love me, Jeffrey?" The sequence ends with the two of them waltzing in the moonlight. What renders this scene particularly interesting, however, is the apparent contradiction between what is heard and what we witness on screen. On the one hand,

Tina confesses that she needs the love of a man, irrespective of whether she knows him as Jeffrey or Venable. On the other hand, Hayward's stellar performance (which is highlighted through the repeated use of close-up) suggests the opposite—that Tina has the capacity to dominate through sheer emotional force. Hayward's biographer Douglas McClelland considers this sequence an example of "acting of the highest rank."[26]

The same contradiction underlies the film's final moments. While Tina willingly accepts Venable's "protection" by taking his hands and embracing him, the fact that the camera focuses on her face bathed in bright light suggests that she is the dominant partner in this relationship. Moreover, it seems significant that no mention is made in the script of whether Tina and Venable intend to marry in the future. This omission seems entirely appropriate for a film that focuses our attention on a star with a reputation as an independent, free-thinking woman. Walter Wanger summed up Hayward's personality in a brief, simple statement: "She has real fire inside."[27]

If Leslie Howard's star persona in films like Berkeley Square offered new versions of manhood in the previous decade, Hayward accomplished much the same feat in the 1940s. Many filmgoers of 1940s and 1950s clearly identified with her; one woman recalled how she admired anyone who, although experiencing "various types of insecurities," did not let them "stand in the way of obtaining her dreams."[28] In her essay "Feminine Fascinations," Jackie Stacey uses the reminiscences of over three hundred correspondents from all parts of the globe to show how many women of the 1940s and early 1950s perceived stars such as Hayward as symbols of liberation from accepted gender roles. By imitating patterns of speech or gesture, or by drawing attention to a particular trait in themselves that resembled that of a star, they discovered new possibilities for self-expression.[29]

Although The Lost Moment's message was one that was characteristic of women's films of the time (and could thus be relied upon to attract filmgoers' interest), the film failed at the box office. Perhaps the subject matter was too sophisticated for audiences—even though the film's use of fantasy sequences, providing some kind of liberation from the humdrum reality of everyday life for the central character, was strongly reminiscent of Berkeley Square. Nonetheless, the film emerged from cinematic oblivion in the early 1970s, at a time when the feminist movement was mounting a full-fledged assault on sexism in all its manifestations. At the same time, critical opinion of The Aspern Papers had also changed; Carolyn G. Heilbrun saw Tina as someone "affronting her destiny and refusing to be trapped by the usual expectations society has for her."[30] Susan Hayward's reputation also improved; many of her most famous films (including *The Lost Moment*) were revived, and she played cameo roles in cult classics such as *Valley of the Dolls* (Twentieth Century Fox, 1967). One writer described her in 1970 as "a Hollywood original and one of the earthiest actresses to grace to screen. . . . With flaming red hair and a voice that ranged from throaty purr to challenging rasp, Hayward played tough with tough guy co-stars."[31] Since her death in 1975, *The Lost Moment* has been regularly shown on television and released on video. Amazon.com's current review section on the film includes several contributions from viewers who describe it as "surprisingly effective," "stylishly made," and "exquisitely done."[32] The film offers an object lesson in how women can disengage themselves from the roles and gestures of a "naturalized" (i.e., imposed) femininity and thereby challenge traditional ways of conceptualizing sexual difference.

Notes

1. Matthew Bernstein, *Walter Wanger: Hollywood Independent* (Minneapolis: University of Minnesota Press, 1994), 236.

2. "The Lost Moment," *Monthly Film Bulletin* 16, no. 182 (February 1949): 25.

3. Paul Taylor, "The Lost Moment," *Time Out* (June 27–July 3, 1980): 50.

4. Tom Milne, "Retrospective: The Lost Moment," *Monthly Film Bulletin*, no. 593 (January 1983): 170–71.

5. Helene Deutsch, *The Psychology of Women* (New York: Grune & Stratton, 1944–1945), 1:289–90.

6. Ferdinand Lundberg and Maryna Farnham, *Modern Woman: The Lost Sex* (New York: Grosset & Dunlap / Universal Library, 1947), 360.

7. Judson J. Landis and Mary G. Landis, *Building a Successful Marriage* (New York: Prentice-Hall, 1948), 34, 77.

8. Deutsch, *Psychology of Women*, 1:302.

9. Deutsch, *Psychology of Women*, 1:295.

10. Lundberg and Farnham, *Modern Woman*, 166–67.

11. Alison Butler, *Women's Cinema: The Contested Screen* (London: Wallflower Press, 2002), 28.

12. *A Code to Govern the Making of Motion and Talking Pictures: The Reasons Supporting It and the Resolution for Uniform Interpretation* (Hollywood: Motion Picture Producers and Distributors of America, 1934), 12.

13. Leonardo Bercovici (1908–1995) was a Hollywood screenwriter whose credits also included *The Bishop's Wife* (1947) with Cary Grant and Loretta Young and *Portrait of Jennie* (1948) for Selznick with Jennifer Jones in the title role. One wonders, given his association with Selznick, whether Bercovici may have conceived *The Lost Moment* as a vehicle for Jones.

14. Wanger was particularly keen to have another success on his hands; of the eight films he produced between 1940 and 1945, only two of them made a profit (Bernstein, *Walter Wanger*, 442–4).

15. "Intelligent Films Aim of Producer Walter Wanger" in press book: *The Lost Moment* (Los Angeles: Universal International Pictures, 1947), 2. The press book also claimed that *The Lost Moment* was the first adaptation of a Henry James novel. Evidently the producers were unaware of the original source for *Berkeley Square*.

16. "Selznick Gets Rights to 'Wings of the Dove,'" *New York Times*, October 25, 1944, 16.

17. Leonard J. Leff, *Hitchcock and Selznick: The Rich and Strange Collaboration of Alfred Hitchcock and David O. Selznick in Hollywood* (Berkeley: University of California Press, 1987), 222.

18. Henry James, *The Aspern Papers and The Turn of the Screw*, ed. Anthony Curtis (Harmondsworth: Penguin Classics, 1986), 85.

19. F. R. Leavis, *The Great Tradition* (Harmondsworth: Peregrine Books, 1983), 21. (Original edition, 1948.)

20. Sigmund Freud, "A Child Is Being Beaten" (1919), in *Sexuality and the Psychology of Love*, ed. Philip Rieff (New York: Collier Books, 1963), 128.

21. Padded shoulders was a style characteristic of many leading actresses at this time. Joan Crawford clashed with the director of *Mildred Pierce* (Warner Bros., 1945), Michael Curtiz, when he asked her to dispose of her shoulder pads: "Those are *my* shoulders!" she was reputed to have said. Shaun Considine, *Bette and Joan: The Divine Feud* (London: Century Hutchinson, 1989), 180.

22. James, *The Aspern Papers*, 82.

23. "Biography of Susan Hayward" (Los Angeles: Paramount Pictures Press Release, 1943), 1.

24. Thomas Wood, "If You Knew Susie," *Picturegoer* (December 29, 1951): 8.

25. Thomas Wiseman, "Susan Hayward Gives Me the Recipe for Her Marriage," *Evening Standard* (London), February 26, 1956, 7. This freedom did not last long. Hayward married her second husband Eaton Chalkley in 1956, a marriage that lasted nine years until Chalkley's untimely death.

26. Doug McClelland, *The Complete Life Story of Susan Hayward, Immortal Screen Star* (New York: Pinnacle Books, 1973), 80.

27. Karen Burroughs Hansberry, "Susan Hayward," in *Femme Noir: Bad Girls of Film* (Jefferson, NC: McFarland, 1998), 249.

28. "Memories of Susan Hayward," at www.geocities.com/audrey_64063/mythoughtsonsusan.html (accessed July 16, 2002).

29. Jackie Stacey, "Feminine Fascinations: Forms of Identification in Star-Audience Relations," in *Stardom: Industry of Desire*, ed. Christine Gledhill (London: Routledge, 1991), 153–55.

30. Carolyn G. Heilbrun, *Towards a Recognition of Androgyny* (New York: Harper and Row, 1973), 95–96.

31. Ken Ferguson, "A Tribute to a Great Actress," *Films and Filming* (April 1970): 24–25.

32. "*The Lost Moment*: Spotlight Reviews," *Amazon.com*, 2000–2004, at www.amazon .com/exec/obidos/tg/detail/-/6300208664/qid = 1134593736/sr = 8–2/ref = sr_8_xs_ap_i2 _xg127/103–5655956–4230241?v = glance&s = video&n = 507846 (accessed December 14, 2005).

CHAPTER THREE

~

The Heiress (1949)

Like *Berkeley Square*, *The Heiress* was based on a Broadway success. It was produced at a time when Henry James's works had suddenly become popular in Hollywood. *The Lost Moment* had appeared in 1947; David Selznick had announced that *The Wings of the Dove* would be filmed with Jennifer Jones; Paramount Pictures, not to be outdone, had also announced a production of *The Portrait of a Lady*, with a script written by Dodie Smith (the author of *101 Dalmatians*). Eventually the idea was abandoned, and Paramount opted instead to buy *The Heiress* as a vehicle for Olivia de Havilland, whose performance in *The Snake Pit* (1948) had won her a Best Actress Oscar.

The Heiress, directed by William Wyler, focuses on a single woman, Catherine Sloper, who—unlike Tina Bordereau in *The Lost Moment*—rejects her suitor, Morris Townsend (Montgomery Clift), in a memorable final scene. She closes all the curtains in her house and sits calmly in her father's chair in the back parlor. Taking a lighted lamp, she coldly walks upstairs, while Morris watches the light move away and diminish in strength. This is shot with a tracking camera that ascends the stairs with her as we hear Morris's knocking at the door. At the top of the stairs, she turns back toward the front door—portraying an isolated, yet towering figure, gaining perverse satisfaction from jilting him. Her final line, "I have been taught by masters," is delivered with tremendous power.[1] In terms of the domestic ideology of the late 1940s, this sequence may be viewed as a warning to female filmgoers of the loneliness they will endure if a suitable marriage partner cannot be found. Peter Swaab compares it to Frank Capra's *It's a Wonderful Life* (Columbia 1946), in which James Stewart's "tactful and devoted wife" (Donna Reed) "is glimpsed, in the nightmare alternative town, as a twitchy frumpish spinster."[2]

However, I suggest in this chapter that Wyler's film takes advantage of de Havilland's dominant on-screen presence to draw a much more positive conclusion, as Catherine matures into a poised, attractive woman who appears to have no need of male company.[3] As Mary Ann Doane observes, she takes a positive pleasure in humiliating Morris, "even if that pleasure is limited by its status as revenge. . . . Catherine climbs the stairs, site of the woman's specularization in the classical cinema, but she is held by no man's gaze."[4] I further suggest that this aspect of women's independence was reinforced in the production design, which deliberately focused on the sets and costumes as objects for consumption, designed to appeal to the wish-fulfilling fantasies of the audience, particularly women. This "sexual sell" was complemented by a publicity campaign in which *The Heiress* was used (among other things) to advertise cars, jewelry, and handbags. Such strategies were characteristic of many women's films that took advantage of the prevailing belief in affluence as a way of sustaining the American way of life to promote an image of female self-liberation entirely bound up with the acquisition of new things, particularly luxury goods.[5]

James himself was not fond of *Washington Square*; in his letters, he dismissed it as a "slender tale, of rather too narrow an interest. I don't, honestly, take much stock in it."[6] By the mid-twentieth century, however, the novella's reputation had undergone a critical renaissance both in academic and journalistic circles. The critic F. O. Matthiessen was someone who undertook a crucial role in reshaping the discussion; he believed that *Washington Square* revealed "a profound sense of moral values" (xi)—as witnessed, for example, in "the simple moral goodness of Catherine [Sloper], in contrast to the cruel egotism of her father and the bare-faced venality of her suitor."[7] Three years later, he identified Catherine as James's center of interest in the novella. He endowed her with none of the usual charm of his heroines, and began by describing her as "plain" and "dull." He then proceeded to develop her, through her unshakable devotion to her one deluded love, into a woman of heroic dignity.[8]

However, it was generally believed that despite the central character's attractions, *Washington Square* could only appeal to those of civilized sensibility. Writing in the *New York Times* in 1947, Brooks Atkinson described James as someone torn between "the dedicated life of the artist" and "the worldly life, which is vulgar but pleasant and comfortable." He was master of one, but longed for success in the other—as seen, for instance, in his unsuccessful attempts to write a play for the London stage. The failure of *Guy Domville* (1895) "wounded him deeply and he crawled back into his literary canon."[9]

In another article written three years later, Atkinson suggested that, despite its relatively straightforward plot, *Washington Square* needed to be rewritten for mass audiences; this is what prompted Ruth and Augustus Goetz to adapt it into a Broadway play—*The Heiress*—incorporating changes "dictated by the theatre where stories have to be seen in orderly consequence and something has to happen decisively in terms of time and action."[10]

An example of this kind of alteration can be seen early on in *The Heiress*, when Morris Townsend first encounters Catherine. James contrives the meeting at a small soirée given by Mrs. Almond, in which the two of them sit "on a little sofa that seemed meant only for two persons."[11] The subsequent conversation is mostly in reported speech, with Morris doing all the talking, while Catherine leans back, admiring his ability to be "so sincere, so natural" in his conversation.[12] The emphasis throughout is on Catherine's gradually increasing affection for Morris, which gradually overcomes her natural tendency towards "self-effacement and sacrifice."[13] The thought of being in love "yielded her a happiness in which confidence and timidity were strangely blended."[14] By contrast, the Goetzes show the two of them meeting for the first time at a party given at Catherine's house; the major focus here is on Catherine's shyness and her lack of social grace. She is a defenseless young woman with a large fortune, easily fooled by Morris's flattery:

MORRIS:	(*smiling at her*) You make me very happy. Do you love me?
CATHERINE:	Yes.
MORRIS:	Dear Catherine! (*He kisses her*)
CATHERINE:	(*holding him*) I love you! I love you!
MORRIS:	I will cherish you for ever.[15]

While there is little suggestion here of the blend of "confidence and timidity" described by James, this alteration paves the way for the climax to the first act. Catherine's love for Morris inspires her to resist her father's wishes—perhaps for the first time—by resolving to marry him, no matter what the consequences.[16]

Critics have remarked on the fact that the Catherine Sloper of *The Heiress* (in both the play and film versions) differs substantially from the Catherine of James's novella. As Jerry Carlson observes,

Whereas James's heroine shows internal moral development, Wyler's heroine displays an abrupt reversal of character: first she is a duped innocent, and then she is a stoic domestic warrior returning injury in kind. Or, to put it differently, whereas

James's narrative is based on a line of moral development, Wyler's film is based on the symmetry of revenge.[17]

I would argue that Wyler's principal intention was not to evoke the complexities of the novella but rather to produce a film built around his star actress that focused on contemporary gender politics.[18] Whereas Olivia de Havilland had once been associated with "sweet" roles (such as Melanie Wilkes in *Gone with the Wind* [1939]), her star persona had radically changed in the 1940s, following her successful court case in 1944 against Warner Brothers to release her from her seven-year contract. She was now characterized as someone whose "steely will" not only gave her the freedom to choose her own films but also rendered her quite capable of surviving on her own resources.[19] *The Heiress* proved an ideal vehicle to reinforce this image. The original play opened on Broadway in September 1947 with the British actors Wendy Hiller and Basil Rathbone in the leading roles; the London production followed two years later. Wyler's biographer reports that De Havilland saw the play in New York and asked Wyler to direct the film version: "It had a great role for her, she said, and she was certain she could help him sell Paramount on the idea."[20]

Ruth and Augustus Goetz's screenplay for *The Heiress*[21] acknowledged de Havilland's presence as the star by focusing more attention on her. For example, the clandestine first meeting between Morris and Catherine, which takes place not on a little sofa (as in the play) but in a gazebo, in the middle of a party celebrating the engagement of Arthur Townsend and Marian Almond. The emphasis here is on the awakening of Catherine's feelings for Morris, which is underlined through a series of tight close-ups. At first, Catherine uses her fan to cover up her embarrassment at being alone with an unmarried man. As he speaks, however, she steals a glance at his unmarked dance card; like herself, he appears not to be a popular partner. This gives her the confidence to look directly into his eyes, as he talks about himself and his past life; it is evident, as James suggests, that this first encounter has prompted her to think that "no one who had first seen him [Morris] would ever forget him."[22]

The film also restores the scene from the novella, omitted from the stage version, where Sloper drinks wine in his dining room with Morris, and reflects to himself on the young man's character: "He is uncommonly well turned out; quite the sort of figure that pleases the ladies. But I don't think I like him."[23] Yet the main focus of interest is on Catherine's apprehensive face as she stands outside the dining room, watching the two of them talking—Morris eagerly trying to please Sloper, while Sloper remains impassive, his eyes "quietly fixed on his [Morris's] bright, expressive face."[24] The scene is shot in a series of long takes, focusing on what Wyler described as "a deliberately slow unfolding of character in dramatic conflict rather than a rapid-fire unfolding of the plot in pictorial action."[25]

The concentration on Olivia de Havilland's performance was intensified by means of some newly created scenes. Having waited in vain for Morris to show up on the night they were due to elope, Catherine understands that he will not come and that she has been jilted. She turns away from the door and walks up the stairs to her room, still clutching her suitcase. Apparently, this scene took a long time to film; after several retakes, Wyler ordered the suitcase to be filled with books and made de Havilland climb the stairs once more. Catherine's exhaustion now became palpable: "Her humiliation and despair seemed to tug at her. She looked as if she were dragging herself up from the bottom of the sea."[26] This scene represents a turning point in Wyler's film; having discovered Morris's true nature, Catherine learns that the only way to maintain her self-respect is to look after herself. Unlike Susan Hayward's Tina Bordereau, she feels she no longer has any need of male company.

The importance of this dictum for Catherine's future is stressed in her subsequent encounters with her father (Ralph Richardson). As he tells her of his impending death, Catherine's impassive countenance is contrasted in a two-shot with that of Maria, the maid (Vanessa Brown),[27] who breaks down in tears. Directly contrary to James's novella, which describes Catherine as "assiduous" in the efforts to nurse her sick father,[28] Wyler's film shows her refusing to see him, even while he lies on his deathbed. Her reaction may seem excessively brutal, but perhaps she is entitled to it; after all, her father had meted out the same treatment to her in the past. Following her six-month European trip, he congratulates her on having become an "entertaining companion." By stressing the consonants in the word "entertaining," Richardson's Dr. Sloper bears witness to James's observation that "it is a literal fact that he almost never addressed his daughter save in the ironical form."[29]

In its concentration on family relations and their problems, *The Heiress* might be thought of as another woman's film—similar in form to *The Lost Moment* in its presentation of a wish-fulfillment scenario. In *The Heiress*, this is not only built into the plot—as Catherine Sloper discovers a voice of her own—but also established through Harry Horner's costume designs. Catherine begins the film dressed in frumpish clothes; her movements clearly suggest that she lacks social grace. On her return from Europe, however, she has acquired elegance and poise; dressed in the latest French fashions, she sits bolt upright in her chair as she cuts the thread from the last letter of her embroidered alphabet and admires her completed work. The sound of Morris pounding his fists on the door outside can be heard. The message is clear: Any woman—provided she has the will to do so—can follow the example of de Havilland's Catherine and symbolically cut the threads of her attachment to anything or anyone.[30] Reviewers of the time were impressed—one drew attention to Catherine's face ("devoid of make-up"), which rendered her the very antithesis of the traditional Hollywood beauty.[31]

The appeal to the audience's wish-fulfilling instincts is evident in other aspects of the film. It was Wyler's belief that, for any film to be a success, every element had to be treated with equal importance—cast, photography, editing, and sets. He collaborated with Horner to create authentic period settings (a strategy that would become much more familiar in James adaptations from the 1970s onwards) that would not give the secrets of the story away. "The story may be a serious one," he observed to Horner, "but this should not show in the designs of the house, since the structure could not know in advance what its inhabitants would do."[32] Eventually, Horner came up with a design concept for Sloper's house that gave the feeling "of having gone through several styles, thus making the first phase of his life which existed only in his memory stand out and become evisible to us."[33]

The entrance hall is dominated by a dramatic staircase, extending upward to the second and third floors. As Wyler himself suggested, "Staircases can give you marvellous camera movement and people can back down them or rise up them to reflect their characters and relationships."[34] In her analysis of Douglas Sirk's *Written on the Wind* (Universal, 1957), Barbara Klinger has shown how the director makes use of the studio's famous "stairway of the stars"—a monumental forty-eight-step structure with a thirty-year history of use. In the film, it not only evokes riches and glamour but also provides an opportunity for Dorothy Malone to make a star entrance, dressed in Bill Thomas's gorgeous gowns. This technique, Klinger argues, is designed to "appeal to the acquisitive fantasies of its spectators, particularly women who were considered the primary purchasers of commodities.[35] In *The Heiress*, the staircase fulfills a different symbolic function: As Olivia de Havilland's Catherine walks up alone to the second floor, having refused to let Morris in during the final scene, she offers a vision of independence to filmgoers—an opulently dressed mistress of the mise-en-scène with no one around to contradict her.

The publicity for *The Heiress* reinforced this idea by suggesting that anyone seeking self-improvement and freedom could follow Catherine's example and achieve it through the acquisition of goods—gowns, jewelry, automobiles, or even property. The posters set the tone for the campaign—especially the taglines for the four teaser ads, heralding the film's opening at the Radio City Music Hall in 1949, which employed words associated with wealth (riches, jewelry) to describe the experience of watching the film. Paramount organized several tie-in campaigns—one invited filmgoers to write reviews of the film, with three Kaiser-Frazer cars valued at over $2,000 each as prizes for the best entries. Any enterprising cinema manager who worked out the best promotional campaign could also win a car; he or she (though presumably he) would be taken to the factory in Willow Rim, Michigan, where he would pick up the car for himself.[36] Those female filmgoers who wanted to follow in Olivia de Havilland's footsteps were given ample opportunity to make their dreams come true. They could try making her costumes for themselves; a sampler design was published in the November 1949 issue of *Good Housekeeping*, with a chart for embroidery based on the film's title being published in the same magazine three months later. Anyone seeking more embroidery could send for a booklet of designs. The press book also proposed an heiress-for-a-day campaign where local businesses were encouraged to provide free services for one lucky girl, who would have the chance to buy the clothes she wanted and enjoy a free beauty treatment.[37] However, the truly fashion-conscious woman had no need to demean herself in competition; she could order her outfits from top New York stores, which offered suits, compacts, hats, jewelry, handbags, and scarves inspired by the film. Even those who neither had money nor prizes could still sample the high life by having a postcard sent to them from the Vanderbilt Hotel, complete with a New York postmark.[38]

The campaign was carefully organized by what Betty Friedan described in her seminal work, *The Feminine Mystique* (1963), as the studio "manipulators and their friends in American business," whose sole intention lay in "flattering the American housewife, diverting her guilt and disguising her growing sense of emptiness."[39] Although Friedan's work summed up the experience of many women in the 1940s and 1950s, perhaps her judgment is a little unfair. Just like Wyler's film, the publicity sought to draw attention to the qualities of the heroine and the actress playing her—qualities that seemed to offer an exciting alternative to the stereotyped roles of wife and mother that were being put forward in the domestic manuals of the time. Perhaps uniquely for a performer of her time, Olivia de Havilland had managed to steer clear of unscrupulous studio bosses and forged her own career path, even if she had to win a court case along the way. She was someone who provided a shining example of what could be achieved if a woman stuck to her convictions and refused to accept the roles offered her by the (male) studio bosses. Elaine Tyler May remarks with justification that many women's films (including *The Lost Moment* and *The Heiress*) sought to represent their central characters differently, as "[once] subservient homemakers moved into center stage" at the expense of "emancipated heroines."[40]

The Heiress opened in New York in October 1949 and in London three months later. In box-office terms, the film's performance might be described as sluggish; it took six months to recoup its costs. Nevertheless, it was nominated for eight Oscars and won four—Best Actress, Best Art Direction, Best Costume Design (Edith Head), and Best Score (Aaron Copland). A movie tie-in paperback text of James's novella, complete with thirteen stills from the film, was published in 1949; a year later, the work was reissued by Random House with a critical introduction by Clifton Fadiman, and in hardback in Britain by the writer-publisher John Lehmann. Clearly, the flurry of Hollywood adaptations of James's works (both actual and proposed adaptations) at the end of the 1940s had brought about a renewed popular interest in his works.

Notes

1. Ruth Goetz and Augustus Goetz, *The Heiress: A Play* (London: Samuel French, 1979), 86.

2. Peter Swaab, "The End of Embroidery: From *Washington Square* to *The Heiress*," in *Henry James on Stage and Screen*, ed. John R. Bradley (Basingstoke: Palgrave, 2000), 63.

3. Much of the argument in this chapter is based on my article "Reconstructing Henry James: *The Heiress*," *Literature Film Quarterly* 30, no. 4 (2002): 243–49.

4. Mary Ann Doane, *The Desire to Desire: The Woman's Film of the 1940s* (Basingstoke: Macmillan Press, 1988), 112.

5. For a fuller discussion of this, see Barbara Klinger's analysis of the promotion and marketing of *Written on the Wind*, in *Melodrama and Meaning: History, Culture and the Films of Douglas Sirk* (Bloomington: Indiana University Press, 1994), 79–94.

6. Leon Edel, ed., *Henry James Letters, 1875–1883*, vol. II (Cambridge, MA: Belknap Press of Harvard University Press, 1975), 313.

7. F. O. Matthiessen, *Henry James: The Major Phase* (London: Oxford University Press, 1944), 122.

8. F. O. Matthiessen, "Introduction," *The American Novels and Stories of Henry James* (New York: Alfred A. Knopf, 1947), xi.

9. Brooks Atkinson, "The Theatre 1947," *New York Times*, October 5, 1947, sec. 2, 1.

10. Brooks Atkinson, "The Theatre 1950," *New York Times*, February 12, 1950, sec. 2, 1.

11. Henry James, *Washington Square*, ed. Michael Swan (Harmondsworth: Penguin Books, 1963), 19.

12. James, *Washington Square*, 20.

13. James, *Washington Square*, 40.

14. James, *Washington Square*, 50.

15. Goetz, *The Heiress*, 26.

16. Goetz, *The Heiress*, 45.

17. Jerry Carlson, "*Washington Square* and *The Heiress*: Comparing Artistic Forms," in *The Classic American Novel and the Movies*, ed. Gerald Peary and Roger Shatzkin (New York: Frederick Unger, 1977), 99–100.

18. Wyler's fellow director Tay Garnett recalled that whenever Wyler "found an idea or story that convinced him it would make a good film, he grabbed it. Truly good story properties are rare, and he regarded himself as lucky when he came across one." "William Wyler," in *Directing: Learn from the Masters*, ed. Anthony Slide (Lanham MD: Scarecrow Press, 1996), 299.

19. Charles Higham, *Olivia and Joan: A Biography of Olivia de Havilland and Joan Fontaine* (Sevenoaks, Kent: New English Library, 1984), 129.

20. Jan Herman, *A Talent for Trouble: The Life of Hollywood's Most Acclaimed Director, William Wyler* (New York: G. P. Putnam's Sons, 1996), 306. Higham reports that Wyler thought her "far too beautiful for the part of Catherine Sloper. Moreover, he found her inflexible, intractable" (Higham, *Olivia and Joan*, 145).

21. Apparently Wyler insisted on the Goetzes being engaged to write the screenplay, even though it cost Paramount Pictures $250,000 plus $10,000 per week. Ruth Goetz recalled Wyler saying, "I'm not going to have it [the film] deformed by somebody who doesn't know what to do with it." Herman, *A Talent for Trouble*, 307–8.

22. James, *Washington Square*, 20.

23. James, *Washington Square*, 37.

24. James, *Washington Square*, 37.

25. Axel Madsen, *William Wyler: The Authorized Biography* (New York: Thomas Y. Crowell, 1973), 296–97.

26. Herman, *A Talent for Trouble*, 311.

27. Peter Swaab calls her Kitty, the name given to the maid in the original play ("The End of Embroidery," 64).

28. James, *Washington Square*, 163.

29. James, *Washington Square*, 22. Richardson was making his Hollywood debut after a long career in British films, notably *The Fallen Idol* (1946). He also played Dr. Sloper in the London stage production of *The Heiress* (1950).

30. The image of Catherine embroidering—which has appeared throughout the

film—is reminiscent of Penelope in Homer's *Odyssey*, who, in the belief that her husband was still alive, put off other suitors by weaving a magnificent cloak for three years.

31. L.H.C., "The Heiress," *Today's Cinema* (London) 6062 (August 18, 1950): 9.

32. Harry Horner, "Designing *The Heiress*," *Hollywood Quarterly* 5, no. 1 (Autumn 1950): 2.

33. Horner, "Designing *The Heiress*," 4.

34. William Wyler interviewed by Adrian Turner, *Films and Filming* 325 (October 1981): 14.

35. Klinger, *Melodrama and Meaning*, 58.

36. Press book: *The Heiress*, 26–27.

37. Press book: *The Heiress*, 28.

38. Press book: *The Heiress*, 28.

39. Betty Friedan, *The Feminine Mystique* (Harmondsworth: Penguin Books, 1965), 200–201.

40. Elaine Tyler May, *Homeward Bound: American Families in the Cold War Era* (New York: Basic Books, 1988), 67.

CHAPTER FOUR

~

I'll Never Forget You (1951)

On the face of it, Roy Baker's *I'll Never Forget You* (aka *The House on the Square*) (1951) would seem to be very different from *The Heiress* or *The Lost Moment*. Conceived as a vehicle for Tyrone Power, who had reigned supreme as Twentieth Century Fox's leading male star since the late 1930s, the film was a remake of *Berkeley Square*, but with the title role slightly rewritten to suit Power's star image. If Leslie Howard's Peter Standish was cerebral—someone who was not frightened of flying in the face of accepted convention by expressing his emotions—Power portrayed him as a romantic leading man, someone whose good looks and essential decency of character rendered him attractive to any woman, particularly Helen Pettigrew (Ann Blyth). It was not surprising that filmgoers sympathized with him at the end of the film; unlike the other characters living in eighteenth-century Britain, he maintained his integrity even in the face of those who called him a madman.

However, I suggest in this chapter that what renders *I'll Never Forget You* more interesting, particularly in terms of when it was released, is that screenwriter Ranald MacDougall has reconceived James's unfinished novella as an invasion narrative, exploring the potentially damaging consequences of scientific knowledge on society. The basic premise remains the same, with the main protagonist traveling back in time and assuming the identity of his ancestor. Whereas Ralph in *The Sense of the Past* is a young man with "a bookish taste for research,"[1] Standish in *I'll Never Forget You* is a physicist invading the past in an effort to prove that past, present, and future can exist simultaneously. He discovers to his cost that people fear him as the outsider with a depth of knowledge extending far beyond their comprehension. It is only as a result of considerable personal suffering that he comes to learn how society depends on love and mutual well-being for its future survival rather than on pursuing scientific knowledge. At the same time, *I'll Never Forget You* follows the example of *Berkeley Square* by stressing the importance of sustaining one's personal beliefs, even at the expense of marriage. It suggests that individuals should have the freedom to choose their own gender roles and reject social convention if they should wish.

Originally titled *Man of Two Worlds*, *I'll Never Forget You* underwent a checkered production history. Initially, Carol Reed was to direct Tyrone Power with Jean Simmons as his leading lady. Roy Baker subsequently assumed the director's chair, while the Irish actress Constance Smith was signed to costar. She in turn was replaced by Ann Blyth.[2] Baker recalled that while "the film was pretty and well mounted," it was "grudgingly accepted" by Darryl F. Zanuck as a vehicle for Tyrone Power, who had been Twentieth Century Fox's biggest star during the late 1930s and 1940s, but whose popularity was now on the wane.[3] The reasoning behind this was simple: Zanuck disliked making any film he hadn't already made at least once before.[4] Unlike Leslie Howard, who embodied the virtues of understatement and gentility, Power—the black-haired romantic hero of countless swashbuckling films—inspired "fanatic[al] passions" among his fans: "A warm look, a shy smile, a gentle pat, a gracious thank you, his every small gesture was magnified and glorified."[5] In publicity interviews he was represented as a fair-minded personality who always tried to look for the good in people—particularly women: "I don't deny that women do have some faults, but they are not so great they cannot be overlooked. I would rather look for the good side of a woman rather than look for her faults."[6] Power was not so much an actor as a screen presence—someone whose screen persona seldom changed, irrespective of what kind of film he made. This, the studio believed, was what his fans wanted: "They won't allow Ty to do anything in which he isn't on the screen, recognizably Power. The Power boy is too valuable a property to be permitted to lose himself in acting alone."[7]

Ranald MacDougall's script for *I'll Never Forget You* reconceives Peter Standish to suit Tyrone Power's star image, portraying him as less of a tortured soul and more of a romantic. In one scene, he takes Helen Pettigrew in his arms and sighs; the camera moves in slowly, framing the two of them as they embrace. On another occasion, Standish sits with Helen by a fountain and takes her hand; Balderston's original play has him seizing it feverishly and Helen withdrawing it almost immediately, exclaiming "I am Kate's sister!" as she does so.[8] *I'll Never Forget You* renders the scene far more passionate, as Baker intercuts close-ups of Helen removing her hand and Standish extending his hand once again towards her, as if to indicate that the two of them are testing the strength of their attraction to one another.[9] In the film's closing moments, the two lovers' clasped hands are shown in close-up, as they sit together for the last time. In a point-of-view shot looking over Standish's left shoulder, we see Helen kissing him on the cheek before walking out of the room. In a voice-over, she reveals that she will love him eternally.

Certain other aspects of the Power image appear in MacDougall's script. Having traveled back in time, Standish tries to seek out the good in everyone he meets—including those who actively despise him. As in other Power vehicles such as *Blood and Sand*, he is faced with a choice between two women—Helen and her older sister, Kate (Beatrice Campbell), who requires a rich marriage partner. Kate consistently rebuffs him until the night of their engagement party when he takes her in his arms, telling her that destiny dictates that she should marry him. Kate responds by telling him to go back to America. In Balderston's play Standish subsequently tries to reason with Kate by telling her that "things *can't* happen that *didn't* happen!"[10] MacDougall's script omits this dialogue, and cuts instead to a scene in the garden, where Standish tells Helen that Kate has split up with him. This is clearly intended to make us sympathize with him, as he has tried and failed to fulfill what he perceives as his destiny.

Critics on both sides of the Atlantic were divided as to the suitability of *I'll Never Forget You* as a showcase for Power's talents. *Time* felt that he lacked Leslie Howard's charm and vulnerability: "His inter-century romance . . . makes something gooey and obsolescent out of what once seemed hauntingly other-worldly."[11] *Variety* reviewed the film twice, on its New York and London premieres. While the first reviewer thought that Power gave "a monotonous performance, that isn't aided any by an unmanageable script," the second considered him "sincere and sympathetic" in a film wherein he appeared "on the screen almost throughout."[12]

So far it would seem that *I'll Never Forget You* is a highly conservative film that reproduces rather than challenges existing gender stereotypes, with Power portraying the kind of romantic hero that he had become accustomed to playing over the previous two decades. But perhaps there is more to the film than meets the eye. In 1943, the critic R. P. Blackmur wrote that in *The Sense of the Past* Henry James had sought to create a fable "for the ulterior purposes of his [artistic] faith . . . the form of the fable, the point of the parable, are brought to extreme use precisely by being embodied in the sensibility of fiction."[13] MacDougall takes up this fable idea in his script. We are told at the beginning that Standish takes his work seriously. His boss Ronson (Ronald Adam)—a newly created character—describes him as someone who graduated from MIT as the top student, and now specializes in nuclear physics at Los Alamos.[14] Standish himself admits that he has been doing quite a lot of research; exactly what that research comprises is revealed later on, as he announces to his friend Roger Forsyth (Michael Rennie)—another newly created character—that "I believe the eighteenth century still exists . . . Henry James expressed it like this: . . . I see the maple trees, the clover field, and around the bend. Your past, your present, and your future. They're all one to the man in the plane. So that time—real time—is all one."[15] To prove the truth of his thesis, he has decided to exchange identities with his ancestor and return to 1784—the Age of Reason.

At this stage, Standish seems engaging if somewhat eccentric: The warning bells start to ring when he informs the eighteenth-century characters about what will happen in the future. In a newly created scene, he congratulates Sir Joshua Reynolds (Ronald Simpson) on having painted Sarah Siddons. Reynolds indignantly replies that the painting has not even been completed yet—which only serves to confirm the suspicions of the eighteenth-century characters that Standish is the devil incarnate. MacDougall's version is very different from James's novel, in which the eighteenth-century characters seem prepared to tolerate the central character. But then, perhaps, this is due to Ralph's modesty, which prevents him from assuming the soothsayer's role: "I only confess to have cultivated my imagination, as one has to in a country where there is nothing to take the trouble off one's hands."[16] By contrast in I'll Never Forget You, Standish is tried and ultimately consigned to Bedlam. When he has been taken into custody, and the contents of his laboratory destroyed, Standish naively assumes that men of science such as the physician (Felix Aylmer) will believe him when he predicts how electricity and chloroform will transform people's lives in the future.[17] The physician's response—to pronounce Standish insane—might seem excessive now but was designed to strike a chord with early 1950s filmgoers, who were accustomed to films dealing with the need to protect one's homeland against possible invaders, or those who would try to upset the balance of the world with too much scientific research.

This suspicion of the scientist permeated other films of the time—for example Howard Hawks's and Christian Nyby's The Thing from Another World (1951), where Dr. Carrington (Robert Cornthwaite) believes that "humans can learn secrets [from beings from other planets] that have been hidden from mankind since the beginning of time." This may be acceptable under certain circumstances, but Carrington develops an altogether unhealthy interest in the eponymous Thing, rendering him oblivious to the threat it poses to human civilization. "Knowledge is more important than life. We split the atom!" he shouts at one point, in a burst of enthusiasm. "That sure made everybody happy" comes the sardonic reply from one of his colleagues. Another film of the same year, Robert Wise's *The Day the Earth Stood Still* (1951), apparently posits a more liberal message. Klaatu, the alien (Michael Rennie), has been sent to inform humanity that its irrationality threatens the universal order. Gort, the robot that Klaatu brings with him (Lock Martin), has the power to destroy the Earth if it does not put its "irrational" differences and petty interests aside. However, Klaatu also originates from a world policed by robots that possess absolute power and punish any aggressors. Like the alien in *The Thing from Another World*, these robots can be remorseless and cruel; negotiations with them are futile, and those who try it may be self-deceiving at best. We should be wary of what Klaatu says; for all his apparent "normality"—his cultured appearance, mild manners, and soft way of speaking—Klaatu is a spokesman for a police state that threatens humanity's future survival. Those who consider him as a "monster" on radio or in the newspapers are absolutely right.

There is little doubt that *I'll Never Forget You* was designed in many ways to recall *The Day the Earth Stood Still*, with Standish as the Klaatu-like figure whose scientific knowledge is perceived as dangerous by the inhabitants of eighteenth-century London. Both were produced by Twentieth Century Fox; the presence of Michael Rennie in both casts (as one of *Variety*'s reviewers noted) "points up the science fiction that seems to have influenced [the studio]."[18] In *I'll Never Forget You*, Rennie played another atomic scientist, Roger Forsyth, who tries to dissuade Standish from making his journey to the past. The fact that he appeared in both films is no coincidence: He had signed a long-term contract with Fox in 1950, after beginning his career in British films.

The fact that people are scared of Standish, in spite of his professed desire to improve their lives through scientific research, does not seem to render him much of a romantic hero. MacDougall's script resolves this tension by making him understand that love is much more essential to the survival of the world than scientific knowledge. As he departs the house in Berkeley Square for Bedlam, accompanied by the magistrate (Martyn Benson), tears stream down his cheeks as he clutches the *crux ansata* (a parting gift from Helen). The thunder rolls, lightning flashes, and Standish returns to the present. Having encountered Forsyth's sister Martha (Ann Blyth), who bears a striking resemblance to Helen, Standish runs upstairs, takes the *crux ansata* out of a drawer, and makes straight for Helen's grave. As he kneels beside the tombstone, Helen's voice can be heard on the soundtrack—to the accompaniment of heavenly voices singing in Latin—saying, "We shall be together always. Not in my time, Peter, or in yours, but in God's time."[19] In a flash, Standish understands that she died only a little while after he left—most likely from a broken heart. Now all he can do is remain true to her memory. He walks slowly away from the tomb arm-in-arm with Martha and Forsyth, before getting into a car and driving away as the action fades out.[20] The scene is far more low key in tone than Frank Lloyd's version of *Berkeley Square*, where Leslie Howard rejects his fiancée and opts for the single life; it is perhaps more appropriate to Tyrone Power's star image as someone who cares for people—particularly women.

However, the principal focus of attention in the closing scenes of *I'll Never Forget You* is not Standish but Helen Pettigrew. Having urged him to stay here in the eighteenth century and not return to his own time, she comes to realize that this is not a viable option. All she can do is ask him not to be too sad in the future about a girl who's been dead so long.[21] As he departs, she promises to love Standish eternally. This appears to fly in the face of received wisdom as to women's accepted role within the family during the late 1940s and early 1950s. Several manuals suggested that social stability was founded on women fulfilling specific duties. She should

- Have kindly attitudes towards others.
- Expect kindly attitudes from others.
- . . . not easily take offense.
- Not [be] unduly concerned about the impressions they make upon others.
- . . . not look upon social relationships as rivalry situations.
- Be cooperative.
- . . . not object to subordinate roles.
- . . . not [be] annoyed by advice from others[22]

I'll Never Forget You repudiates these recommendations, on the grounds that they fail to acknowledge the importance of individuals taking responsibility both for themselves and the worlds they inhabit. Helen would have accepted a subordinate role, if she had married Standish; by choosing to make what James himself describes as the "indispensable, unspeakable sacrifice,"[23] she demonstrates that women have as significant a part to play as men in ensuring the future health of their societies. Several cinematic texts of the period offer similar recommendations. Nikki Nicholson, the heroine of *The Thing from Another World* (Margaret Sheridan), fulfills a similar role in bringing about the successful dénouement. Her participation is essential, as the human beings struggle to exterminate the Thing.

I'll Never Forget You received a lukewarm reception on its opening in 1951. One critic charitably described it as "not a dud by any means, but a sort of self-conscious film."[24] Costing $1.6 million to make, it recouped its costs in domestic rentals, but only ended up fourteenth in Twentieth Century Fox's list of top films for 1951, tying with the Clifton Webb comedy *Mr. Belvedere Rings the Bell*. There are two likely explanations for its poor showing—first, that Fox marketed it rather half-heartedly, and second, that Tyrone Power's status as a star was beginning to fade. In 1950, he had fallen out of the list of top-ten stars for the first time in fifteen years. Perhaps the time was ripe for a reconsideration of *I'll Never Forget You* as a text that (like *The Lost Moment* and *The Heiress*) promotes individual responsibility as the foundation of a secure world. To ignore this would be to encourage conformity, something that leads to an overincreasing reliance on the views of so-called geniuses or other experts. They may offer well-intentioned advice (for example, those writing manuals on how to establish a successful marriage), but they might also pose a threat to social stability. As Reinhold Niebuhr observed in 1952, the scientific or technocratic enemy within was a force to be reckoned with.[25] *I'll Never Forget You* challenges this view by suggesting that if people follow Helen's example and act in society's interests, as well as their own—even if that involves a personal sacrifice—they can neutralize any potential threat to their way of life, whether internal or external.

Notes

1. Henry James, *The Sense of the Past* (London: W. Collins, n.d), 247.

2. Dennis Belafonte and Alvin H. Marill, *The Films of Tyrone Power* (Secaucus, NJ: Citadel Press, 1979), 30.

3. Roy Baker, *The Director's Cut: A Memoir of 60 Years in Films* (Richmond, Surrey: Reynolds and Hearn, 2000), 61.

4. Hector Arce, *The Secret Life of Tyrone Power* (New York: Bantam Books, 1979), 89.

5. Arce, *Secret Life*, 90.

6. James Robert Parish and Don E. Starke, *The Swashbucklers* (New Rochelle, NY: Arlington House, 1976), 222.

7. Leonard Wallace, "Star-Spangled Weddings," *Picturegoer* (December 9, 1950), 10. Once Power had been released from his studio contract, he became more frank in interviews. He remarked in 1956 that "I've made 42 films . . . and I am dissatisfied with 90 per

cent of them. If you ask me what kinds of films I liked, I can name you about three—and then I have to start thinking." Thomas Wiseman, "Mr. Power Dismounts," *Evening Standard* (London), July 20, 1956, 6.

8. Balderston, *Berkeley Square*, 71.

9. The unpublished script for *I'll Never Forget You* (using the U.K. title *The House in the Square*) is now housed in the library of the British Film Institute, London.

10. John L. Balderston, *Berkeley Square: A Play in Three Acts* (New York: Macmillan, 1929), 80.

11. Quoted in Belafonte and Marill, *The Films of Tyrone Power*, 172.

12. "House in the Square," *Variety*, October 12, 1951, 7; "House in the Square," *Variety*, December 11, 1951, 5.

13. R. P. Blackmur, "In the Country of the Blue," *Kenyon Review* 5, no. 4 (Autumn 1943): 697.

14. Ranald MacDougall, "I'll Never Forget You," unpublished script No. 53493, (Los Angeles: Twentieth Century Fox Film, 1951), 12.

15. MacDougall, "I'll Never Forget You," 18–21. James uses the metaphor somewhat differently. He talks of Ralph's desire "to remount the stream of time, really to bathe in its upper and more natural waters, to risk even, as he might say, drinking of them" (*Sense of the Past*, 47). The clover and maple leaf metaphor appears in Balderston's *Berkeley Square*, but there is no direct reference to Henry James:

Suppose you are in a boat, sailing down a winding stream. You watch the banks as they pass you. You went by a grove of maple trees, upstream. . . . I'm up in the sky above you, in a plane. I'm looking down on it all. I can see all at once the trees you saw upstream, the field of clover that you see now, and what's waiting for you, around the bend ahead! *All at once!* So the past, present and future of the man in the boat are all *one*, to the man in the plane. (*Berkeley Square*, 26)

16. James, *Sense of the Past*, 247–48.

17. MacDougall, "I'll Never Forget You," 126–29.

18. "House in the Square," 5.

19. Balderston, *Berkeley Square*, 118.

20. MacDougall, "I'll Never Forget You," 148–49.

21. MacDougall, "I'll Never Forget You," 138.

22. Judson J. Landis and Mary G. Landis, *Building a Successful Marriage* (New York: Prentice-Hall, 1948), 119.

23. James, *Sense of the Past*, 341.

24. Eric Barrett, "Have They Done Any Better?" *Picturegoer* (December 13, 1951): 13.

25. Reinhold Niebuhr, "Our Country and Our Culture," *Partisan Review* 29, no. 3 (May–June 1952): 302.

CHAPTER FIVE

〜

The Innocents (1961)

Critics have generally treated Jack Clayton's *The Innocents* as one of the more successful attempts to film Henry James. James W. Palmer praises the director's "rich and balanced" treatment of the novella, which renders spectators uncertain as to whether Miss Giddens hallucinates the ghosts in her own mind, or whether the ghosts are real, seeking to corrupt the children.[1] Edward Recchia makes a detailed comparison between the novella and a copy of the screenplay that originally belonged to Clayton himself. He believes that the director conveys "a very vital sense of the terrible presence of evil. . . . [This is] the greatest homage a film adaptor can make to the ambiguity which James sees as the essence of life."[2] Val Wilson suggests that Clayton expanded on the novella by introducing "yet another turn of the screw . . . [an] uncertainty about the fate of Miss Giddens,"[3] while Anthony J. Mazzella attributes this uncertainty to the film's deliberate oscillation between "subjective shots undercut by objectified data."[4]

While acknowledging Clayton's achievement in translating James's ambiguities into cinematic terms, I think that more attention needs to be paid to the film's conditions of production.[5] Much had changed in Hollywood in the decade separating *I'll Never Forget You* from *The Innocents*. Censorship had been relaxed; in December 1956, the Production Code was rewritten to allow references to previously forbidden subjects such as drug addiction, abortion, prostitution, and miscegenation, although topics like sexual perversion were banned. By the mid-1960s, even this last bastion had been breached. As a result, the major studios began to produce films with explicit social, psychological, and/or sexual problems at their core. Barbara Klinger suggests that they were conceived as adult films with specific conventions, "such as psychosexual and romantic conflicts, tormented characters, and erotic performances, [designed] to foster an ideological identity for the film which was commensurate with the era's strong emphasis on sex and sexuality."[6] Clayton's film appeared at a time when polemical works of first-wave feminists such as Betty Friedan's *The Feminine Mystique* had prompted many women to ask the kinds of questions about their lives that hitherto they had only asked in their own homes. Was there to be nothing more in life than accepting the conventional gender roles of a wife or a "deviant" spinster, doomed to be regarded as an outsider in a patriarchal society? What was it all for? And how did this ideal of marriage square with the rising divorce rate, with the high percentage of female alcoholics, and the sense of sterility that many women seemed to be experiencing in their lives? Friedan was uncompromising in her conclusions. Having interviewed several high school girls in the late 1950s, she detected "new dimensions to the problem of feminine conformity"; many of them were so terrified of becoming like their mothers that they could not see themselves at all. They were afraid to grow up in a world where women seldom used their minds, "played [their] own part in the world, and also loved, and had children."[7] In *The Innocents*, Clayton shows Miss Giddens using her mind—perhaps for the first time—as she acknowledges the presence of powerful sexual desires within her. The ghosts she sees at Bly House might be apparitions of dead people, or they may be nothing more than projections of her fevered imagination; but the film suggests this is not important. What is more significant is the fact that Clayton represents the sexual awakening of the heroine explicitly on screen—something that *The Heiress* could only hint at a decade earlier.

In the late 1950s, Twentieth Century Fox had already enjoyed considerable success with films of similar subject matter such as *Peyton Place* (1957), *No Down Payment* (also 1957), and *The Long Hot Summer* (1958). The independent producer Jerry Wald—who was responsible for all three films—announced plans to produce further adult material derived from literary classics "which have been neglected in the past for reason of complexity, daring subject matter or off-beat story."[8] These included *Sons and Lovers*, *The Sound and the Fury*, and *Ulysses*. The *Ulysses* project was eventually shelved (Joseph Strick's version, made in Britain for an independent company, appeared in 1967), but *The Sound and the Fury* (1959) and *Sons and Lovers* (1960) reached the screen. Jack Cardiff's Lawrence adaptation was nominated for seven Academy Awards, winning one for Freddie Francis's cinematography.

Clearly, Fox hoped to repeat the success of *Sons and Lovers* with *The Innocents*, which was based on a stage adaptation of *The Turn of the Screw* by

William Archibald, first performed in New York in 1950, and in London two years later.[9] The studio had acquired the screen rights following the successful off-Broadway revival in 1959, which (according to the *New York Times* reviewer) proved that Archibald's "psychological melodrama of abounding evil influences is still a spellbinding work."[10] Fox's film version was planned in collaboration with Achilles Productions, with Albert Fennell and Jack Clayton as coproducers, and Clayton as director. He was a big name at the time, having enjoyed considerable success with *Room at the Top* (1958), and had already rejected *Sons and Lovers* on account of the fact that "[it] bore a resemblance to *Room at the Top* in theme."[11] Fox insisted on casting Deborah Kerr as Miss Giddens; at forty years of age, she was hardly the "young, untried, nervous" woman of James's novella, flinching at the grim prospect of "serious duties and little company" at Bly.[12] However, it had become something of a tradition for the role to be played by older actresses. Beatrice Straight was thirty-four and Flora Robson was fifty when they starred in *The Innocents* on Broadway and in London; in two of the television adaptations, the leading role was played by Sarah Churchill (forty-three) and Ingrid Bergman (forty-four). Kerr's participation in Clayton's film also made sound box-office sense; Donald Chase observes that after a twenty-year career, "she dominated American movies of the Fifties as surely as, though more quietly than, the orthodox distaff trinity of Monroe, Taylor and Audrey Hepburn."[13]

Several critics have focused on the shortcomings of Archibald's adaptation; Neil Sinyard thinks that it lacks "the novel's . . . sense of suggestiveness and ambiguity."[14] Nonetheless, it seems to observe some of the conventions of basic storytelling—especially the three-act structure—that are characteristic of a mainstream Hollywood film (and helps to explain why Fox secured the rights to it). The first act introduces the audience to the world of the story, and its principal characters—Miss Giddens (Archibald's new name for the governess), Miles, Flora, and Mrs. Grose. It also sets up the main conflict around which the story will be built, as Miss Giddens becomes aware of the ghosts and their influence over the children. The second act outlines Miss Giddens's difficulties in more detail, as she comes to believe that Miles and Flora are deceiving her. This results in a change of character; she is no longer the timid personality of Act I, as she resolves to confront the children—even if that means subjecting them to intense stress. In Act III, the action is brought to a dramatic close, leaving the audience feeling that the conflict is over. Miss Giddens contrives to be alone with Miles, and forces him to say Quint's name out loud. Miles screams, "Leave me! Leave me! Ah—leave me!" as he dies in her arms, while Miss Giddens exclaims, "You're free—Miles, you're free" as the curtain falls.[15]

The screenplay for *The Innocents* went through several drafts, with many different people—including Archibald, Clayton, and the writers John Mortimer, Nigel Neill, Rhys Adrian, and Truman Capote—contributing to it.[16] The action begins with a childish voice heard on the soundtrack, followed by a shot of Miss Giddens's hands and face materializing out of the darkness, as she protests that she loves the children and only wants to protect them. The song "O Willow Waly"—written especially for the film by Paul Dehn—is sung by a childish voice that we later identify as that of Flora (Pamela Franklin). It will become something of a leitmotiv in the subsequent action, as Flora hums it on two occasions prior to the appearance of the ghosts. This scene raises a number of questions—and refuses to answer them. Where exactly is Miss Giddens? The bird song on the soundtrack suggests that she might be outside, but the darkness prevents us from being sure of this. She subsequently observes that the children need someone who will look after them. Why should this be the case? Judging from her tortured expression, perhaps she is not the right person to undertake this task.

The ending of *The Innocents* poses similar uncertainties, as we are left wondering whether Quint (Peter Wyngarde) actually exists or whether he is just a figment of Miss Giddens's imagination. At one point, the screenplay suggests that Miles's and Quint's faces seem to merge together, almost as if Miss Giddens were about to faint.[17] In a later sequence, Miles (Martin Stephens) appears to be oblivious of Quint's presence, even though the spectators can see him on the right of the frame. As Miles screams, the figure disappears, and Miles dies with a confused look on his face, as if unsure whether there is anyone there at all.[18] James's novella ends in much the same way, as the governess cries, "It's there—the coward horror [at the window], there for the last time!" and Miles stares at her "in a white rage, bewildered, glaring vainly over the place and missing wholly . . . the wide overwhelming presence."[19] Even when the governess points to the apparition, he sees nothing: "he had already jerked straight round, stared, glared again, and seen but the quiet day."[20]

The screenplay includes a sequence that apparently resolves these uncertainties, as Miss Giddens reflects on her time at Bly and speculates on the relationships, both past and present, among the children, Miss Jessel, and Quint. It comprises a montage of images superimposed over her reclining figure—the cracked photograph of Quint, Quint on the tower, Flora's hand holding her pet tortoise with a wreath of flowers around his neck, a musical

box trilling "O Willow Waly." The dream ends with Miss Giddens imagining
how the children have been possessed by the ghosts, with Miss Jessel (Clytie
Jessop) dancing in silhouette with Flora, Quint putting a possessive arm
around Miles's shoulder, and Miss Giddens herself praying for deliverance to
the sound of a chiming clock. Unlike Archibald's play, which includes the
ghosts among the dramatis personae, this sequence suggests that they have
been conjured up by Miss Giddens's macabre imagination. She is the kind of
person who could be suffering from delusions—inspired, perhaps, by her love
of gothic fiction ("Was there a 'secret' at Bly—a mystery of Udolpho or an
insane, an unmentionable relative kept in unsuspected confinement?").[21]

At first glance, this treatment of Miss Giddens would appear to reinforce
the kinds of stereotypical assumptions about unmarried women that dictated
previous James adaptations (as well as other films of the late '50s and early
'60s). Like Tina Bordereau in *The Lost Moment*, she is a pitiful creature,
whose lack of a suitable partner renders her liable to unnatural thoughts and
deeds. The work of Tennessee Williams offered several studies of the neurotic
single woman, such as Katharine Hepburn's Mrs. Venable in *Suddenly, Last
Summer* (1959), clutching the memory of her homosexual son by attempting
to have niece Elizabeth Taylor lobotomized, or Geraldine Page's aging spinster in *Summer and Smoke* (1961), whose obsessive fantasies about the doctor
next door make his ultimate rejection the cause of her breakdown. Even
someone who experienced difficulties trying to find a husband, such as Katharine Hepburn's Lizzie in *The Rainmaker* (1956)—was considered deviant. At
one point she asks her father, "Can a woman take lessons in being a woman?
. . . Pop, I'm sick and tired of me. I want to get out of me and be someone
else." Audiences may sympathize with Miss Giddens in *The Innocents*, but
they are also aware of the fact that she is a spinster, whose lack of a male
"protector" renders her liable to unnatural thoughts or to possession by evil
forces. This interpretation was clearly emphasized in the film's publicity
material. Some posters tantalized prospective filmgoers by asking them "Dare
YOU face—as she did—the evil that possessed THE INNOCENTS?"); others posed the question "Do they ever return to possess the living?" without
identifying who "they" were. All material featured Deborah Kerr's face, half
in darkness and half illuminated, as she stared fixedly at something in the
middle distance, her eyes wide open in terror.

However, it soon becomes clear that Clayton offers a more positive view
of the unmarried woman. Instead of being querulous or self-protective (like
Tina Bordereau or Catherine Sloper), she can gain strength simply by understanding—in the words of Kate Chopin—that "the past . . . offered no lesson

which she was willing to heed. The future was a mystery which she never attempted to penetrate. The present alone was significant; was hers."[22] An example of Clayton's approach can be seen in her contradictory responses to the ghosts' presence at Bly House, which might seem "strange" in rational (i.e., masculine) terms, but which demonstrate her gradually coming to terms with the present. In James's novella, the governess encounters the ghost of Miss Jessel for the third time in the schoolroom. She sees a pathetic woman, "Dark as midnight in her black dress, her haggard beauty and unutterable woe," whose expression prompts the governess to believe, somewhat guiltily, that "her [the ghost's] right to sit at my table was as good as mine to sit at hers." She responds with a "wild protest" of pity and fear: "You terrible, miserable woman!"[23] Clayton follows the novella until Miss Giddens encounters Miss Jessel, at which point he introduces a new sequence, with Miss Giddens noticing a teardrop on a slate lying on the teacher's desk. As she puts her finger in the teardrop, to test whether it is real or not, the camera cuts to a close-up of her face, which registers sadness rather than fear. Her expression suggests that she may understand Miss Jessel's suffering: Perhaps the ghost should be pitied rather than feared. For one critic who had hitherto been convinced that *The Innocents* sought to expose the "wishful fantasies" of Miss Giddens's "spinsterish heart," this moment proved "a maddening interpolation."[24]

Miss Giddens's reactions to Quint (Peter Wyngarde) are even more startling. On the one hand, he is someone to be feared; this is emphasized in her second sighting of him, while playing hide-and-seek with the children. Hiding behind the living-room curtain, she catches sight of her own reflection in the window, and then jumps back with a scream, as her face is replaced by that of Quint, his breathing audible on the soundtrack. Her eyes open wider and wider in consternation as Quint retreats into the blackness. On the other hand, he has the capacity to awaken her sexual yearnings. Throughout the film, Miss Giddens remains convinced that the ghosts have corrupted the children, forcing them to play monstrous games.[25] An example of this "indecency" occurs when Miles kisses Miss Giddens goodnight on the mouth; we might expect her to recoil in horror, but instead she gets up from her kneeling position, her face contorted with confusion. She gives the dead Miles an equally passionate kiss on the lips at the end of the film, which suggests that she might be attracted to the boy or to Peter Quint's spirit.[26] Both kisses might be viewed as further examples of Miss Giddens's diseased mind, yet she is herself aware of the fact that Quint might exist, as she observes to Mrs. Grose (in a speech not in the novella): "If it isn't true, if I didn't see him, how could I have described him so accurately?"[27] At one point, the novella shows the governess admiring Miles's "secret precocity." Nonetheless, she is troubled by "the poison of an influence that I dared but half-phrase," which makes him "appear as accessible as an older person," and forces her to "treat him as an intelligent equal."[28] *The Innocents* implies that this "influence"—whether it can be attributed to Miles or to Quint's spirit working through Miles—is especially problematic for Miss Giddens, being simultaneously poisonous yet attractive. She is certainly frustrated, but at least she begins to acknowledge that such frustrations may be caused by the presence of strong—and often uncontrollable—sexual desire.[29] This represents a first step in the process of discovering her identity. Such insights, according to Penelope Gilliatt of the London *Observer*, seemed "startlingly apt" at the time of the film's release.[30]

Recalling her work on *The Innocents* twenty-five years later, Deborah Kerr suggested that, while the experience at Bly "could have been nurtured in her [Miss Giddens's] own imagination," she preferred to believe that the character was "perfectly sane."[31] Unlike other actresses who had essayed Jamesian roles on film, such as Susan Hayward and Olivia de Havilland, Kerr's star image was not that of a strong-willed person but rather an English rose whose demure exterior concealed a passionate nature. In *Black Narcissus* (1947), she played Sister Clodagh, one of a group of nuns living in a remote Himalayan community having to fight the locals as well as their own inner conflicts. In *Tea and Sympathy* (1956), she was a teacher's wife trying to help a young boy (John Kerr) come to terms with his homosexuality, who becomes attracted to him. Her apparently happy marriage is thereby destroyed. As her biographer Eric Braun suggests, in *The Innocents* Kerr exploited her star image "to suggest the moral rectitude of a well-bred Victorian governess—or was it the fevered imaginings of repressed sex? Miss Giddens remains an enigma, and one of Deborah Kerr's subtlest characterizations."[32]

The fact that Miss Giddens remains an "enigma" serves to underline Clayton's intention to challenge the prevailing view of spinsters as witches or people suffering from mental problems. The subject of women's independence had been sympathetically explored in British neorealist films such as Tony Richardson's *A Taste of Honey* (1961), which showed how a single woman (Rita Tushingham) could not only come to terms with her pregnancy but also maintain a fierce pride in her independence, as she set up home with a gay man (Murray Melvin) who nursed her through childbirth. In *The Innocents*, Miss Giddens is certainly frustrated, but she confronts her sexual desires in an attempt to think beyond the limits of her position as a governess, living her life through the children. She becomes dimly aware of the need to follow the example of other women and (in the words of Betty Friedan) to "stretch and stretch until their own efforts will tell them who they are."[33] If this involves acknowledging the existence of powerful sexual desire, at least this represents a positive step in the right direction.

The Innocents opened without previews in London in November 1962, with a New York opening a month later. Stephen Rebello has suggested that most reviews were raves, with the only reservations centering "on what was perceived as Clayton's . . . spoiling the ambiguous fun of the whole story," or on the apparently distancing effect of "the film's elegant production values."[34] The film's box-office performance has been disputed; Clayton himself claimed that it made over $25 million, but this is contradicted by Aubrey Solomon's research into the financial history of Twentieth Century Fox, which shows that The Innocents came tenth in the studio's list of U.S. rentals for 1962, making $1.2 million. At the top were Darryl Zanuck's war epic The Longest Day ($17.5 million) and Mr. Hobbs Takes a Vacation with James Stewart ($4 million).[35] This discrepancy can be explained by the fact that Clayton based his calculation on the film's gross income since 1962, including revivals and the sale of television and video rights.

In the four decades since its premiere, The Innocents has become popular with art-house filmgoers; Rebello reports that following a screening at the Los Angeles County Museum in 1983, "rapt audiences responded as though they had rediscovered a lost treasure." Compared to such "fast-food, fast-fade shockers" such as Poltergeist, The Innocents represented "a four-course gourmet feast."[36]

Clearly, The Innocents is a product of changing times, both inside and outside Hollywood. It appeared at a time when women—both on and off screen—were beginning to come to terms with the discrepancy between the reality of their lives and the images to which they were expected to conform. Miss Giddens has to work for a living in a profession that expects ladies to be good mannered, well educated, and selflessly devoted to the care of children. She is what might be described as a tabooed woman coming to terms with falling in love—either with Miles or Quint—even though she realizes that such love is unthinkable. Clayton analyzes her mental conflicts sympathetically, taking care not to portray her as a spinster whose chief problem is her inability to find a suitable male partner. More importantly, Clayton's film provides concrete evidence of the fact that anyone who tries to explain the ambiguities of The Turn of the Screw in a logical (or "masculine" manner) is doomed to be frustrated. Linda Ann Williams has stressed the importance of a "tactful," rather than a "vulgar" reading of James's novella, which resists drawing fixed truths from the text, and allows it instead to withhold its secrets, ambiguities, and discontinuities.[37] On this view, *The Innocents* is certainly a "tactful" film.

Notes

1. James W. Palmer, "Cinematic Ambiguity: James's *The Turn of the Screw* and Clayton's *The Innocents*," *Literature Film Quarterly* 5 (1977), 213–14.

2. Edward Recchia, "An Eye for an I—Adapting Henry James's *The Turn of the Screw* to the Screen," *Literature Film Quarterly* 15 (1987), 34.

3. Val Wilson, "Black and White and Shades of Grey: Ambiguity in *The Innocents*," in John R. Bradley, *Henry James on Stage and Screen* (London: Palgrave, 2002), 117.

4. Anthony J. Mazzella, "The Story . . . Held Us: *The Turn of the Screw* from Henry James to Jack Clayton," in *Henry James Goes to the Movies*, ed. Susan M. Griffin (Lexington: University Press of Kentucky, 2002), 22.

5. Much of the following discussion is based on my article "Hollywoodizing Henry James: Jack Clayton's *The Innocents* (1961)," *Henry James Review* 25, no.1 (March 2004): 36–61.

6. Barbara Klinger, *Melodrama and Meaning: History, Culture and the Films of Douglas Sirk* (Bloomington: Indiana University Press, 1994), 56. Other adaptations of the period included films of Tennessee Williams's *Baby Doll* (1956), *Cat on a Hot Tin Roof* (1958), and *Suddenly, Last Summer* (1959).

7. Betty Friedan, *The Feminine Mystique* (Harmondsworth: Penguin Books, 1965), 65–67.

8. Jerry Wald, "This Is Why We'll Film James Joyce," *Films and Filming* (September 1958): 30.

9. Ivan Butler claims that Archibald's play was "a failure" on stage, on account of the fact that "it was difficult for two young children, however admirably cast, to sustain the necessary emotional level through lengthy performances." Ivan Butler, *Horror in the Cinema*, 3rd ed. (Cranbury, NJ: A. S. Barnes, 1979), 65. Several critics attending the first night of *The Innocents*—in both New York and London—expressed precisely the opposite view. Brooks Atkinson of the *New York Times* thought the two children "superb" in the Broadway production; Wolcott Gibbs of the *New Yorker* called them "eerily self-possessed" (Brooks Atkinson, "*The Innocents*: A Ghost Story from Henry James' *The Turn of the Screw*," *New York Times*, February 2, 1950, 30; Wolcott Gibbs, "Black Magic and Bundling," *New Yorker* (February 11, 1950): 46.

10. Louis Calta, "The Innocents," *New York Times*, April 21, 1959, 41. James's original novella proved equally popular; it was adapted three times—in 1955, 1957, and 1959; the last adaptation starring Ingrid Bergman won Bergman her first Emmy award.

11. Jack Clayton, "Accepting the Challenge," *Films and Filming* (December 1961): 7.

12. Henry James, *The Aspern Papers and The Turn of the Screw*, ed. by Anthony Curtis (Harmondsworth: Penguin Classics, 1986), 150.

13. Donald Chase, "Clayton's *The Innocents*," *Film Comment* 34, no. 1 (January/February 1998): 73.

14. Neil Sinyard, "Pearl of Ambiguity: *The Innocents*," in *Jack Clayton* (Manchester: Manchester University Press, 2000), 84.

15. William Archibald, *The Innocents* (New York: Random House, 1950), 142, 144.

16. The unpublished script for *The Innocents* is now housed in the library of the British Film Institute, London.

17. William Archibald and Truman Capote, "The Innocents" (unpublished film script, 1961), 133.

18. Archibald and Capote, "The Innocents," 136.

19. Henry James, *The Turn of the Screw, The Aspern Papers and Other Stories*, ed. Michael Swan (London: Collins, 1963), 408.

20. James, *Turn of the Screw*, 408–9.

21. James, *Turn of the Screw*, 332.

22. Kate Chopin, *The Awakening* (New York: Bantam Books, 1982), 59.

23. James, *Turn of the Screw*, 377.

24. John Coleman, "Amusette," *New Statesman* (London), December 1, 1961, 14.

25. Archibald and Capote, "The Innocents," 88.

26. This kiss was the most controversial sequence of the entire film. Twentieth Century Fox urged Clayton to remove it, on the grounds of decency; the director recalled that Spyros Skouras, the studio's president, called him "every two days for two solid weeks . . . begging me to change the ending, which I would not and did not do." Stephen Rebello, "Jack Clayton's *The Innocents*," *Ciné-Fantastique* 13, no. 3 (Autumn 1983): 17.

27. Archibald and Capote, "The Innocents," 72.

28. James, *Turn of the Screw*, 381.

29. The novella suggests that the governess's description of Quint is of such detail that it enables Mrs. Grose to identify him easily: "He's tall, active, erect,' I continued, 'but never—no, never!—a gentleman.' My companion's face had blanched as I went on; her round eyes started and her mild mouth gaped. 'A gentleman?' she gasped, confounded, stupefied: 'a gentleman he?'" (James, *Turn of the Screw*, 339).

30. Penelope Gilliatt, "The Innocents," *Observer* (London), November 26, 1961, 42.

31. Eric Braun, *Deborah Kerr* (London: W. H. Allen, 1977), 184.

32. Braun, *Deborah Kerr*, 184.

33. Friedan, *The Feminine Mystique*, 331.

34. Rebello, "Jack Clayton's *The Innocents*," 17.

35. Aubrey Solomon, *Twentieth Century-Fox: A Corporate Financial History* (Metuchen, NJ: Scarecrow Press, 1988), 143.

36. Rebello, "Jack Clayton's *The Innocents*," 17.

37. Linda Ann Williams, *Critical Desire: Psychoanalysis and the Literary Text* (London: Edward Arnold, 1995), 86.

CHAPTER SIX

The Nightcomers (1971)

It may appear that *The Nightcomers*, Michael Winner's imaginative speculation about what happened to the characters before *The Turn of the Screw* began, represents a minor contribution to the canon of Henry James adaptations. On its American premiere in 1972, it was variously described as "a rather untidy sex-and-violence melodrama"—or, worse still, "a particularly listless and greedy parody [of James's novella]."[1] Since then its reputation has hardly improved; it has been called "one of the dullest and most unimaginative British films ever made" that "doesn't have a modicum of understanding about English country-house life seventy years ago."[2] To an extent, these comments might be justified; *The Nightcomers* is unnecessarily explicit, while Marlon Brando's presence as Quint challenges the audience's belief in the credibility of the plot. He might speak with an Irish accent, but he eschews any depth of characterization in favor of conforming to his screen persona of a social misfit, at once repellent yet brutally attractive. Brando admitted that he enjoyed working with Winner, who told him that "I was a great actor and he wasn't a great director. So I could do what I liked."[3]

Nonetheless, I believe that *The Nightcomers* deserves critical reappraisal. By situating the film in its context of production—the early 1970s—this chapter demonstrates that one of the principal attractions of *The Turn of the Screw* for Winner and his screenwriter Michael Hastings lies in its portrait of a dysfunctional family. Miles's and Flora's parents have died; their legal guardian is not really concerned for their welfare, and other characters—in this case, Quint—assume a paternal role. Winner and Hastings opt for a literal reading of James's novella: Quint and Miss Jessel are not projections of the governess's imagination, but living presences. Quint exerts a tyrannical influence over Bly House, while Miss Jessel unwittingly aids and abets him.

As there is no one to restore patriarchal authority in a more just (i.e., less visibly domineering) form, the children are corrupted. Many of the film's more extreme elements, notably the sadomasochistic scenes, bear witness to this corruption. If *The Innocents* showed Miss Giddens gradually discovering the presence of sexual feelings within her, *The Nightcomers* depicts a world where sexual freedom runs rampant. The implication is clear—perhaps men and women do need to conform to specific behavioral roles to sustain the social order (an idea that gained currency in the 1970s as opposition to the feminist movement mounted, particularly from the American "New Right").

More significantly, this chapter shows how sexually explicit material was essential to the box-office success of an upmarket horror film, conceived at a time when censorship laws in the U.S. and U.K. were more relaxed than ever before. Whereas Jack Clayton could only hint at the novella's sexual undertones in *The Innocents*, Winner could portray them in realistic detail. *The Nightcomers* might not be especially good, but it does help us to explore popular attitudes towards James in the early 1970s—attitudes that would shape more "faithful" adaptations of his work, such as Peter Bogdanovich's *Daisy Miller* (1974).[4]

In the early 1970s, the horror film was at the peak of its popularity. One commentator observed in 1971 that "whereas comedy or drama must first assume a prospective audience that it will be funny or dramatic; the horror film does not have to guarantee that it will be frightening."[5] The majority of films remained safe and undemanding, but there were directors who created more experimental work that combined horror themes with complex social and psychological material. Peter Sasdy's *Countess Dracula* (1971) explored the tensions between maternal power and the social roles assigned to women in a patriarchal society through its eponymous heroine (Ingrid Pitt), who sought to become a mistress, friend, and mother in one. Peter Sykes's *Demons of the Mind* (1972) portrayed the family as a repressive institution dominated by a father (Patrick Magee) whose children represent little more than extensions of his being in some grotesque way. He is eventually destroyed, while the other surviving members of his family are driven insane. Robert Mulligan's *The Other* (1972) shows a child possessed by demonic destructive forces that persuade him to rebel against his middle-class parents. No longer the victim, he becomes the victimizer himself.

These films seemed especially important at a time when the growth of first-wave feminism had prompted speculation as to the future of the nuclear family. The British writer Sheila Rowbotham suggested in 1973 that the family restricted women's freedom "in order to maintain the interest men have in terms of compensation from the exploitation and alienation capitalism forces on them at work." It provided "a continued source of aggression and resentment as human beings fail to live up to their impossible ideal stereotypes of one another."[6] Both *Countess Dracula* and *The Other* can be seen as responses to the perceived "threat" of feminism as they create nightmare visions of what might happen if a woman or child were to transgress the expectations of the patriarchy.

Some critics of Henry James's work thought in much the same way. S. Gorley Putt wrote in 1966 that the governess was "no protectress, but a vampire. She is most dangerously self-deluded, and Miles is the most pitiful victim of all James's long list of emotional cannibals."[7] Winner's *Nightcomers* apparently rejects this interpretation. In 1973 Pan Books published Michael Hastings's novelization of the screenplay, whose preface contained a quotation from Willard Thorpe, co-editor of the *Literary History of the United States* (1949): "A reader who wishes to . . . see in the harassed governess a sex-starved spinster . . . must ignore some of James's deliberately contrived controls . . . [such as] the narrator (who framed the story), who testifies to the 'character' of the governess . . .' she would have been worthy of any position whatever."[8]

In Winner's and Hastings's view, the responsibility for the corruption of the children rests solely with the uncle and Peter Quint. The uncle (Harry Andrews), a tall, imperious personality, is clearly not interested in Bly House or the children's welfare. He delegates responsibility to Quint, advising him that he might have to look after the nanny as well as the children. The reason for this is clear: The patriarchy in the house must be maintained, even if Quint is manifestly unsuitable for the task.[9]

Quint's dominance over the children is stressed in the film's opening sequences. One scene shows him placing a cigarette in the mouth of the children's pet toad, informing them as he does so that it loves to smoke.[10] The toad eventually bursts into pieces. The children do not seem especially shocked; on the contrary, Miles (Christopher Ellis) accepts Quint's explanation without demur in the belief that loving something passionately will almost invariably result in death.[11] As Flora (Verna Harvey) rides home in a pony-and-trap with Mrs. Grose (Thora Hird) and Miss Jessel (Stephanie Beacham), she describes the life of a particular species of butterfly whose life consists of finding a mate and dying. Mrs. Grose contemptuously dismisses such speculation, but Miss Jessel is not so sure. Winner cuts to a close-up of her looking around Bly's grounds until she espies Quint standing on the tower. She is well aware of who has encouraged Flora to think like this and of how such words could have an adverse effect on the children's minds.

In a 1978 interview, Winner observes that the inspiration for *The Night-comers* came from "two or three strong hints" in James's novella "that Quint was responsible for the children's turn of mind."[12] Such hints include Mrs. Grose's recollection that "Quint was much too free. . . . With every one!"; the governess's observation that "Quint and the boy have been perpetually together"; and her later statement that the ghosts wanted to possess the children "For the love of all the evil that, in those dreadful days [when they were alive], the pair put into them."[13] *The Nightcomers* depicts this evil in two forms—in the children's fondness for deadly games and in an unhealthy obsession with sex (shared by all the principal characters). At one point, Miss Jessel and Mrs. Grose have to dash to the top of the tower to prevent Miles from throwing Flora over the edge. But Flora is far from happy at being rescued—she screams at Mrs. Grose that the game she was playing had to end with her death, and that the housekeeper had ruined it.[14] The children interpret Quint's aphorism—to love is to die—quite literally; having seen how attracted Quint and Miss Jessel are to one another, they believe it is their responsibility to kill them. In one scene they are shown standing on either side of the frame, with two chamber pots in front of them. They take the corn dolls of Quint and Miss Jessel (which Quint has made for them) and set them alight, watching them turn to ashes in the chamber pots.[15] This foreshadows Quint's death scene as Miles shoots him twice with a bow and arrow. As he pushes the corpse into the lake, Miles observes that Miss Jessel is waiting for Quint (the governess having already drowned when her boat sank).

With no one to restrain him at Bly, Quint indulges himself sexually, with Miss Jessel's willing participation. He ties her hands and feet to the bed and subsequently trusses her up like a chicken with a rope around her neck and beats her. The two of them indulge in passionate sex, presented in a series of dissolves with orchestral music as an accompaniment, without realizing that Miles is watching them through the keyhole of the bedroom door.[16] The boy subsequently imitates what he sees in a series of feverishly absurd little sequences with Flora. As he puts a rope round her neck, she squeals with pain and he replies that the ritual should be as painful as possible, as Quint has said this is the only way of discovering the truth behind it. In another scene, Miles informs Flora that the two of them are passionately in love, throws her down on the bed, and tries to take her knickers off. Both the screenplay and the novelization feature explicit sex scenes between the two children that are not in the film. In the screenplay, a naked Flora is covered with ink and paint bands of a bright color. Miles ties a rope across her face and tries to punch her.[17] The novelization has the children stripping naked and looking at one another's pubic hair with interest, prior to making love (unsuccessfully) for the first time.[18]

While the sex scenes in the film may fulfill Winner's stated aim to show how "we are perverted by what we see,"[19] there remains the distinct impression that they are designed to appeal to filmgoers' voyeuristic instincts. Like Miles, we can take a vicarious pleasure in watching Brando's first ever nude sex scene, described by one reviewer as "one of the sweatiest . . . on film,"[20] and then watch the children reenact it for themselves. James's novella hints that the governess finds Quint's ghost attractive; he may be "like nobody" but he gives her "a sort of sense of looking like an actor."[21] Jack Clayton's *The Innocents* brought this out in Miss Giddens's dream sequence. By opting for "sensationalism rather than subtlety," *The Nightcomers* appears to give filmgoers "everything we never wanted to know about the events that occurred before those in *The Turn of the Screw*."[22]

However, this film was likely to find an audience in the 1970s—a time when liberation seemed to be the watchword. In Britain, censorship laws had been relaxed to the extent that Andy Warhol's *Flesh* (1968) was given a limited release, while sex comedies such as *The Statue* (1970)—about a sculptress who makes a statue of her husband with someone else's genitalia—and *Percy* (1971)—where a man has the world's first penis transplant—were both box-office hits. Some critics argued that horror films such as *Countess Dracula* had helped to create a new genre—the liberated woman's picture that, unlike the woman's film of the 1940s, did not propose marriage, home, and family as the ultimate goals in life. Instead, it sought to explore what liberation really meant for women in the early 1970s, as they were forced to create their own roles without any real understanding of what such roles might be.[23]

But just how much freedom did women enjoy in the films of the early 1970s? In British horror films they were often placed in dangerous or life-threatening situations, menaced by (invariably) male psychotic killers.[24] Alternatively, they were represented as heroines who, despite valiant attempts to resist, were ultimately forced to submit to the dictates of the patriarchy. Stephanie Beacham's Miss Jessel cannot resist Brando's sexual roughness. In mainstream cinema, the achievements of first-wave feminists of the 1950s and 1960s were simply left unrecognized. From this point of view, *The Nightcomers* is a conservative film that, while suggesting the children and Miss Jessel are victimized by Quint, implies that this domination is in some way inevitable. Winner characterizes the governess as a sex-starved spinster—a perpetual object of desire both for Quint and the male director, who involve her in sequences that according to one reviewer "would make a fine benefit show for the S&M society."[25] If Jack Clayton's Innocents used The Turn of the Screw to hint at new possibilities for women, Winner uses the same text to reinforce patriarchal attitudes and values.[26] The women's movement was here to stay, but this did not mean that male directors had to accept it. Even horror films such as Countess Dracula, which apparently focused on tensions within the family, sought to suggest that the female challenge to male authority could be "quickly contained and neutralized."[27]

The Nightcomers had a bumpy ride before it was finally put on general release. Winner originally set up the picture with Brando in the leading role but was unable to find anyone to finance it. The actor was at that time box-office poison after ten straight flops and also had a reputation for professional awkwardness. A private source of finance was eventually found, and both director and star worked without pay. Following a successful premiere at the Venice Film Festival in 1971, an American distributor—Joseph E. Levine of Avco Embassy—agreed to market the film, and gave it a limited release in the U.S. in 1973. The Nightcomers only achieved more general acclaim after The Godfather opened, and Brando had recovered some of his lost reputation. In Britain The Nightcomers was marketed as a sexploitation flick based on a classical text rather like Burke and Hare (1971), Vernon Sewell's version of the nineteenth-century tale (which also starred Harry Andrews, who played the guardian in The Nightcomers). Jonathan Petley treats The Nightcomers as characteristic of a period in British cinema when "a film's exploitable ingredients had to be foregrounded more garishly than ever before in the attempt to keep [audience] interest alive."[28] The film eventually reached number three in the list of top London box-office grosses and returned a small profit.

Notes

1. Quoted in "The Nightcomers," Film Facts (April 1972): 84–86.

2. David Pirie, A Heritage of Horror: The English Gothic Cinema 1946–72 (London: Gordon Fraser, 1973), 185; David Shipman, Marlon Brando (London: Sphere Books, 1989), 184.

3. Quoted in Shipman, Marlon Brando, 183.

4. Much of the material in this chapter is based on my article "Horrific Henry James: Michael Winner's The Nightcomers (1971)," Literature Film Quarterly 31, no. 3 (2003), 193–99.

5. Michael Armstrong, "Some Like It Chilled," *Films and Filming* (February 1971): 28.

6. Sheila Rowbotham, *Woman's Consciousness, Man's World* (Harmondsworth: Penguin Books, 1973), 53.

7. S. Gorley Putt, *A Reader's Guide to Henry James* (Ithaca, NY: Cornell University Press, 1966), 26.

8. Michael Hastings, *The Nightcomers—A Speculation* (London: Pan Books, 1973), v–vi.

9. Shipman remarks that "[Quint] would never have been kept on by a guardian or housekeeper. . . . Photographs of the period give a lie to all this: he might have found employment as a corporation dustman, but never as a groom (let alone a valet)" (*Marlon Brando*, 184).

10. Michael Hastings's original screenplay for *The Nightcomers* is now housed at the library of the British Film Institute, London.

11. Michael Hastings, *The Nightcomers: A Screenplay* (London: Scimitar Films, 1971), 11.

12. Quoted in Bill Harding, *The Films of Michael Winner* (London: Frederick Muller, 1978), 68.

13. Henry James, *The Turn of the Screw, The Aspern Papers and Other Stories*, ed. Michael Swan (London: Collins, 1963), p. 342, 352, 366

14. Hastings, *The Nightcomers: A Screenplay*, 84.

15. In Hastings's screenplay, the children originally set fire to their tortoise—a pet that (according to their twisted logic) has to die because they love him so much (Hastings, *The Nightcomers: A Screenplay*, 107).

16. According to one (uncredited) reviewer, Quint was supposed to be impotent. This is not indicated in the screenplay.

17. Hastings, *The Nightcomers: A Screenplay*, 43–48.

18. Hastings, *The Nightcomers—A Speculation*, 62–64.

19. Harding, *The Films of Michael Winner*, 72.

20. Harding, *The Films of Michael Winner*, 72.

21. James, *Turn of the Screw*, 339.

22. Nigel Andrews, "The Nightcomers," *Monthly Film Bulletin* (May 1972): 99; "The Nightcomers," *Film Facts* (April 1972): 86.

23. Ken Wlaschin, "Liberated Women," *Films and Filming* (November 1971): 27.

24. Julian Petley, *English Gothic: A History of Horror in Cinema* (Richmond, Surrey: Reynolds and Hearn, 2000), 186.

25. Margo Skinner, "Michael Winner Directs Brando in 'The Nightcomers,'" *Hollywood Reporter*, October 14, 1971, 60.

26. Winner's biographer Bill Harding considers *The Nightcomers* superior to *The Innocents*, on the grounds that Deborah Kerr in Clayton's film was "miscast, being too wholesome an actress to project the duality James implied in the psychology of the second governess." By contrast Stephanie Beacham was quite capable "of suggesting both a rigid

respectability and the heated sexuality of Miss Jessel" (Harding, *The Films of Michael Winner*, 70).

27. Peter Hutchings, *Hammer and Beyond: The British Horror Film* (Manchester: Manchester University Press, 2000), 183.

28. Petley, *English Gothic*, 187.

CHAPTER SEVEN

~

Daisy Miller (1974)

If Paramount Pictures' publicity is to be believed, Peter Bogdanovich's film of *Daisy Miller* would seem to be very different from *The Nightcomers*. The American press book marketed it as a costume drama that continued the tradition of other adaptations of Henry James ("the celebrated American novelist") such as *The Lost Moment*, *The Innocents*, and *The Heiress*.[1] Theater managers were encouraged to organize a competition in which viewers were asked to name the original sources for these adaptations; the winners would be entitled to a free pass to see *Daisy Miller*. Television and radio presenters could "give the clue for the movie," and request viewers and/or listeners to telephone in with the novel's title.[2] Another competition focused attention on the star of *Daisy Miller*, Cybill Shepherd, who had evidently shown great strength of character in sacrificing a successful career in modeling to become an actress. Newspaper and radio listeners had to guess the identity of other women who had taken a similar route to stardom, including Suzy Parker, Ali MacGraw, and Deborah Raffin. In a preproduction interview, Shepherd admitted that she identified with Daisy: "I suppose you could say she was liberated. . . . Or trying to be. I suppose I am, too. Or trying to be."[3] Bogdanovich agreed; in the same article, he was quoted as saying that "You'd think Henry James wrote it for her [Shepherd]. . . . Certain qualities in the part are qualities that Cybill also has, in the sense of her flirtatiousness and her Americanness and her enthusiasm."[4] The principal tagline for the posters summed up his point of view: "She did as she pleased."

In this chapter, I show that, contrary to what the publicity implies, Bogdanovich's film seeks to restrict Daisy's opportunities for self-expression.[5] This is not only evident in terms of plot, where Daisy's opportunities for self-expression are limited by her social circle (who expect her to observe certain standards of behavior) but also in terms of structure, as Winterbourne (Barry Brown) continually treats her as the object of his gaze. Some of these ideas have been discussed by David Cross in his recent essay on the film; his main interest lies in determining whether Bogdanovich has found an appropriate means to convey "Jamesian themes" and "the novella's tragic tones."[6] My purpose is rather to suggest that Bogdanovich's point of view has been limited by the conventions of a mid-1970s mainstream Hollywood film. Winterbourne remains at the center of the film's consciousness; many sequences end with him continuing to gaze while the other characters leave the frame. Daisy's resistance might encourage the audience to identify with her, but she ends up "paying" for her crusade with her life—in other words, conforming to the stereotype of a femme fatale. Joan Mellen observed in 1975 that this was a characteristic strategy of Hollywood products of the period: "When women cease to be 'pure' in these films, that is, dependent and demure, they forfeit the protection given to domesticated women. . . . After all, goes the accepted if unstated premise, she—the 'free' woman—only gets what she deserves."[7] Like Miss Jessel and Flora in The Nightcomers, Daisy Miller ends up being victimized by a patriarchal society.

Following three enormous commercial successes (The Last Picture Show [1971], What's Up, Doc? [1972], and Paper Moon [1973]), Peter Bogdanovich decided to make a film that might not find too much favor with the moviegoing public but that rather appealed to him personally as an interesting subject. Originally, he had wanted to film John Galsworthy's The Apple Tree but changed his mind when he failed to obtain the rights. Having visited Rome in 1969, he had become intrigued by "the whole idea of an Italian versus American background," which prompted him to film Daisy Miller.[8] James's story also appealed to Bogdanovich because it provided a starring vehicle for Cybill Shepherd—his current partner—and gave him the chance to reconsider the ways in which women were perceived in Hollywood films. Daisy Miller was an attractive personality for Bogdanovich—"a symbol of the vitality and life [characteristic of] the New World," who wanted to remain independent by refusing to conform to the expectations of the Euro-American old world.[9]

The film demonstrates how difficult it is for her to find opportunities for self-expression. Much of the action is filtered through Winterbourne's (Barry Brown's) viewpoint, as he observes Daisy or is photographed in such a way that we seem to be looking over his shoulder. In one sequence, Winterbourne, down left of frame, with back of head to camera, looks up at Daisy who faces the camera in close-up as he tells her, "I'm puzzled if you want to know," and his gaze is directed at her face for clues about how to "read" it. In another scene written especially for the film by Bogdanovich and screen-writer Frederic Raphael,[10] she is shown enjoying herself at the piano with Giovanelli (Diulio del Prete) at the Millers' hotel. Winterbourne enters and sits down on a red velvet chair, while Daisy sings two songs—"Pop Goes the Weasel" and "Maggie"—framed against the bright sunlight of the window. His expression, serious at first, melts into one of pleasure as he listens to her. She represents a vision of loveliness, both for him and the spectators; it is part of his tragedy that he is unable to express his feelings.

Such sequences represent Daisy as fundamentally passive, an object to be molded according to other characters' whims. Bogdanovich follows the novella in the scene taking place at Chillon Castle when Winterbourne looks longingly at Daisy's "white dress and, on the great staircase, her little, rapid confiding step" and "felt as if there was something romantic going forward."[11] Later on, Mrs. Walker (Eileen Brennan)—described by James as "a very accomplished woman"[12]—advises Daisy to refrain from walking with Giovanelli in the Pincio, to avoid being "talked about" or worse still, being considered "a very reckless girl" by her peers.[13] Bogdanovich's camera focuses on her face, then cuts to a two-shot of Daisy and Winterbourne, as Daisy asks, "Does Mr. Winterbourne think that . . . to save my reputation—I ought to get into [her] carriage?"[14] This is followed by a series of cross-cuts between Winterbourne, Mrs. Walker, Daisy, and Winterbourne, implying that this represents an attempt to subjugate Daisy to the demands of polite society.

Later on, Winterbourne talks with his friend Charles (Nicholas Jones) who expresses many of the opinions put forward by James in reported speech ("these shrewd people [Winterbourne's acquaintances] had quite made up their minds that she was going too far").[15] Winterbourne's and Charles's dialogue shows their willingness to pass judgment on her, especially when she is not there to defend herself.

CHARLES:	She's certainly pretty.
WINTERBOURNE:	Yes, she's a mystery. I can't decide whether she's really reckless or really—
CHARLES:	Innocent?
WINTERBOURNE:	Yes—I suppose.
CHARLES:	Well, no one can say you aren't gallant. I hear she's about all hours with that Italian and not always in the most refined surroundings.

WINTERBOURNE:	Maybe she's just an American girl and that's that.
CHARLES:	All right. What do you say we both go back to Geneva this summer?
WINTERBOURNE:	Well, it's a hopeless puzzle anyway, and if there's anything I've missed about her, it's too late now. She's obviously carried away with Giovanelli.
CHARLES:	I don't think you've missed a thing.

However, there are moments when Daisy participates more actively in the film. In James's novella, the visit to Chillon provides an opportunity for the narrator to observe ironically that "Miss Miller's observations [on the castle] were not remarkable for logical consistency."[16] Bogdanovich alters the emphasis of this scene with some new dialogue that shows Daisy subverting Winterbourne's efforts to instruct her in local culture. Her insistent chatter about the meaning of an oubliette, followed by a rapid change of subject where she asks Winterbourne whether he has any brothers and sisters, reduces him (in John C. Shields's phrase) to "a panting, fondling puppy."[17]

At Mrs. Walker's apartment, Daisy and her mother (Cloris Leachman) continually reduce their hostess to virtual silence with their talk about Schenectady, Dr. Davis, Winterbourne's alleged meanness in refusing to remain at Vevey, and Daisy's intention to bring Giovanelli to Mrs. Walker's party. During this one-sided conversation, Mrs. Walker never once looks Daisy in the face; from her expression it is clear that she disapproves, even though Daisy at the moment is blissfully unaware of this. Several critics also registered their distaste; John Simon described her as "a ponderous coquette—a verbal Lizzie Borden."[18] By refusing to conform, however unwittingly, to the Euro-Americans' notions of polite behavior, Daisy is making her bid for freedom. She embodies vitality and spontaneity; Winterbourne and Mrs. Walker, on the other hand, are victims of an identity crisis, trapped between the old and new worlds. Daisy herself suggests at the beginning of the film that, for all his verbal sophistication, Winterbourne speaks more like a German than an American.[19]

The contrast between Daisy and Winterbourne is reemphasized later on, as the camera frames them in a two-shot while Daisy asks Winterbourne his full name. He replies, "Frederick Forsyth Winterbourne," which prompts Daisy to run out of the right side of the frame exclaiming that she cannot say the whole name. By refusing to stay within the frame, and participate in small talk, Daisy quite literally breaks with tradition; she resists any attempt either on Winterbourne's or the cinematographer's (Alberto Spagnoli's) part to constrain her. I have already quoted the passage from the novella where Winterbourne imagines that something romantic is developing between them; the film suggests that Daisy's view is completely different. On the Chillon ferry, the two of them are once again photographed in a two-shot as Daisy observes, "You're funny." Intrigued, Winterbourne replies "Am I?" to which Daisy mumbles "Uh-huh" before running out of the left side of the frame, leaving Winterbourne staring after her in astonishment. Clearly, this is not how he expects a romantic heroine to react.[20]

However, the structure of the film also suggests that Daisy's fight for freedom is little more than an illusion. In a seminal essay "Visual Pleasure and Narrative Cinema," written in 1973 and published two years later, the British feminist Laura Mulvey drew a distinction between the representation in mainstream Hollywood cinema of "woman as icon" and the active male figure who "controls events. . . . The male protagonist is free to command the stage, a stage of spatial illusion in which he articulates the look and creates the action."[21] In this construction, the female is "isolated, glamorous, on display, sexualized."[22] Mulvey uses psychoanalysis to justify this distinction; for the male unconscious, woman represents a danger, her lack of a penis implying a threat of castration and hence a lack of pleasure. There are two ways to neutralize this threat—fetishistic scopophilia, or building up the physical beauty of the object, transforming it into something satisfying in itself; or voyeurism, asserting control and subjugating the guilty person—normally the woman—through punishment or forgiveness. Mulvey elaborates her argument with references to *Vertigo* and *Rear Window*.

Like Hitchcock, Bogdanovich makes use of both strategies in *Daisy Miller*; this comes as no coincidence, given the fact that he is a "cinephile," whose filmmaking style has been heavily influenced by classic Hollywood directors. In interviews, Bogdanovich compared Winterbourne's condition to that of James Stewart's paralyzed state at the end of *Vertigo* (1958); he remains a voyeur, unable (or unwilling) to engage with people on a personal level. Thomas J. Harris suggests that this is part of Bogdanovich's "distanced approach" to directing, which emphasizes that "merely looking is no substitute for the real thing."[23] This would seem to be the case in another newly written scene where Daisy and Winterbourne witness a Punch and Judy show. Bogdanovich intercuts between close-ups of Winterbourne staring at Daisy and Daisy's face in profile, her white bonnet, blonde hair, and delicate features illuminated by the sun. As Winterbourne gives a small smile, Daisy turns her head once again towards the show. Winterbourne essays another glance towards her but only succeeds in catching the eye of an unnamed woman coming towards him from the distance. Once again, his reluctance to openly declare his feelings leads to disappointment.

However, Winterbourne is not as passive a figure as Harris would have us believe. James's novella ends with an ironic comment on Winterbourne, who has returned to Geneva, from whence came a report that he is "studying hard—an intimation that he is much interested in a very clever foreign lady."[24] Clearly, Daisy's death does not deter him from pursuing another socially advantageous alliance. The film omits this coda altogether, and ends with Winterbourne alone in the cemetery after Daisy's burial. As the camera draws away from this solitary figure, the song "Maggie"—first heard when Daisy was sitting at the piano with Giovanelli—is played on a harmonica. On one level, this sequence reiterates the theme of lost love and how Winterbourne cannot break his social shackles. On another level, the use of this music recalls Winterbourne's idealized vision of Daisy playing the piano, framed against the sunlit window—suggesting once again that even after her death, he is attempting to minimize her potential "threat" to his masculine identity through fetishistic scopophilia. Eric Birdsall suggests that "old Winterbourne has learned a painful lesson" in the last scene of the film,[25] but the fact that he is the last person to be seen on the screen indicates precisely the opposite. Bogdanovich persistently controls the image in order to demonstrate how Winterbourne clings to patriarchal authority in his efforts to control Daisy.

At this point, it is worthwhile to consider more closely the sociohistorical conditions in which *Daisy Miller* was produced. Unlike Michael Winner—a journeyman director who undertook any project, so long as it had money-making potential—Bogdanovich was perceived as one of the so-called Movie Brats, a new generation of cine-literate directors who were either film school graduates or had served their apprenticeship in television. At the forefront of this group were Francis Ford Coppola, Brian DePalma, Martin Scorsese, John Milius, George Lucas, and Steven Spielberg. Many of them were aware of auteur theory and of film history in general and aspired to become auteurs themselves, working within the industry but at the same time establishing their individual personae. Lucas observed in an interview that they were wresting power from the studio chiefs: "We're the pigs. . . . We are the ones who snuff out the truffles. You can put us on a leash, keep us under control. But we are the guys who dig out the gold."[26] For a while, it seemed as if this claim were true, with the auteurists achieving financial success with one film and subsequently being given carte blanche to pursue projects of their own. Bogdanovich's reputation had been founded on the success of *What's Up,*

Doc? and *The Last Picture Show* (which occupied numbers four and six of the 1972 list of top box-office hits). *Daisy Miller* itself was made by the Director's Company—a cooperative venture set up by Bogdanovich, Coppola, and William Friedkin.

But just how much leeway did this generation of directors have to create films of their own? One inescapable fact remained: Their reputation depended on continued success at the box office. Those who tried too hard to create unusual, personal films became marginalized; Robert Altman was a famous example after the box-office failure of *McCabe and Mrs. Miller* (1971). Consequently, the majority of directors reproduced the kind of gender stereotypes that had become part of the classical Hollywood films, to render their work accessible to the largest possible audience. *Daisy Miller* fits securely into this tradition, with the characters being assigned a particular set of traits that are sustained throughout the film. Winterbourne is the voyeur; Daisy is the social misfit because she repudiates his patriarchal protection, and her desire for self-expression, for all its superficial attractiveness, remains nothing but a dream. In spite of his professed enthusiasm in the publicity for her Americanness and her enthusiasm, Bogdanovich ends up by depicting her as a victim of her own stubbornness.

As with *The Nightcomers*, *Daisy Miller* points to the fact that in the early 1970s most mainstream filmmakers implied that the women's movement simply did not exist; there were only individual women who felt personally constrained. Martin Scorsese's *Alice Doesn't Live Here Any More* (1974) provides another good example. Alice, a widow (Ellen Burstyn), unsuccessfully tries to pursue a singing career as a way of recovering her self-respect. She meets a nonoppressive man (Kris Kristofferson) to whom she can relate on equal terms and with whom she can experience a satisfying relationship. On the one hand, the film's ending contains a certain ambiguity: We have no way of knowing whether this relationship will last or whether it will bring Alice any lasting happiness. On the other hand, the ending also suggests that women have no need to seek independence, so long as there are strong protective males around to look after them. Their search for independence is accordingly reduced to a gesture, "an irrational 'feminine' whim," as Robin Wood suggests.[27]

Since that period there have been considerable shifts of opinion, both in the way women are perceived onscreen and how it might affect one's reading of a film. Laura Mulvey herself wrote in a 1983 essay (published 1986) that "the either/or binary pattern" she employed in her earlier work "seemed to leave the argument trapped within its own conceptual frame of reference."[28]

She proposed instead a model derived from the Bakhtinian notion of the carnivalesque, in which women could occupy a space "between silence and speech, the terrain in which desire almost finds expression . . . [which] could provide the basis for change."[29] Other commentators have argued that the fetishization of the female body has the potential for producing the alternative pleasure of a masochistic relationship between the male moviegoer/voyeur and the female star. As this bond refuses the symbolic power of the father, masochism challenges established gender and sexual differences; the female star represents a power found in performance, which transforms the pleasure and control of the male gaze.[30]

From this point of view, Winterbourne can be thought of as being involved in a motion picture of his own life, wherein he has retreated from the world of male competition and where Daisy is placed on a series of romantic pedestals of his own making. After her death, he looks at her grave—a moment that, according to one critic, "suggests a swelling in two ways ironic. As a female swelling, it is an image of death in the place of pregnancy. . . . As a phallic protuberance, it suggests death's cause and Winterbourne's stiff loss [of masculinity]."[31]

Such views, I would suggest, were beyond the scope of Bogdanovich's film, which apparently supports Daisy in her efforts to escape the confines of her society. On the other hand, the liberalism of this message is undercut by the suggestion that, however justifiable or attractive their cause might be, women should continue to participate in patriarchal narratives. This point of view is similar to that of *The Nightcomers*, even though the two films are very different in terms of subject matter. This, I suggest, is the consequence of Bogdanovich working in a Hollywood that was trying to accommodate a new generation of directors yet determined to sustain the conventions— particularly concerning the representation of male and females—on which its reputation had been built over the previous half century. Douglas Kellner suggests that Hollywood in the 1970s, "like society, was very much a contested terrain, with the future of society and culture up for grabs."[32] Bogdanovich's *Daisy Miller* offers an example of how such contests were often ignored in the films appearing at that time.

Notes

1. *Daisy Miller*'s high-cultural credentials were further emphasized through book displays of James's works to be displayed in local libraries (including school libraries). Among

the novels included in the display were *The Ambassadors, The Portrait of a Lady, The Turn of the Screw*, and, of course, *Daisy Miller*.

2. Press book, *Daisy Miller* (Los Angeles: Paramount Pictures, 1974), 2.

3. Press book: *Daisy Miller*, 4.

4. Press book, *Daisy Miller*, 3. For further discussion on the implications of casting Shepherd—Bogdanovich's girlfriend at that time—as Daisy Miller, see Peggy McCormack, "Reexamining Bogdanovich's *Daisy Miller*," in Griffin, *Henry James Goes to the Movies*, ed. Susan M. Griffin (Lexington: University Press of Kentucky), 34–60.

5. Much of the following discussion is based on my article "Observing Femininity: Peter Bogdanovich's *Daisy Miller*," *The Henry James E-Journal* no. 4, 2001, at www.new paltz.edu/~hathaway/ejourn4.htm (accessed January 22, 2003).

6. David Cross, "Framing the 'Sketch:' Bogdanovich's *Daisy Miller*," in *Henry James on Stage and Screen*, ed. John R. Bradley (London: Palgrave, 2000), 127–43.

7. Marjorie Rosen, *Popcorn Venus: Women and Their Sexuality in the New Film* (London: Davis-Poynter, 1975), 25–26.

8. Quoted in Thomas J. Harris, *Bogdanovich's Picture Shows* (Metuchen, NJ: Scarecrow Press, 1990), 160.

9. Harris, *Bogdanovich's Picture Shows*, 165.

10. Raphael alone received screen credit, though Bogdanovich fought to have his name included for deciding to reject the initial version of the script and stay close to James's novel.

11. Henry James, "Daisy Miller," in *Selected Short Stories*, ed. Michael Swan (Harmondsworth: Penguin Books, 1963), 158. James himself described *Daisy Miller* as a "nouvelle." I use the term novella for convenience.

12. James, "Daisy Miller," 163.

13. James, "Daisy Miller," 173.

. 14. James, "Daisy Miller," 173.

15. James, "Daisy Miller," 184.

16. James, "Daisy Miller," 159.

17. John C. Shields, "*Daisy Miller*: Bogdanovich's Film and James's Nouvelle," *Literature Film Quarterly* 11, no. 2 (1983), 106.

18. John Simon, "Jacobin—not Jacobite" (1974), in *Reverse Angle: A Decade of American Films* (New York: Crown, 1981), 155.

19. Shields suggests that Bogdanovich's intention was to caricature Winterbourne as one of those "pretentious Americans in Europe . . . an ensnared gull who ecstatically allows himself to be duped" ("*Daisy Miller*," 106–7). This was part of the overall intention to provide a "screen pastiche" of James's novel, something that most reviewers at the time of the film's release "completely failed to grasp" (110).

20. Some reviewers took an active dislike to Shepherd's interpretation. For a brief survey, see Shields, "*Daisy Miller*," 106–8.

21. Laura Mulvey, "Visual Pleasure and Narrative Cinema," (London: Macmillan Press, 1999), 20.

22. Mulvey, "Visual Pleasure and Narrative Cinema," 21.

23. Harris, *Bogdanovich's Picture Shows*, 169–70.

24. James, "Daisy Miller," 192.

25. Eric Birdsall, "Interpreting Henry James: Bogdanovich's *Daisy Miller*," *Literature Film Quarterly* 22, no. 4 (1994): 277.

26. Quoted in Kristin Thompson, *Storytelling in the New Hollywood: Understanding Classical Narrative Technique* (Cambridge, MA: Harvard University Press, 1999), 5.

27. Robin Wood, "Images and Women," in *Hollywood from Vietnam to Reagan*, ed. Robin Wood (New York: Columbia University Press, 1986), 204.

28. Mulvey, *Visual and Other Pleasures*, 162.

29. Mulvey, *Visual and Other Pleasures*, 174.

30. Paul McDonald, "Reconceptualising Stardom," in *Stars*, ed. Richard Dyer, new ed. (London: BFI Publishing, 1998), 189–90.

31. Robert Weisbuch, "Winterbourne and the Doom of Manhood in *Daisy Miller*," in *New Essays on Daisy Miller and The Turn of the Screw*, ed. Vivian R. Pollak (Cambridge: Cambridge University Press, 1993), 80.

32. Douglas Kellner, "Hollywood and Society," 1996, at www.gseis.ucla.edu/courses/ed253a/Mckellner/HOLSOC.html (accessed December 15, 2003).

CHAPTER EIGHT

~

On a Clear Day You Can See Forever (1970) and Somewhere in Time (1980)

If *The Nightcomers* exploited the relaxation in film censorship in the late 1960s and 1970s, both *On a Clear Day You Can See Forever* (1970) and *Somewhere in Time* (1980) reacted against it. Loosely based on James's *The Sense of the Past* and John Balderston's *Berkeley Square* (even though neither film included any acknowledgment of these sources), both films were conceived as period romances for family audiences. In the case of *On a Clear Day*, this gave director Vincente Minnelli the chance to stage the kind of fantasy sequences that rendered his MGM musicals of the 1950s so successful at the box office. In *Somewhere in Time*, Jeannot Szwarc sought to re-create the kind of idealism he perceived as characteristic of romances produced in the so-called Golden Age of the studio system in the 1940s. To render their material even more attractive to filmgoers' wish-fulfilling instincts, both directors placed particular emphasis on visual detail—historic locations, sets, and costumes. Sometimes this detail emphasizes the contrast between past and present, but there are occasions in both films (particularly formal scenes such as dinner parties and balls) where narrative development is suspended in favor of visual spectacle.

Despite the directors' best intentions, both films resemble *The Nightcomers* in the sense that all of them appear particularly conservative in their treatment of gender issues. The existence of *On a Clear Day* is almost entirely dependent on Barbra Streisand's status as superstar, giving her the opportunity to undertake two completely different roles interspersed with plenty of songs. One of the characters she plays, Melinda Tentrees, is a strong eighteenth-century English woman who refuses to conform to what society expects of her. Not only does she divorce her first husband in favor of Robert Tentrees (John Richardson), a wastrel and a gambler, but she freely admits in court that she will stay with the younger man, even if she is found guilty of high treason. Yet the film suggests that while Melinda offers a good example of female independence, she is ultimately nothing more than an illusion conjured up by Daisy Gamble's (also Streisand) and Marc Chabot's (Yves Montand's) imaginations.

Somewhere in Time transforms Christopher Reeve into a romantic leading man by giving him much the same kind of role that Tyrone Power played in I'll Never Forget You nearly three decades earlier. By contrast, Elise McKenna—the principal female character (played by Jane Seymour)—is treated very differently. While the earlier film has Helen Pettigrew (Ann Blyth) making an "indispensable, unspeakable sacrifice" by persuading Standish (Power) to return to his own time, Elise is portrayed as a victim of circumstance (as constructed by the male director), as her fiancé Richard (Reeve) disappears back to 1979 before her very eyes, condemning her to a life of isolation and suffering. Somewhere in Time suggests that she should expect nothing else in a patriarchal society, having sacrificed her reputation by falling in love with a social misfit. This message seems typical of mainstream Hollywood films of the 1970s and 1980s (including Daisy Miller), which took little note of the changes wrought by first-wave feminism and reemphasized stereotypical role models for women instead.[1]

Unlike I'll Never Forget You, which treats the time traveler with suspicion (especially as he is a scientist by profession), the two later adaptations suggest that such people enjoy a freedom of thought and expression denied to anyone living solely in the present. In On a Clear Day, Chabot yearns to be transported back two centuries so that he can dance with Melinda in front of an illuminated Royal Pavilion in Brighton, England. He breaks into a song that begins with the question "What's the matter with me, there was never Melinda?" and ends with "You're no mere dream, Melinda." The workaday psychiatrist transforms himself into a romantic leading man. Richard Collier, the hero of Somewhere in Time (Reeve) relishes the experience of the past; standing in front of a sepia photo of Elise, he touches her face with his fingers and leans his cheek against it. It is both an exhibit—a memory of the past captured by the camera—and a living being, someone with whom he enjoyed a passionate affair. The experience of time travel proves equally memorable in James's original novella, as Ralph Pendrel (in the guise of his nineteenth-century ancestor) takes his bride-to-be, Molly Midmore, in his arms and kisses her, thereby generating "a freshness of interest in this adventure [that] surged through our young man's blood."[2]

In general, however, both *On a Clear Day* and *Somewhere in Time* are structurally very different from *The Sense of the Past*. *On a Clear Day* rewrites the novella to incorporate a fantasy sequence, something that is characteristic of Vincente Minnelli's oeuvre. The ballet interlude in *An American in Paris* (1951) contrasts the black-and-white of the central character's (Gene Kelly's) sketch of Paris with the vibrant, colorful, three-dimensional images of the city projected from his mind onto the screen. These images are breathtaking while they last, but they vanish all too quickly into thin air, with grimy reality intruding itself once again in the form of the sketch.[3] The film ends happily as Kelly embraces the girl of his dreams (Leslie Caron) while the final bars of Gershwin's piece that gave the film its name echo triumphantly on the soundtrack. There is no such fairy-tale ending to the fantasy sequence in *On a Clear Day*. Chabot imagines Melinda whispering to her lover Robert (John Richardson), while Robert plays roulette. Minnelli cuts to a close-up of their hands clasped, then tracks upwards to show them in a passionate embrace. The dream evaporates with Chabot's voice-over ("What does she see in him, that gigolo?"); and grim reality returns in the form of a shot of the psychiatrist sitting alone in his consulting room. In the film's most spectacular sequence, Chabot can be heard on the soundtrack singing "Come Back to Me" to Melinda, while the camera offers breathtaking panoramas of early 1970s New York from the air and on the ground. The contrast between his sterile vision of the past and the vibrancy of the present-day city is palpable.[4] Chabot's fantasy ends on a bathetic note, as his song is interrupted by Daisy (who had conjured up Melinda in the first place as part of her own vision) asking him not to bother her.

Somewhere in Time restructures *The Sense of the Past* as a passionate romance that develops in a series of dramatic set pieces accompanied by a swirling romantic score (by John Barry). Szwarc was quoted in the film's press book as saying he had never encountered such a romantic story,[5] while another interview quoted him as saying that he had been inspired by the great Hollywood romances of the 1940s with their images, words, and emotions.[6] The production notes developed this idea by identifying Richard and Elise's first encounter as the moment when the romantic story began.[7] This sequence begins with a series of intercut close-ups, as Elise looks at Richard as if she cannot believe he has appeared. Szwarc cuts to a two-shot of the lovers framed against Lake Michigan as Richard asks how she is and whether he startled her. As in *On a Clear Day*, however, the intimacy of this moment is abruptly curtailed by another voice-over, this time from Elise's Svengali-like manager W. F. (William) Robinson (Christopher Plummer) asking her to accompany him to dinner. In another scene, Richard is pictured in close-up on the hotel balcony on the right of the frame, looking despondently at the ground. The garden stretches out toward the horizon behind him. Szwarc holds this shot for what seems like an age, but suddenly we see a white speck in the distance and realize that Elise is coming toward us, screaming Richard's name as she does so. The sequence ends predictably with a close-up of the lovers, the music reaching a crescendo as they embrace. Such saccharine moments, one male reviewer predictably complained, were most likely intended for "middle-aged women who read Barbara Cartland."[8]

Both adaptations place particular emphasis on scenic detail, something that is conspicuously absent from the original novella. *The Sense of the Past* only includes description if it relates to the characters' state of mind; Ralph experiences a "sharp special thrill" as he enters the hall of the Mansfield Square house—especially the floor "paved in alternate squares of white marble and black, each so old that the white was worn merely to yellow and the black nearly to blue." The mere sight of this gives him "on the instant, under his first flush, the measure of a possible experience" of traveling into the past.[9] Jeremy Tambling has recently suggested that the figure of the ghost in narratives such as *The Turn of the Screw* and *The Sense of the Past* represents "that which is not in the picture and yet which fills the picture, *punctum* to any *studium*, as Barthes uses these terms in *Camera Lucida*—the *punctum* piercing the certainties usually held." In a Jamesian narrative, "the unsettling and ghostly" of the unconscious transforms the text from "a record of the known and the observable" into something that views "the ghostly as the buried, erotic, disturbing history."[10] This can also apply to characters in Jamesian adaptations—for example, Deborah Kerr's Miss Giddens in *The Innocents*, whose "buried, erotic [and] disturbing" thoughts are brought to the surface at Bly House.

By contrast, *On a Clear Day* and *Somewhere in Time* celebrate "the known and the observable" through their locations, sets, and costumes. Minnelli is at pains to show off the architectural splendor of the Royal Pavilion; in one sequence Melinda and her first husband Percy (Laurie Main) draw up in front of it in a carriage.[11] As they dismount, the camera cuts to a shot of the east front with its numerous minarets and pinnacles, with small groups of lords and ladies conversing in the grounds. The interior scenes are, if anything, even more opulently staged. Percy and Melinda are invited to a dinner held in the great banqueting room completed in 1820. The camera looks down from the ceiling past the main chandelier and swoops to ground level, showing the servants offering food to the guests in massive silver tureens. In the rear of the shot we can see the crimson window draperies. The entire scene—including the prince-regent's (Roy Kinnear's) presence as guest of honor—recalls John Nash's picture of the banqueting room, part of his "Views of the Royal Pavilion" (1824). Another sequence takes place in the great kitchen—also completed in 1820—where the staff are lined in serried ranks while the prince-regent congratulates the head chef on his salmon mousse. While this scene bears little significance to the development of the plot, it permits us to admire the fireplace with its ingenious mechanism for turning spits, and delight in the reds, yellows, and gold of the guests' costumes.[12] Melinda's outfits for the regency sequences in *On a Clear Day* were designed by Cecil Beaton, who had won Oscars for his work on two previous Alan Jay Lerner musicals—*Gigi* (1958) and *My Fair Lady* (1964). He came up with some stunning creations—a pencil-thin evening gown and silver bonnet, and a scarlet robe and headdress for her appearances in court.

Somewhere in Time was mostly filmed at the Grand Hotel, Mackinac Island, on Lake Michigan. Built in 1887, the hotel is situated in a 500-acre park with its own gardens, on an island that has banned motorized vehicles since 1901. In a report for *American Cinematographer*, one reporter described this location as "a charming and historic spot, a place where, perhaps, time ought to stand still. . . . With such an atmosphere around them, it didn't take long for the filmmakers to conjure up déja vu pictures of elegant living in 1912."[13] Throughout the film, Szwarc punctuates the narrative with shots designed to show the period atmosphere off to its best advantage. As Richard emerges from the elevator on his first morning in the world of 1912, he looks out on the lobby thronged with guests. Szwarc employs a variation on this shot later on, as the camera tracks Richard threading his way through the dining room filled with people eating and chattering in equal measures. Elise makes a grand entrance accompanied by William, looking like a duchess rather than an actress. The exterior shots of the hotel are equally colorful; one focuses on the magnificent gardens, as a brougham carrying guests up the driveway crosses the frame left to right. Szwarc cuts to a close-up of Richard trying to talk to Elise; in the background the hotel's neoclassical front entrance with its massive 900-foot porch can be seen. Even those reviewers (such as Philip French of the London *Observer*) who disliked the romantic plot admitted that the location evoked "something of the lost romantic grandeur" of pre–World War I America.[14]

The ambience in both films is very similar to that described by Jeremy Tambling in an essay on James's *The American Scene* (1907): "The hotel [or royal palace] cocoons the subject from the world outside . . . it may be thought of as the attempt to suspend meaning in its embrace, so that it discourages the search for anything 'behind and beyond.' "[15] In *Somewhere in Time*, the Grand Hotel and its environs are photographed in soft focus with wide-angle lenses,[16] creating an idealized world in which the potentially unsettling consequences of Richard's journey back in time (both for Richard himself and the people around him) are removed as he discovers true love. While the ending of *On a Clear Day* suggests that the past represents nothing more than a sterile illusion compared to the present, the illusion is nonetheless attractive visually for Chabot and the audience alike.

Both directors sought to appeal to filmgoers' wish-fulfilling instincts in an attempt to challenge the prevailing beliefs of the 1970s, which considered sex and violence as the major ingredients of a box-office success (as seen, for example, in *The Nightcomers*). Marjorie Rosen complained in 1973 that most male directors seemed so preoccupied with sex that they were destroying "the old intimacy" between men and women, redefining it in its most clinical and external terms: "Because of the new permissiveness, a number of filmmakers who have created their body of work in climates of restraint are now overindulging personal fantasies or obsessions never before allowed to surface undisguised."[17]

Maybe she had a point; in the week of June 16, 1970—when *On a Clear Day* opened in New York—the other releases includes an art-house sex film (*Censorship in Denmark* [1969]) and a routine Hollywood action film (*The Hawaiians* [1970]) offering leprosy, lust, loyalty, frigidity, American imperialism, and bare breasts among its attractions. One *New York Times* reviewer tartly observed that filmgoers were "turning blasé with the spate of sex films, both factual and fictional, flooding local screens."[18] The cinematic climate had scarcely changed much a decade later: Szwarc complained in an interview that most mainstream releases either contained too much sex and violence or "achieved even greater technical proficiency, while becoming even more cold and sterile."[19]

As with other big-budget musicals of the period such as *Star!* (1968), *Paint Your Wagon* (1969), and Streisand's previous musical hit *Hello, Dolly!* (1969), *On a Clear Day* was aimed at family audiences, especially those who appreciated period style. One recommended publicity strategy for theater managers consisted of organizing a reincarnation ball where the guests could come dressed as their favorite character from history. Alternatively, free tickets could be offered to those filmgoers bold enough to come to the cinema in historic costumes. Whatever strategy could be employed, it was important that publicity was given to all of them.[20] A fashion show might be staged, in which models wearing period costumes could share the catwalk with those wearing merchandise currently available. Posters showing Streisand in the various Beaton creations could be prominently displayed in local department stores, particularly on the main streets.[21] The publicity for *Somewhere in Time* portrayed Mackinac Island as a natural resource hitherto undiscovered by Hollywood, while the historic location of the Grand Hotel contributed much to the film's romantic aura.[22]

Yet there remains the strong suspicion that, while the period settings are undoubtedly attractive, they nonetheless reinforce the films' fundamentally conservative stance on gender. Both directors suggest that women should devote their lives to finding a suitable male partner. Melinda Tentrees overflows with self-confidence, speaking in ringing tones worthy of a theatrical grande dame; the *Hollywood Reporter* applauded Streisand's characterization, observing that although Minnelli had "forced [her] to do a British accent, she does it with the nature of a mimic born. . . . She is with the technique and conviction beyond many more experienced actresses."[23] However, Melinda's strength of character poses no threat to the patriarchy; she is a reincarnation conjured up in Daisy Gamble's imagination, who subsequently figures in Chabot's romantic vision. By contrast, Daisy is a social misfit who, while rejecting a proposal of marriage from her long-term boyfriend Warren Pratt (Larry Bryden), still strives to be a good wife in the making. At one point, she is shown learning how to bake a cake in domestic science classes. Unfortunately, all her efforts come to nothing as she discovers that Chabot has only ever considered her an intermediary, enabling him to communicate with Melinda. Minnelli cuts to a close-up of her face contorted with rage and frustration as she sits alone in the psychiatrist's consulting room. The camera dollies outwards to show her looking at some potted plants in dire need of water.[24] She had previously given them to Chabot as a mark of her affection for him; their shriveled state aptly sums up her current state of mind.

Elise McKenna in *Somewhere in Time* would appear to be much more fortunate. Although she protests her independence to William, she is prepared to sacrifice everything—even her career—for love. At one point, she interrupts a performance to declare her feelings for Richard, who sits in the audience; he is the sort of man, apparently, whom every woman dreams about. Szwarc shoots the entire scene in soft focus, investing the action with a fairy-tale quality, far removed from the modern world. This atmosphere does not prevail for long, however, as Richard is twice expelled from the hotel. On the first occasion, William has him bound, gagged, and thrown into a stable; on the second, Szwarc transports him back to 1979, thereby condemning Elise to a life of suffering with nothing to comfort her but the memory of one passionate night alone with Richard. While the film ends with the lovers restored to one another in death, we are left with the impression that the (male) director and screenwriter have punished Elise for falling in love with someone who lacks the appropriate social and cultural knowledge to integrate successfully into 1912 Californian society.

On a Clear Day and Somewhere in Time might indulge in idealized re-creations of the past, contrasting with the humdrum world of the present, but their message is conservative—almost reactionary—in tone, invoking traditional Hollywood stereotypes of the unmarried or submissive woman. While On a Clear Day offers plenty of opportunities for Streisand to show off her acting skills, it offers no criticism of the patriarchal order. Apparently designed to recall Hollywood romances of the 1940s, Somewhere in Time overlooks the fact that many films of that period featured strong women played by Susan Hayward (The Lost Moment) or Olivia de Havilland (The Heiress). It is thus hardly surprising that many critics should have considered Szwarc's film old-fashioned by 1940s standards, let alone those of the early 1980s.[25]

Perhaps we ought not to dismiss On a Clear Day and Somewhere in Time as flawed adaptations of a James novella but rather treat them as examples of a particular moment in film history when producers were trying to tempt family audiences back to the theater. If that meant spending a large proportion of the budget ($10 million for On a Clear Day) on re-creating the past, and reaffirming traditional role models in the process, then so be it. James adaptations such as Daily Miller might have been antifeminist in the sense that they sought to deny women the privilege of self-expression. I suggest that perhaps this is not the case with On a Clear Day or Somewhere in Time; rather the producers acknowledged the fact that, if they were going to tempt audiences away from the television and back into the movie theater, they would have to draw on the stereotypes that had dominated some of the major series of the period. Hal Himmelstein's Television and the American Mind (1994) has emphasized the enduring popularity of the notion of community and stability in family life based on well-defined gender roles in series such as Marcus Welby MD (premiering in 1968), The Waltons (1972–1979), and Little House on the Prairie (1974–1981). Marcus Welby was the community

patriarch, "kind, gentle, competent and humble;"[26] the other series celebrated the values of strong family bonds, based on the notion of the man as
breadwinner, and the woman as wife and loving mother. Anyone failing to
conform to such stereotypes was either inadequate (Daisy Gamble) or potentially subversive (Melinda Tentrees, Elise McKenna). This theme will be further explored in the next chapter, which concentrates on *The Turn of the
Screw*, a U.S. network television adaptation from 1974.

Despite the producers' best intentions, both *On a Clear Day* and *Somewhere in Time* had a rough ride with the studios and subsequently at the box
office. *On a Clear Day* was scheduled to run nearly three hours, but Paramount cut it to 128 minutes, omitting four songs completely.[27] Szwarc had
no control over the final cut of *Somewhere in Time*, and had to suffer the
indignity of a major flop, as the film opened at 800 American theaters and
closed after three weeks. The film's British release was equally disastrous; one
critic observed that on the afternoon he saw it, he appeared to be completely
alone, although he could hear "sobbing coming from somewhere in the cinema."[28] Like *The Lost Moment*, both films have subsequently become cult hits
but perhaps for different reasons.[29] Whereas Gabel's film has proved particularly appealing to feminist filmgoers, both *On a Clear Day* and *Somewhere
in Time* are welcomed by those who appreciate romantic stories and period
atmosphere. Compared to the earlier novels, *The Sense of the Past* occupies a
minor place in the Jamesian canon. However, thanks to films such as *On a
Clear Day* and *Somewhere in Time*, the novella's basic time-traveling plot has
become a favorite with film-going audiences—even if they are not always
aware of where it comes from.

Notes

1. Much of the material in this chapter is based on my article "Preserving Henry
James' *Sense of the Past*: *On a Clear Day You Can See Forever* (1970) and *Somewhere in
Time* (1980)," *Interactions* 13, no. 1 (Spring 2004): 81–91.

2. Henry James, *The Sense of the Past* (London: W. Collins, n.d.), 125.

3. David John Fleck, "On a Clear Day . . . Lucid Fantasies," *Cinéfantastique* 3 (Winter
1978): 49.

4. Jim Cook, "On a Clear Day You Can See Forever," *Movie* 24 (February 1977): 62.

5. *Universal News: Somewhere in Time* (Los Angeles: Universal City, 1980), 3.

6. Jordan R. Fox, "Somewhere in Time with Jeannot Szwarc," *Cinéfantastique* 10, no.
4 (Spring 1981): 19.

7. *Production Notes: Somewhere in Time* (Los Angeles: Universal City, 1980), 3.

8. John Brosnan, "Somewhere in Time," *Starburst* 1, no. 7 (1981): 17. It is likely that

Szwarc would have taken such comments positively, in view of his professed aim (as expressed in the publicity) to create a film that represents "a return to pure romanticism. . . . It's about idealistic love, which I think it's the way it should be" (*Universal News*, 1).

9. James, *Sense of the Past*, 61–62.

10. Jeremy Tambling, *Henry James* (Basingstoke: Macmillan Press, 2000), 18–19.

11. Robert Stam remarks that this technique is characteristic of Minnelli's style of filmmaking ("The Minnelli Magic," *Literature through Film: Realism, Magic and the Art of Adaptation* (Malden, MA: Blackwell, 2005), 165–75.

12. The publicity made much of the fact that *On a Clear Day* was to be filmed inside the Royal Pavilion in Brighton, England. Press book: *On a Clear Day You Can See Forever* (Los Angeles: Paramount Pictures, 1970), 2.

13. "Behind the Scenes of 'Somewhere in Time,'" *American Cinematographer* (July 1980): 669.

14. Philip French, "Somewhere in Time," *Observer*, January 4, 1981, 35.

15. Tambling, *Henry James*, 14–15.

16. Isidore Mankofsky, "Filming in the Time Warp of Two Different Eras," *American Cinematographer* (July 1980): 683, 686.

17. Marjorie Rosen, *Popcorn Venus: Women and Their Sexuality in the New Film* (London: Davis-Poynter, 1975), 331, 333.

18. A. H. Weiler, "Zodiac Couples Adds to Spate of Sex Films," *New York Times*, June 18, 1970, 56.

19. Fox, "Somewhere in Time," 19.

20. Press book: *On a Clear Day*, 7.

21. Press book: *On a Clear Day*, 7.

22. Production Notes: *Somewhere in Time*, 12.

23. James Powers, "Koch Produced, Minnelli Helmed," *Hollywood Reporter*, June 17, 1970, 3.

24. This scene is discussed in more detail in Fleck, "On a Clear Day," 53–54.

25. Brosnan, "Somewhere in Time," 17.

26. Hal Himmelstein, *Television Myth and the American Mind*, 2nd ed. (Westport, CT: Praeger, 1994), 220.

27. "Wait 'til We're Sixty Five" and "She Isn't You" were songs that were from the original Broadway production of *On a Clear Day*. "Who Is There among Us Who Knows?" and "E.S.P." were two of the four new songs written especially for the film, but all of which were cut.

28. Brosnan, "Somewhere in Time," 16.

29. There are websites devoted to both; *Somewhere in Time* has its own fan club INSITE (International Network of *Somewhere in Time* Enthusiasts), one of only three single films to enjoy that privilege. The other two films are *Gone with the Wind* and *The Wizard of Oz*.

CHAPTER NINE

~

The Turn of the Screw (1974)

John Ellis claimed in 1982 that most broadcast television institutions proceed on the assumption that their everyday audiences consist of nuclear families—in other words, two parents (working husband, a wife who may also work but also looks after the home) and two or possibly three school-age children.[1] This belief still governs the majority of television's output on both sides of the Atlantic—for example, in advertising material, in the way statistics are interpreted on the news, in the types of contestants selected for quiz programs and/or reality shows,[2] and in "families" portrayed in television dramas of all kinds. Ever since the end of the Second World War, the notion of the nuclear family had been particularly potent on American television during times of social and political strife. Lynn Spigel observes that 1940s advertisements emphasized the link between television and family values, "a world that must have been quite different from the actual experiences of returning GIs and their new families in the chaotic years of readjustment to civilian life."[3] Nearly three decades later, America "almost came apart at the seams" as a result of the Watergate scandal,[4] prompting the major television networks to screen series such as *Little House on the Prairie* (1974) that reinforced the idea of the family as a source of social and moral strength.

In the 1970s, the networks also broadcast dramas focusing on an individual, a family, or an entire community struggling with the forces of evil that threatened to undermine the stability of their world. This chapter shows how Dan Curtis's adaptation of *The Turn of the Screw* (1974) provides a good example of this type of program, as James's novella is transformed into a ghost story reminiscent of Curtis's highly successful ABC daytime soap *Dark Shadows* (1966–1971), in which mortals encounter a succession of ghosts, witches, a vampire, and even the devil incarnate. In *The Turn of the Screw*, the governess (Lynn Redgrave) is repeatedly assailed by the ghosts of Quint and Miss Jessel as she tries to rescue the children's innocent souls from their malign influence through maternal affection (something they have not previously experienced). However, Curtis stresses that as a single woman, Jane Cubberly can never accomplish the task successfully. Starved of male company since her childhood, she is plagued by sexual urges and ultimately tormented by guilt for having contributed to Miles's death. As with Bogdanovich's *Daisy Miller*, this *Turn of the Screw* emphasizes the importance of the nuclear family to the health of society by suggesting that any single woman who cannot benefit from the "protection" offered by a husband or a father is doomed to perpetual suffering. This ideology had been popular ever since the 1950s when "representations of television continually addressed women as housewives and presented them with a notion of spectatorship that was inextricably intertwined with their useful labor at home."[5] Gregory A. Waller observes that such conservatism was characteristic of most made-for-television horror films of the 1970s and early 1980s, which had "less in common with the atypical households featured on situation comedies in the wake of 'All in the Family' . . . than with the families in, for example, other made-for-television movies and in commercials for insurance and toothpaste."[6]

The first episode of *Dark Shadows*, aired on June 27, 1966, began with the journey of Victoria Winters, a young governess traveling by train to Collinwood, an old Gothic mansion, to tutor young David Collins. The first few episodes centered on the governess's experiences in this new environment, but poor viewing figures persuaded Curtis to introduce a ghost story. Nine months into the show's run, the reluctant vampire Barnabas Collins (Jonathan Frid) was released from imprisonment in the family vaults, and *Dark Shadows*'s Nielsen ratings skyrocketed. So popular was this new character (and actor) that other supernatural entities such as ghosts and werewolves were soon added, including Angélique (Lara Parker)—an evil witch who condemned Barnabas to vampirism in the first place—and Quentin Collins (David Selby), a Byronic hero affected with the werewolf curse. Barnabas was especially popular because—like Dr. Spock in *Star Trek*—he appeared to challenge authority. At the same time, he had human (and vampiric) weaknesses, as he fell in love with Victoria yet found himself unable to express his feelings adequately because he was a bloodsucker, a vampire who could just as easily kill her as kiss her. At the height of *Dark Shadows*'s popularity,

Jonathan Frid commented that "Youngsters today are looking for a new morality. And so is Barnabas. . . . He hates what he is and he's in terrible agony. Just like the kids today, he's confused, lost, screwed up and searching for something."[7] By 1970, the series attracted an audience of more than fifteen million viewers, and the production received five thousand letters and cards a week from viewers who wanted to know everything about Barnabas and the actor who played him. The series ended in April 1971 after 1,225 episodes.[8]

Curtis's version of *The Turn of the Screw* seeks to capitalize on the popularity of *Dark Shadows* by rewriting the novella as an orthodox ghost story taking place in a haunted house. This is certainly not what James intended; in a notebook entry for January 12, 1895, he records that the inspiration came from a story recounted by the Archbishop of Canterbury, "being all that he had been told (very badly and imperfectly) by a lady who had no art of relation, and no clearness. . . . It is all obscure and imperfect, the picture, the story, but there is a suggestion of a strangely gruesome effect in it."[9] The fact that the original tale had been recounted imperfectly lies at the heart of the novella's ambiguity: we never know for certain whether the ghosts are real or products of the governess' fevered imagination. Even before Quint appears for the first time, she dreams of how "it would be as charming as a charming story suddenly to meet someone."[10] She pictures herself as the heroine of a gothic romance revealing Bly's dark secret—"a mystery of Udolpho or an insane, an unmentionable relative kept in unsuspected confinement."[11] By contrast, we are left in no doubt in Curtis's version that the ghosts are living presences (as in *The Innocents*, William Archibald's play that inspired the 1962 adaptation). But perhaps we should not be too quick to criticize the director's decision; as Waller remarks, the bulk of 1970s and 1980s telefilms (irrespective of genre) were cheaply made for audiences who generally preferred the pleasures of familiarity to anything challenging. They drew upon tried-and-tested formats involving "a small number of clearly delineated individual characters—heroes and villains—who are 'causal agents' in plots that inevitably move forward toward a closed resolution with no 'questions or enigmas' left open."[12] The opening moments of *The Turn of the Screw* should be recognizable to anyone acquainted with *Dark Shadows*, as the governess Jane Cubberly arrives at Bly House in a cart driven by the servant Luke (Benedict Taylor). The ambience seems peaceful enough; but Jane informs us in a voice-over of her suspicions that something dreadful will happen. And so it proves, as she catches sight of Quint (James Laurenson) looking at her standing on the tower. The camera zooms into a close-up of her startled face and then cuts back to ground level where Quint had stood; he is no longer there.

The basic *Dark Shadows* scenario of human beings threatened by supernatural forces is repeatedly employed in this adaptation.[13] On one occasion, Miles (Jasper Jacob) invites Jane to play a macabre game called "Fetch" wherein she has to bring them a Chinese doll from the tower. As she climbs up the stairs, the door slams shut; she looks up to find Miss Jessel (Kathryn Scott) standing threateningly opposite her. Curtis cuts to a shot of a disembodied hand opening the door, and tracks backwards to reveal that it belongs to Miles who has come to look for her. Curtis retains the scene from the novella where the governess encounters Miss Jessel in the schoolroom, but adds a dramatic coda as Jane rushes out of the room and sees Quint coming towards her. Screaming that the ghost will not take the children from her, she throws a candlestick at him and falls down the stairs in a faint as the scene fades to black.[14]

Jane's concern for the children is shared by the director who makes it clear that they are the blameless victims of a dysfunctional family. As in *The Nightcomers*, the uncle—renamed Mr. Fredericks (John Barron)—has neglected his responsibilities as a guardian; he is certainly not the "bold and pleasant, off-hand and gay and kind" personality of the novella who "pitied the poor chicks and had done all he could [for them]."[15] He has no concern for the children, whom he considers a menace to his peace of mind. Apparently, they had stayed with him in London for a few days, but they neither took to him nor he to them; consequently he banished them to Bly House. While informing Jane in an imperious voice that does not wish to be troubled by the children, he has no qualms about troubling *her*. At the end of what has proved an uncomfortable interview, he asks whether she thinks he is a dreadful man, leering at her as he does so. She nods her head in assent and quits the room before he has the chance to act on his lascivious impulses.

Once the action shifts to Bly, we learn that until his untimely death Quint took on a role similar to that in *The Nightcomers* by ruling the children as a surrogate father. Mrs. Grose (Megs Jenkins) informs Jane about the strong bonds between Quint and Miles.[16] James has Mrs. Grose admitting that it was Quint's pleasure to spoil Miles, and that he was much too free, without going into any specific detail; Curtis offers specific examples of Quint's misdeeds. Apparently he gave Miles whiskey to drink, but no one cared—least of all Miss Jessel, who had Flora all to herself.

The adaptation follows the example of *The Nightcomers* by suggesting that the children were privy to Quint's and Miss Jessel's lovemaking, prompting them to start an incestuous affair for themselves. Jane wakes up one night as she hears the sound of heavy breathing. She makes her way to the children's room, to find Miles and Flora sitting together on the bed. While Miles explains that he was innocently tickling his sister, the guilty smile on his face suggests that something more sinister had occurred. Our suspicions are confirmed once Jane has left the room, as a loud moan of orgasmic pleasure bursts forth from behind the door.

As a governess, Jane believes that the only way to reeducate the children is to lead by example. In the novella, the governess recalls that they became so fond of her that "they got their little tasks as if they loved them; they indulged, from the mere exuberance of the gift, in the most unimposed little miracles of memory."[17] Curtis includes extra material to show how Jane makes every effort to become the children's substitute mother. She takes them on a picnic (on what looks like a very cold autumn day!); plays hide-and-seek on the stairs; and even organizes a little soirée where the children can recite their own poetry. At one point, she observes in a voice-over that the boy's fate is in her hands, and it is incumbent on her to ensure his future well-being.

In spite of her best intentions, Jane falls victim to the corruption pervading Bly House. At one point, Quint materializes in a doorway; the camera zooms to a close-up of his haggard face, then cuts to another close-up of Jane staring at him, unable to move. There is no doubt she finds him attractive with his unkempt hair, white shirt open to the waist, and skin-tight black pants.[18] She subsequently admits in a voice-over that Quint exerts a malign influence; in a dream sequence later on, she is shown lying in bed waiting for him to have sex with her. This is followed by a dissolve to a close-up of the two of them engaged in passionate lovemaking; Jane's moans of pleasure can be heard on the soundtrack. The scene ends with her waking up to see Miles leaning over her, wondering (in a deliberate innuendo) whether he could "help" her.

Compared to the dream sequence in *The Innocents*, which depicts Miss Giddens's gradual sexual awakening, Curtis suggests that Jane's fantasies are unnatural, rendering her unfit for the role of governess. This is stressed in two short sequences, the first of which begins with Miles giving her a good-night kiss on the lips. The camera zooms into a reaction shot of her face, which registers astonishment and pleasure. In the second, Jane sits on Miles's bed while Miles massages her shoulders. Unlike the novella, where the boy is described as ten years old, this Miles is a powerfully built adolescent seducing a governess who believes that, by permitting him to do so, she can commune with Quint.

Although striving to suppress her instincts, Jane finds herself unequal to the task. In the climax to the adaptation, Miles runs toward the ghost; Jane screams at him, which prompts the little boy to turn round and rush into her arms. Curtis cuts to a shot from Jane's point of view of Miles dressed as Quint; he comes towards her and administers yet another passionate kiss. Jane jerks herself away, as she realizes then that she has fallen for a minor. But the damage has already been done; Miles falls down dead; and the governess is left all alone cradling his head and sobbing as the camera tracks backward and the scene fades to black.

Curtis leaves us in no doubt why she should do such a thing: Jane is not only a single woman but (like the children) she has never known "normal" (i.e., nuclear) family life. In some newly written dialogue, she tells Mrs. Grose how her mother died when she was a child and that her father was so strict that she learned to keep out of his way. Mrs. Grose cannot offer much help; her mother also died young, while her tradesman father ran away when the children were scarce into their teens. Like Jane, she has been alone for many years.

Curtis had previously dramatized an affair between a mortal and a supernatural being in *Dark Shadows*. However, the approach is very different; despite Barnabas's affection for Victoria Winters, he refuses to commit himself for fear of corrupting her. He remains an essentially decent man—a villain by circumstance (on account of Angélique's curse) but with goodness inside. Jane Cubberly's concern for the children might be equally selfless, but she sacrifices her ideals once she falls for Quint. A comparison between the two programs tells us a lot about attitudes towards gender on American television during the 1960s and early 1970s. Whereas males such as Barnabas possess sufficient moral strength to resist temptation, the same is obviously not true of single females. They need to be brought up in a stable two-parent family where the father sets an example to his children. Curtis implicitly suggests that once women have reached adulthood, they need to get married so that they have a male to guide them toward right action.

Although not as sexually explicit as *The Nightcomers* (the television networks would never have allowed it), this *Turn of the Screw* follows Winner's example by dramatizing the governess's love life in detail. Once she arrives at Bly, she is transformed from a repressed virgin into a sexual predator. Until she gets married herself, she will always pose a threat to the stability of society. John Ellis suggests that this view is characteristic of most television drama:

> For many people living in ways that differ from this supposed norm [of the nuclear family], these ways of living are experienced as exceptions or temporary departures from the norm. The presence of a grandparent, or other relatives, the single-parent family, the childless household, all of these common and by no means 'radical' forms are taken as a passing phase rather than as a real way of living. Such is the power of the conception of the nuclear family in its present form [on television].[19]

On this view, Jane Cubberly's experiences at Bly should be viewed as a "passing phase" rather than suggesting "a real way of living" for women.

Curtis's *Turn of the Screw* was first broadcast on ABC in two parts on April 15 and 16, 1974. Reviews were mixed; the *Los Angeles Herald Examiner* commended the acting, which apparently had "the glisteningly fine finish of the English period film"; but nine years later, the British trade paper *Video Business* gave it a damning review: "The voice-over narration is a bad blunder, the sound is lavatorial, the spooks are all too reminiscent of talcum-powder and track lighting, and the older child, the boy Miles . . . is a great hulking lout of a prop forward."[20] Nonetheless, the presence of Dan Curtis as director has given this adaptation a certain popularity (notoriety?) in the video/DVD market; it is currently available as part of a four-disc set entitled "The Dan Curtis Macabre Collection." The other three adaptations are *Dr. Jekyll and Mr. Hyde* (1968), *Dracula* (1973), and *The Picture of Dorian Gray* (also 1973)—all of which transform the original texts into ghost stories very similar in terms of content to *The Turn of the Screw*. Apparently nothing succeeds like imitation.

Notes

1. John Ellis, *Visible Fictions: Cinema: Television: Video* (London: Routledge, 1982), 113–14.

2. This is especially true of historical reality shows such as the British-made *The 1900 House* (1997) or *The 1940 House* (1999), where nuclear families of a husband, wife, and two children were invited to spend a month living as their ancestors might have done.

3. Lynn Spigel, *Make Room for TV: Television and the Family Ideal in Postwar America* (Chicago: University of Chicago Press, 1992), 41.

4. Hal Himmelstein, *Television Myth and the American Mind* (Westport, CT: Praeger, 1994), 221.

5. Spigel, *Make Room for TV*, 75.

6. Gregory A. Waller, "Made-for-Television Horror Films," in *American Horrors: Essays on the Modern Horror Film*, ed. Gregory A. Waller (Urbana: University of Illinois Press, 1987), 156.

7. Quoted in John Kenneth Muir, *Terror Television: American Series 1970–1999* (Jefferson, NC: McFarland, 1999), 294.

8. *Dark Shadows* was later turned into two films *House of Dark Shadows* (1970) and *Night of Dark Shadows* (1971). The television series was rerun on American TV stations and PBS from 1975 onwards; in 1990 the Sci-Fi Channel purchased the rights to the show, where it was regularly broadcast in America throughout the subsequent decade. *Dark Shadows* was revived in 1991 on NBC with a new cast, but canceled after a two-month run. For further information, see the *Dark Shadows* website at www.darkshadows .com (accessed March 12, 2005).

9. Henry James, *The Complete Notebooks of Henry James*, ed. Leon Edel and Lyall H. Powers (New York: Oxford University Press, 1987), 342.

10. Henry James, *The Turn of the Screw, The Aspern Papers and Other Stories*, ed. Michael Swan (London: Collins, 1963), 330.

11. James, *Turn of the Screw*, 332. Shoshana Felman observed in 1977 that the very act of "seeing" ghosts in the original novella involves the perception of ambiguous and contradictory signifiers. In her endeavor to reduce the contradictory and ambiguous to "but one meaning," the governess's method of reading her own adventure is thus not substantially different from that of James's readers, according to the critics of the text. Shoshana Felman, "Turning the Screw of Interpretation," in *Literature and Psychoanalysis: The Question of Reading: Otherwise*, ed. Shoshana Felman (Baltimore: Johns Hopkins University Press, 1977), 154–55.

12. Waller, "Made-for-Television Horror Films," 147.

13. See, for example, the picture on the box for the VHS release (1991) and the DVD version (2001), which shows Redgrave in close-up staring fearfully at the camera.

14. Cf. *The Innocents*, where Miss Giddens (Deborah Kerr) suddenly becomes aware of Miss Jessel's suffering, as she puts her finger in a teardrop on a slate lying near the teacher's desk in the school-room.

15. James, *Turn of the Screw*, 318–19. The actor's name has been incorrectly spelled as "John Baron" in the credits.

16. Megs Jenkins played the same role in *The Innocents*.

17. James, *Turn of the Screw*, 355.

18. Quint's costume and manner deliberately recalls Quentin Collins in *Dark Shadows*.

19. Ellis, *Visible Fictions*, 115.

20. "The Turn of the Screw," *Los Angeles Herald-Examiner*, April 22, 1974, 66; "The Turn of the Screw," *Video Business*, May 23, 1983, 60.

CHAPTER TEN

~

The Portrait of a Lady (1968) and The Golden Bowl (1972)

So far we have seen that in the 1970s and early 1980s most James adaptations posited a reactionary view of gender relations by suggesting that women's primary duties consisted of marriage and the family, while those who favored the single life remained somehow unfulfilled. It would appear that the women's movement's struggle for equality in the previous decade had been in vain; most filmmakers preferred to reaffirm the strength of the patriarchy. However, there were at least two adaptations produced at this time that challenged this view: James Cellan Jones's BBC television versions of *The Portrait of a Lady* (1968) and *The Golden Bowl* (1972). In this chapter, I demonstrate that, unlike his counterparts on American network television, Cellan Jones had the freedom to develop an idiosyncratic perspective, unfettered by commercial imperatives (for example, ratings or advertisements).[1] By the late 1960s, the classic serial formed a mainstay of the BBC's schedules; through weekly scheduling in seasonal blocks, it had established enough regularity to build an audience, and enough identity to fulfill the corporation's remit as a public service broadcasting organization.[2] A 1972 book *Television and the People* congratulated the BBC on its achievement in making great literature accessible to mass audiences and thereby rendering "obsolete the former divisions which stratified the public into high, low and middle brows."[3] Directors were actively encouraged to experiment with new approaches to adaptation, secure in the knowledge that their work would be scheduled at a regular time and would attract a loyal audience. Shaun Sutton, a former head of BBC Drama, observed in 1982 that television drama required "a continuing flow of new ideas and fresh approaches. A diet of old success and safe formula leads to enervation and death by dramatic starvation."[4]

In the second part of this chapter, I argue that Cellan Jones adopts an idiosyncratic approach to James adaptations by supporting the female protagonists of *The Portrait of a Lady* and *The Golden Bowl*—Isabel Archer, Maggie Verver, and Charlotte Stant—in their bids for self-determination. Isabel rejects a financially advantageous marriage to Lord Warburton and chooses to return to England to comfort the dying Ralph, in defiance of Osmond's wishes. On the majority of occasions, she sustains her independence through less direct means, ones that Cellan Jones highlights televisually: He frequently frames her face in close-up as she chides her friends for asking too much from her or expecting her to behave in a particular manner. Both Charlotte Stant and Maggie Verver in Cellan Jones's *Golden Bowl* opt for silence as a method of resistance. On the surface they appear to be committed to marriage, home, and family, but no one really knows them. The on-screen narrator Bob Assingham makes repeated attempts to explain their motives; it is clear from his speeches, however, that his judgments are riddled with uncertainties. Cellan Jones's emphasis on female potential might now be considered sexist (it clearly reinforces women's position on the periphery of society); for first-wave feminists of the late 1960s and 1970s, however, this viewpoint was of paramount importance. Carol Andreas's *Sex and Caste in America* (1971) suggested that a greater awareness of female potential could open up "new possibilities for freedom" for both men and women who hitherto had been "kept in anxiety about their worth and identity as human beings because they must 'make it' as a man or woman member of a sexist society."[5] In *Towards a Recognition of Androgyny* (1973), Carolyn G. Heilbrun exalted "feminine traits," in the belief that "since they have [hitherto] been so drastically undervalued, [they] must now gain respect, so that a sort of balance is achieved among those in power, and within individuals."[6]

The classic serial of the 1960s and early 1970s was the ideal medium to disseminate these ideas to viewers who (in the directors' minds at least) were considered perfectly capable of listening to as well as watching what took place on screen. Whereas Dan Curtis's *Turn of the Screw* recasts the novella in a popular format—the ghost story—in the belief that this is what audiences wanted, Jack Pulman's screenplay for Cellan Jones's *Portrait of a Lady* likewise incorporates large quantities of Jamesian text. In one sequence, the action moves from the scene where Madame Merle (Rachel Gurney) promises to talk to Isabel (Suzanne Neve) on Mrs. Touchett's behalf to the moment where Osmond (James Maxwell) wonders what to do with Pansy.[7] The dialogue remains much the same as in the novel, save for the omission of Isabel's observation to Osmond ("I think that wouldn't do much towards making her resemble me").[8]

Pulman's faith in the Jamesian text is equally evident in Cellan Jones's adaptation of *The Golden Bowl*. In one newly written sequence, Bob Assingham (Cyril Cusack) observes Maggie Verver (Jill Townsend) waiting for her husband to return home: "So Maggie waited, her heart I'm sure beating very fast." The prince (Daniel Massey) returns without a greeting from Maggie. In the next scene, Bob admits that "what she [Maggie] might have said, what she longed to say, I suppose, was . . . ," followed closely by Maggie's own voice-over of a passage taken almost verbatim from the novel:

> Why have I made this evening such a point of our not dining together? Well, because I've all day been so wanting you all alone that I finally couldn't bear it, and there didn't seem to be any great reason why I should try to. You seem these last days, I don't know what, more absent than ever before, too absent for us merely to go on so. It's all very well and I perfectly see how beautiful it is all around. But there comes a day when something snaps and the cup flows over. That's it. The cup all day has been too full to carry, so here I am with it spilling over you, because it's my life after all, and I don't have to explain, do I, that I'm as much in love with you now as on the first hour we met, except there are some hours, which I know when they come because they frighten me, that you are even more so, and they do come, oh how they come, how they come.[9]

The cup image is used earlier on in the novel, when James describes the prince's eyes meeting Charlotte's on the balcony: "So therefore while the minute lasted it passed between them that their cup was full; which cup their very eyes, holding it fast, carried and steadied and began, as they tasted it, to praise."[10] Charlotte subsequently observes that she feels "like a great gold cup that we [i.e., the prince and herself] must somehow drain together."[11] Cellan Jones retains Charlotte's line, but emphasizes the strength of her attraction to the prince—as expressed through the gold cup image—by having Mr. Blint (Terry Mitchell) play the love song "Plaisir d'Amour" on the piano in the background.[12] The fact that Maggie is unaware of this when she makes use of the golden cup image to express her feelings for her husband renders her speech even more poignant.

Throughout Maggie's long speech, the camera focuses on her expressionless face until Bob observes in a newly written line that "of course she couldn't say that." In fact the only words spoken in the scene are by the prince, who talks about what he has been doing, then excuses himself with the phrase "I must go and bathe." The clear implication is that he seeks to cleanse himself of Charlotte's smell, leaving Maggie alone in the darkness as the scene fades to black. The entire sequence seeks to render the novel's interior states as being visible; viewers contemplate Maggie as she reflects on her husband's behavior and comes to understand what he has been up to.[13]

The experience of watching classic serials of this kind is very different from watching that of Curtis's *Turn of the Screw*, which has been divided into fifteen segments to accommodate commercial breaks. Each segment—lasting between eight and fifteen minutes—ends in a climax to sustain the audience's attention while the advertisements are shown. As Julian Critchley remarked in his review of Cellan Jones's *Portrait of a Lady*, "We concentrate not on action but on character, and watch with growing pleasure the application of a large talent to the very slightest of stories."[14] Bearing in mind the likelihood that many viewers were encountering *The Portrait* and *The Golden Bowl* for the first time, Pulman and Cellan Jones emphasize that both novels are as much concerned with states of mind as character and incident. Little attempt has been made to liven up both plots with gratuitous action; viewers should listen to as well as observe what unfolds on screen.[15] These adaptations might seem flat and undramatic; nonetheless, they provide excellent examples of how the classic serial sought to educate as well as entertain television audiences of the late 1960s and 1970s.[16]

Sometimes it seems as if Cellan Jones deliberately interrupts the narrative to enable viewers to reflect on the characters' behavior. Isabel's journey from Gardencourt to Italy is not described in James's *Portrait* (we only learn that she finds Italy "a land of promise, a land in which the love of the beautiful might be comforted by endless knowledge."[17] In the adaptation, Isabel's voyage is symbolically represented by means of an interlude in which an etching of a ship at sea is shown onscreen, accompanied by Ralph's (Richard Chamberlain's) voice-over telling his father (Alan Gifford) that he seeks to "get just the good I said a few moments ago I wished to put into Isabel's reach—that of having met the requirements of my imagination."[18] In the background, the opening bars of the first movement of the Ravel Trio for piano, violin, and cello can be heard.[19] As studio time was limited in 1968, and most classic serials had to be recorded quickly (within ten to fourteen days), it is likely that sequences such as this were deliberately introduced to enable the actors to move from one set to another. Nonetheless, this strategy—a legacy of the days when all BBC dramas were broadcast live—has a thematic as well as a practical function. Just like Winterbourne scrutinizing Daisy in

Bogdanovich's *Daisy Miller* or Marc fantasizing about Melinda in *On a Clear Day*, Ralph conceives Isabel as a canvas on to which he can project his dreams of success. This interlude also adumbrates the next scene in the adaptation where Madame Merle tells Osmond that drawing is his sole accomplishment, even if it does reveal his "adorable taste."[20]

Such devices were no longer necessary by 1972, as the technology of videotape recording had improved. However, Cellan Jones frequently interrupts the action to allow Bob Assingham (Cyril Cusack) to address the viewers directly on camera or to comment on the other characters through voice-over. On one occasion, Maggie sits in a tea-shop staring into the middle distance while Bob tells us how she had been courted by the prince. Later on—in a newly written speech—he reflects on Charlotte's (Gayle Hunnicutt's) forthcoming marriage to Verver:

> I think in her own way she was bent on making the marriage work. When she thought about it consciously I think she meant all that she had said to Verver that day on the pier at Brighton. She did want to get married. She did like him; she was immensely grateful to him and perhaps at first she didn't know what was truly at the back of her mind.

Writing in the London *Times* after the opening episode was broadcast in May 1972, Leonard Buckley complained that the use of Bob as an on-screen narrator was "irksome," as Cusack's voice was not "the sort to sustain a long narration without grating."[21] It is certainly true that Bob's voice-overs divert our attention away from the visual image, as we concentrate on what is happening mentally and emotionally (through the words) rather than physically (through the action).[22] But perhaps this is the most effective way of rendering James's exploration of his characters' state of mind explicit on screen.

Not all critics were happy with this style of adaptation, which had remained much the same since the BBC started transmitting classic serials on a regular basis in the years immediately following the end of the Second World War. Commenting on John Davies's 1972 *War and Peace*, one writer complained that the genre had become too predictable: "Sometimes you feel as if the same serial has been going on for five years. It changes title once every six months. Some time ago it was called *Portrait of a Lady*; then *Pride and Prejudice*. Still later they called it *Middlemarch*, and for the moment they refer to it as *War and Peace*."[23]

Even a recent critic such as Lee Clark Mitchell, who was generally sympathetic towards Cellan Jones's *Golden Bowl*, described the production as "bare-bones . . . with restrained costumes, uncluttered rooms, shot in under-stated studio sets."[24] By contrast, Curtis's *Turn of the Screw* was shot entirely on location in Lincolnshire, England. Yet a studio-bound approach to presentation seems to suit Henry James; by concentrating almost exclusively on the characters and their reactions, through close-ups, medium, or two-shots, it can reveal (in Jonathan Freedman's words) how "human beings must not only reckon with the relations that construct them, but also work to build new, more efficacious ones."[25] This certainly seems the case in *The Portrait of a Lady*. At one point, Isabel admits in some newly written lines that "if it hadn't been for the money, I'd never have married him [Osmond]." Yet she refuses to take Henrietta Stackpole (Sarah Brackett's) advice and end her marriage. Her reasons are plain enough: "Why—because I know him better now than when I married him. That would be a paltry thing to do. I must make him like me better. While it remains unspoken, there's a chance it may improve. I think I owe him that. I think I owe it to myself."

The entire sequence is filmed in a series of medium shots and close-ups, with Isabel standing next to a large marble statue, its gleaming whiteness providing an apt metaphor for the sterility of her marriage. Her determination to try and make things better is also expressed symbolically, as she moves away from the statue and sits in a chair sipping tea in the shadow of a tree. Clearly, she is searching for more fertile ways to communicate with her husband.

This quest proves futile, however, as Osmond accuses her of having played "a very deep game" in driving Lord Warburton away, and thereby preventing Pansy from contracting a financially advantageous marriage.[26] Cellan Jones shoots this scene in a series of two-shots, with Osmond standing threateningly over Isabel. On at least two occasions, the action cuts to a point-of-view shot of Osmond looking at his wife sitting on the sofa, with all of his ornaments (vases, bronze figures) illuminated by candlelight in the background. On one level, this point-of-view shot stresses Isabel's confinement; like Daisy Miller in Bogdanovich's film, she cannot evade the male gaze. On another level, the shot suggests that Osmond treats her as just another item in his collection of antiques.

In *The Golden Bowl*, Charlotte's burgeoning affair with the prince is expressed through a close-up of their hands linked together. The prince's head is seen on the right of the frame as he moves towards Charlotte; as he does so, the camera tracks backwards to show her smiling face. What makes this moment more interesting is that, as the action unfolds, we hear Bob telling us that his wife, Fanny (Kathleen Byron), could not understand "whether anything was going on between them or not. One moment she thought there was, the next she thought she was mistaken." Clearly, Charlotte and the prince are thoroughly enjoying their affair—particularly when no one else appears to know about it.

Later on, Maggie's growing suspicion about their relationship is suggested in a sequence that begins with a close-up of Charlotte playing the piano. The camera tracks backward once again to a medium shot of the prince, Maggie, and Adam Verver (Barry Morse), who are listening to her recital. Two medium close-ups of Maggie's face, her eyes fixed on the prince, are separated by another shot of Charlotte playing "Plaisir d'Amour." Clearly this song, with its romantic message, alerts Maggie to the fact that it might not be intended for everyone's pleasure.

Another technique Cellan Jones employs to focus attention on the relationships in both adaptations is the use of visual symbolism. I have already shown how the marble statue functions as a metaphor for Isabel's marriage; the same image appears in the sequence where Isabel and Lord Warburton (Edward Fox) are shown walking in the grounds of Gardencourt—the only scene filmed on location in the entire adaptation. This says a lot about Isabel's status in society; she is only permitted to walk outdoors when faced with a proposal of marriage. The two of them are shown sitting by a large marble statue placed in the center of an ornamental pond. Clearly, we are meant to understand that whereas the union might bring Isabel wealth and social position, it will prove as lifeless as the statue. She is thoroughly justified in telling Warburton "not to hope at all" for her consent.[27] The most obvious symbol to appear in *The Golden Bowl* is the bowl itself. The prince is the first to identify the flaw in its structure; as he considers whether this might be a bad omen or not,[28] Cellan Jones cuts to a close-up of the bowl with Charlotte's fingers running round the edge. The same shot is used later on, once Maggie discovers the truth about her husband's infidelity, only this time it is Maggie's hand, rather than Charlotte's, which is shown running round the bowl.[29]

So far, we have concentrated mainly on Cellan Jones's approach to adaptation and how it sought to fulfill the BBC's public service responsibility to inform, educate, and entertain audiences. What we have not yet considered is how both *The Portrait of a Lady* and *The Golden Bowl* focus on the question of female identity. Neither Isabel, Maggie, nor Charlotte suffers the same experience as Catherine Sloper in Wyler's *The Heiress*, who rejects her father and Morris by showing the same kind of brutality that her father meted out to her in the past. Rather, they endeavor to create a specifically feminine language for themselves that is irreducible to a masculine language based on power and authority. In Isabel's case, this is evident through her reticence, which renders her difficult to accommodate within the patriarchal order. To Ralph, she is "a clever girl—with a strong will and a high temper,"[30] possessed of "a rare mind." He invites her to "be frank" about her marriage to Osmond,[31] to which Isabel replies (in a newly written line): "I didn't marry to please my friends, and I can't complain just to please them either." Cellan Jones cuts to a close-up of Ralph's crestfallen face—despite his friendship for her, Isabel will not give him access to her "rare mind."

On another occasion, Lord Warburton admits that he cannot make out what Isabel is "up to," and suggests that her mind is "a most formidable instrument" that "looks down on us all; it despises us."[32] Cellan Jones adds the following lines:

ISABEL: I do not like the picture you draw of me.
WARBURTON: It might be exaggerated. Perhaps you're right. Perhaps we
                should join the others.

Creating a "portrait of a lady"—either physically or in one's mind—constitutes a masculine strategy that imposes order and unity on her by capturing her for eternity in a particular attitude. Isabel resents this; she seeks to remain "perfectly free" and not have to justify her behavior to others, even if she could.[33]

This is further emphasized at the end of the adaptation. As someone who has based her career on manipulating others for Osmond's benefit, Madame Merle might have expected some reaction from Isabel to the revelation that it was Ralph who had imparted "that extra lustre . . . to make you a brilliant match." James's novel implies that this is the case, as Merle observes "in a kind of proud penance" that Isabel is unhappy.[34] In Cellan Jones's adaptation, Isabel remains silent, refusing to betray her emotions. After a few seconds, she turns away, delivering the line "I think I should like never to see you again" with a long pause between the words "like" and "never."[35] She opens the door and quietly exits, leaving Merle alone, a pathetic figure whose scheming has left her with nothing—not even the pleasure of sustaining some kind of hold over Isabel.

To anyone who relies on Bob Assingham's judgment in Cellan Jones's *Golden Bowl*, Maggie Verver's and Charlotte Stant's behavior must seem equally unpredictable. On one occasion, Bob likens Maggie to a bird who "had flapped her little wings as a token of wanting to fly a little, not merely as a plea for a more gilded cage."[36] The result, according to Bob's patriarchal view of the world, was that Maggie "felt suddenly immensely alone." This summation is undermined by the events that follow, as Maggie admits that Charlotte has "always been so good, so perfect, to me—but never as wonderfully as just now. We have somehow been more together—thinking for the time almost only of each other; it has been quite as in old days."[37] Cellan Jones emphasizes the closeness of their relationship by means of a split-screen image, with Charlotte on the left of the frame, and Maggie on the right. Such contradictory impulses—where Charlotte chooses to remain close friends with someone who suspects her of having an affair with her husband—are beyond the scope of Bob's imagination. Like Winterbourne in Bogdanovich's *Daisy Miller* two years later, he evaluates the two women according to his patriarchal view of society; they are either visions of loveliness or femmes fatales (once their marriages start to fall apart). He cannot conceive of the fact that they might rely on one another for moral support. The strength of their friendship is further emphasized in a newly created sequence when Maggie purchases the golden bowl. The shopkeeper recalls the time earlier on when Charlotte looked at it, and asks Maggie whether Charlotte is her sister. Maggie's countenance is shown in tight close-up as she replies, "No—my friend."

Bob's attempts to explain Charlotte's behavior prove equally misleading. Once the details of her affair with the prince have been brought to light, he remembers in a newly written speech that

> When Fanny said "Poor Charlotte," I knew exactly what she meant. For whatever you may think of Charlotte, it was the cruelest thing imaginable that could be done to a woman as much in love as she was. To leave her suspended in mid-air and just wondering. . . . She [Maggie] could sense the panic rising in Charlotte's heart, as if she were a bird in a cage, suspended in a room into which a cat had just walked. She saw the flutterings, the beating of wings, the trembling of feathers around the throat.

What happens next does not appear so dramatic, as Charlotte and Maggie exchange confidences on the Castledeans' balcony, as if nothing had happened. Charlotte guides groups of tourists around her husband's house, while Bob solemnly intones in a voice-over that she "knew what her doom was, that she was to be separated from her lover and to all intents and purposes never to see him again." Charlotte neither confirms nor refutes his observations; like Isabel Archer, she appears to be enjoying "her cheerful submission to [wifely] duty."[38] The last we see of her in the adaptation is just before she departs for American City, where she stresses that "our real life isn't here [in England]" and points out, much to Maggie's chagrin, that she speaks both for herself and her husband: "Let me admit it—I *am* selfish. I place my husband first."[39] While such brazenness is an act designed to cover up her private anguish, it seems hardly characteristic of a woman fluttering like a "bird in a cage" and proceeding inexorably to her doom, as Bob would have us believe. Just like the readers of James's novels, viewers have to form their own interpretations of events, asking the same kinds of questions, and reaching the same kinds of tentative conclusions as the characters themselves. Like Bob, we might find our judgments disproved by events.[40]

Cellan Jones's adaptations cannot be considered radical in the sense that they redefine existing television production practices. The narratives may not be directly concerned with the nuclear family, but they focus on numerous issues related to it—for example, heterosexual romance, the stability of marriage, masculine careers and feminine domesticity, and the division of the world into public and private spheres.[41] While the focus of attention shifts from rational male discourses to the linguistic in-between (something characteristic of women's language),[42] we must nonetheless bear in mind that these adaptations have been created by a male director, who might seek to underline women's marginal position in a patriarchal society. Yet perhaps we should not be too critical; as this chapter has sought to suggest, Cellan Jones's representation of women is very different from the kinds of images that were characteristic of other James adaptations of the 1960s and 1970s. While Isabel, Charlotte, and Maggie appear to subject themselves to patriarchal authority, their refusal to explain themselves suggests some kind of repudiation of masculine (i.e., rational) values. This represents a considerable advance on *The Innocents*, for example, where Miss Giddens remains a frustrated spinster but at least comes to understand that her frustrations may be caused by powerful sexual desire.

Jane Gaines argued in 1984 that a feminist film should seek to "destroy the codes of mainstream entertainment and ultimately replace them with a cinema that provokes thought and encourages analysis." Her ideal approach was Brechtian inspired, based on a refusal to allow audiences to identify with characters, and thereby provoke them into critical analysis of what unfolds before them.[43] Cellan Jones's *Portrait of a Lady* and *The Golden Bowl* do not go that far; but by permitting the female protagonists to leave certain things unexplained, and thereby undermining the sense of closure in the endings, he prompts us to consider the limitations of mainstream classical narrative.

Both *The Portrait of a Lady* and *The Golden Bowl* are very much products of a particular period in British television history, with their studio sets, restrained costumes, and rather stilted visual style oscillating between medium shot and close-up. This was a deliberate directorial choice, prompted partly by a desire to conform to the BBC's house style of classic adaptations and partly by the desire to make the viewer listen to as well as observe what took place on screen. In Alistair Cooke's view, Henry James's "calm and wary analysis of the emotions of people" was "just what the small screen craves." Pulman and Cellan Jones stressed this by showing how "television is not so much a miniature theatre as a powerful microscope for scanning the emotions concealed under gestures so small as a licked lip . . . or a defensive chuckle."[44] At the same time, both adaptations reveal the extent to which feminism had penetrated the television industry in the late 1960s and 1970s. The majority of directors and writers may have been male, but some of them began to understand that women had a different way of looking at the world. The BBC producer Irene Shubik complained in 1970 that "one of the most disappointing things" about British television drama at that time was "that if you try to do anything at all off the beaten track nobody seems to want to understand or know."[45] I suggest that the very opposite was true, that directors like Cellan Jones explored the limits of the genre in an attempt to comment on gender relations of the period.

Notes

1. Much of this chapter is based on my article "James Cellan Jones's View of Female Potential in *The Portrait of a Lady* (1968) and *The Golden Bowl* (1972)," *Henry James E-Journal* no. 7, September 2003, at www2.newpaltz.edu/~hathawar/ejourn7.html (accessed November 6, 2005).

2. Lee Clark Mitchell suggests wrongly that this was a "Masterpiece Theatre production" produced for the BBC. Unlike later adaptations, which were supported by WGBH Boston, *The Golden Bowl* was entirely financed by the BBC, and first broadcast in America as part of the 1972–1973 Masterpiece Theatre season. Lee Clark Mitchell, "Based on the Novel by Henry James," in *Henry James Goes to the Movies*, ed. Susan M. Griffin (Lexington: University Press of Kentucky, 2002), 297.

3. Brian Groombridge, *Television and the People: A Programme for Democratic Reform* (Harmondsworth: Penguin Books, 1972), 23.

4. Shaun Sutton, *The Largest Theatre in the World: Thirty Years of Television Drama* (London: British Broadcasting Corporation, 1982), 28.

5. Carol Andreas, *Sex and Caste in America* (Englewood Cliffs, NJ: Prentice-Hall, 1971), 25.

6. Carolyn G. Heilbrun, *Towards a Recognition of Androgyny* (New York: Harper and Row, 1973), xvi.

7. Henry James, *The Portrait of a Lady* (Harmondsworth: Penguin Books, 1979), 277, 284.

8. James, *Portrait*, 285.

9. Henry James, *The Golden Bowl*, ed. Patricia Crick (Harmondsworth: Penguin Books, 1987), 337.

10. James, *Golden Bowl*, 290.

11. James, *Golden Bowl*, 292.

12. This song first appeared in the film *Love Affair* (1939), starring Irene Dunne and Charles Boyer. In William Wyler's *Heiress*, Morris Townsend (Montgomery Clift) declares his love for Catherine through the same song. That Cellan Jones should also include the song in his James adaptation seems to be more than just coincidence.

13. I am indebted for much of this discussion to Mitchell, "Based on the Novel," 297–301.

14. Julian Critchley, "Divorce as a Holiday Theme," *Times* (London), June 3, 1968, 4.

15. James himself was well aware of the structural differences between *The Turn of the Screw*, *The Portrait of a Lady*, and *The Golden Bowl*. Whereas the two later novels concentrated on the analysis of character rather than on plot, James wrote in a letter to Frederic William Henry Myers (December 19, 1898) that *The Turn of the Screw* was "a very mechanical matter . . . an inferior, a merely *pictorial* subject & rather a shameless pot-boiler." Henry James, *A Life in Letters*, ed. by Philip Horne (Harmondsworth: Penguin Books, 2000), 314.

16. Neil Berry observes that *The Portrait* was only the second BBC adaptation to be shot in color. Twice transmitted in 1968 on BBC2, it was shown again on BBC1, this time attracting seven million or more viewers: "Here was a sequence of events that must have gladdened the heart of the BBC's Presbyterian founder, Lord Reith." Neil Berry, "Enduring Ephemera: James Cellan Jones, Henry James and the BBC," in *Henry James on Stage and Screen*, ed. by John R. Bradley (Basingstoke: Palgrave, 2000), 120.

17. James, *Portrait*, 223.

18. James, *Portrait*, 186.

19. This theme recurs throughout the adaptation as a way of bridging particular scenes.

20. James, *Portrait*, 242.

21. Leonard Buckley. "The Golden Bowl." *The Times* (London), May 5, 1972, 9.

22. Mitchell, "Based on the Novel," 300.

23. Monica Lauritza, *Jane Austen's Emma on Television: A Study of a BBC Classic Serial* (Göteborg: Acta Universitatis Gothoburgensis, 1981), 30.

24. Mitchell, "Based on the Novel," 297.

25. Jonathan Freedman, *Professions of Taste: Henry James, British Aestheticism and Commodity Culture* (Stanford, CA: Stanford University Press, 1990), 6.

26. James, *Portrait*, 481.

27. James, *Portrait*, 106.

28. James, *Golden Bowl*, 123.

29. The shot of disembodied hands also occurs in *The Lost Moment*: At the beginning of the film they are seen opening a large leather-bound book, which is shown to be Jeffrey Ashton's biography. The hands then turn the pages to show a poem, "To Juliana in Venice," with the lines "And your face so fair, / Stirred in a dream, / As rose leaves with the air." This sequence adumbrates the fact that history will repeat itself: Venable expresses precisely the same feelings for Tina at the end of the film.

30. James, *Portrait*, 42.

31. James, *Portrait*, 467.

32. James, *Portrait*, 80. This phrase is also used by the narrator for Osmond's mind, as described by Isabel. Perhaps the word "despise" is a word particularly associated with those who would seek to impose their viewpoint on others, and who resent the fact that there are those who refuse to conform to their behavioral standards.

33. James, *Portrait*, 331–32.

34. James, *Portrait*, 559.

35. James, *Portrait*, 559.

36. James, *Golden Bowl*, 355. The text has been slightly rewritten in the adaptation.

37. James, *Golden Bowl*, 365.

38. James, *Golden Bowl*, 526.

39. James, *Golden Bowl*, 542.

40. "The BBC's *The Golden Bowl* conjured up a fabulous haut bourgeois London of exquisite manners and limitless leisure. What it made no attempt to do was to pack with gratuitous action an essentially aesthetic work much concerned with states of mind, impressions, reveries, suspicions and dim apprehensions." Berry, "Enduring Ephemera," 122.

41. John Ellis, *Visible Fictions: Cinema: Television: Video* (London: Routledge, 1982), 115.

42. Jane Gaines, "Women and Representation," in *Issues in Feminist Film*, ed. Patricia Erens (Bloomington: Indiana University Press, 1990), 78.

43. Gaines, "Women and Representation," 81–82.

44. Alistair Cooke, *A Decade of Masterpiece Theatre: Masterpieces* (New York: Alfred A. Knopf, 1981), 92.

45. Irene Shubik, "Drama," in *The New Priesthood: British Television Today*, ed. Joan Bakewell and Nicholas Garnham (London: Allen Lane / Penguin Press, 1970), 90.

CHAPTER ELEVEN

~

The Jolly Corner (1975)

Arthur Barron's adaptation of the short story "The Jolly Corner" (1907) was one of a twenty-one-part series *The American Short Story Collection*, cofinanced by the National Endowment for the Humanities, the Corporation for Public Broadcasting, and the Xerox Corporation.[1] It was one of the first six to be filmed—and came about as a result of a collaboration between Barron (a veteran documentary filmmaker), Robert Geller (a former executive of the American Film Institute), and Alfred Kazin (the distinguished critic and professor of literature at Stony Brook). The guidelines were clear: All the stories had to be chosen for their literary values, entertainment qualities, and cinematic potential. The three came up with a list of 100 possible entries to include in their initial proposal to the National Endowment of the Humanities. The response was—find six good ones for the series. "The Jolly Corner" was selected on the grounds that, as it was largely an interior monologue, no one else would dare try to film it. First aired on PBS in the United States in 1977, the adaptation was subsequently released on video cassette as a resource for schools and colleges, available for purchase both separately and as part of a twenty-one-volume set. Currently it is still available on video and DVD.

This chapter discusses how the public service ethos played a major part in the conception of this production. Not only did the screenplay (by Barron himself) endeavor to stay as close as possible to the spirit (if not the letter) of James's original short story, but the production values were designed to reinforce the story's status as a classic of American literature. Although filmed mostly in the studio with very little use of outdoor location, the costumes and settings were meticulously designed to re-create the atmosphere

117

of early twentieth-century New York. Casting was equally important; the central roles were played by Fritz Weaver and Salome Jens, both of whom had extensive previous experience of working in classical adaptations for television. The adaptation was prefaced with a talk by Henry Fonda that described why the story was written and what its main themes were. His presence—as a major star of Hollywood and Broadway—further emphasized the "classic" credentials of *The Jolly Corner* as it attempted to inform, educate, and entertain viewers in much the same fashion as *Masterpiece Theatre*, which was first broadcast on PBS in 1971, and whose repertoire in the 1970s overwhelmingly consisted of imported adaptations and/or classic dramas made by the BBC and Independent Television in Great Britain.

In the second part of this chapter, I show how, in contrast to an adaptation conceived for U.S. network television (for example, Dan Curtis's *Turn of the Screw*), *The Jolly Corner* focuses attention on words rather than action, as Barron focuses attention on central character Spencer Brydon's turbulent state of mind as he undergoes the experience of confronting his past self, "a man of his own substance and stature."[2] This seems appropriate to the later work of James, which pushes to new limits the presentation of, or rather the fusion through metaphor of, the perceiving mind and the external (or supposedly external) world. More significantly, *The Jolly Corner* focuses on the construction of masculinity in capitalist societies, as Brydon wrestles with the problem of whether to maintain his "frivolous, scandalous life" as a European expatriate or give in to "this lively stir, in a compartment of his mind never yet penetrated, of a capacity for business and a sense for construction."[3] Barron also challenges accepted wisdom (particularly in network television adaptations such as Curtis's *Turn of the Screw*) by allowing a strong single woman—Alice Staverton (Salome Jens) to assume the dominant role in the story. Such representations could only be found in PBS productions, with their professed commitment to creative innovation.[4]

It might seem from the beginning of Barron's version of *The Jolly Corner* that we are about to witness a ghost story in the style of *The Turn of the Screw*, with a central character visiting a deserted house and becoming aware of an invisible presence therein. The opening scene begins with a shot of a black-and-white photograph of Brydon while his voice can be heard on the soundtrack describing his age and the experience of returning to this childhood home—the Jolly Corner. This is followed by an exterior view of the building (with Brydon's carriage arriving at the front), followed by shots from Brydon's point of view of the deserted interior. The camera tilts as he admits having made several previous visits to the house, which had become ever more frequent and ever stranger. The sequence ends with a shot of him standing moodily by the window, a solitary drum intoning in the background.

None of this exists in the original story, which opens with a conversation between Brydon and Alice, and records Brydon's impressions on returning to America as he becomes aware that "the 'swagger' things, the modern, the monstrous, the famous things, those he had . . . come over to see, were exactly the sources of his dismay."[5] Yet Barron's alteration is not especially significant; perhaps it represents nothing more than a deliberate attempt to challenge viewer expectations. What seems like a ghost story actually turns out to have a strong romantic element, as Brydon stands by the window and admits that his return to America was also prompted by the desire to see Alice—someone who, although in the afternoon of life, still possessed a certain "grace of appearance" for him. More significantly, Barron's script lifts the line "grace of appearance" from James's story, which refers to "that slim mystifying grace of her appearance."[6] This determination to stay close to the original is characteristic of a production designed to fulfill the public service remit of rendering classic tales such as "The Jolly Corner" accessible to a wider audience, particularly for educational purposes.[7]

If alterations had to be introduced into the adaptation, their main purpose was to clarify what was already contained in the original story. This can be seen, for instance, in Barron's rewriting of the scene where Brydon and Alice visit the new apartment building, and Brydon discovers that he has a "real gift" for business—something that makes him "thrilled and flushed . . . very much as if he might have been met by some strange figure, some unexpected occupant, at a turn of one of the dim passages of an empty house."[8] Barron transforms this moment into a dramatic set piece, with Brydon discussing the new building with a newly created character, Mr. Wilkes (James Greene). When Brydon criticizes him for overspending, Wilkes asks what is wrong with money and asks Alice to "talk some sense into him".[9] Barron cuts to a close-up of Wilkes smoking a fat cigar, and then cuts back to a medium shot of Brydon sitting behind a desk, riffling papers in a businesslike manner. For all his apparent indifference, he is obviously delighted by the fact that he has forced the builders to cut their costs on the grounds that they have spent too much on copper. As Alice observes (in a newly created line), he is someone who speaks the same language as the builders.

Such changes emphasize the two sides of Brydon's nature—the idle expatriate who "loafed about his 'work' undeterred"[10] and the hard-headed businessperson perpetually speculating about "what he personally might have been, how he might have led his life and 'turned out,' if he had not so, at the outset, given it up."[11] In another newly created scene, Barron shows Brydon attending a séance, where he seeks to reconnect with his past, to find out more about what his life might have been like had he not chosen to live in Europe. As the medium speaks, Barron cuts to a medium close-up of Brydon in the house, a candle in his hand, looking for the mysterious figure. This alteration has been inspired by Brydon's remark that he wanted to see this "just so totally other person. . . . And I can. And I shall."[12] Alice's observation that she has "seen him [Brydon's past self] in a dream . . . twice over"[13] is transformed in the adaptation into a full-scale dream sequence that combines black-and-white shots of Brydon dressed as a young gentleman playing croquet on the lawn (while Alice runs delightedly into his arms) with lurid images of Brydon the tycoon, his face illuminated by a lurid red light, grasping Alice in his arms and planting a harsh kiss on her lips. This illustrates the extent to which Alice understands the contradictory sides of Brydon's nature—the romantic socialite and the man whose pursuit of wealth rendered him "unhappy" and "ravaged."[14] She observes at one point that she knows who Brydon is and what his capabilities might be.

Yet textual fidelity is only one of a number of strategies Barron employs to establish the high cultural credentials of his adaptation. The sets and costumes are meticulously designed to reflect the tastes of polite society in early twentieth-century New York; each room seems stuffed full of ornaments and other bric-a-brac. Occasionally, exterior sequences are inserted into the narrative with the express purpose of showing off historic locations. One such scene occurs towards the end, when Brydon and Alice take a boat trip on a lake in front of an (uncredited) mansion. The camera lingers lovingly on the two of them, as their swan-shaped boat moves around and around in circles, the house's reflection clearly visible on the water. In terms of plot, this scene shows the two of them drawing closer together, as Alice reassures Brydon that he will always be good enough for her. However, there remains the distinct impression that this scene fulfills a primarily decorative function. Giddings and Selby remark that in the British context at least, directors of the 1970s (especially at the BBC) favored Henry James on account of the fact that his "fascination with European middle-class social mores offered tempting pickings for colour television—handsome clothes for men, beautiful dresses for the ladies, sumptuous, frequently palatial, locations."[15] I suggest that Barron's intentions were much the same in The Jolly Corner; in spite of the limited budget, he sought to render the adaptation as visually appealing as possible.

He also appears to have taken considerable care in his choice of actors. Fritz Weaver (Brydon) had enjoyed a long career as a supporting actor until the early 1970s, when he began to appear in numerous classical adaptations for television including *Antigone* (as Creon) and *A Touch of the Poet* (as Cornelius Melody). His costar Salome Jens had completed several TV movies, including *Parker Adderson Philosopher* (1974), another installment in the *American Short Story Collection* based on a work by Ambrose Bierce, which was also directed by Barron.[16] Following the precedent established by Alistair Cooke in *Masterpiece Theatre*, *The Jolly Corner* includes an introductory piece sketching in the background to the story and its main themes, which were designed to prompt viewers to question their motives and actions and consider the implications of their cultures—something that should be considered particularly American in focus. By doing so, one could hope to justify or legitimize "the good fortune, abundance, and relative freedom that our country has enjoyed."[17] The two-minute piece (illustrated with black-and-white photos of James himself, as well as early twentieth-century views of New York) was delivered directly to the camera by Henry Fonda, sitting on a chair against a foliage-lined background. Clearly, Fonda's presence was designed to increase the production's cultural prestige—a Hollywood legend introducing viewers to the work of a literary giant.

In visual terms, this version of "The Jolly Corner" is quite repetitive; on several occasions, the narrative unfolds through a combination of two-shots and close-ups of the two main characters. However, it is clear that the main focus of attention is on dialogue rather than action. This is especially evident in the scene where Brydon tells Alice that he continually regrets the fact that he could have made his fortune if he had chosen to stay in America— even though it might have had an adverse effect on his personality. His conclusion is clear; he believes that he possesses "a strange *alter ego* deep down somewhere within . . . as the full-blown flower is in the small tight bud but . . . I just transferred him to the climate, that blighted him for once and for ever."[18] All these lines have been lifted verbatim from the original story, as Barron demonstrates how James fuses the external with the fluctuating exercise of mind and feeling—a technique that may help to explain why "The Jolly Corner" has acquired its reputation as one of James's last great short stories. Such intentions seems particularly appropriate for a PBS production whose primary function was to fulfill what Hartford Gunn, president of the Public Broadcasting Service, defined in 1972 as "a continuing national need—helping to fulfill citizens' requirements for education, information and culture through the greatest system of communication now available—broadcast television."[19]

The enduring appeal of "The Jolly Corner" also stems from its treatment of masculinity; Eric Savoy argues that its main concern is "the precarious situation of the bachelor, his liminal position in dominant culture and his permeable psychic boundaries which admit the rigors of homosexual panic."[20] Barron's adaptation focuses on issues of masculinity that were particularly significant during the mid-1970s. Two best-selling books, Joseph H. Pleck's and Jack Sawyer's edited collection *Men and Masculinity* (1974) and James Levine's *Who Will Raise the Children?* (1976), argued for new models to be developed, taking into account the social changes of the previous half century, such as the loss of interest in the traditional male "breadwinner" role, increased divorce, rising unemployment, the impact of feminism, and the growth of the men's liberation movement.[21] In Barron's adaptation of "The Jolly Corner," Brydon wonders whether he would have become a monster if he had assumed the breadwinner role—with all the power that goes with it—in America. He asks Alice whether she would have liked him that way, and Alice replies "How should I not have liked you?"[22] Barron cuts to the dream sequences described earlier on, with the two of them playing croquet and dancing in one another's arms, followed by the embrace in the lurid red light. Clearly, Alice doubts her own words; if Brydon had remained in America, would he have been romantic and likeable (as she has already informed him) or would he have become a monster who treated women as mere objects? Such sequences demonstrate how difficult it is to expect any male to conform to accepted behavioral notions of "masculinity"—particularly in the 1970s when, as Tom Williamson observes, the very act of questioning the male condition "was to appear weak and unstable and to lose credibility."[23]

These issues had been addressed almost three decades earlier in Frank Lloyd's *Berkeley Square*, where Peter Standish (Leslie Howard) repudiates the idea of marriage and family in favor of a single life that attaches no shame to an open display of emotion. As he puts it, he wants to be himself rather than trying to fulfill society's expectations of him as an eligible bachelor. Spencer Brydon in Barron's *Jolly Corner* undergoes a similar process of self-discovery. Throughout the adaptation, we are made well aware that the apparition ("spectral yet human, a man of his own substance and stature"[24]) represents his alter ego—a nightmarish vision of what he might have been like if he had spent his working life in America. In the climactic sequence, Brydon is shown climbing the stairs and suddenly becoming aware of the apparition's shadow on the wall next to him—a hunchbacked figure in a battered fedora. Barron cuts to a point-of-view shot of the apparition coming towards Brydon and making a grab for him; Brydon sinks to the floor, smashing the candlestick he is holding into smithereens.[25] The screen fades to black, and the next thing we see is Brydon waking up the next morning in Alice's arms. In many ways, this sequence recalls the confrontation between Miles and Quint at the end of *The Turn of the Screw*; but unlike the little boy, Brydon survives, and by doing so discovers the clue to his own identity. He admits to Alice that "it can only be that I died. You've literally brought me back to life."[26] In some ways this is absolutely true: Brydon has "died" in the sense that he has thrown off the self-doubts about his identity that plagued him earlier on. He can now say with certainty that the apparition he encountered was not his alter ego or a ghostly apparition of what he might have been. Like Standish, he realizes that it is no shame to reject capitalist society and all the social expectations associated with it, and to pursue an existence allowing "in the most liberal and intelligent manner, for brilliancy of change"[27]—allowing for the fact that one's identity can alter according to circumstances. This decision is not without its complications; we may wonder whether he will continue to support himself with the income from his apartments, which "(thanks precisely to their original excellent type) had never been depressingly low."[28] If so, how can he ever free himself from the apparition's malign influence? But clearly this is not Barron's concern; as Henry Fonda's introductory piece points out, this version of *The Jolly Corner* concerns itself with the rights and wrongs of people's choices in life. On this view, Brydon discovers how "wrong" it would have been for him to assume the role of breadwinner by spending his entire life in America.

The ending of this adaptation also shows Alice Staverton assuming a dominant role as she admits that she knew all along that Brydon would encounter the apparition and emerge unscathed from the experience. Barron enforces the idea of dominance in visual terms: Alice sits on the stairs cradling Brydon's head in her arms, as if assuming a maternal role rather than just being a good friend. But it is evident that she will not be satisfied with this either; she wants to sympathize with whomever she wishes, even the apparition, who in her view was "grim, worn, and many things have happened to him."[29] The adaptation ends with Brydon and Alice locked in an embrace; but the romantic climax is undercut somewhat by Alice's line "And he isn't—no, he isn't—*you!*"[30] Salome Jens delivers this line with two long pauses after the repeated word "isn't"—suggesting that she is, at present, reluctant to commit herself to anyone, whether Brydon or anyone else. Barron implies that what holds true for men must also prevail for women: They should have the freedom to determine their own course of action, even if that means subverting the expected happy ending to the tale.[31]

Compared with other James adaptations that appeared around the same period, *The Jolly Corner* remains little known. To date it has attracted very little critical comment; at the time of writing (June 2006), no reviews have yet appeared either on amazon.com or on the Internet Movie Database (www.imdb.com). There is also a significant absence of references in academic publications; the only reference to the adaptation comes in J. Sarah Koch's "Henry James Filmography" in the 2002 anthology *Henry James Goes to the Movies.*[32] Nonetheless, this *Jolly Corner* seems quite advanced for its time; like James Cellan Jones's *Portrait of a Lady* and *The Golden Bowl*, it seeks to put forward possibilities for men and women to challenge existing gender roles and construct new identities for themselves. This should come as no surprise; all three adaptations were produced for public service broadcasting companies, which, during the 1960s and 1970s, sought to offer new and/or challenging interpretations of canonical texts, without necessarily being concerned about ratings and/or commercial concerns. Production budgets might have been limited, but many directors took advantage of such constraints to produce material that forced viewers to concentrate on words and gestures as well as visual display. This was the case with *The Jolly Corner*; although designed for educational purposes, this did not mean that Barron had to become a slave of the original story. The entire *American Short Story Collection* may now be almost three decades old, but it is still available on video and/or DVD and (so far as one can gather) still selling well to educational institutions. It remains one of PBS's most ambitious and most successful productions, well meriting the praise heaped upon it by the *New York Times* as "an extraordinary experiment in the blending of scholarship, cinematic art, patience, dedication—and money."[33] If Spencer Brydon had been exposed to such work that combined financial investment with a concern for maintaining artistic integrity, then perhaps he would have not suffered his internal struggles with his alter ego.

Notes

1. The other titles in the collection include Richard Wright, "Almos' a Man"; William Faulkner, "Barn Burning"; F. Scott Fitzgerald, "Bernice Bobs Her Hair"; Stephen Crane, "Blue Hotel"; Flannery O'Connor, "Displaced Person"; Ring Lardner, "Golden

Honeymoon"; James Thurber, "The Greatest Man in the World"; Hortense Calisher, "Hollow Boy"; Sherwood Anderson, "I'm a Fool"; Katharine Anne Porter, "The Jilting of Granny Weatherall"; Harold Brodkey, "Love and Other Sorrows"; Mark Twain, "The Man That Corrupted Hadleyburg"; John Updike, "Music School"; Ambrose Bierce, "Parker Addison Philosopher"; Willa Cather, "Paul's Case"; Nathaniel Hawthorne, "Rappacini's Daughter"; Mary E. Wilkins Freeman, "The Revolt of Mother"; Ernest J. Gaines, "The Sky Is Gray"; and Ernest Hemingway, "The Soldier's Home."

2. Henry James, *The Jolly Corner and Other Tales*, ed. Roger Gard (Harmondsworth: Penguin Books, 1990), 187.

3. James, *Jolly Corner*, 171, 163.

4. Ralph Engleman, *Public Radio and Television in America: A Political History* (London: Sage, 1996), 52.

5. James, *Jolly Corner*, 162.

6. James, *Jolly Corner*, 164.

7. In a 1990–1991 survey conducted by the CPB (Corporation for Public Broadcasting) focusing on the way audiences responded to public television programs over the previous two decades, it was shown that 79.4 percent of all teachers used television or video programs in their classrooms, for 60.6 percent of all students. The most popular subjects for instructional television were English (including all literature courses), social studies, and history. *Facts and Figures about Public Broadcasting in America* (Washington, DC: Corporation for Public Broadcasting, 1991), 14.

8. James, *Jolly Corner*, 165.

9. All extracts from the screenplay for *The Jolly Corner* are taken directly from the VHS Video release (Thousand Oaks, CA: Monterey Media, 1999)

10. James, *Jolly Corner*, 163.

11. James, *Jolly Corner*, 169.

12. James, *Jolly Corner*, 172.

13. James, *Jolly Corner*, 172.

14. James, *Jolly Corner*, 193.

15. Robert Giddings and Keith Selby, *The Classic Serial on Television and Radio* (Basingstoke: Palgrave, 2001), 38.

16. The casting for all the adaptations contained some notable names, such as Tommy Lee Jones (*Barn Burning*), Shelley Duvall (*Bernice Bobs Her Hair*), David Warner (*The Blue Hotel*), two-time Oscar nominee James Whitmore (*The Golden Honeymoon*), and Robert Preston (*The Man That Corrupted Hadleyburg*).

17. "The Jolly Corner" screenplay.

18. James, *Jolly Corner*, 170.

19. Hartford Gunn, "Public Television Program Financing: A Proposal for the PBS Station Program Cooperative (SPC)," *Educational Broadcasting Review*, October 1972, at www.current.org/pbpb/documents/spc72.html (accessed November 25, 2005).

20. Eric Savoy, "The Queer Subject of 'The Jolly Corner'" *Henry James Review* 20, no.1 (Winter 1999), 1–21.

21. Cf. a comment made by the radical feminist theorist Valerie Solanas, founder of the Society for Cutting Up Men, in 1968: "Every man, deep down, knows he's a worthless piece of shit. Overwhelmed by a sense of animalism and deeply ashamed of it; wanting, not to express himself, but to hide from others his total physicality's total egocentricity, the hate and contempt he feels for other men, and to hide from himself the hate and contempt he suspects other men feel for him." Valerie Solanas, *S.C.U.M.: Society for Cutting Up Men Manifesto* (New York: Olympia Press, 1968), 5.

22. James, *Jolly Corner*, 171.

23. Tom Williamson, "The History of the Men's Movement" in *Men Freeing Men: Exploding the Myth of the Traditional Male*, ed. Francis Baumli (Jersey City, NJ: New Atlantis Press, 1985), at www.amazoncastle.com/feminism/menhist.shtml (accessed November 27, 2005).

24. James, *Jolly Corner*, 187.

25. Cf. the description in the original story, as Brydon finds the apparition so "evil, odious, blatant, [and] vulgar . . . a rage of personality before which his own collapsed" that "his head went round; he was going, he had gone" (James, *Jolly Corner*, 188). Clearly, the capitalist view of life has the power to destroy the cultured European mentality (a theme that would be explored in greater detail in later adaptations such as Merchant-Ivory's *Golden Bowl* [2001]).

26. A slightly adapted version of the original lines in the story: "Yes—I can only have died. You brought me back to life" (James, *Jolly Corner*, 190).

27. James, *Jolly Corner*, 162.

28. James, *Jolly Corner*, 162.

29. James, *Jolly Corner*, 193.

30. James, *Jolly Corner*, 193.

31. Tom Williamson observes that, like the women's movement, the men's movement of the 1970s tried to embrace the concept of equal rights between the sexes; however, it has often been the case that it has been interpreted very differently. Many men's groups used it as a tool to "end discrimination against themselves. Nowhere was this more evident than in the father's rights movement." Williamson, "History of the Men's Movement."

32. J. Sarah Koch, "A Henry James Filmography," in *Henry James Goes to the Movies*, ed. Susan M. Griffin (Lexington: University Press of Kentucky, 2002), 345.

33. Daniel Stern, "An Ambitious New Series Brings the American Short Story to TV," *New York Times*, April 3, 1977, 92.

CHAPTER TWELVE

~

The Europeans (1979) and The Bostonians (1984)

Over the past three decades, the films of Ismail Merchant, Ruth Prawer Jhab-vala, and James Ivory (collectively known as Merchant-Ivory) have been viewed by critics as prime examples of the kind of conservatism that domi-nated the mainstream film industries in Britain and America during the 1980s and early 1990s. Martin A. Hipsky suggests that they conjure up a world of "exquisite affordable luxuries . . . self-indulgent, delicious and intel-lectually fattening."[1] A New York Times article of 2001 thought that Mer-chant-Ivory's films were "terrible because they are so terribly self-important."[2] This chapter concentrates on Merchant-Ivory's first two James adaptations—The Europeans (1979) and The Bostonians (1984)—in an attempt to reassess the importance of the team's contribution to the cinema of the past twenty-five years or so.

I begin by arguing that perhaps their detractors are right. As in earlier adaptations such as On a Clear Day, Ivory creates pleasurable images of the past, encouraging filmgoers to "read individual images for their display of authentic period detail rather than for narrative symbolism."[3] Issues of tex-tual fidelity no longer assume importance, as viewers are invited to take plea-sure in locations, sets, and costumes for their own sake. On the other hand, I suggest that both The Europeans and The Bostonians should be treated seri-ously as contributions to the debates on gender and sexuality that emerged in the late 1970s and early 1980s, and continue to this day. Sue Sorensen has already shown how Ruth Prawer Jhabvala's screenplay for The Bostonians communicates a feminist message, especially at the end when Olive Chan-cellor (Vanessa Redgrave) is given a "credible final speech, expressing her intention to continue the struggle for equal rights."[4] I believe that Ivory's main focus of interest in *The Europeans* and *The Bostonians* lies elsewhere; by means of Jhabvala's screenplays and the casting of specific actresses (Lee Remick and Vanessa Redgrave) in the respective leading roles, they seek to focus attention on women in contemporary Western societies. This strategy is nothing new—as we saw earlier on, both *The Lost Moment* and *The Heiress* employed similar techniques—but what differentiates Ivory's James adaptations is that they extend their analyses beyond marriage and the family to include issues of sexuality. In particular, they question the idea that sexuality should be tied to gender by linking masculinity with activity and control and femininity with passivity and acquiescence. In *The Europeans*, the Baroness Eugenia seeks to play an active part in forging an advantageous union for herself, while gently exposing the gender-specific pretensions of those around her. Nonetheless, it could also be argued that by endeavoring to dominate them, she is merely reproducing rather than overturning binary restrictions. The same goes for Olive Chancellor in her relationship with Verena, where she assumes the active/dominant role. As the action develops, however, she comes to understand that the most effective strategies of female self-expression constitute an alternative to, not a reproduction of, those of her male counterparts. Both films should be viewed as dissident interventions that seek to question or undermine existing binary oppositions (male/female; active/passive).

From the start, it is clear that the settings will assume a prominent role in *The Europeans*. We first encounter Gertrude Wentworth (Lisa Eichhorn) walking away from a gazebo set in a forest a short walk from her family home. The reds, browns, and yellows of the autumn leaves positively shimmer in the late afternoon sun. Gertrude's first exchange with Felix Young (Tim Woodward) begins in the gazebo and continues as they walk toward the house, the camera framing them against the background of trees. This represents a radical change from the novella where (as with later works) James is more interested in the interplay between characters rather than the situation. As someone fond of the *Arabian Nights*, Gertrude perceives Felix's arrival as a fulfillment of her romantic dreams, "a wondrous, delightful answer to her vague wish that something would befall her."[5]

Ivory introduces Eugenia (Lee Remick) by means of another visually spectacular sequence, as she is shown riding in a trap with her brother toward the Wentworths' house. The action cuts to an aerial shot of the forest, and dissolves to a tracking shot of the trees passing by at ground level, as if we were looking at them from the passengers' point of view. Ivory employs a variation on the same shot later on, as Eugenia goes for a ride with Robert Acton (Robin Ellis), where the action subsequently cuts to a medium shot of the trap coming over the brow of the hill. A quick two-shot of Eugenia and Acton is followed by another point-of-view shot of the trees and the azure-blue sky overhead. The sequence concludes with a tracking shot of the trap going through a small pond, the splashing of the horses' hooves clearly audible on the soundtrack.[6]

The treatment of the interior sequences is no less precise. In a 1991 book, Ivory recalled that The Europeans was the first film to employ what he describes as a "state-of-the-art" approach to set and costume design. Compared to most period films, which evidently "looked pretty sloppy," his designers "steeped themselves in the Victorian past by way of old photographs, paintings and extant evidence," which gave them the chance to develop "almost an archeological, or a scientifically detailed approach to the film's overall design."[7] Ivory is scrupulous to show off their efforts in the best possible light. He creates a ball scene that does not exist in the novella[8] in which the principal female characters are shown sitting at the side of the room, with Mr. Brand (Norman Snow) standing behind them, the plainness of his black garb standing out amidst the finery of the women's party dresses. Shots of Lizzie Wentworth (Kristin Griffith) dancing are intercut with close-ups of Eugenia standing alone, as if unsure how to respond to such merry-making. Acton rescues her from potential embarrassment as he takes her arm and leaves the room, while the camera cuts to a shot of the musicians playing. The spectacle of the ball contrasts with the precision of the scenes taking place in the Wentworths' house. In one scene, Charlotte (Nancy New) is shown lighting candles in the living room, putting them on the mantelpiece and subsequently passing through to the parlor where she sits down in a rocking chair. Clearly, she is concerned about her familial responsibilities, which she believes give her the justification to berate her sister for her indifference towards Mr. Brand: "He helped you to struggle with your peculiarities. You told me that he had taught you how to govern your temper."[9]

Despite Robert Emmet Long's insistence that the visual elements stress the contrast between the great outdoors and "the New Englanders' world that, however admirable, is lived essentially indoors,"[10] there remains the distinct impression that Ivory uses them to create a nostalgic vision of the past in which all hardship has been removed. The same could be said for The Bostonians; the British journal Sight and Sound reported that the film included extensive work on location at a rocky cove, "an hour's drive from Boston"; an alley on Beacon Hill "which is apparently thoroughly accustomed to film crews, since it preserves its gas lamps and very bumpy cobblestones"; and a music hall in Troy, upper New York State, where "some four hundred extras will be mustered."[11] In the finished film, the music hall's interior splendors are proudly shown off, as the camera pans the vast expanse of empty seats before focusing on the huge arena stage. In the center of the frame, a small speck can be seen; this turns out to be Basil Ransom (Christopher Reeve), who has come to find Verena (Madeleine Potter) before her lecture begins. The action cuts to a shot of the music hall's neo-Gothic exterior with coaches drawing up alongside, before returning to another interior shot of the stage (by now full of worthies) and the auditorium filling up with some of the four hundred extras. James's novel tells us that at this moment "Boston seemed to him [Basil] big and full of nocturnal life, very much awake and preparing for an evening of nocturnal pleasure."[12] Ivory seems determined to exploit this observation to the full.

On other occasions, however, Ivory's penchant for visual detail tends to overwhelm the plot. James tells us in the novel that Olive imagines Verena as a femme fatale in a melodrama: "She [Olive] saw the boat overturned and drifted out to sea, and (after a week of nameless horror) the body of an unknown young woman, defaced beyond recognition, but with long auburn hair and in a white dress, washed up in some far-away cove."[13] Ivory's film replaces the narrator's satiric comment with a sequence that intercuts shots of Olive (Vanessa Redgrave) running wildly on the beach with close-ups of Basil and Verena embracing one another. Our attention is diverted from the plot by a kaleidoscope of colors: the reddish-yellow of the setting sun contrasted with the graying sea, Verena's flaming red hair standing out against the horizon; the blackness of Olive's angular form silhouetted against the darkening night sky. Interludes like this are designed to stimulate the viewers' sense of nostalgic consumerism; as with *The Heiress*, over three decades earlier, we are presented with an idealistic portrait of life that might be enjoyed so long as (like our nineteenth-century counterparts) one possesses plenty of money and/or leisure time.[14]

If both films are situated in their respective contexts of production, with particular reference to the development of feminist film theory, then it soon emerges that they are more complex than this reading might suggest. As I suggested in connection with *Daisy Miller*, throughout the late 1970s and 1980s, many writers realized that women—either represented on screen or watching in the audience—might not be as subjugated by the male (or the male gaze) as might once have been assumed. Writing in 1988, Tania Modleski identified in Hitchcock's films some limited expression of female desire:

"despite the often considerable violence with which women are treated . . . they remain resistant to patriarchal assimilation."[15] Both *The Europeans* and *The Bostonians* focus on the lives of socially constructed, active females. It is clear from the early sequences of *The Europeans* that Gertrude possesses a will of her own. Mr. Brand complacently assumes that she will listen to "one thing [he has] to say" about marriage, and is shocked to find her putting her fingers in her ears and running out of the right of the frame.[16] Later on, he asks if he might walk home with her; while the novella indicates that she agrees to this request ("and when she said that he might if he wanted"),[17] Ivory shows her once again escaping from the frame, exclaiming that she will not go back home. Despite her obvious affection for Felix, Gertrude treats his attempts to control her with equal disdain. While agreeing to have her portrait painted, she refuses to acquiesce to his wish for her to keep the same expression and stalks out of the frame. Ivory repeats the shot later on as Gertrude scurries out of the kitchen of the family home, leaving Charlotte to exclaim in astonishment, "You *are* wicked, you *are* changed."[18] This is clearly untrue; Gertrude has always been a free spirit, resisting any attempts to confine her either in the prison house or in the limited focus of the cinematic frame. In another newly created sequence, she is shown in the kitchen throwing an egg from one hand to another; Charlotte takes it from her, which prompts the younger girl to get up from her chair, threaten to scream, and run upstairs. Charlotte pursues her, but only after pausing to close the oven door. The contrast between the two sisters could not be more obvious; one willingly embraces the domestic life, while the other struggles to find alternative means of self-expression.

Whether Gertrude actually fulfills her wish is debatable. The novella suggests that she and Felix remain "imperturbably happy" in one another's company.[19] By contrast, Ivory creates another new scene in which Eugenia helps Gertrude to put on her fashionable European-style clothing, observing as she does so that Europe is the place where cultivated women are truly appreciated. The pensive expression on Gertrude's face indicates that she is not convinced of her superiority. She lacks the worldliness of Isabel Archer or Charlotte Stant in Cellan Jones's *Portrait* or *Golden Bowl* that encourages them to remain silent and thereby repudiate any attempts by their respective male partners to contain them.

Ivory's treatment of Eugenia is far less straightforward. On the face of it, she remains doomed to lead a nomadic existence. This is suggested in the opening sequences, when we first see her arrival in New England in a trap, a lake in the background. In the novella, Felix describes the Wentworths and the Actons to her over dinner; the film shifts this dialogue to an exterior scene with the two of them riding toward the Wentworths' house. Despite her professed interest in Acton's fortune,[20] we sense that she will never settle down and thereby take advantage of it.[21] It soon becomes evident that they are an ill-matched couple; in one scene, Eugenia claims that she has always longed for the "natural relations I should find here" in preference to the "artificial relations" in Europe.[22] The banality of this statement is emphasized a little later when Acton proposes marriage and Eugenia replies in French, using exactly the kind of artificial language she claims to have left behind. A series of intercut close-ups at the end of the film, contrasting Acton's kind smile with Eugenia's pained expression, emphasize the fact that her search for a husband has ended in failure. She looks at herself in the bedroom mirror before packing her bags to the accompaniment of the melancholy tones of Clara Schumann's Trio Op. 17 on the soundtrack—the same music that signaled her arrival in New England at the beginning of the film.[23] The wheel has come full circle; she leaves as she came—a lonely, isolated woman.

Yet there is also much to admire about her. In a stolid, deeply patriarchal society she represents a much-needed breath of fresh air, as she uses her sexuality to turn situations to her advantage without resorting to the conventionally masculine strategies of domination and control. As she outlines to Acton the details of her marriage, she toys with an ornament, suggesting that she enjoys playing verbal games with him. Far from being moved by his insincere expression of flattery ("a woman looks the prettier for having unfolded her wrongs or her sufferings"),[24] she picks up a cornflower and separates the flower from its stalk as she outlines the choice she apparently faces between revenge and liberty. In another sequence, Eugenia and Acton are shown in Acton's house walking through a long gallery filled with family portraits. No doubt he has taken her there to impress her; like Gilbert Osmond in Cellan Jones's Portrait, he considers her a potentially valuable addition to his collection of curios. Eugenia remains blissfully unmoved by his strategies as she plays with her fan and asks him whether she should sign the paper releasing her from her marriage. Although she has no intention of heeding his advice, she knows how to pretend that he exerts an influence over her.

Eugenia's cavalier treatment of Clifford Wentworth (Tom Choate) might be considered reprehensible, as she suggests that he accompany her to Europe as her lover and that he should not mind "because that would be uncivil."[25] Nonetheless, there is something beguiling about the way she gently exposes the New Englanders' pretensions to sophistication. She passes

Clifford a scone as if nothing untoward was happening, despite the fact that the younger man is slurping tea from a saucer rather than from the china cup provided. Personal feelings clearly count for little in this society, and Eugenia is prepared to exploit this to the full. Ivory includes a sequence similar in structure to Bogdanovich's *Daisy Miller* that intercuts close-ups of Eugenia playing the piano with shots of Acton observing her from outside the window of her house. Whereas this represents a strategy of control in *Daisy Miller* (as the heroine is contained by the male gaze), it is clear in *The Europeans* that Eugenia knows how to resist it. Ivory cuts to a close-up of her ushering him into the house, politely explaining as she does so that as he has committed a social gaffe by staring at her for so long.

Ivory's reading of Eugenia's character has been greatly enhanced by the casting of Lee Remick in the role. In a career spanning three decades, the actress had acquired a reputation for versatility, playing everything from a sexy majorette in Elia Kazan's *A Face in the Crowd* (1957) to Jack Lemmon's alcoholic wife in *Days of Wine and Roses* (1962). By the 1970s she had moved to Britain (staying for eleven years) and subsequently acquired a reputation for playing prominent, self-possessed women such as Jennie, Lady Randolph Churchill, in the ATV series of the same name (1975), and Maria Gostney in the BBC Play of the Month adaptation of James's *The Ambassadors* (1977). Her presence in *The Europeans* constituted one of the film's major selling points; her name was placed above the title in the publicity, while the poster for the initial British release showed her face in medium close-up, with a cart traveling left to right underneath, emphasizing her nomadic existence. Unlike *The Lost Moment*, in which the leading actor's star persona prompts an ambiguous response to the plot (we doubt whether Susan Hayward's Tina Bordereau has willingly accepted Louis Venable's marital "protection"), Ivory's *The Europeans* draws on Remick's reputation to suggest alternatives for female self-expression. This viewpoint had been expressed as long ago as 1960 by Richard Poirier, who claimed that "at the end of the novel James's compassion and admiration are given more to Eugenia than to her American friends."[26] Ivory seeks to evoke something more than "compassion and admiration" by portraying Eugenia as someone prepared to defend her integrity, unencumbered as much as possible by the restraining hand of male authority.[27] Whether her behavior constitutes an act of resistance to dominant conceptions of gender and sexuality, however, is another matter. By trying to "feminize" her suitors through playing the active "masculine" role, Eugenia reproduces the kind of discourses that, as Judith Butler remarks, determine "what a person feels, how a person acts, and how a person expresses herself sexually."[28]

Verena Tarrant in Ivory's *The Bostonians* also seeks to act in a "masculine" way, but lacks the self-knowledge and the experience to transform her dreams into reality. She remains a passive "feminine" figure, observing at one point (in a newly written line) to Olive that, were it not for the younger woman's presence, she might not be so active in campaigning for women's rights. Toward the end of the film, she tries to sustain a heterosexual relationship with Basil Ransom (Christopher Reeve) while continuing to promise herself to Olive. This renders her liable to exploitation by others. The film opens with a shot of an organist preparing to play "My Country 'Tis of Thee"; we see a close-up of his feet, then his hands, and subsequently the organ pipes as he begins. This serves as an apt metaphor for Verena's existence; as her father, Selah (Wesley Addy), observes, someone needs to "start her up" before she can express an opinion, either in public or private.[29] At Miss Birdseye's (Jessica Tandy's) house, Verena is shown sitting in front of him, her head bowed, while he places his hands on her shoulders, murmuring "Quietly—quietly. . . . It will come."[30] We hear organ music once again on the soundtrack as Verena rises from her chair and admits that she feels the calling, before launching into her speech about the "just revolution" of women.

Throughout the film, Basil makes it his business to persuade her to abandon her lesbian relationship and marry him instead. Eventually he succeeds, leading her by the hand away from Olive and silencing her with a kiss. However, Ivory suggests that this represents no real alternative for Verena; she has allowed herself to be exploited by someone else. Basil covers her head with his large black cape and spirits her away, observing as he does so that "we shall take the night train for New York."[31] This visual image would seem to corroborate Leland S. Person's view that Ivory's *Bostonians* catches the mood of America during the first Reagan presidency, wherein marriage and the nuclear family were prioritized above women's and/or gay and lesbian rights.[32] The casting of Christopher Reeve, whose "iconographic appeal as Superman shadows his characterization of Ransom [and] helps to fulfill the wish . . . that some 'super' man would save America from the 'most damnable feminization' and restore the 'masculine tone' to a 'womanized' generation [of males]."[33]

This reading can be challenged on three counts. First, it fails to acknowledge that audiences read films differently in different contexts. There is certainly a justification for this, in view of the fact that it is an Anglo-American coproduction financed in part by the British companies Rediffusion, Curzon Film Distributors, and the Rank Organization, with the participation of the

BBC. Secondly, one of Christopher Reeve's biographers has suggested that, far from exerting an "iconographic appeal," the actor's reputation was considered harmful to the film's potential box-office success: "Several backers vetoed the 'Reeve idea' and thought that Chris wasn't marketable in a serious literate film—that the art crowd would guffaw at Superman playing in an adaptation of a Henry James novel."[34] Merchant-Ivory fought to retain him, arguing that Reeve possessed considerable technical range, having played in other costume dramas on stage and screen (notably *Somewhere in Time*, which was beginning to acquire cult status in the mid-1980s). Thirdly, Person pays insufficient attention to the subtleties of Vanessa Redgrave's characterization of Olive Chancellor. While she begins the film by attempting to reproduce "normal" sexual distinctions in a nonheterosexual relationship, she gradually discovers subversive possibilities for causing "gender trouble."

Superficially, it would seem that Olive's sexuality condemns her to a life of loneliness. She assumes the dominant "masculine" role in her relationship with Verena but ultimately discovers that Verena would rather be the passive partner in a heterosexual relationship with Basil Ransom. After Verena goes for her "little daily walk" with him,[35] Olive is shown alone outside her house, burying her head in her hands. Eventually Verena returns with Basil; Ivory cuts to a shot of Miss Birdseye binding his foot with a bandage, having cut it on a piece of glass. Olive enters at the rear of the frame and recoils in horror at the sight of Basil. The unthinkable has happened—Basil has usurped her territory and ingratiated himself with her fellow women. Olive's feelings of isolation are reinforced later on when Verena fails to return from one of her walks. The novel describes in detail the "immeasurable load of misery" that settles on her soul, prompting her to reflect on "how women had from the beginning of time been the sport of men's selfishness and avidity."[36] Ivory's film replaces this inner reflection with a point-of-view shot from Olive's perspective as Verena walks slowly away from the house to the wasteland beyond. The camera subsequently tracks left through 180 degrees to show Olive's face wistfully gazing at her through the window.

As Julianne Pidduck reminds us, however, the cinematic image of the woman at the window, particularly when juxtaposed with a shot of a landscape, can suggest female potential as much as loneliness. She quotes examples from Merchant-Ivory's *A Room with a View* (1986), as well as more recent adaptations such as *Sense and Sensibility* (1995), which might be read as condensing a number of layered types of desire: "A passive desire for romance . . . an acquisitive desire for property and the wealth and rights it imparts; and a class-based desire for social mobility and individual freedom.

Such gendered desires are . . . a form of potentiality that is at once corporeal, discursive and deeply felt.[37]

From this perspective, the shot of Olive looking out at Verena can be read as an expression of her desire to challenge the conventions of a heterosexual society and discover new possibilities for herself. There are other examples of this throughout the film; on one occasion, she embraces Verena, quoting Poe's "Annabel Lee" as she does so ("We loved with a love that was more than love / I and my Annabel Lee"). In another newly written scene, she sits in her bedroom with Verena and tells her that she feels passionate both about women's lack of a vote and the plight of young women treated as sex objects by men. Another new sequence depicts both women in their undergarments; Olive kneels at Verena's feet and arranges her dress, while Verena asks that she should be trusted.[38] Olive responds by kissing her on the cheek.

Ivory's faith in Olive's intentions is greatly enhanced by the casting of Vanessa Redgrave in the role. In an article published in the British film journal *Sight and Sound*, he recalled that at the time of filming *The Bostonians* the actress was experiencing a difficult time professionally, having not worked for fourteen months on account of her support for the Palestine Liberation Organization.[39] As one journalist remarked, she resembled Olive Chancellor in the sense that both were "famous—if not notorious—for [their] committed political beliefs." In the same article, Redgrave was described as someone who, although heterosexual herself, could bring her own particular qualities to the role, as someone who "expresses her views with no hint of the demagogue that the popular press have made her out to be, but rather of a serious—and searching actress." Redgrave admitted to being "intrigued by my character—a woman who grows as she develops."[40]

This process of development is particularly evident at the end of the film, as Redgrave's Olive begins to understand the importance of behaving differently. If society expects her to articulate her sexual politics in a certain way (e.g., by publicly expressing her antipathy toward the male sex or by assuming the dominant masculine role), then the best way to subvert such expectations is to develop new forms of expression—and hence initiate "gender trouble." She appears to raise no objection to Verena's departure for New York with Basil, preferring instead to deliver the speech that the younger woman was scheduled to give (which does not exist in James's novel), outlining the great cause for which women will be harsh and uncompromising, never giving ground to anyone. Whereas Olive might previously have uttered such sentiments in a hectoring voice, now she speaks softly—trying to persuade by argument rather than by force.[41] To dismiss her speech as "elegaic, perhaps even dismissive" of the feminist movement is to misunderstand its purpose, as it seeks to subvert notions of sexuality and gender that consist of observing particular behavioral conventions laid down by one's society.[42]

Both The Europeans and The Bostonians enjoyed considerable box-office success. The Europeans cost $700,000 to make; it was originally slated as the British entry for the 1979 Cannes Film Festival but was withdrawn by the Film Producers' Association on the grounds that it was not a British film (despite the fact that the bulk of the finance had come from the British National Film Finance Association). Nonetheless, its six-month run at the Curzon Cinema, London, proved the longest in the theater's history. Robert Emmet Long observes it was also the first Merchant-Ivory film to find a significant audience across the Atlantic, even though it was not widely shown due to distribution difficulties.[43] The Bostonians experienced no such problems; it cost $3.5 million and grossed more than $1 million alone in its first sixteen weeks at one New York theater. On the one hand, neither film can be considered especially radical; with their lush color photography and detailed sets and costumes, they are designed to appeal to filmgoers' visual imagination. On the other hand, I have tried to show in this chapter how the narratives of The Europeans and The Bostonians raise questions about the infinite variety of roles that women can potentially fulfill. They do not have to respect previously formulated social or biological classifications; they can focus instead on the "infinite sensibility" of their personalities. This is especially true of The Bostonians, which was praised by Gilbert Adair for showing how the suffragettes pursued "an amorous dimension of their own, a Courbet-like physicality, which divests Olive's love for Verena of any 'taint' of lesbianism in the narrow sense [i.e., as something 'unnatural' compared to heterosexuality]."[44] For this, perhaps Ivory should be recognized as one of the few contemporary filmmakers prepared to challenge accepted cinematic wisdom by producing innovative work that proposes more flexible social, psychological, and sexual relations, while simultaneously sustaining its appeal at the box office. Perhaps this helps to explain why The Bostonians is such a moving and important intervention in the canon of Jamesian adaptations.[45]

Notes

1. Martin A. Hipsky, "Why Does America Watch Merchant-Ivory Movies?" *Journal of Popular Film and Television* 22, no. 3 (Fall 1994): 103.

2. Franz Lidz and Steve Rushin, "How to Tell a Bad Movie from a Truly Bad Movie," *New York Times*, August 5, 2001, B4.

3. Andrew Higson, *Dissolving Views: Key Writings on British Cinema* (London: Cassell, 1996), 244. As James Ivory is invariably the director of the films, I am using his name for convenience in preference to the collective term "Merchant-Ivory."

4. Sue Sorensen, "'Damnable Feminization': The Merchant Ivory Film Adaptation of *The Bostonians*," *Literature Film Quarterly* 25, no. 3 (Autumn 1997): 233.

5. Henry James, *The Europeans* (Harmondsworth: Penguin Books, 1964), 25.

6. The program note for a National Film Theater, London, season of Merchant-Ivory films (1982) quotes from John Coleman's *New Statesman* review of *The Europeans*: "Ivory and lighting photographer Larry Pizer turn the forced exigencies of shooting in late autumn to glorious advantage, with the turbulent reds, golds, russets and greens of New England flora adding a natural richness to the large simplicities of the Wentworth mansion." Program Notes, National Film Theatre Season: *"Merchant Ivory at Twenty-One"* (London: National Film Theatre, 1982), 12.

7. Robert Emmet Long, *The Films of Merchant Ivory* (New York: Harry N. Abrams, 1997), 102.

8. Ruth Prawer Jhabvala pointed out in a publicity interview that "Jim [Ivory] likes to have a big party in his films. A big party and lots of meals. There were lots of meals in the book but not a big party." Quoted in "Where Could I Meet Other Screenwriters?" *Sight and Sound* 48, no. 1 (Winter 1979), 18.

9. James, *The Europeans*, 105.

10. Long, *The Films of Merchant Ivory*, 99.

11. Penelope Houston, "The Bostonians on Location," *Sight and Sound* 53, no. 1 (Winter 1984): 2–3.

12. Henry James, *The Bostonians*, ed. Charles B. Anderson (Harmondsworth: Penguin Classics, 1986), 413.

13. James, *The Bostonians*, 398–99.

14. Andrew Higson has shown how this longing has been exploited in the publicity for later Merchant-Ivory adaptations, notably *The Remains of the Day* (1993), where a competition linked to the film offered "two luxurious weekend breaks to the elite" as first prizes and "ten hampers by Crabtree and Evelyn" as second prizes. Andrew Higson, *Dissolving Views: Key Writings on British Cinema* (London: Cassell, 1996), 243.

15. Tania Modleski, *The Women Who Knew Too Much: Hitchcock and Feminist Film Theory* (London: Methuen, 1988), 3.

16. James, *The Europeans*, 25.

17. James, *The Europeans*, 69.

18. James, *The Europeans*, 106.

19. James, *The Europeans*, 172.

20. James, *The Europeans*, 34.

21. In a sequence not used in the final version, Ivory has Eugenia looking out from her hotel room upon the white church spires that to her represent the provincial life she despises so much. She mumbles to herself, "It's too horrible. I shall go back. I shall go

back." Allen Hirsh, "*The Europeans:* Henry James, James Ivory, and That Nice Mr. Emerson," *Literature Film Quarterly* 11, no. 2 (1983): 115.

22. James, *The Europeans*, 77.

23. Richard Robbins, collaborating for the first time on a Merchant-Ivory production, recalled that Schumann's piece not only "belonged to European culture" but "suited Eugenia's background and feelings, as an assertive but sensitive character." Quoted in Long, *The Films of Merchant Ivory*, 102.

24. James, *The Europeans*, 82.

25. James, *The Europeans*, 112.

26. Richard Poirier, *The Comic Sense of Henry James: A Study of the Early Novels* (New York: Oxford University Press, 1960), 144.

27. Not all critics of the film agree. In a 1979 review, Nicola Bradbury, author of *Henry James: The Later Novels*, complained that Ivory's shift away from authorial manipulation "requires that the Baroness be more outspoken. She is given speeches she would never have made aloud, or in company." Nicola Bradbury, "Filming James," *Essays in Criticism* 29, no. 4 (October 1979): 297.

28. Quoted in Kathryn Woodward, *Identity and Difference* (London: Sage, 1997), 215.

29. Addy also played Mr. Wentworth in Ivory's *The Europeans*, one of two actors (the other being Nancy New [Charlotte Wentworth/Adeline Luna]) who appear in both films. The casting of both seems to be deliberate, drawing attention to their shared interest in both films in preserving the patriarchal status quo.

30. James, *The Bostonians*, 83.

31. James, *The Bostonians*, 430.

32. Cf. Robert Zaller's review of *The Bostonians* (published in 1985) that opens with the sentence "Two recent classic adaptations of classic novels by veteran directors [the other being Volker Schlöndorff's *Swann in Love*] illustrate the deepeningly reactionary cast of our current social climate, and particularly its hostility toward women." Robert Zaller, "*The Bostonians* and *Swann in Love*: A Note on the New Misogyny," *Film and History* 15, no. 4 (December 1985), 91.

33. Leland S. Person, "Still Me(n): Superman Meets *The Bostonians*," in *Henry James Goes to the Movies*, ed. Susan M. Griffin (Lexington: University Press of Kentucky, 2002), 121–22.

34. Adrian Havill, *Man of Steel: The Career and Courage of Christopher Reeve* (London: Headline Book, 1996), 144.

35. James, *The Bostonians*, 372.

36. James, *The Bostonians*, 394–96.

37. Julianne Pidduck, "Of Windows and Country Walks: Frames of Space and Movement in 1990s Austen Adaptations," *Screen* 39, no. 4 (Winter 1998): 383.

38. James, *The Bostonians*, 297.

39. James Ivory, "The Trouble with Olive: Divine Madness in Massachusetts," *Sight and Sound* 54, no. 2 (Spring 1985): 96.

40. Philip Bergson, "Feeling the Quality," *What's On* (London), September 27, 1984, 41.

41. "Taking her place on the platform, speaking at first in a faltering voice, then with an increasing assurance, she demonstrates that the flame of feminism is not to be dimmed by any one defection from the cause, however prestigious." Gilbert Adair, "The Ivory Tower: *The Bostonians*," *Sight and Sound* 55, no. 4 (Autumn 1984), 621.

42. Person, "Still Me(n)," 121.

43. Long, *The Films of Merchant Ivory*, 98.

44. Adair, "The Ivory Tower," 621.

45. It could be argued that *The Innocents* in its way was equally innovative, but it certainly enjoyed nothing like the same box-office popularity.

CHAPTER THIRTEEN

~

The Turn of the Screw (1989)

Throughout the 1980s, cable television had begun to challenge the three major American networks for a share of the mass audience, by offering a combination of recent Hollywood movies plus series of their own. Some of the most successful were the horror anthologies *The Hitchhiker* (HBO 1983–1987 and USA Network 1987–1991), *Tales from the Crypt* (HBO 1989–1997), and *The Ray Bradbury Theater* (HBO 1985–1986, USA Network 1987–1992). *Nightmare Classics* (1989) represented Showtime's contribution to the genre; produced by Shelley Duvall—who had previously been responsible for the children's series *Fairy Tale Theater*—it was a short-run (four-episode) anthology adapting famous gothic novels and stories from the previous two centuries. These included *Dr. Jekyll and Mr. Hyde*, Ambrose Bierce's "The Eyes of the Panther," Joseph Sheridan Le Fanu's "Carmilla," and Henry James's *The Turn of the Screw*. Each episode was impressively cast; the James adaptation, directed by Graeme Clifford, starred Amy Irving and David Hemmings, with an introduction by Linda Hunt (who had played Dr. Prance in Ivory's *Bostonians*).[1]

Cable channel networks such as HBO and Showtime, dependent on viewer subscriptions for their existence, were able to show R-rated or adult movies uncut and unedited, without running into censorship difficulties; likewise, their series could feature sexually explicit or violent scenes. Initially this proved something of a novelty for viewers, but as the 1980s wore on, as John Kenneth Muir remarks, the majority of cable series featured nudity or simulated sex scenes for their own sake, while "the stories tended to feel secondary or rather insubstantial."[2] This would seem to be the case with Showtime's fifty-four-minute adaptation of *The Turn of the Screw*, which transforms the uncle (renamed Mr. Harley) into a lecherous paterfamilias with a penchant for collecting pornographic objects d'art, and includes explicit sex scenes involving Quint and Miss Jessel.

However, I demonstrate that, contrary to what Muir suggests, such material is not simply intended to titillate viewers; rather Clifford invites us to consider it from the governess's (Amy Irving's) point of view. The film highlights her inability to resist Harley's and Quint's unwelcome advances; in the final sequence, for example, we hear Quint's heavy breathing on the soundtrack as the governess stands on top of the tower, clearly suggesting that he has penetrated her against her will. What is truly horrific in this version of The Turn of the Screw is not the presence of evil but rather male attitudes of lust towards women. Clifford might not propose any alternatives to established gender roles, but nonetheless he conducts a surprisingly critical analysis of male sexual desire and the accompanying objectification of women, by linking this kind of visual objectification to acts of violence and sexual abuse against those least able to defend themselves in this version. If James Ivory's Europeans and Bostonians focused on women's potential for self-expression, this Turn of the Screw criticizes existing power relations within patriarchal societies that seek to frustrate this potential. The governess's experiences should inspire women to fight for their rights with even greater vigor.[3]

The severity of her ordeal when she takes the job at Bly is underlined in the opening sequence, which takes place in a restaurant. As she admits in a voice-over that Harley (David Hemmings) appears a most charming person, the camera tracks a waiter passing through a crowded room into a curtained-off alcove, where she sits primly in her Victorian costume, while Harley puffs on a cigar as if it were a surrogate penis. He is obviously infatuated with her; at one point, he questions whether he has made the right decision in sending her to Bly, when he would far rather have her sitting by his side. Clifford makes his intentions explicit by cutting to a close-up of his hands threading a rolled-up napkin through a metal ring, followed by a reaction shot of the governess staring at him incredulously. None of this exists in James's novella, where the governess visits the uncle's London home and idealistically views him "in the glow of high fashion, of good looks, of expensive habits, of charming ways with women."[4] Clifford's interpretation recalls The Nightcomers or Dan Curtis's 1974 Turn of the Screw as it reaffirms the stereotypes of the predatory male and the female as his (frequently unwilling) victim. However, the reaction shot of the governess implies some kind of criticism of such roles. She refuses to be drawn into Harley's seduction ritual, being aware of her inferior social position, as well as realizing that any overt reaction on her part would simply fuel his lustful intentions.

Harley's obsessions are further emphasized when the action switches to Bly House, as the camera pans the entrance hall, salon, and dining room, which are all decorated with a variety of pornographic paintings and sculptures. The governess looks at them in consternation, and immediately orders Mrs. Grose (Micole Mercurio) to remove them. Having received the governess's letter concerning Miles's behavior,[5] Harley returns to Bly and immediately orders that the statues and paintings be put back on display. He has no time for scruples, assuming (quite arbitrarily) that women enjoy pornography as much as men in an essentially amoral society. When asked by the governess to be mindful of the children's innocence, he scornfully remarks that anyone who believes in innocence must be a fantasist—just like those who believe in ghosts.

Such licentiousness is bound to affect other members of the family as well as the servants. As in Curtis's version, Miles (Balthazar Getty) in Clifford's film is a strapping young lad of fourteen whom Mrs. Grose already predicts will be as sexually predatory as Harley. He neither exhibits any "great glow of freshness" nor "positive fragrance of purity" as in the novella;[6] on the contrary, he hopes to become a sexual athlete—like William the Conqueror—and to sire bastard children by the age of fifteen. He grins broadly as the governess takes down a book from the shelf and discovers—to her horror—that it contains a lithograph of a woman showing off her vagina; later on, he fondles a nude female statue as he expresses contempt for the governess's perpetual references to love. These ideas are totally alien to Bly, where Quint's ghost (M. K. Harris) enjoys total freedom to seduce any woman he encounters. At one point, the governess discovers Quint making love to Miss Jessel (Cameron Miller) on her bed. He momentarily looks up with a lecherous expression before maneuvering Miss Jessel's head towards his penis. On another occasion, he asserts his authority through Miles; at one point, the boy tells the governess in Quint's voice that if he doesn't have sex with her, then someone else will.[7]

Clearly, the governess has little option other than to accept that, at Bly, pleasure has been reduced to male pleasure and equated with male power. Quint gazes at her sleeping with scopophilic desire—that is, treating her as a passive erotic object for his active male gaze—and disappears as she wakes up. After having searched the house, the governess comes to the top of the stairs and espies Quint and Miss Jessel in the entrance hall, playing with a hairbrush. As Quint beckons her to join them, her immediate reaction is to run back to her bedroom in terror. Such sequences recall Dan Curtis's version of *The Turn of the Screw*, which likewise includes a bedroom scene followed by a climax where Quint seduces the governess. However, both directors treat their material very differently. Curtis has Miles (dressed as Quint) coming up the stairs and kissing Jane; as he does so, the director cuts to a close-up of Miles/Quint from Jane's point of view, followed by a medium shot of her recoiling in terror as she realizes that she has fallen for an adolescent boy. The implication is that despite her concern to set a good example to the children, she has succumbed to her sexual urges. By contrast, Clifford's version suggests that the governess remains a perpetual victim of male sexual harassment, due to her subordinate social position.[8] This is accomplished by shooting the entire sequence from the governess's point of view, except for a medium shot at the end when Quint appears on the right of the frame, as the governess runs out of the left side. The only sound we can hear is Quint's heavy breathing on the soundtrack, suggesting that the governess can never escape his ubiquitous presence. Clifford's treatment of James's novella recalls the words of the nineteenth-century feminist Charlotte Perkins Gilman, who argued that women's existence depended on being "noticed, studied, commented on [by men] and incessantly interfered with. . . . How can they grow up without injury?"[9] Evidently little had changed eight decades later.

However, there were others who interpreted the novella more positively. In a lengthy discussion of the novella appearing in 1994, T. J. Lustig observed that James seems to abandon "the traditional masculinist views" of an omniscient narrator "by producing a writing which 'working (in) the in-between,' deploys the very fluidities and resonances which [Hélène] Cixous associates with feminine writing. . . . James's text is a charged border which resists absolutes of difference or an exclusive commitment to a simple dynamic."[10]

Clifford's interpretation does not go that far, but nonetheless he seeks to identify an alternative to the masculinist and/or patriarchal view of the world. Immediately prior to Quint's third ghostly appearance, Flora (Irina Cashen) sits in bed and asks the governess what love feels like. The older woman replies it is safe and comforting—rather like the little girl's toy rabbit. As she speaks, she puts her arm around Flora—who starts, as if unaccustomed to this kind of human warmth. In a few moments, she falls asleep in the governess's arms, clutching her teddy bear. The sequence lasts only one and a half minutes, but its representation of the child's and the governess's mutual affection recalls Olive Chancellor and Verena Tarrant in James Ivory's *Bostonians*. There are no sexual undertones;[11] rather, Clifford emphasizes how this same-sex relationship is based on love—a simple virtue (as the governess describes it) that does not depend on one person dominating another.[12] This is very different from the equivalent scene in James's novella, where the governess refuses to believe that Flora tells the truth about why she was looking out of the bedroom window: "At the moment, in the state of my nerves, I absolutely believed she lied; and if I once more closed my eyes it was before the dazzle of the three or four possible ways in which I might take this [matter] up."[13]

It would seem that Flora in Clifford's film is an innocent little girl—something reinforced by her appearance (blonde-haired, about seven or eight years old, invariably dressed in white). However, our assumptions are shattered in a sequence beginning with Harley riding into the forest, and culminating in his untimely death at Quint's hands. The governess, Mrs. Grose, Miles, and Flora set out to look for him and eventually discover his corpse dangling from a branch of a large oak tree. Clifford intercuts close-ups of Miles's and Flora's delighted expressions with a reaction shot of the governess's doleful countenance. Harley might be no more, but Quint is still very much in charge at Bly. Despite her efforts to forge a relationship with the children (especially Flora) based on trust and mutual kindness, they will never extricate themselves from what the governess describes as the all-pervasive evil perpetrated by the male characters around the house.

The governess's experiences in the final scene serve to verify this observation. As Quint propels Flora toward the edge of the parapet, the governess tells him to leave her alone and goads Miles into acknowledging Quint's presence. The boy yells his denial, runs toward the ghost, and falls fifty feet to his death. Mrs. Grose tries to revive him before looking up at the governess standing triumphantly with her arms around Flora. Quint's heavy breathing can be heard once more on the soundtrack as Mrs. Grose screams, and the action cuts to a close-up of the governess's scowling face. Far from rescuing the children from Quint, she has become his latest victim, who has been transformed from a pious woman into a fiend. One might ask why she capitulates so quickly—was this not the same person who declared earlier on that she would use all her religious training passed on to her by her father to deliver the children from evil?[14] Unfortunately, love and religion provide poor protection against Quint's animal desires. Clifford's ending is very different from James's text—perhaps the only connection between the two is the idea of possession. The governess in the novella observes triumphantly to Miles that "What will he [Quint] *ever* matter? *I* have you . . . but he has lost you for ever."[15] Clifford underlines the irony of this statement: We are well aware that Quint *does* matter, as he dominates the governess and the children. The film's ending seems closer in spirit to Charlotte Perkins Gilman's novella *The Yellow Wallpaper* (1892), where the narrator fights as best as she can against women "creeping" (i.e., being forced to accept a subordinate role in a patriarchal world) but ends up a victim of that world, as she peels off yards and yards of wallpaper and creeps around the floor.[16]

Despite the impressive casts and an extensive publicity campaign offering viewers the prospect of terror stemming "from the deepest depths of our imagination . . . this is where you'll find the things that really frighten us,"[17] HBO's *Nightmare Classics* anthology (including *The Turn of the Screw*) found little favor with audiences and critics. John Kenneth Muir points out that it aired "from late-summer 1989 to November of the same year, and quietly disappeared after its quartet of shows."[18] To my knowledge, the series has not been rebroadcast either on network, cable, or satellite television. The video of *The Turn of the Screw* was released a year later on the (now-defunct) Cannon label; it is now difficult to find. Nonetheless, the adaptation provides a good example of how American cable television treated the classics (as opposed to the major networks), as well as offering a powerful analysis of the difficulties encountered by women in patriarchal societies. They might struggle for freedom, but frequently they end up victims of existing power relations, as they are treated as sex objects. I do not think it coincidental that Clifford's adaptation recalls Charlotte Perkins Gilman's work; she was a contemporary of James, and had enjoyed something of a revival of interest in the 1970s and 1980s, with many of her writings—both factual and fictional—being reissued. Although there is no evidence to suggest that Clifford had read anything of hers, I venture to suggest that he was acquainted with some of the issues she discusses.[19] The critic Barbara H. Solomon wrote in 1992 that despite the improvements in women's status in the twentieth century, more and more of them were struggling (like Gilman) to "improve the quality of [their] lives in a [patriarchal] world that seems increasingly materialistic, violent, stressful and indifferent to individuals."[20] Clifford's adaptation of *The Turn of the Screw* bears witness to the truth of this statement.

Notes

1. By the late 1980s, Hemmings had become something of an established figure in American terror television series, having directed seven episodes of Fox's *Werewolf* (1987–1988).

2. John Kenneth Muir, *Terror Television: American Series 1970–1999* (Jefferson, NC: McFarland, 1999), 104.

3. Cynthia A. Freeland, "Feminist Frameworks for Horror Films," in *Post-Theory: Reconstructing Film Studies*, ed. David Bordwell and Noel Carroll (Madison: University of Wisconsin Press, 1996), 213–14.

4. Henry James, *The Turn of the Screw, The Aspern Papers and Other Stories*, ed. Michael Swan (London: Collins, 1963), 318.

5. James, *Turn of the Screw*, 383.

6. James, *Turn of the Screw*, 328.

7. Despite Harley's assurances to the contrary, Clifford's adaptation stresses the fact that the ghosts are living presences at Bly. Partly this has been dictated by the demands of the horror anthology format (which invariably includes such classic elements as witchcraft and/or monsters) (Muir, *Terror Television*, 568). The publicity also focused on this aspect: "Could it be that Quint and Miss Jessel had returned for revenge? Were the children precariously close to losing their souls?" "Nightmare Classics: *The Turn of the Screw*" (Los Angeles: Viacom, 1989), 1.

8. This is also the case in the novella; despite her conviction—expressed at the beginning—that she is "strangely at the helm!" of Bly House (James, *Turn of the Screw*, 324), the governess remains just as much of a servant as Mrs. Grose or Miss Jessel.

9. Quoted in Elaine R. Hedges, "Afterword," in Charlotte Perkins Gilman, *The Yellow Wallpaper* (New York: Feminist Press, 1973), 51.

10. T. J. Lustig, *Henry James and the Ghostly* (Cambridge: Cambridge University Press, 1994), 184.

11. This is certainly not the case in the novella, where the governess describes Flora's communication with the ghost of Miss Jessel thus: "Hidden, protected, absorbed, she evidently rested on the sill—the casement opened forward—and gave herself up" (James, *Turn of the Screw*, 360). Robert Weisbuch observes that such moments demonstrate that "every sighting of the ghosts [in the children's company] includes a potentially sexual implication . . . as the Governess is by now far more concerned with her own dramas than with protecting her charges." Robert Weisbuch, "Henry James and the Idea of Evil," in *The Cambridge Companion to Henry James*, ed. Jonathan Freedman (Cambridge: Cambridge University Press, 1998), 107.

12. Clifford makes only one direct reference to the title of James's novella, occurring immediately after this scene, when the governess vows to herself in an aside that, as a result of the turn of the screw of ordinary human virtue, the ghosts never corrupt the children.

13. James, *Turn of the Screw*, 359.

14. The publicity was in no doubt that, for all the governess's good intentions, she was "impressionable and naïve" ("Nightmare Classics," 1). This is not what the film itself suggests.

15. James, *Turn of the Screw*, 408.

16. Hedges, "Afterword," 53.

17. "Nightmare Classics," 1.

18. Muir, *Terror Television*, 586.

19. The year 1966 marked the republication of *Women and Economics*, the first of her works to be reissued during the following years. *The Yellow Wallpaper* was published in 1973 by the Feminist Press, followed by her other works (e.g., *Herland and Selected Stories* [1992]) in the subsequent two decades.

20. Barbara H. Solomon, "Introduction," *Herland and Selected Stories by Charlotte Perkins Gilman* (New York: Signet Classics, 1992), xxix.

CHAPTER FOURTEEN

The Turn of the Screw (1992)

Superficially, Rusty Lemorande's Anglo-French adaptation of *The Turn of the Screw* (1992) appears very much in tune with contemporary critical thinking about the novella. In this version, the role of the narrator is played by an unidentified female patient in a psychiatric hospital participating in a group therapy session. As the action unfolds, we learn that she has had access to a diary written by the governess (renamed Jenny Gooding) written not long after "he" died; but we are not told who "he" is. Only in the final scene do we discover that the patient/narrator is none other than Flora, who holds the governess responsible for her brother Miles's demise. Whether her judgment can be relied upon is another matter, in view of the fact that she has spent her entire life coming to terms with her childhood experiences at Bly. This would seem to confirm Lustig's opinion that *The Turn of the Screw* deliberately subverts the controlling "masculine" presence of a narrative voice.[1] David McWhirter suggests that this technique represented James's attempt to "make an investment in the feminine," decentered style of writing and thereby "express the experience of in-betweenness."[2]

However, I argue in this chapter that Lemorande's treatment is aggressively "masculine," as he suggests that the governess should take full responsibility for what happens at Bly. Peter G. Beidler sums up this point of view: "Her [the governess's] passion for the uncle controls most of the actions of the story. . . . [G]ripped by her paranoia and exhausted beyond measure, [she] thinks she sees ghosts . . . she determines to ride out the crisis on her own, not realizing that there is no crisis."[3]

In Lemorande's film, Jenny Gooding (Patsy Kensit) not only lacks experience of looking after children, but her entire existence has been blighted by her father—a minister of the church—who abused her when she was young. In her mind, Quint's ghost poses a similar threat to Miles and Flora. Despite the fact that she finds herself attracted to the uncle (renamed Mr. Cooper in the film), she assumes that he is equally dangerous, even though, as a drug addict, he is more likely to abuse himself rather than the children. Despite the fact that she considers the uncle rather attractive, she believes that—like her father or Quint—he poses a threat both to herself and the children. Her deteriorating mental state is signaled through a series of dream sequences comprising a series of images of her father, Cooper, Quint, liquid flowing from a bottle, and an image of a child slashing her wrists. Far from saving the children from the ghosts, she crushes the life out of Miles in her attempts to make him acknowledge Quint's existence, and condemns Flora to lifelong mental anguish.

I also suggest that Lemorande's reading of the novella has been influenced by his decision to resituate the action in the mid-1960s, rather than the last decade of the nineteenth century (as in the original). Frequently he invites us to reflect on the seamier aspects of that time, when young women such as Jenny who led sheltered lives were unable to survive. In a world committed to the liberalization of social and sexual morality, Quint has assumed total control at Bly, while those characters who are supposed to set a responsible example have neglected their duties: Jenny's father is an abuser, Cooper a drug addict, Grose an alcoholic.

Lemorande's *Turn of the Screw* makes a fascinating contribution to the canon of James adaptations. While following Clifford's version in portraying the governess as a victim of an unjust society, it suggests that this unjustness is caused not by gender inequalities but by a decline in social standards of behavior. This represents a characteristically "New Right" conservative interpretation of the 1960s as a period when British and/or American society began to fall apart, as individuals fought for their freedom (women's rights or sexual equality) while paying scant attention to maintaining collective stability.

The director's purpose is rendered explicit early on in the film when the narrator (a new character especially written for the film, played by Marianne Faithfull) points out that the post at Bly is Jenny's (Patsy Kensit's) first, and that she might therefore be vulnerable. Cooper (Julian Sands) exerts a powerful effect on her; Lemorande intercuts close-ups of her staring fixedly into his eyes with shots of Cooper telling her that she will not get along with Mrs. Grose (Stéphane Audran), who is a French woman. For the present, Jenny appears to be in control of her passions, admitting in a letter to her school friend Claire (in a newly written scene) that she is living out a beautiful and ghastly episode in a storybook. However, we are soon made aware that any romantic feelings she might have for Cooper have been corrupted by her childhood experiences. Lemorande creates another new sequence beginning with an aerial shot of a little girl on a beach beside a sandcastle. As the camera dollies down toward her, we see two black-trousered legs standing threateningly in the background. The action cuts to a shot of Jenny's father (Thomas Krygier) entering a room, followed by a scene with Jenny in the schoolroom, marking the children's homework. She puts pen to paper but blood gushes forth from its nib; this is followed by shots of someone slashing his or her wrists and a close-up of Jenny's horrified face. The narrator observes that there are certain things about her life that she did not tell Mr. Cooper, things that happened to her when she was a child that she could not understand but which left an indelible scar on her.

None of this exists in the novella; all we are told is that the governess considers herself the victim of a seduction by the splendid young man (the uncle) after two meetings.[4] Lemorande stressed in an interview that he had sought to "read between the lines of the novella while gutting and exposing how much of it was a projection of her [the governess's] sexuality in turmoil."[5] Whether his alterations add anything more to the novella is debatable; one reviewer found the experience of "watching a sledge-hammer being taken to this most delicate of stories . . . a distressing experience."[6] More significantly, Lemorande's rewriting of the novella imposes a (masculine) controlling perspective on the narrative by suggesting that the governess's feelings of guilt and loathing render her incapable of looking after the children competently.

This is particularly evident in the rather repetitive dream sequences. While Jack Clayton's *The Innocents* and Dan Curtis's *Turn of the Screw* use this technique to suggest the governess's burgeoning awareness of her sexuality, Lemorande stresses that Jenny will never experience such self-development. As in the novella, she is imprisoned by her imagination, but her mental experiences could not be more different. The governess in James's work is starved of male company, prompting her to fantasize about how charming it would be, "as charming as a charming story suddenly to meet someone" who would "stand before me and smile and approve." This reflection occurs immediately prior to the first of the ghostly apparitions—"my imagination had, in a flash, turned real"—but instead of the uncle, it turns out to be Quint.[7] If we accept that the ghosts are projections of the governess's mind, their appearance can most likely be attributed to "self-reproof, displacing itself into the idea of [the ghosts being] a threat to others—exactly the others whom she ought herself to be protecting with the eyes of love."[8] Lemorande's film is more preoccupied with Jenny's sexual fantasies; in her mind, all men seem to take advantage of women and consign them to eternal damnation. Even death cannot restrain them. This is suggested by the images that recur throughout her dreams: Miles disguised as a satyr; Flora moving up and down as if a man were making love to her; an exposed nipple; a corpse emerging from milky-white water; Quint and Miss Jessel in bed; Cooper asking if she can help him; and her father staring into space.

Jenny's fantasies quite literally drive her to distraction. In the final scene, she shakes Miles (Joseph England) so hard that he falls to the ground; as he does so, Lemorande cuts to two shots of Quint (Olivier Debray) taking his shirt off, and Flora (Clare Szekores) lying in bed waiting for him. Jenny makes a final attempt to make Miles acknowledge the ghost's presence and thereby drive him away; unable to comprehend what she says, the boy now realizes that he is fighting for his life. He hits her twice on the skull with a blunt instrument; as Jenny looks at the blood trickling down her face, the narrator draws our attention to her feeling that the boy might be innocent— and if so, what has happened to her. But this pang of conscience comes too late to save Miles, who dies in her arms from a heart attack.

Yet perhaps Jenny cannot be entirely blamed for what happens at Bly. She admits at one point that she has spent so much time teaching self-reliance in children, and thought of herself so little, that she is still mentally a child. No one sets an example for her nor offers her any advice. In the opening scene, she enters Cooper's office to find him stretched vacantly on a chaise-lounge under the influence of drugs. The narrator comments that although she likes him, Jenny needs his help. She looks into his eyes, exclaiming as she does so that she wants to protect the children from harmful things, the evils of modern society. What she fails to understand is that perhaps the members of modern society of the 1960s—like Cooper himself—pose a danger to themselves and their dependents with their self-indulgence. Much the same criticism can be leveled at Mrs. Grose. Superficially, she appears as someone whose down-to-earth practicality contrasts with Jenny's wild imaginings. At one point, she entreats Jenny to consider the children as sweet little flowers; it's a pity that Jenny fails to heed this advice before confronting Miles in the final scene. However, Grose's competence as a housekeeper is questioned in a short sequence where she sits in the front room reading a newspaper and sipping a large glass of wine, taking little notice of the governess. Grose herself admits that alcohol provides a convenient way to forget about her responsibilities at Bly—for example, informing Cooper about Quint and Miss Jessel's antics.[9]

The consequences of such behavior are inevitable; with no one to set any moral standards for them, the children become obsessed with sex and sexual display. On her first night at Bly, Jenny is offered roast beef elephant-style—apparently the children's favorite dish—consisting of a leg of meat with a parsnip protruding like an erect penis from the carved side. Later on that night, she discovers a casket under her bed with a suspender belt inside. Miles enters, disguised as a satyr in horns and tail, and informs her in a matter-of-fact tone that even though Miss Jessel (Bryony Brind) used to wear it, Jenny would look much sexier if she put it on herself. In the novella, the governess observes that the children seem to possess an apparently inexhaustible capacity to take pleasure in "the mere exuberance of the gift, in the most unimposed little miracles of memory."[10] Lemorande treats these "little miracles" as examples of licentiousness; Miles wears an elephant mask as he runs round a bonfire and kisses the governess full on the lips. Later on, the children stage a play for the adults' benefit that begins with Miles lifting his sister's skirts up and sticking his tongue out, simulating oral sex. For her part, Flora clasps two half-coconuts to her chest as if they were breasts.

Jenny might find such moments offensive, but despite her best intentions she falls victim to the moral corruption pervading Bly House. This is suggested by means of a repeated shot of a white owl flying away from the house. We first see it immediately prior to her first vision of Quint; it reappears when she sees Miss Jessel and again when she encounters Miles in the garden. The image suggests that Jenny's innocence cannot survive the onslaught of what the narrator describes as an inexplicable phenomenon—the spirit of the 1960s, with its emphasis on the destruction of social and sexual taboos. Our awareness of Jenny's predicament is greatly helped by the casting of Marianne Faithfull as the narrator; as a 1960s icon herself, Faithfull underwent a similar process of corruption. She was well qualified to comment on the action of the film: In a 2001 interview, she claimed that drugs had destroyed her career as an actress.[11] Lemorande observed that Faithfull "had strong feelings about the film, and rather than use direct lifts from James's prose as planned, she reinterpreted them with a Nineties sensibility using her own powerful Sixties viewpoint."[12]

Lemorande's *Turn of the Screw* did not enjoy wide distribution; following its premiere at the Sitges Film Festival, Canada, in 1992, it went straight to video in Great Britain and America. Reviews were largely unenthusiastic;

Robert Cummings as Jeffrey Ashton and Susan Hayward as Tina Bordereau in the final scene of *The Lost Moment* (Walter Wanger Productions, 1947).

Olivia de Havilland as Catherine Sloper in the final scene of
The Heiress (Paramount Pictures, 1949).

Ann Blyth as Helen Pettigrew and Tyrone Power as Peter Standish in *I'll Never Forget You* (U.K. title: *The House in the Square*) (Twentieth Century Fox, 1951).

Deborah Kerr as Miss Giddens and Martin Stephens as Miles in
The Innocents (Twentieth Century Fox/Achilles Productions, 1961).

Barbra Streisand as Melinda Tentrees in *On a Clear Day You Can See Forever* (Twentieth Century Fox, 1970).

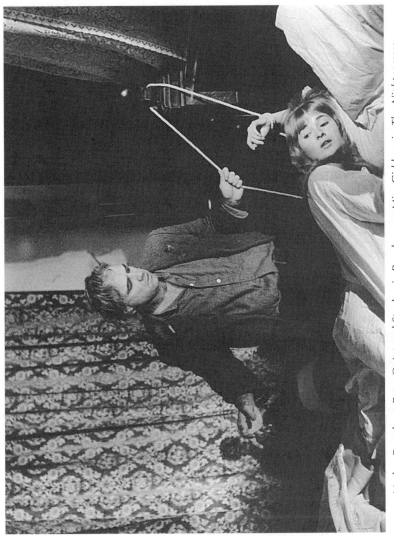

Marlon Brando as Peter Quint and Stephanie Beacham as Miss Giddens in *The Nightcomers* (Scimitar Films/Elliott Kastner-Jay Kanter-Alan Ladd Jr. Productions, 1971).

Detail of autumn landscape from *The Europeans* (Merchant-Ivory Productions, 1979).

Jane Seymour in *Somewhere in Time* (Rastar Pictures/Universal Pictures, 1980).

Vanessa Redgrave as Olive Chancellor and Madeleine Potter as Verena Tarrant in *The Bostonians* (Merchant-Ivory Productions, 1984).

Christian Bale in *The Portrait of a Lady*
(Polygram Filmed Entertainment/Propaganda Films, 1996).

Helena Bonham Carter as Kate Croy and Linus Roache as Merton Densher in *The Wings of the Dove* (Miramax Films/Renaissance Dove, 1997).

Uma Thurman as Charlotte Stant, Anjelica Huston as Fanny Assingham, and Jeremy Northam as the prince in *The Golden Bowl* (Merchant-Ivory Productions/TF1 International, 2001).

Variety described the film as "lacking any flair or originality."[13] Despite the insights of earlier Jamesian adaptations, Lemorande failed to acknowledge that women could control their own destinies. Angela McRobbie wrote in 1991 that by the end of the previous decade a feminist intellectual culture had been established, "or to put it another way, a strongly feminist critique has found its way into the orthodoxies of sociology, history, psychology, politics and so on. . . . Possibly the most important achievement in the developments . . . has been precisely the revealing of some of women's hidden oppressions, both past and present."[14] Lemorande disregarded such notions, preferring instead to remain within the safe boundaries of established gender relations. Perhaps he saw this as an effective way to attract large audiences to a "safe ghost story" that took as its central premise the idea of the young woman threatened by forces beyond her control.[15] The fact that this version of *The Turn of the Screw* failed to attract much interest (it barely recouped its $1.5 million cost, even after video release) shows how much filmgoers' tastes had changed. Although Lemorande confidently claimed in an interview that his film sought to bring *The Innocents* up-to-date by recognizing "the essential truths contained in the original text,"[16] the "essential truth" about his film is that, for all its attempts to update James's novella, its gender perspective—as far as women are concerned—remains resolutely old-fashioned.

Notes

1. T. J. Lustig, *Henry James and the Ghostly* (Cambridge: Cambridge University Press, 1994), 183.

2. David McWhirter, "In the 'Other House' of Fiction: Writing, Authority and Femininity in *The Turn of the Screw*," in *New Essays on Daisy Miller and The Turn of the Screw*, ed. Vivian R. Pollak (Cambridge: Cambridge University Press, 1993), 142.

3. Peter Beidler, *Ghosts, Demons and Henry James: The Turn of the Screw at the Turn of the Century* (Columbia: University of Missouri Press, 1989), 6–9.

4. Henry James, *The Turn of the Screw, The Aspern Papers and Other Stories*, ed. Michael Swan (London: Collins, 1963), 320.

5. Alan Jones, "Turn of the Screw," *Shivers: The Global Magazine of Horror* no. 6 (March 1993): 21.

6. "Call Yourself a Scientist!—*The Turn of the Screw* (1992)," at http://twtd .bluemountains.net.au/Rick/liz_ts.htm (accessed January 25, 2004).

7. James, *Turn of the Screw*, 330.

8. Adrian Poole, *Henry James* (Hemel Hempstead: Harvester Wheatsheaf, 1991), 153.

9. Cf. the novella: "He didn't really in the least know them. The fault's mine" (James, *Turn of the Screw*, 379). Lemorande suggests quite early on that Mrs. Grose might not be

quite up to the job, by having Cooper observe that she is French. One wonders what the film's French financiers must have thought of this remark.

10. James, *Turn of the Screw*, 355.

11. Lynn Barber, "You Know, I'm Not Everybody's Cup of Tea!" *The Observer* (London), June 15, 2001, B7.

12. Jones, "Turn of the Screw," 21.

13. Peter Besas, "The Turn of the Screw," *Variety*, November 2, 1992, 91.

14. Angela McRobbie, *Feminism and Youth Culture* (London: Macmillan Press, 1991), 62.

15. Jones, "Turn of the Screw," 20.

16. Jones, "Turn of the Screw," 19.

~

CHAPTER FIFTEEN

The Portrait
of a Lady (1996)

Jane Campion's adaptation of *The Portrait of a Lady* has attracted a range of critical responses since its release in 1996. At worst, it has been described by Ellen Cheshire in her book on Campion as "thoroughly depressing . . . the extreme close-ups of beautiful people, in elegant drawing rooms, is akin to watching the paint dry on a series of portraits."[1] Having watched the film for the first time, Karen Michele Chandler thought that it was "merely . . . a flawed dramatization of James's novel." After a second viewing, however, she concluded that Campion sought "to evaluate the social constraints on nineteenth-century womanhood," even though by doing so the director "unnecessarily simplifies many of its [the novel's] characters and their conflicts."[2] Feminist critics have taken a particular interest in the film; Priscilla L. Walton argues that Isabel (Nicole Kidman) remains "an object of [male] scrutiny," whose efforts "to control and develop her subjectivity are subverted and her sexuality constrained by the times in which she lives."[3] By contrast, Nancy Bentley believes that Campion seeks to create "a portrait of a woman that manipulates its own medium to try and sustain conflicting possibilities about the imagination, desires and 'fate' of a woman who is an object of 'conscious observation.'"[4]

This chapter develops Bentley's thesis by showing how this version of *The Portrait* focuses on a series of discourses—social, political, and cinematic—and their methods of ordering experience in order to expose the gaps (the repressions) and the contradictions within them. As someone who begins the film with a conscious desire to determine her own fate, Isabel Archer

(Nicole Kidman) becomes an object of "conscious observation"; everyone seeks to impose his or her will on her, either by settling a fortune on her or by encouraging her to get married. When she accepts Osmond's proposal (and thereby places herself under someone else's control), Ralph Touchett (Martin Donovan) accuses her of having sacrificed herself for someone narrow and selfish—a dilettante.[5] The fact that Ralph cannot recognize the contradictions within Isabel's existence reveals the extent to which the social and political discourses of *The Portrait* depend on language and the (patriarchal) ideology on which they are based.

However, I suggest that Isabel transcends the roles imposed on her by discovering a mode of expression that cannot be reduced to a language based on power, authority, and rational explanation. Despite her loathing for Osmond, Isabel opts to remain within the "prison-castle" of her marriage, in the belief that she should accept the consequences of her own actions. While finding him repellent, she appears to derive some form of masochistic pleasure from his treatment of her. At the end of Campion's film, we are left uncertain as to whether Isabel will return to her previous life in Rome or stay in England and forge a new existence as a single woman. But then, perhaps this is not particularly significant: As in Cellan Jones's *Portrait* and *Golden Bowl*, Campion suggests that the notion of female "freedom" is not identified with direct action but expressed through statements—either verbal or nonverbal—that repudiate rational (i.e., masculine) values and provide for the encouragement of multiple perspectives (Isabel suffers at her husband's hands yet finds the experience curiously pleasurable).

What renders Campion's film unique is that this objective is reinforced in terms of form as well as content, as she deliberately seeks to challenge the conventions of the period adaptation. While several earlier adaptations such as Cellan Jones's *Golden Bowl* or Merchant-Ivory's *Bostonians* explore James's novels in terms of contemporary feminist thinking, they do so within a narrative that explicitly situates the action in its appropriate sociohistorical context through period sets and costumes. By contrast, Campion includes deliberately anachronistic elements—in the opening scene, for instance, where several young Australian women from the mid-1990s talk about their experiences of love or in a sequence comprising images in a variety of cinematic styles ranging from the look of a Valentino silent epic to the bizarre effects of a surrealist film. Such moments invite the viewer "to construct and contradict simultaneously, to make connections and suggest distinctions. Startle the viewer with the juxtaposition of seeming opposites."[6]

Of course, this is not to say that the inclusion of fantasy sequences in a cinematic narrative is an exclusively feminist strategy. There are other James adaptations that make use of this technique—notably *On a Clear Day* and the two versions of *The Turn of the Screw*, by Dan Curtis (1974) and Rusty Lemorande (1992). In these three films, however, we are left in no doubt that the fantasies are legitimized by the patriarchy; Marc Chabot imagines Daisy Gamble as Melinda Tentrees in *On a Clear Day*, while the governess's dreams in the two films of *The Turn of the Screw* underline the extent to which they have been corrupted by the experience of living at Bly House, where the uncle (and subsequently Peter Quint) reign supreme. Campion creates fantasy sequences combining multiple, even contradictory, images that resist logical explanation.

Such difficulties are clearly articulated at the beginning of the novel and the film. She makes her first appearance as an eligible marriage prospect at Gardencourt framed by the ample doorway leading to the garden—an image that foreshadows her future imprisonment in the discourses of late Victorian bourgeois society.[7] The image recurs later on when Ned Rosier (Christian Bale) sees her "framed in the gilded doorway" of Osmond's house, where "she struck our young man as the picture of a gracious lady."[8] Warburton (Richard E. Grant) offers her marriage with the "splendid" security of money and influence in return; for Isabel, however, this opportunity "so offered her was not the greatest she could conceive."[9] Goodwood (Viggo Mortensen) tries the same strategy; after Ralph's death, he tells her that "You don't know where to turn. Turn straight to me. I want to persuade you to trust me."[10] Although Ralph has no apparent interest in marrying her, his concern for Isabel is a function of his desire to control her future as a gracious lady. He considers it "an entertainment of a high order" to find out "what she was going to do with herself."[11] He fetishizes her thus in an aside: "A character like that . . . a real little passionate force to see at play is the finest thing in nature. It's finer than the finest work of art—than a Greek bas-relief, than a great Titian, than a Gothic cathedral."[12]

By settling an inheritance on her, Ralph believes that he can transform her into an independent woman who will realize his "charming vision" of her future: "I had amused myself with planning out a high destiny for you."[13] Ralph's somewhat contradictory desires (i.e., giving Isabel financial freedom yet simultaneously trying to organize her life) turns out to be little different from those of Warburton and Goodwood. For him, Isabel represents a commodity whose love and respect for him depends on her acquiring a large fortune and the security that goes with it. Laura Jones's screenplay for this scene refers to Isabel's pain and bewilderment as she discovers Ralph's true motives; the finished film has her standing in front of one of the pens in the Palazzo Crescentini's stables, suggesting her confinement within the prison house of male desire.[14]

This type of image recurs in different forms throughout the film. At one point, Isabel is shown walking with Osmond in the garden of his house, the iron railings clearly visible in the foreground. On another occasion, she is discovered standing by the window at Gardencourt; despite her wealth, she cannot walk unaccompanied in the garden. In a ball scene later on, Campion suggests that most women of Isabel's social position share the same fate. Unlike Ivory's *Europeans* (where the ball sequence comprises a series of long shots focusing on the historically accurate sets and costumes), Campion uses a series of close-ups to emphasize the preparations for the ball—a tracking shot of the servants putting top hats on a table, a close-up of the ladies offering their dancing cards, and the gentlemen filling in their names. This is followed by an aerial shot of couples dancing in circular formation. They seem like automata as they make circular patterns that should remind us of the sequence earlier on in the film when Campion cuts to a medium shot of Osmond twirling Isabel's parasol prior to seducing her.[15] Clearly, the whole ritual of finding a suitable marriage partner resembles a business with no place for human feelings. Campion emphasizes the callousness of the ball by showing some ladies being carried out of the room on the servants' shoulders, while others, too exhausted to continue, are given smelling salts to revive them. According to the capitalist logic of the occasion, they are inferior goods—unlike Pansy, who (as Warburton observes) has several young men who are more than willing to dance with her.[16]

It would seem that any woman who tries to flout the system by choosing her own destiny is doomed to fail. Campion suggests this in a short sequence that expands on the scene in James's novel where Mrs. Touchett accuses Isabel of being "too fond of her own ways" and Isabel replies that she wants to "know the things one shouldn't do . . . so as to choose."[17] The film includes some extra dialogue as Mrs. Touchett (Shelley Winters) reproves Isabel for not heeding her advice.[18] Campion cuts to a close-up of Isabel's hand pulling some scraps of paper on which a series of words have been written (including honesty, probity, and nihilism) off her wardrobe door. Such terms summarize the contradictory experiences of an independent woman in a bourgeois patriarchal society. While she might be admired for her nihilism and her honesty, she may be admonished for abnegating her appointed roles as wife, mother, or potential marriage partner, and thus regarded as an aberration. Campion herself suggested, in the production notes to *The Portrait*, that scenes like this were included to emphasize the contemporary aspects of the story, giving women the chance to identify with the heroine.[19]

What renders this *Portrait* even more bold, modern, and provocative is Isabel's gradual discovery that female autonomy depends less on outright resistance to the patriarchal order and more on finding a form of expression that confounds masculine logic. This process is indicated through repeated close-ups of her looking at herself in a mirror. From one point of view, this type of shot may emphasize "control from the periphery of the image . . . 'the object of the shot is not what she [the central character] is looking at, not even her look; it is: looking at her looking.' . . . This totalizing force and organization of vision works to efface, or at the very least contain, the female look."[20] From another point of view, I would argue that this denotes female potentiality, as Isabel comes to understand something about herself and her future (compare, for instance, the shots of Vanessa Redgrave's Olive Chancellor looking out of the window in Ivory's *Bostonians*). As the production notes observe, it is at moments like these that Isabel "awakens to a curious freedom."[21]

By masculine standards, this "freedom" is certainly curious. At one point, Osmond assaults her not just with psychological violence but with physical indignities as well—picking her up and sitting her down on a heap of cushions, and subsequently standing on her dress so that she falls to the floor, claiming all the while that she has played "a very deep game" in preventing Pansy's marriage to Warburton.[22] Isabel reacts by moving toward him as if expecting a kiss; clearly, she is still sexually drawn to him, in spite of her suffering. Ken Gelder suggests that this strain of masochism runs throughout Campion's *Portrait*; it is also evident in Isabel imagining the possibility of being promiscuous (as in the dream sequence where she is fondled by all her suitors) even while she acknowledges the restrictions that marriage imposes on her.[23] In James adaptations such as *The Nightcomers*, scenes like this put filmgoers in the position of voyeurs taking pleasure in female suffering. By contrast, Campion suggests that the experience of masochism might give Isabel the chance to experience power or pleasure within the given limits of the patriarchal constraints imposed on her.[24] Isabel is punished, to be sure, but she receives pleasure in return; moreover, her experiences encourage the audience to empathize with her suffering. Her sense of power is implied in the final shot of the scene, with Isabel's right profile fully visible in medium close-up, while Osmond can only be seen in reverse. This reading of Isabel, a battered wife, as somehow powerful may "unbalance . . . the drama" for critics such as Philip Horne, but it only appears unbalanced in terms of the (masculine) cultural law that separates the "dominant" from the "dominated."[25] By contrast, Campion shows Isabel negotiating a contradictory position between these two poles: She is passive yet active, humiliated yet fulfilled.[26]

In the film's final sequence, Isabel is shown running back to Gardencourt; we watch her dark skirts flash over the snow, but her progress is jerky, heightened by the deliberate use of step-printing.[27] Through the windows of the house we can see a room lit attractively by candlelight. Isabel's hand turns on the doorknob leading to this room, but suddenly she turns back toward the landscape, her body held in freeze-frame, as if Campion wanted to end by depicting "the portrait of a lady" looking slightly to the viewer's right. In Cellan Jones's version of the novel, Isabel treats any attempt to capture her in a portrait (whether literal or figurative) as a masculine strategy to impose order and unity on a personality that seeks to remain "perfectly free."[28] Likewise, Campion's version ends with Isabel rejecting order and unity; we do not know whether she will open the door and return to her past life or stay outside and fend for herself. But perhaps this does not really matter for a woman who has discovered a means of expression for herself. Far from rejecting one life choice for another, she seeks to construct a multiple perspective that encompasses both.

The ambiguous ending also emphasizes Campion's desire to repudiate the conventions of the classical narrative film, and thereby force the viewer to make connections between apparently disparate elements. This is evident at the outset, where we see a blank screen with the sound of women speaking on the soundtrack about the joys of being kissed or kissing themselves. Campion cuts to a sequence—photographed in black-and-white and color—comprising a series of shots of modern young women either moving slowly or standing still. In an interview published to coincide with the film's American release, Campion pointed out that this was designed to show "what the romantic hopes of young girls could be. . . . [It] serves as a link to our era . . . a poem before the journey of a young woman."[29] They look for a mirror—in other words, someone who might respond in kind to the young women's feelings and emotions—by staring directly into the camera lens, as if expecting the audience to fulfill that role.

Such moments signal that this *Portrait* is going to be very different from previous James adaptations. In Bogdanovich's *Daisy Miller*, for instance, Daisy becomes the object of pleasurable looking both for the viewer and for Winterbourne. By contrast, the women in this sequence are active agents who approach the viewer on equal terms and expect the same in return. In a skillful transition between present and past, Campion shows Isabel in medium close-up, having spurned Warburton's proposal of marriage. As the camera zooms in towards her, her tear-filled eyes look from right to left and then stare directly at the viewer, as if searching—like the young women—for someone who does not expect her to marry and might therefore provide the clearest mirror of her feelings at this moment. The same shot recurs later on in the film, as Isabel talks to Ralph after having rejected Goodwood's proposal. Ralph's gaze emphasizes his desire to control her, but Isabel turns away from him and looks straight into the camera, as if searching for someone less threatening. As we have seen, it is only when she looks at herself in a mirror that she understands the importance of self-reliance.

Another sequence disrupting the classical narrative form occurs just after Goodwood exits (having promised to leave Isabel alone for two years) and Isabel experiences a fantasy of making love to Goodwood, Warburton, and Ralph simultaneously. Structurally speaking, this scene is very reminiscent of Jack Clayton's *The Innocents*; like Miss Giddens, Isabel seeks to resist patriarchal authority by acknowledging her powerful sexual desires. Campion herself suggested in an interview that Isabel possessed "very strong sexual aspirations, who wants to be loved."[30] The images in the film—and the swelling musical score accompanying it—correspond closely to the erotic implications of James's prose:

> [S]he was trembling—trembling all over. Vibration was easy to her, was in fact too constant with her, and she found herself now humming like a smitten harp. . . . [T]he sense was there, throbbing in her heart, it was part of her emotion, but it was a thing to be ashamed of—it was profane and out of place. It was not for some ten minutes that she rose from her knees, and even when she came back to the sitting-room her tremor had not quite subsided. It had had, verily, two causes: Mr. Goodwood, but it might be feared that the rest was simply the enjoyment she found *in the exercise of her power*.[31] (emphasis added)

A third black-and-white fantasy sequence suggests that Isabel has relinquished that power once she has accepted Osmond's hand in marriage. Nominally intended to be a record of her travels on honeymoon, the sequence also serves as a surrealist depiction of her entrapment. A large pair of lips repeat Osmond's declaration ("I'm absolutely in love with you"); a plate of transmogrified beans repeat the words once more, while the circular motion of the parasol—with Osmond's face emerging at the rear of the shot—becomes a vortex into which Isabel's nude body plunges. Michael Anesko complains that the sequence "deliberately forecloses Isabel's imagined freedom"; something he perceives as characteristic of a film that "yields to the simplifications of an overriding agenda."[32] The truth of this observation depends very much on what is meant by Isabel's "imagined freedom"; even while suffering physical abuse from her husband, she enjoys the freedom to experience pleasure, as well as solicit the viewer's sympathies. Bearing this in mind, I would argue that this sequence has a positive rather than a negative connotation, encouraging multiple and/or contradictory perspectives. Campion herself has indicated how Isabel is "fascinated by images of domination and suppression," even while she finds them repugnant: "She believes that she's looking for light, when she's attracted by shadow, by a somber adventure that's going to swallow her up. When Osmond makes his declaration of love, it's in a place plunged in darkness, with beams of light."[33]

Some critics have complained that such sequences willfully distort James's text. John Carlos Rowe believes that, in her attempts to provide an alternative for Isabel to dominant "heterosexual normativity" (as expressed in the black-and-white honeymoon sequence), Campion has oversimplified Ralph's role by transforming him into a "late nineteenth century decadent or aesthete, bringing to mind such figures of the aesthetic and avant-garde as Lytton Strachey, Oscar Wilde and John Aldington Symonds." When Isabel climbs into bed with him and makes passionate love without intercourse, Rowe complains that he has been forced to "perform the symbolic work of cultural sacrifice for the sake of feminine catharsis."[34] It is debatable whether Ralph endures a "cultural sacrifice" at all, either in the novel or the film. In a 1995 article, Chris Foss argues that on his deathbed in the novel Ralph endeavors to control Isabel by sustaining his idealized vision of her:

> This is why he does not wish her to return to Rome, instead requesting of her, "You must stay here." Indeed, he tells her that no matter what might happen, "for me you'll always be here." In the end he dies refusing to believe she will not return to how he once conceived her to be—he insists she will "grow young again": her "generous mistake" cannot hurt her "for more than a little."[35]

Most of these lines are retained in the screenplay; the fact that Isabel responds in the film by planting passionate kisses on his lips suggests that she has willingly sacrificed herself to him. This seems coherent in terms of Campion's interpretation; Isabel does not seek to repudiate patriarchal authority but to discover ways of experiencing pleasure within it, and thereby feels closer to Ralph than she has ever been before.

While accepting that the film failed to exert mass appeal, I would argue that this adaptation represents a bold attempt to make the cinematic form serve the content—in other words, to provide a narrative that forces the viewer to make connections between apparently disparate elements, and to allow for the presence of multiple, even contradictory, perspectives. The film is characteristic of Campion's work in the sense that it seeks to combine apparent opposites; in subsequent films such as *Holy Smoke* (1999), the narrative marries fantasy and realism so that the central characters Ruth and PJ, having undergone their own tortured and extreme awakenings (like Isabel) become reconciled to compromise. *In the Cut* (2003) incorporates fantasy sequences reminiscent of *The Portrait* as well as concentrating once again on the idea of female masochism. In 1985, Mary Gentile proposed that feminist filmmakers should avoid a cinematic language "that seeks to create meaning by focusing, scheduling, narrowing down a proposed concept" but rather develop a form that "attempts to open out into various directions, to suggest new correlations and interrelations."[36] *The Portrait* is perhaps the first James adaptation to attempt to put this into practice.

Notes

1. Ellen Cheshire, *The Pocket Essential: Jane Campion* (Harpenden, UK: Pocket Essentials, 2000), 75.

2. Karen Michele Chandler, "Agency and Social Constraint in Jane Campion's *The Portrait of a Lady*," *Henry James Review* 18 (1997): 191.

3. Priscilla L. Walton, "Jane and James Go to the Movies: Post Colonial Portraits of a Lady," *Henry James Review* 18 (1997): 188.

4. Nancy Bentley, "Conscious Observation of a Lovely Woman: Jane Campion's *Portrait* in Film," *Henry James Review* 18 (1997): 177. Bentley's, Walton's, and Chandler's essays all appear in a special section of the *Henry James Review* 18 (1997) devoted to the film.

5. Laura Jones, *The Portrait of a Lady: The Screenplay Based on the Novel by Henry James* (Harmondsworth: Penguin Books, 1997), 63–64.

6. Mary C. Gentile, *Film Feminisms: Theory and Practice* (Westport, CT: Greenwood Press, 1985), 72.

7. Henry James, *The Portrait of a Lady* (Harmondsworth: Penguin Books, 1979), 15.

8. James, *Portrait*, 367.

9. James, *Portrait*, 108.

10. James, *Portrait*, 589.

11. James, *Portrait*, 63.

12. James, *Portrait*, 63.

13. James, *Portrait*, 344.

14. Jones, *The Portrait of a Lady: The Screenplay*, 63.

15. The association of the parasol with ideas of possession is nothing new—Billy Wilder uses a similar image in *Sunset Boulevard* (1950), where Norma Desmond (Gloria Swanson) twirls her parasol in front of Jay (William Holden).

16. Jones, *The Portrait of a Lady: The Screenplay*, 84.

17. James, *Portrait*, 68.

18. Jones, *The Portrait of a Lady: The Screenplay*, 8.

19. Production Notes: *The Portrait of a Lady* (Beverly Hills, CA: Gramercy Pictures, 1996), 19.

20. Mary Ann Doane, *The Desire to Desire: The Woman's Film of the 1940s* (Basingstoke: Macmillan Press, 1988), 100.

21. Production Notes, 18.

22. James, *Portrait*, 482–83.

23. Ken Gelder, "Jane Campion and the Limits of Literary Cinema," in *Adaptation: From Text to Screen, Screen to Text*, ed. Deborah Cartmell and Imelda Whelehan (London: Routledge, 1998), 163. Mark Nicholls has suggested that Campion herself relishes female masochism, particularly the fact that Isabel's yearnings for independence remain unsatisfied. This may be true, but only if one identifies "independence" with repudiating the patriarchal order. Mark Nicholls, "She Who Gets Slapped: Jane Campion's *Portrait of a Lady*," *Metro* 111 (August 1997): 43–47.

24. As Linda Williams has proposed, films with scenes of female masochism contain "a strong mixture of passivity and activity, and a bisexual oscillation between the poles of each." Linda Williams, "Film Bodies: Gender, Genre and Excess," in *Feminist Film Theory: A Reader*, ed. Sue Thornham (Edinburgh: Edinburgh University Press, 1999), 278.

25. Philip Horne, "Varieties of Cinematic Experience," in *Henry James on Stage and Screen*, ed. John R. Bradley (London: Palgrave, 2000), 42.

26. Campion's version of this scene may be closer to the novel than critics like Horne might suggest; at one point in the novel, the narrator observes how Isabel makes strenuous efforts to ensure "that her unhappiness should not have come to her through her own fault. She had no near prospect of dying, and yet she *wished to make her peace with the world*—to put her spiritual affairs in order" (James, *Portrait*, 486; italics added). Campion's new scene shows that Isabel is equally capable but on her own terms.

27. A type of printing in which both original and print films are stationary during exposure.

28. James, *Portrait*, 331–32.

29. Michel Ciment, "Voyage to Discover Herself," in *Jane Campion Interviews*, ed. Virginia Wright Wexman (Jackson: University Press of Mississippi, 1999), 180.

30. Ciment, "Voyage," 180.

31. James, *Portrait*, 163–64.

32. Michael Anesko, "The Consciousness on the Cutting Room Floor: Jane Campi-

on's *The Portrait of a Lady*," in *Henry James on Stage and Screen*, ed. John R. Bradley (London: Palgrave, 2000), 181, 184.

33. Ciment, "Voyage," 181.

34. John Carlos Rowe, "For Mature Audiences: Sex, Gender and Recent Film Adaptations of Henry James's Fiction," in *Henry James on Stage and Screen*, ed. John R. Bradley (London: Palgrave, 2000), 201–2.

35. Chris Foss, "Female Innocence as Other in *The Portrait of a Lady* and *What Maisie Knew*: Reassessing the Feminist Recuperation of Henry James," *Essays in Literature*, September 22, 1995, at www.highbeam.com/library/doc3.asp?DOCID = 1P1:28616278& refid = ip_almanac_hf&ctrlInfo = Round9d%3AProd2%3ATYF%3AContinue (accessed January 31, 2004).

36. Gentile, *Film Feminisms*, 71.

CHAPTER SIXTEEN

The Wings
of the Dove (1997)

In a recent article on the publicity campaign for Iain Softley's *The Wings of the Dove* (1997), I showed how Kate Croy (Helena Bonham Carter) was represented as a strong woman—someone who might appeal to contemporary filmgoers, especially in the all-important eighteen-to-thirty-five age group.[1] Softley himself expressed his viewpoint in a "Director's Statement" included in the press book: "How can a person reconcile their heart with their ambitions in a world that puts tremendous pressure on both?"[2] In another interview, he claimed that he was interested in characters like Kate, "who question and discover the world for themselves." James's novel had been deliberately rewritten to accommodate "moments which are similar to our time—a girl coming to her boyfriend's apartment unchaperoned, and lying on the bed, or hidden in a lift in the Underground, where characters can grab each other physically."[3]

Bonham Carter emphasized in another interview that unlike most of her early twentieth-century contemporaries, Kate appeared as someone who might have been portrayed by Bette Davis as "deliciously unsympathetic, but alluring at the same time."[4] In similar vein, the film's screenwriter, Hossein Amini, drew a parallel between *Wings* and women's films of the 1940s. He likened Kate's motives to those of Barbara Stanwyck in *Double Indemnity* (1944) in the sense that both of them put murderous ideas into their lovers' minds in pursuit of material gain.[5] In another article, Amini observed that Kate was "ahead of her time . . . who wants like only a man is allowed to do at that time [the early twentieth century]."[6]

Using these observations as a starting point, this chapter compares *Wings of the Dove* with *The Lost Moment*; both films boast strong women who assume the dominant role in their relationships with men. The heroines are femmes fatales in the sense that they refuse to admit the truth of what they are doing to themselves. Tina Bordereau (Susan Hayward) shuns the realities of her life as a spinster by assuming the identity of her aunt Juliana as a young woman. Kate Croy hides behind cryptic words and phrases, hoping that Merton Densher (Linus Roache) will express her opinions for her. On the other hand, the structure of the two films could not be more different. Hayward's stellar performance in *The Lost Moment* offered women of the late 1940s the prospect of release from accepted gender roles; no longer would they have to be housewives and mothers. This was characteristic of many star vehicles of that period (including *The Heiress*). By contrast, *The Wings of the Dove* associates a strong woman—Bonham Carter's Kate Croy—with immorality and exploitation—someone trapped by the belief that human relationships exist solely for personal and material gain. She is someone to be simultaneously feared yet pitied. Softley's alternative is personified by Milly Theale (Alison Elliott), who believes that most people are fundamentally good and can be rescued so long as their innate qualities are recognized. This version of *Wings* follows Rusty Lemorande's *Turn of the Screw* by advancing the neoconservative view that too much freedom—particularly where women are concerned—causes moral corruption. Softley proposes that both men and women should follow Milly Theale's example by pursuing a celibate existence based on the suppression of one's sexual instincts, rejecting self-gratification and working—if at all possible—for the benefit of others. As John Carlos Rowe remarks, this point of view may have been inspired by the early 1990s apprehensions about "the threats of AIDS and other sexually transmitted diseases."[7]

Kate Croy's personality is revealed in the film's opening moments as she stares directly at the camera—a sequence that recalls the opening of Campion's *Portrait*. Unlike Isabel Archer, however, Kate Croy's intentions remain crystal clear throughout the film as she strives to control those around her.[8] Inspired, perhaps, by James's description of her rendering Densher's "long looks . . . most completely her possession,"[9] Softley shows her putting her arm round the back of Densher's head and ordering him to kiss any woman he chooses to dance with.[10] Later on, Densher climbs the stairs of his lodgings, while Kate waits for him above. This shot leaves us in no doubt as to who dictates this relationship; although Densher protests that he will not go to Venice,[11] we know that he will eventually accede to Kate's request.

Kate treats Milly in much the same way—as shown in a sequence taking place at the Serpentine Gallery (the National Gallery in James's novel), which begins with Kate taking Milly's arm and propelling her towards an erotic portrait by Klimt. Densher follows behind them. The three of them are shown in medium close-up before Softley cuts to a reverse shot of them staring at the canvas. Kate walks out of the left of the frame with a small sigh, leaving the other two staring at one another in embarrassment, as if realizing that they have been the unwitting protagonists in Kate's scheme. The scene concludes with Kate telling Milly that Densher is nothing more than an "old family friend," and staring directly at the camera, as if sharing a confidence with the audience. Meanwhile, Milly looks up at the paintings and smiles faintly—clearly, Kate has persuaded her to "provisionally take everything [that happens] as natural."[12]

Softley has cast Bonham Carter against type in a masculine role. Kate might resemble many of the heroines the actress had hitherto portrayed on screen (e.g., Lucy Honeychurch in Merchant-Ivory's *Room with a View* [1985]), in the sense that she had been trapped and emotionally manipulated by others. However, the character of Kate represented a new departure for Bonham Carter, as the character had, in the actress's words, "a maturity in her, a knowingness, and I was keen to play her with her hair down and not as an ingénue."[13] Kate was not frightened to cross-dress—witness her costume for the carnival in Venice, where she is shown wearing a mustache. Although Martin Gabel's *The Lost Moment* (released exactly half a century earlier) does not go that far, the film is dominated by a strong female personality. This may serve to support Softley's and Amini's claim that their version of *Wings* was inspired as much by 1940s films as James's novel.[14] Tina Bordereau (Susan Hayward) manipulates Louis Venable (Robert Cummings) as she ignores his question about why certain parts of her house are off limits to him, and poses another question instead: "Why are you willing to pay such an extravagant price [for lodging]?" As in *Wings*, Tina's relationship to Venable is summed up by a shot of her standing on the stairs outside her house with Venable looking up as if expecting approval. Even when Tina reveals her human side—as, for example, when she asks Venable, "You do love me, don't you?"—we know that this is part of a performance with Tina as director and leading actor casting herself as the young Juliana and Venable as Jeffrey Ashton (Aspern in James's novella). Tina dominates in the role, dressed in a patterned white frock while playing the piano. Gabel shoots this sequence in a series of close-ups designed to focus attention on her range of facial expressions.

Both Tina and Kate show a reluctance to confront the realities of their lives. In Tina's case, the tendency to retreat into a world of make-believe was perceived as a characteristic response women unable to find male partners in 1940s women's films. Kate Croy in Softley's *Wings* shares Tina's inability to acknowledge her innermost feelings. When Densher asks her how she loves, she refuses to answer the question on the basis that it plays no part in the success or failure of her plans.[15] She is far more preoccupied with Milly's wealth, asking her whether it all belongs to her as soon as she enters the Palazzo Leporello. Milly replies democratically that it does.[16] Later on, Kate tells Densher that "We're all she [Milly] has"; Amini's stage directions emphasize that this remark shows how easily the American girl can be manipulated: "She seems to be telling him something with her eyes, something she doesn't want to say in words."[17] Softley indicates through the repeated use of prison imagery that Kate's scheming constitutes her principal weakness; she is trapped by the belief that people are nothing more than objects of exploitation, both sexually and socially. In the film's opening moments, Kate is seen embracing Densher behind the iron bars of the elevator in the London Underground; she subsequently peeps at him through the gold bars of his bedstead—a shot that recurs later on in the film when she strips naked, prior to getting on top of him. The two of them are simply pale ghosts going through the motions of having sex, like Casanova with his mechanical doll.

The narrator of James's novel implies that Kate and Densher cannot speak plainly either about themselves or others. Towards the end, Densher spends several "private hours of wondering what had become of his sincerity" or whether "he had it all in use."[18] The only remedy, as he sees it, is for both of them to disregard the truth, to "bury in the blindness of each other's arms the knowledge of each other that they couldn't undo."[19] Softley suggests that Kate never had any opportunity to acknowledge her sincerity, having been brought up in a dysfunctional family with a drug-addicted father (Michael Gambon) and headed by the ruthless Aunt Maud (Charlotte Rampling), who treats love as nothing more than a commodity to be bought and sold in exchange for social and financial favors. Maud insists at one point that she will no longer take financial responsibility, either for Kate or her father, if Kate continues to see Densher and rejects a financially advantageous marriage.[20] To emphasize the brutality of her worldview, Softley has her deliver this line in a two-shot as she towers over Kate and grasps her chin as if she were a rag doll.

Kate treats Milly in similar fashion by dragging her into the males-only section of a bookshop and showing her an explicitly pornographic illustration in a Victorian tome—for the sole purpose of showing off her knowledge of sexually explicit material.[21] This sequence recalls Graeme Clifford's *Turn of the Screw*, as Mr. Harley (David Hemmings) insists that his collection of pornographic sculptures should be kept on display at Bly House, even if they may offend the children or the governess. In his opinion, innocence no longer exists; anyone who still believes in it must be a fantasist, just like those who are frightened of ghosts. Kate Croy's view of life in Softley's *Wings* is equally degenerate. Lord Mark (Alex Jennings) observes that behind her pretty eyes there lurks a corrupt nature. Such remarks are delivered in jest, but Kate's nervous smile indicates that they are uncomfortably close to the truth.[22]

Softley's view of an independent single woman is very different from the films of the 1940s. There were heroines such as Daisy Kenyon (Joan Crawford) in the picture of the same name (1947) who repressed their emotions—especially where men were concerned—citing pressure of work as an excuse. Eventually, Daisy is forced to confront the truth about herself as she returns to her husband, Peter (Henry Fonda), at the expense of her lover (Dana Andrews). *The Lost Moment*, like *The Heiress* two years later, challenges the accepted belief that women had to opt for marriage, home, and family in order to survive. On the contrary, Tina demonstrates that she has no need for a lover to experience pleasure; in the closing frames of *The Lost Moment*, she is shown in medium close-up with her eyes closed, as if unable to believe that she is free at last.

The ideal single woman in Softley's *Wings* is personified by Milly Theale (Alison Elliott)—a modern American dream of elegance that contrasts starkly with the corruption of her English friends. We first encounter her at one of Aunt Maud's dinner parties, where her behavior strikes us as direct and spontaneous. When she admits that she has been looking at Kate throughout the meal, the note of yearning is unmistakable.[23] Although taken aback by the explicitness of the picture Kate shows her in the bookshop, Milly's subsequent laughter demonstrates her ability to take a quite unselfconscious pleasure in what she sees. Robin Wood observes that she has the ability to communicate emotion to the audience—something that Kate might interpret as a sign of weakness. As Milly looks down from the parapet of St. Mark's Cathedral in Venice, "[We see her] delight, exhilaration, despair, joy in living combined with full awareness of her condition (mopping throat and face with a handkerchief after her impetuous exertions). Milly looks as if she might just possibly throw herself off, despite her delight in being alive."[24]

This reading of Milly is very different from James's novel, whose narrator warns us against trusting in her too implicitly. Like Isabel Archer in *The Portrait*, she resists any attempts to categorize her socially by behaving in a manner that "wasn't definite or phraseable"[25] and flourishing her public mask "as [she] might have flourished Spanish fans."[26] However, James is often critical of her idealism that (according to Lord Mark) renders her incapable of feeling her losses,[27] and blinds her to Kate's motives in befriending her.

The advantages of trusting in Milly's idealism are further emphasized in Softley's film through the use of visual imagery. At one point, she is seen holding a parasol as she walks with Densher beside the canal in Venice. In Campion's *Portrait*, this image emphasizes Osmond's domination over Isabel (as in the fantasy sequence where a rotating parasol is seen in close-up with Osmond's voice intoning "I'm absolutely in love with you" on the soundtrack). Softley uses it to suggest Milly's serenity as she listens to Merton intently in support of her claim—made the night before—that she believes in him. This "belief" has nothing to do with personal profit, but consists rather of a naïve faith that "everything's going to happen for you, Merton. Sooner than you think."[28]

And things certainly do happen for Densher—for example, in the sequence taking place in the Church of Santa Maria della Salute. Milly begins by looking at all the marble frescoes covered with white covers and work drapes and wonders why no one is working.[29] The two of them subsequently climb up the tower—Milly leading the way—until they reach a cordoned-off room at the top. When they kiss passionately behind the curtains, we see the edge of the fresco behind them, with the angels pointing towards several other frescoes that litter the Venetian scene. This moment not only alludes to Milly's condition (she will soon be joining the angels in heaven) but suggests how she seeks to redeem Densher from a life of materialism and exploitation. Even before they reach the church, Milly has tested Merton's resolve by offering to accompany him to his rooms; Merton refuses.[30] Clearly, he has begun to learn the benefits of restraining his sexual desires.

In a later scene, Densher visits Milly with the intention of persuading her to believe that Kate's intentions remains strictly honorable. Through a series of intercut close-ups, Softley shows how Densher understands that this issue is no longer important, either for himself or Milly; as Milly herself observes, Kate's intentions are simply not important any more.[31] Softley cuts to a close-up of Densher's agonized face, his chin quivering, his eyes cast down as he apologizes in a small voice, as he realizes how inadequate those words are to sum up his feelings at this moment. The violins swell on the soundtrack as Densher buries his face in Milly's lap, while Milly caresses him. Softley cuts to a long shot of the two of them—Milly stretched out on the divan, Densher kneeling before her—while the camera tracks slowly to the left, drawing attention to the ornate decoration of the room. Although this moment may be melancholy in the sense that this is the last time Densher will see Milly, it nonetheless reveals how he tried to compensate for the follies of his past life by kneeling before her in an act of symbolic worship.

Softley's treatment of Milly Theale and Kate Croy as angel and monster implies a view of femininity that, as Sandra M. Gilbert and Susan Gubar observed as long ago as 1979, not only constitutes a major literary tradition but forms a strategy by which men limit women's capacity for self-expression: "[They] attempt to enclose her in definitions of her person and her potential which, by reducing her to extreme stereotypes (angel, monster) drastically conflict with her own sense of her self—that is, of her subjectivity, her autonomy, her creativity."[32]

By contrast, James's novel depicts Densher's attempts to control Milly and Kate as ultimately futile. He forces Kate to accept a bargain whereby he will stay in Venice so long as she visits his rooms "on your honour."[33] Once she agrees (albeit reluctantly), Densher experiences a sharp pleasure, "too sharp for mere sweetness—at the vividness with which he saw himself master of the conflict."[34] By the end of the novel, however, this sense of mastery has been transformed into overwhelming guilt; Densher remains "a haunted man"[35]—haunted by the awareness that he was not only complicit in the plan to destroy Milly but sought to limit Kate's freedom of movement as a condition for participating in that plan.

Why should this alteration to the novel have been introduced? One reason may be that Softley endorses Milly's life of celibacy. The original printed screenplay ends with a barge carrying Milly's coffin moving through the water like an arrow. Densher's voice can be heard off-screen speaking the lines: "My heart is sore pained within me, And the terrors of death are fallen upon me, Fearfulness and trembling are come upon me, and horror hath overwhelmed me. And I said, Oh that I had wings like a dove, for then I would fly away, and be at rest."[36]

Clearly, he is haunted by the belief that he will never be at peace, having been involved in Kate's plan to acquire Milly's wealth. In the finished film, Softley creates an entirely new ending, as Densher arrives in Venice by gondola and walks away from the camera. On the soundtrack, Milly's voice can be heard repeating the phrases "I believe in you. I just do. I have a good feeling. I think everything's going to happen for you, Merton." However, this statement is paradoxical in the sense that everything will only happen for Densher as long as he keeps his sexual instincts under control. The same certainly cannot be said for Kate, whose way of life—based on unrestrained freedom of expression—is equated with corruption.[37] Although this message may strike a chord with those concerned about the threat of sexually transmitted diseases such as AIDS, it is nonetheless neoconservative in the way it casts women as either angels or whores.

On the other hand, Softley's revised ending is clearly designed to appeal to mass audiences whose general preference tends towards melodrama rather than faithful literary adaptations.[38] Christine Gledhill argues that one of the characteristics of the melodrama genre that distinguishes it from others is its tendency to render interior psychology in terms of external signs—bodily gesture, dress, or environment and setting. This leads to an anthropomorphic use of setting, lighting, and other theatrical devices, and to a rhetorical, hyperbolic use of language, music, and sound effects, in which speech becomes gestural and kinetic rather than intellectual and analytic. Characters become agents of causality through the externalization of personality in action.[39] Softley's *Wings* draws on such conventions in the closing moments. In the penultimate scene, Densher and Kate have passionless sex in a room lit by harsh gray light with the rain pouring down outside. Clearly, their lives are as grimy as the apartment they inhabit. By contrast, we are invited to share Milly's "good feeling" as we watch Densher in Venice walking away from the camera, to the accompaniment of the sound of water splashing against the canal bank and a closing theme (by Edward Shearmuir) played on woodwind, piano, and violin.

Softley and Amini fulfilled their task admirably; unlike Campion's *Portrait* (which failed at the box office), *The Wings of the Dove* was a notable critical and box-office success. The film was selected for the Royal Film Performance in London of 1997 and subsequently received four Oscar nominations for Best Actress (Bonham Carter), Best Adapted Screenplay, Best Cinematography, and Best Costumes (winning none of them).[40] For the first time, a James adaptation opened to what Helena Bonham Carter described as "fantastic business" in New York, taking over $12 million in its first three months. The U.K. release was equally popular; after two months the gross topped £2 million.[41] However, the film pays a price for its success, as its view of gender relations represents a throwback to the 1940s, rather than being up-to-date as Softley and Amini claimed in their publicity interviews. Mary Ann Doane suggests that several "women's pictures" of that period portrayed female desire as nourished by an overactive imagination. If such desires are allowed to flourish, then the woman has to die or be cast out in order for the patriarchy to reassert its authority.[42] Softley puts forward a similar scenario in *Wings*: Kate Croy's desires have been unrestricted for too long, and thus she needs to be "punished" by being eliminated from the film's ending. If *The Lost Moment* depicts the female central character acquiring an inner strength that enables her to break free of patriarchal control, *Wings of the Dove* represents the other side of the coin as the patriarchy (represented, in this case, by the male director) takes revenge on an independent woman.

Notes

1. Laurence Raw, "Making Meaning: Publicizing Iain Softley's *The Wings of the Dove* (1997)," *Literature Film Quarterly* 32, no. 3 (2004): 175–76.

2. Press book: *The Wings of the Dove* (Los Angeles: Miramax Films / Renaissance Dove, 1997), 13.

3. Nick Hasted, "The Wings of the Dove," *Independent* (London), January 2, 1998, 6.

4. Press book, *The Wings of the Dove*, 23.

5. Hossein Amini, "Introduction" in *Henry James' The Wings of the Dove—A Screenplay* (London: Methuen Film, 1998), vii. Cf. Richard Williams's review of the film in *The Guardian*: "[Kate and Densher] could be . . . well, who? Bogart and Gloria Grahame, perhaps, in Nick Ray's *In a Lonely Place*. Or Mitchum and Jean Simmons in Preminger's *Angel Face*." Richard Williams, "Sex and Sensibility," *The Guardian*, January 2, 1998, sec. 2, 4–5).

6. Hossein Amini, "Adapting *The Wings of the Dove*," *Scenario* 3, no. 3 (1997): 201. This film had troubled origins. Originally it was to be produced by Bridgewater Films as a vehicle for Uma Thurman (who would later star in James Ivory's *The Golden Bowl*) with Alastair Reid as director and Rufus Sewell, Polly Walker, and Fiona Shaw in the cast. Thurman withdrew, and Ralph Fiennes was subsequently slated for the role of Densher, while Reid was replaced by Iain Softley. Bridgewater Films sold the rights to Renaissance Films (who had previously made such hits as *Henry V* and *Much Ado*, both starring Kenneth Branagh), who themselves struck a deal with Miramax Films to provide a version of *Wings* that would appeal to the market for more cerebral, "adult" costume dramas (like Anthony Minghella's *The English Patient*). For the origins of *Wings*, see *Screen International*, no. 934 (October 15–21, 1993), no. 979 (October 14–20, 1994), no. 1029 (October 13–19, 1995), and no. 1125 (September 12–18, 1997). For the announcement of the original production of *Wings*, see Baz Bamigboye, "De Niro and Uma Put Love Tryst before a Film Date," *Daily Mail* (London), March 4, 1994, 33.

7. John Carlos Rowe, "For Mature Audiences: Sex, Gender and Recent Film Adaptations of Henry James's Fiction," in *Henry James on Stage and Screen*, ed. John R. Bradley (London: Palgrave, 2000), 202.

8. Alan Nadel complains that this is characteristic of a film that "reduces the problem

of Milly Theale to simple melodrama. . . . Softley removes James's murkiness, giving the plot the crispness of a 1930s melodrama or a 1950s soap opera." Alan Nadel, "Ambassadors from an Imaginary 'Elsewhere:' Cinematic Convention and the Jamesian Sensibility," in *Henry James Goes to the Movies*, ed. Susan M. Griffin (Lexington: University Press of Kentucky, 2002), 203.

9. Henry James, *The Wings of the Dove*, ed. John Bayley with notes by Patricia Crick (Harmondsworth: Penguin Books, 1986), 94.

10. Hossein Amini, *Henry James' The Wings of the Dove: A Screenplay* (London: Methuen Film, 1998), 25. There are in fact two versions of the published screenplay. The first (based on a 1995 draft) was published in *Scenario* 3, no. 3 (1997): 7–46. The second draft was published by Methuen in 1998. All references to the screenplay in this chapter are to the Methuen version.

11. Amini, *Henry James' The Wings of the Dove: A Screenplay*, 38.

12. James, *Wings*, 243. The gallery scene does not appear in the published screenplay; instead Amini has Milly and Kate visiting a photography shop in an antique market, and encountering Merton by chance. The three of them subsequently go to a coffee shop, where Densher looks at some photographs taken of Milly lying on a chaise longue. The two of them laugh nervously, before Densher leaves for work; the scene concludes with Kate and Milly laughing as Kate says Densher is nothing more than "a friend" while Milly raises an eyebrow (Amini, *Henry James' The Wings of the Dove: A Screenplay*, 28–31). The finished film shows Milly making no response to Kate's comment.

13. Matt Wolf, "In Time for Uncle Oscar," *The Times* (London), December 22, 1997, 14.

14. Amini wrote in the published screenplay that he had focused on "the love triangle [in the novel] at the expense of the minor characters" and "changed the order of certain events so that the audience would follow the story like a thriller, rather than be ahead of it as James had intended" (Amini, *Henry James' The Wings of the Dove: A Screenplay*, viii).

15. Amini, *Henry James' The Wings of the Dove: A Screenplay*, 61. This is very different from the novel, where Kate insists to Densher that she is telling "the proper lie" all the time, to ensure the success of her plan. At heart, however, she is "the most honest woman in the world" (James, *Wings*, 294).

16. Amini, *Henry James' The Wings of the Dove: A Screenplay*, 42. The printed screenplay adopts a rather idiosyncratic approach to the characters' names, calling Milly "Millie" and Aunt Maud "Maude." I follow the spellings given in James's text.

17. Amini, *Henry James' The Wings of the Dove: A Screenplay*, 53.

18. James, *Wings*, 464.

19. James, *Wings*, 500.

20. This sequence does not exist in Amini's published screenplay.

21. The published screenplay writes this scene differently, with Kate translating a pornographic passage from French into English. The owner looks disapprovingly at her, whereupon she picks another book off the shelf containing photographs of naked men

and women in the guise of Greek gods. Amini, *Henry James' The Wings of the Dove: A Screenplay*, 20–21.

22. Amini, *Henry James' The Wings of the Dove: A Screenplay*, 21–22.

23. The printed screenplay gives this line to Kate, which prompts Milly to smile shyly (Amini, *Henry James' The Wings of the Dove: A Screenplay*, 17).

24. Robin Wood, *The Wings of the Dove* (London: BFI Publications, 1999), 67–8.

25. James, *Wings*, 243.

26. James, *Wings*, 339.

27. James, *Wings*, 157.

28. Amini, *Henry James' The Wings of the Dove: A Screenplay*, 64. Marcia Ian complains that Milly must be a "dumb bunny" to utter these words in front of a man who possesses both belief and passion. If Softley and Amini are naïve enough to believe that this "good feeling" represents redemption for Densher, then perhaps they have not understood James's novel, in which "belief does not signify amity or romantic credulity, but a different, more tangible type of credit; belief means money." Marcia Ian, "How to Do Things with Words: Making Language Immaterial in *The Wings of the Dove*," in *Henry James on Stage and Screen*, ed. John R. Bradley (London: Palgrave, 2000), 218. This may be true, but fails to acknowledge the moral scheme that the adaptors have introduced into the film, which is very different from the novel.

29. Amini, *Henry James' The Wings of the Dove: A Screenplay*, 68.

30. Amini, *Henry James' The Wings of the Dove: A Screenplay*, 65.

31. Amini, *Henry James' The Wings of the Dove: A Screenplay*, 77.

32. Sandra M. Gilbert and Susan Gubar, "Infection in the Sentence: The Woman Writer and the Anxiety of Authorship" (1979), in *Feminisms: An Anthology of Literary Theory and Criticism*, ed. Robyn R. Warhol and Diane Price Herndl (New Brunswick, NJ: Rutgers University Press, 1997), 23.

33. James, *Wings*, 397.

34. James, *Wings*, 398.

35. James, *Wings*, 469.

36. Amini, *Henry James' The Wings of the Dove: A Screenplay*, 82. The version of *Wings* published in *Scenario* omits this passage.

37. Dianne F. Sadoff takes a completely opposite view, arguing that Softley has created a cross "between soft-core porn and indie film [that] finally, recalls the history of pornography's emergence and its eventual move into the mainstream." Dianne F. Sadoff, "Hallucinations of Intimacy: The Henry James Films," in *Henry James Goes to the Movies*, ed. Susan M. Griffin (Lexington: University Press of Kentucky, 2002), 273.

38. Mark Eaton, "Henry James Films as Middle-Brow Culture," in *Henry James on Stage and Screen*, ed. John R. Bradley (London: Palgrave, 2000), 172–73.

39. Christine Gledhill, "Between Melodrama and Realism," in *Hollywood Narrative: The Paradigm Wars*, ed. Jane Gaines (Durham: Duke University Press, 1992), 140.

40. For the record, Best Actress went to Gwyneth Paltrow (*Shakespeare in Love*) and Best Adapted Screenplay to Bill Condon (*Gods and Monsters*).

41. Statistics from *Screen International* no. 1132 (February 21–28, 1998). The U.S. box office totaled $13.7 million, nearly four times that of *Portrait of a Lady* ($3.7 million) and seven times that of Agnieszka Holland's *Washington Square* ($1.7 million).

42. Mary Ann Doane, *The Desire to Desire: The Woman's Film of the 1940s* (Basingstoke: Macmillan Press, 1988), 117–18.

CHAPTER SEVENTEEN

~

Under Heaven (1998)

In an essay from the anthology *Henry James Goes to the Movies* (2002), Marc Bousquet argues that Softley's *Wings of the Dove* specifically appealed to Gen X filmgoers in its portrayal of a generational struggle and generation-specific exploitation. Both Linus Roache's Merton Densher and Helena Bonham Carter's Kate Croy

> belong to a generation whose parents have consumed their future and expect to be supported in self-gratifying profligacy by their children. The parents . . . have colonized the idea of youth . . . which accounts for the special repugnance and sense of violation that the Gen X audience feels when the aging bohemian Lionel Croy [Michael Gambon] suggests to his daughter, "We're the same, you and I."[1]

Characters like Densher "produce distinction in all senses (beauty, categorical knowledge, social differentiation), but members of the dominant class . . . enjoy the product of their labor."[2] This thesis might be challenged on two counts: First, it fails to acknowledge the fact that the film was received very differently in different contexts. Whereas it certainly might have struck a chord with Gen X filmgoers in the United States, in Great Britain it was still perceived on its initial release as an example of so-called heritage cinema (with the added spice of nude scenes). Geoff Brown of the London *Times* observed that "He [Softley] and his adapter Hossein Amini raise the sex quotient, and allow late-20th century fears and frustrations to penetrate the characters' heads."[3] Secondly, I think one has to take into account the statements made by Softley and Amini in press interviews concerning the film's portrayal of Kate Croy as a woman ahead of her time. Far from having her future consumed by her father, she is someone who believes in questioning and discovering the world for herself—to such an extent that she represents a threat to the established patriarchal order. This issue was explored earlier in chapter 16.

What is certain, however, is that 1998 witnessed the appearance of a specifically Gen X interpretation of *The Wings of the Dove: Under Heaven*, directed by Meg Richman. The small independent production deliberately adopts a Gen X view of filmmaking by rejecting the traditional conventions associated with a mainstream classical adaptation (for example, elaborate sets and costumes), and instead resituates James's novel in the swirling, confused world of contemporary Seattle—the center of the Pacific Northwest culture that produced grunge, which William Strauss argues was "the first Generation X-produced and consumed music."[4] The story features a young waitress, Cynthia (Molly Parker), and her dropout boyfriend, Buck (Aden Young), in the roles of Kate and Densher. Cynthia leaves her job to become the live-in companion of a wealthy young woman, Eleanor (Joely Richardson), who is dying of cancer. Eventually, Cynthia persuades Eleanor to engage Buck as the gardener; Eleanor's subsequent crush on Buck leads to a three-way love affair. In this chapter, I begin by analyzing the way in which the film rewrites James's novel to incorporate Gen X values, focusing in particular on a lack of faith in institutions such as marriage, the nuclear family, or orthodox religion, a disillusion brought about by unemployment or financial hardship, and a desire to reject the traditional values and linear reasoning of the dominant culture.[5] I subsequently demonstrate that, unlike Softley's version, *Under Heaven* hints at the possibility of complex affection between the three main characters; both Eleanor and Cynthia are attracted to one another as well as to Buck. Through this strategy, Richman allows for the creation of sexual and gender identities based not on social conditioning but on individual choice. This is especially evident at the end of the film when Buck and Eleanor vow to love one another eternally (in a scene very reminiscent of the earliest James adaptations [such as *Berkeley Square*]) while Cynthia, having been spurned by both of them, invites her mother and three sisters to live with her in Eleanor's old house. One may pursue a solitary existence (sustained only by memories of past romances) or one may opt instead for a Gen X–inspired rethinking of family life as a unit characterized by shifting roles, involving two or more people who may or may not be married and who might also be members of the same sex.[6] This is in stark contrast to the idea of the nuclear family that nurtured previous generations in America—and that still predominates in many mainstream Hollywood products.

The Gen X way of looking at the world was well expressed in Douglas

Coupland's 1991 novel, *Generation X*: "We live small lives on the periphery; we are marginalized and there's a great deal in which we choose not to participate."[7] Coupland continues, "There invariably comes a certain point where our youth fails us; where college fails us; where Mom and Dad fail us. . . . My crisis wasn't just the failure of youth but also a failure of class and of sex and the future and I still don't know what. . . . The point of all this was that I reached a clean slate with no one to read it. I needed to drop out even further."[8] "Dropping out" in this sense had little or nothing to do with experimentation and protest or pursuing a life of sex, drugs, and rock 'n' roll (as in the 1960s and 1970s) but rather maintaining a cynical, detached perspective, with little conviction about the future of institutions such as government, church, or the family. This should come as no surprise; the Gen X worldview was shaped by a society whose divorce rates rose from 10 percent in 1950 to almost 20 percent in 1980. Such things as a close-knit family life seemed a thing of the past. One character in Coupland's novel reminisces about the time when his family decided to abandon the nuclear model "and the shimmering but untrue promise it made to us. This is the year we decided to call it quits, normality-wise; the year we went the way families just *do*, the year everyone finally decided to be *themselves* and to hell with it." He has no memory of "being hugged by a parental unit. . . . No, I think *psychic dodge ball* would probably better define our family dynamic."[9] Another character remarks, "You know, I really think that when God puts together families, he sticks his finger into the white pages and selects a group of people at random and then says to them all, 'Hey! You're going to spend the next seventy years together even though you have nothing in common and don't even *like* each other."[10]

Career prospects for the majority of Gen Xers seemed equally unattractive; most college graduates took menial jobs with little or no prospect of advancement. Coupland describes this kind of occupation as a "McJob—a low pay, low prestige, low-dignity, low-benefit, no-future job in the service sector. Frequently considered a satisfying career choice by people who have never held one."[11] The Gen X outlook can be summarized as a "sad Everyplace where citizens are always getting fired from their jobs at 7-Eleven and where the kids do drugs and practice the latest dance crazes at the local lake, where they also fantasize about being adult and pulling welfare-check scams as they inspect each other's skin for chemical burns from the lake water."[12] But this does not mean that Gen Xers are simply angry and pessimistic; on the contrary, they retain a sense of humor and self-respect about their own sad plights. Moreover, they can understand how society's ills could be cured, if there were sufficient inspiration at the grassroots level.[13] This is especially important if we are to understand the significance of what happens at the end of *Under Heaven*.

The world of James's *Wings of the Dove* is populated by characters sharing the same jaundiced view of life. Kate Croy has little faith in anything—especially her family, whose life is likened to "some fine florid voluminous phrase, say even a musical, that dropped first into words and notes without sense and then, hanging unfinished, into no words or any notes at all." The narrator speculates on why the family members—Kate's father, her sister, her two lost brothers, as well as Kate herself—should have started out "with such an air of being equipped for a profitable journey," only to break down "without an accident, to stretch themselves in the wayside dust without a reason?"[14] Kate believes that this breakdown owes a lot to her father's self-interest as she looks at him and muses, "She felt afresh, and with the memory of their old despair, the despair at home, how little his appearance ever by any chance told about him. . . . If he [Lionel] recognized his younger daughter's happy aspect as a tangible value, he had from the first still more exactly appraised every point of his own."[15] With no one to offer her a way forward, Kate believes that her future "put on a bareness that already gave her something in common with the Condrips."[16] She is a product of a fin-de-siècle world—encompassing both England and Italy—which in Densher's view seems to be overflowing with people "huddled, stranded and wageless, bored and cynical, under archways and bridges."[17]

In *Under Heaven*, Meg Richman shifts the *Wings* plot to Seattle and renames the three principal protagonists: Kate Croy becomes Cynthia, a young waitress; Merton Densher, Buck, a feckless drifter addicted to drugs and alcohol; and Milly Theale is transformed into Eleanor, a wealthy ex-teacher. Their family lives appear equally as unrewarding as in the novel. Cynthia's mother (Krisha Fairchild) married four husbands, all of them alcoholics; she cynically remarks that the entire town seems to be populated by alcoholics. Although Cynthia loves her mother, she remains convinced that being poor is not the life to follow. But perhaps being rich is not much better; despite her privileged upbringing, Eleanor never knew her mother and father and was brought up by her grandparents, who sent her away to boarding school when she was still a child. Although we know nothing about Buck's background, it is obvious that the only "family" he really trusts are his close friends. If Cynthia should leave him, he believes that he would be "decapitated in shit." Eleanor likewise treats Buck and Cynthia as her family as she yearns for the occasion when money worries might no longer plague them.

All three characters share the Gen Xers' sense of disillusion, with little faith either in themselves or their futures. Buck cannot see himself conforming to the traditional male role in a capitalist society of breadwinner; he believes that he is such a loser that the only solution for him is to go out and get drunk. Cynthia feels much the same about his lack of "maleness"; at one point during a hallucination—brought on by drinking too much cough syrup—she imagines God telling her that he will never become a man and that she should therefore stay with him. Cynthia's life has been equally difficult; having failed to complete a university course, she has eked out an existence in a series of McJobs (to use Coupland's term) in the service sector. Nor is there much hope of relief; at one point, Cynthia and Buck are shown making love in Eleanor's bedroom behind a metal bedstead, suggesting confinement.[18]

Although Eleanor likes to believe in the present, she is nonetheless painfully aware that cancer has already dictated her future, and that no one can change it. Richman emphasizes her sense of loneliness at this moment by framing her in medium close-up, as she stares moodily to the right of the camera.

By comparison with Softley's *Wings*, Richman's version seems more pessimistic, as she suggests that all three main characters are victims of circumstance. The novel's positive aspects—for example, Kate's attempts to free herself from her patriarchal society and its expectations of her or Densher's and Milly's naïve belief in idealism—appear to have been expunged—no one believes in the possibility of changing the future in any way, shape, or form. This is emphasized in Marc Olsen's grunge-inspired soundtrack, which includes songs with titles like "No Surprise," "Reckless," and "Never Seen Beauty." One number, "First Cut," accompanies a sequence of extended close-ups where Cynthia, having found out that Buck is in love with Eleanor, mutilates herself with a hatpin and subsequently tries to commit suicide with a mixture of vodka and sleeping pills. The "cut" is both mental and physical: Cynthia has been injured by the person she once considered closest to her, which prompts her to cause injury to herself. Such drastic action would have been anathema to the Kate Croy of James's novel and Softley's film. Softley himself described her as someone combining "a childlike vulnerability" and "a womanly sexuality."[19] Although Kate is clearly insecure as she implores her father to stand by her ("We won't worry in advance about how or where; we'll have a faith and find a way"), she nonetheless takes to heart his exhortation to be "as bold as [she] like[s]" and not rely on others for advice.[20] It was this capacity for self-determination that persuaded Softley to film the novel in the first place; he suggested in another interview that Kate resembled the "classic heroine trying to change the hand fate has dealt her by manipulating the situation."[21]

Yet Richman's Cynthia is not as nihilistic as she might initially appear. As the story unfolds in the idyllic surroundings of Eleanor's mansion, she discovers how to change her life by embracing the idea of carpe diem—enjoying the pleasures of the moment without concern for the future. In two lengthy sequences, Cynthia and Eleanor are shown preparing and subsequently eating their evening meal. Richman's camera work (comprising repeated close-ups and two-shots) stresses the close relationship developing between them as they shift from lighthearted topics such as edible underwear to more serious issues such as the possibility of Cynthia helping Eleanor to commit suicide. Silences assume more significance than words as Eleanor stares into Cynthia's eyes and informs her that she will not ask for help unless she needs it, taking a long pause between the words "ask" and "unless." Cynthia responds by looking nervously down at her dinner plate and toying with her food. Clearly, some kind of physical attraction exists between the two of them. This represents some kind of awakening—especially for Cynthia, who experiences for the first time the transgressive pleasure offered by alternative sexualities.[22]

Like Cynthia, Eleanor finds herself equally attracted to women *and* men. In a later sequence, she accepts Buck's offer to listen to grunge for the first time, and admits that it is more pleasant than she had anticipated. Buck asks her to dance; she accepts, and the two of them gyrate slowly in front of the fireplace, their eyes fixed on one another. In other James adaptations—for example, Cellan Jones's or Campion's versions of *The Portrait of a Lady*—dances form the centerpiece of a social occasion, an opportunity for people to see and be seen in the search for suitable marriage partners. By contrast, Richman stages the dance as a private moment where Buck and Eleanor fall in love, although neither of them had foreseen it. Susan Wendell observes that women with disabilities or those who have undergone serious operations are "othered" in the sense that they are viewed "as symbolic of something else—usually, but not always, something we reject and fear. . . . [They] symbolize, among other things, imperfection . . . and everyone's vulnerability to weakness, pain and death."[23] The same process of "othering" on the grounds of "imperfection" can also be applied to any man lacking those qualities conventionally deemed masculine—independence, rationality, assertiveness, physical strength, and protectiveness. By presenting Eleanor and Buck as subjects rather than objects of our experience (with whom we might identify), Richman underlines how restrictive such classifications can be. Anyone can fall in love if he or she is given the opportunity to do so. This is clearly illustrated in a later sequence when the two of them are discovered in bed. Initially, Eleanor reacts according to her social conditioning, by refusing to show off her mastectomy scars in the belief that these are what render her an "imperfect" woman; Buck responds by admitting that, as someone who has likewise been regarded as a social misfit, such scruples have little importance for him. At last, Eleanor has found someone prepared to treat her on her own terms rather than as a cancer victim; she responds by taking her top off and letting Buck run his hands over her scars.

John Bayley suggests that James was preoccupied with the idea of consciousness, which he likened to the "secret converse of lovers"—in other words, a form of discourse characterized by contradiction and complication. This is especially evident in his depiction of the central love triangle of *Wings* involving Kate, Milly, and Densher; all three of them share a "special and personal intimacy."[24] *Under Heaven* demonstrates how the characters' shared experiences of adversity—illness, unemployment, or an unstable family life—helps them create this "secret converse," offering them alternative ways of living that challenge conventional constructions of the family and/or gender roles. Neither Eleanor nor Buck desires a civil marriage ceremony; they prefer to create one of their own in the garden Buck has created especially for the dying woman. This small area of flowers and shrubs assumes an Edenic quality for both of them, a place of refuge where established social rituals no longer have any significance. Eleanor dies in Buck's arms while looking at the flowers, murmuring under her breath that she thinks she will meet him in the afterlife. Buck concurs; as he speaks, Richman cuts to a pan of the entire garden, with the two of them in the center of the frame. On the soundtrack a song can be heard likening Eleanor to an angel flying up to heaven.[25] The tone of this sequence is unashamedly sentimental—reminiscent of the earliest James adaptations such as *Berkeley Square* (1933), where Peter Standish (Leslie Howard) and Helen Pettigrew (Heather Angel) vow to meet again "not in my time, not in your time, but in God's." The film's tone has utterly changed; whereas it began pessimistically, its ending introduces a note of optimism that is absent from James's text. One reviewer criticized Richman for introducing such "sugary sweetness" into such an "emotionally and sexually convoluted" tale: "That Buck, who customarily brought home dinner by shoplifting, should suddenly develop a conscience at the end of the film seems a bit farfetched."[26] This criticism is certainly justified, but if we approach Richman's script on its own terms, perhaps both

Buck and Eleanor deserve to experience life's "sugary sweetness," having overcome the social constraints that hitherto had condemned them to the margins of society. Their affair leaves open the possibility that life's so-called misfits might have experiences as good as or even better than those who pursue conformity.

Cynthia achieves a similar kind of fulfillment as she inherits Eleanor's house and sets up a commune for her mother and three sisters, designed to repudiate the prevailing organizational strategy of domination that customarily excludes or marginalizes women. Her mother observes that she never believed they would experience this kind of life in which Cynthia (who always wanted to be a princess when she grew up) can experience freedom of expression without having to seek male approval. Their existence is based on mutual trust rather than competition; a transformational organizing principle through which women of different generations are linked together to accomplish what none of them can separately—to achieve a stable family unit. Henceforth, they can set up home in a way that suits them.[27]

To the majority of journalists in mainstream media, Gen Xers have frequently been identified with slackers. Reviewing Douglas Coupland's novel *Girlfriend in a Coma* (1998), Laura Miller complained in the *New York Times* that, while the main characters enjoyed a comfortable life, they were "still not satisfied" with a world dedicated to "empty confidence and workaholic 'efficiency.'" Rather than working themselves, they preferred to stand apart from the world and pontificate on its shortcomings.[28] *Under Heaven* suggests that the Gen X view of the world has little or nothing to do with being work shy; rather, it seeks to run counter to conventional wisdom on the family, sex, and gender. Geoffrey T. Holtz's book *Welcome to the Jungle*, which focuses explicitly on Gen X (or, as he terms it, "Free Generation") values, suggests that this is characteristic of a generation that grew up "in a world that offers more choices than have ever before been available. . . . With the breakdown of many gender-based traditions and racial stereotypes, we enjoy a much broader ranger [sic] of lifestyle and career choices than any generation which preceded us."[29] For the Gen Xer, established traditions are identified with corruption or exclusion: Cynthia believes her life has been ruined, Buck considers himself "unmanly" because he cannot fulfill the role of breadwinner, while Eleanor is automatically marginalized by society on account of her illness. Instead, the three main characters reorder their priorities and relationships, and in the process discover new ways of living based on individual choice and community rather than domination. In many ways, their outlook on life could be deemed postmodern on three distinct counts: first, that they value feelings and relationships rather than logic and reason; second, that they believe in the importance of community and/or sticking together (as compared to modernists who compartmentalized knowledge and exalted the individual); and third, because they seek to deconstruct the categories through which we understand our world, and thereby call attention to how these constructions are used to marginalize certain individuals.[30] That Richman should have chosen *Wings* for this kind of treatment seems particularly apt; although the endings of the two works are very different, James is preoccupied with showing how the "masculine-realist" approach to life (based on power and domination) embodied by Kate is gradually superseded by Milly Theale's radically inconclusive *écriture feminine*, as she finally manages to convert Densher to her way of thinking. Like many other adaptations appearing at the same time—notably Agnieszka Holland's *Washington Square*, and Paul Unwin's *American*—Richman recasts the Jamesian text to offer a way forward for audiences—an invitation to strike out on one's own and discover a life for oneself rather than following the example of one's peers, either within the family or within society at large.[31]

Notes

1. Marc Bousquet, "Cultural Capitalism and the 'James Formation,'" in *Henry James Goes to the Movies*, ed. Susan M. Griffin (Lexington: University Press of Kentucky, 2002), 228.

2. Bousquet, "Cultural Capitalism," 230.

3. Geoff Brown, "Nasty Bugs but Nastier People," *The Times* (London), January 1, 1998, 29.

4. Quoted in Gemma Tarlach, "Out: Ten Years after Cobain, Can Grunge Speak to Spirit of a Generation?" *Milwaukee Journal Sentinel*, April 8, 2004, 16.

5. Douglas Rushkoff, *The GenX Reader* (New York: Ballantine Books, 1994), 6.

6. Karen Ritchie, *Marketing to Generation X* (New York: Lexington Books, 1995), 42–43.

7. Douglas Coupland, *Generation X: Tales for an Accelerated Culture* (New York: St. Martin's Press, 1991), 11.

8. Coupland, *Generation X*, 30–31.

9. Coupland, *Generation X*, 134.

10. Coupland, *Generation X*, 36.

11. Coupland, *Generation X*, 5.

12. Coupland, *Generation X*, 39.

13. Rushkoff, *The GenX Reader*, 8.

14. Henry James, *The Wings of the Dove*, ed. John Bayley with notes by Patricia Crick (Harmondsworth: Penguin Books, 1986), 56.

15. James, *Wings*, 61.

16. James, *Wings*, 83.

17. James, *Wings*, 415.

18. The same shot also occurs at the end of Softley's *Wings*, when Densher and Kate meet in Densher's apartment following Milly's death, and vow to remain "as we were" (James, *Wings*, 509).

19. "Seven Questions with Iain Softley, the Director of 'The Wings of the Dove,'" 1997, at www.indiewire.com/people/int_Softley_Iain_971120.html (accessed September 30, 2005).

20. James, *Wings*, 68–69.

21. "About the Production: Iain Softley and Hossein Amini Approach the Novel," in Press book: *The Wings of the Dove* (London: Miramax Films and Renaissance Dove, 1997), 14.

22. More than one reviewer of *Under Heaven* noted the physical resemblance between Joely Richardson (as Eleanor) and her mother Vanessa Redgrave. Ruthe Stein, "Under Heaven: Love Triangle Focuses on Fatal Patient," *San Francisco Chronicle*, June 26, 1998, at www.sfgate.com/cgi-bin/article.cgi?f=/c/a/1998/06/26/DD54053.DTL (accessed December 24, 2005). I would suggest that the similarity is particularly evident in this scene, when compared with Redgrave's performance as Olive Chancellor in her exchanges with Verena Tarrant (Madeleine Potter) in Ivory's *Bostonians*. Hugh Stevens suggests that the notion of queerness as a transgressive homoerotic passion that is simultaneously "highly private [and] heroic" was evident in most of James's work, from the early fiction onwards. Hugh Stevens, "Queer Henry *In the Cage*," in *The Cambridge Companion to Henry James*, ed. Jonathan Freedman (Cambridge: Cambridge University Press, 1988), 124.

23. Susan Wendell, "Women and Disability," in *Encyclopedia of Feminist Theories*, ed. Lorraine Code (London: Routledge, 2000), 138.

24. John Bayley, "Introduction," in Henry James, *The Wings of the Dove* (Harmondsworth: Penguin Books, 1986), 8–9.

25. Richman alludes to this moment in the final scene, where Buck touches a locket given to him by Eleanor just before she died, which now hangs from the rear-view mirror of his truck.

26. Barbara Shulgasser, "Under Heaven: Bad Copy of 'Wings of the Dove.'" *San Francisco Examiner*, June 26, 1998, at www.sfgate.com/cgi-bin/article.cgi?f=/e/a/1998/06/26/WEEKEND3821.dtl (accessed December 24, 2005).

27. Luce Irigaray, "Women-amongst-Themselves: Creating a Woman-to-Woman Sociality," in *The Irigaray Reader*, ed. Margaret Whitford (Oxford: Basil Blackwell, 1991), 190–97.

28. Laura Miller, Review of Douglas Coupland, *Girlfriend in a Coma*, *New York Times*, April 12, 1998, sec. 7, 9.

29. Geoffrey T. Holtz, *Welcome to the Jungle: The Why behind Generation X* (New York: St. Martins Griffin, 1995), 3.

30. Mark Tittley, "Generation X Papers: The Postmodern Generation," at www.to morrowtoday.biz/generations/xpaper1005.htm (accessed October 2, 2005).

31. Unfortunately, very few filmgoers actually got to see the film. Made on a shoestring budget by the independent company Banner Entertainment, it was shown at the Sundance Festival of 1998, and subsequently received a limited theatrical release in art-house cinemas on the west and east coasts of the United States. It was sold to cable television and video; Richman herself made very little money out of the film, and it did not enhance her reputation.

~

CHAPTER EIGHTEEN

The Turn of the Screw
(1995 and 1999)

By comparison with the 1960s and early 1970s, when James Cellan Jones and Jack Pulman created their versions of *The Portrait of the Lady* and *The Golden Bowl*, the climate of television drama in the 1990s had radically changed. Following the deregulation of terrestrial broadcasting in 1990, a U.K. requirement that 25 percent of all output had to be commissioned from independent producers was extended to the BBC and the independent television companies. As a result, individual producers began to look toward coproduction as a way of raising the necessary finance to mount a classic adaptation. This represented a radical break with the past: Whereas U.S. companies such as WGBH Boston had once purchased ready-made BBC and Independent Television (ITV) programs for their Masterpiece Theatre strand, they now played a major part both in the financing and distribution of classic adaptations. American finance and American taste overdetermined British television production. Several adaptations deliberately acknowledged American worldviews—for example, by representing Britain as a "mythological and geographically distinct 'Old World.' . . . Far removed from actual historical locations and events . . . [that] catalyses emotional and sexual awakenings for Anglo-American travelers."[1]

At the same time, the BBC (and ITV to a lesser extent) were under increasing pressure to increase revenue from sales of television programs abroad, and to maintain high ratings at home.[2] The best way to achieve this with the classic adaptation was to approach it as a "quality" production, with considerable care and attention paid to assembling star casts, selecting suitable locations, and maintaining historical authenticity in set and costume

193

designs. In the 1970s, the majority of classic adaptations had been low-budget, studio-bound affairs, deriving much of their force from characterization or through the emphasis on visual symbols (e.g., the golden bowl in Cellan Jones's adaptation of the James novel).[3] Two decades later, the emphasis had shifted to high production values in an attempt to maximize the adaptation's commercial potential. John Caughie observes somewhat caustically that this represented "the horizon of aspiration for a medium which increasingly suffered from a poverty of desire. . . . The advocates of 'quality' [television] seemed to content themselves with production values and with making sure that the money appeared on screen."[4]

This chapter focuses on how these conditions of production affected two versions of *The Turn of the Screw*—one produced by an American company (Rosemont Productions) for CBS in 1994, the other mounted five years later as a coproduction between Meridian Television, the British independent company Martin Pope Productions and WGBH Boston, for broadcast in the Masterpiece Theatre strand.[5] The first of these, directed by Tom McLoughlin and retitled *The Haunting of Helen Walker*, provides a good example of a "quality" production designed with consumer interests in mind. Filmed entirely on location in Britain, it attached great importance to historical accuracy in its locations and settings. McLoughlin sought to stimulate the viewers' desires; if they were prepared to pay the airfare and/or the price of admission, they could recreate for themselves the experience of the film by visiting the locations for themselves. Apart from the American star (the comedy actress Valerie Bertinelli), the cast comprised the best of British theatrical acting talent—Diana Rigg, Michael Gough, and Paul Rhys. The appeal (and advertising) of theatrical performance may also be linked to the attraction of the use of spoken English, particularly for American audiences.[6]

In Ben Bolt's Masterpiece Theatre version, James's novella has been deliberately restructured to provide a cameo role for Colin Firth as the uncle—in the belief, no doubt, that Firth's popularity as a television star (*Pride and Prejudice* [1994], *Nostromo* [1997]), would help to sell the adaptation on both sides of the Atlantic.[7] The narrative is pictorial rather than dramatic in structure; on many occasions, visual techniques are employed in ways that are ostentatious or just pleasing in themselves. This technique not only draws attention to the surface "quality" of the adaptation, but re-creates an American worldview of Britain as an "Old World" of cricket matches and endless tea parties, peopled by eligible young men and women seeking partners. The image seems particularly appropriate for someone like James, who was preoccupied with "the relationality of national feeling at the moment of international intermingling. It is only when they travel to Europe, after all, that James's Americans are able to define their own national identity."[8]

I suggest that it is not only the viewing public who are invited to reflect upon their identities through exposure to this Old World. Both adaptations show the governess's desires being aroused by the "excessive visuality" of the settings[9]—to such an extent that she dreams of becoming a permanent fixture at Bly House. In *The Haunting of Helen Walker*, the governess is seduced by Bly's "consumer culture" (understood in this context as a culture of conspicuous expenditure rather than the accumulation of bare necessities), to such an extent that she ultimately loses the capacity to distinguish good from evil. This renders her easy prey for Quint. By contrast, the governess in Bolt's adaptation draws on her experience of consumer culture to develop a version of femininity that rejects self-gratification and dedicates itself to helping others.

Far from revealing a "poverty of desire," both adaptations of *The Turn of the Screw* demonstrate a commitment to the cinema of attraction, in which the fictional world of the narrative is continually ruptured by self-conscious moments of spectacle. This strategy not only serves a commercial purpose (to stimulate consumption among viewers)[10] but also focuses attention on whether consumers—particularly women—can make creative use of images of "quality" to develop a "quality" of life of their own.

Earlier James adaptations produced for the cinema—notably *On a Clear Day, Somewhere in Time*, and the two James Ivory films—had placed similar emphasis on visuals; Ivory recalled in an interview with Robert Emmet Long that the art direction and costumes for *The Europeans* invested the film with "a very precise knowledge . . . a kind of scholarship, you could say."[11] Within two decades, the concentration on visual detail had become a prerequisite of all classic adaptations on film and television. As Simon Langton, the director of BBC's *Pride and Prejudice* (1995), explains, this is what audiences over a wide international cultural range had come to expect from the genre: "Now virtually every expensive drama is done on film, as opposed to being done on tape, and so a whole generation of people who have grown up entirely weaned on all film productions, will not stand for the more limited standards of tape. . . . Things have changed and people are far more concerned about the look of things."[12]

The old public service ideal—based on informing, educating, and entertaining the viewer—no longer seemed significant (particularly for adaptations produced in Britain); any classical adaptation had to be marketable in a wide variety of contexts. This was the only way in which their funding could be justified.

With this objective in mind, both adaptations of *The Turn of the Screw* place particular emphasis on authentic historical details. Filmed at Englefield House near Reading, west of London, *The Haunting of Helen Walker* takes great care to show the landscape surrounding the house—the green hills, the village church, the neatly manicured fields full of deer and horses grazing. Later on, the governess (Valerie Bertinelli)—renamed Helen Walker in this adaptation—enjoys her first experience of the game of cricket as part of her initiation into country-house life; Miles (Aled Roberts) helpfully explains that "Now you are an English country governess in an English country house, you've got to learn to play cricket." She turns out to be rather good at it, hitting Miles's bowling to all parts of the field. Once the game has concluded, Helen, the children, and Mrs. Grose are shown having tea on the lawn with a magnificent view of the house in the background. The director, Tom McLoughlin, creates several new domestic servants, none of whom exist in James's novella—for example, Barnaby the gardener (Michael Gough) who clears fallen leaves from the pathways, or Peggy the cook (Tricia Thorns), who is shown preparing Miles's favorite dinner—steak and kidney pie—in a well-stocked kitchen. These sequences are shot in a series of long takes designed to show off the iconography with which the 1990s classic adaptation is most popularly associated: buildings, landscapes, and costumes. This represents one of the film's main selling points for the television audience.[13]

Another selling point lies in the casting. Bertinelli's experience of classic drama was confined to the television special *The Secret of Charles Dickens* (1979), but her popularity as the star of the CBS sitcom *One Day at a Time* provided McLoughlin with suitable justification for casting her as Helen. The British supporting cast included Gough and Rigg, the Tony-award winning actress known to older viewers as the costar of the original *Avengers* series. Her presence in *Helen Walker* invested the production with "quality," as Bertinelli pointed out in an interview. At first, she "just watched this great actress [Rigg] from the sidelines. . . . Then one day, she came up to me and asked if we could work on an upcoming scene over dinner. I was flattered to say the least and I learned a great deal from her."[14] Hugh Whitemore's screenplay self-consciously advertises its "quality" by incorporating quotations from Shakespeare—as, for example, when Helen introduces *Hamlet* to Miles and Flora as part of their schoolwork. She asks them whether they believe in ghosts, but her enthusiasm rapidly dwindles when Miles dismisses Shakespeare's work as "not real life after all, only a play."

Ben Bolt's Masterpiece Theatre version likewise wears its "qualities" on its sleeve. Nick Dear's script has Miles (Joe Sowerbutts) quoting directly from *Hamlet* ("Angels and ministers of grace defend us! . . . Thou com'st in such a questionable shape / That I will speak to thee").[15] The cast includes Firth, Pam Ferris as Mrs. Grose (who also appeared in the Masterpiece Theatre productions of *Middlemarch* [1996] and *Our Mutual Friend* [1998]) and Jodhi May (*Last of the Mohicans* [1993]) as the governess. This adaptation seems to be inspired as much by *Helen Walker* as James's novella; there is another cricketing scene where the governess is bowled out by Miles (Joe Sower-butts). Flora (Grace Robinson) exclaims that it was "a jolly game; we have such sport with you!"; clearly, viewers are encouraged to think the same. Country-house life seems calm and unhurried, with every need quietly taken care of by the staff. Dinners are long, leisurely affairs, involving the children, Mrs. Grose, and the governess, punctuated by snatches of polite conversation. For the governess, experiencing this kind of life for the first time, the attractions of Bly seem irresistible; at one point she exclaims, "Am I dreaming?"

In both adaptations, the attractions of Bly's "consumer culture" and its representatives—the house, the uncle, and the children—prove irresistible to the governess. Through repeated close-ups of her smiling face, intercut with shots of the front exterior, *The Haunting of Helen Walker* suggests that she has been captivated by Bly's "broad, clear front [and] its open windows."[16] Her sense of wonder increases later on when she first encounters Miles, who possesses an "indescribable air of knowing nothing in the world but love";[17] McLoughlin suggests this through close-ups of Miles's smiling face and Helen staring wide-eyed at him, as they ride home in the carriage. Even before she arrives at Bly for the first time, the governess in Bolt's *Turn of the Screw* has fallen for the uncle, whom she views "all in a glow of high fashion, of good looks, of expensive habits, of charming ways with women."[18] At one point, Bolt cuts to a close-up of his hands clasping hers; the camera tilts upwards to show the governess looking doe-eyed at him as he admits (in a newly written speech) to having "the highest estimation of [her] abilities." Flattered by his attention, the governess gulps twice; on the soundtrack a solo flute can be heard, underlining the fact that for her "this prospective patron proved . . . such a figure as had never risen, save in a dream or an old novel."[19] Everything seems almost *too* perfect: when Flora—a cherubic figure, her long blonde hair done up with two blue ribbons—meets her at the front door for the first time, she offers the governess a bunch of violets. Bolt cuts to a long shot taken from inside the house looking outward at the two of them crossing the threshold, suggesting that for the governess this represents a life-changing moment as she enters a new life of grace and favor that surpasses her wildest expectations.

One of the main attractions of consumer culture—as portrayed in the cinema of attraction—lies in its potential for spectator identification, or in some cases complete transformation. Jackie Stacey's research on female cinemagoing habits of the 1940s and 1950s reveals that many women recognized in their favorite stars qualities they sought to possess, mostly through fashion.[20] The major studios sought to exploit this phenomenon; Paramount's campaign to publicize Wyler's *Heiress* (1949) included a competition, offering an opportunity for someone to become an heiress for a day through a complete makeover at her local department store. Both McLoughlin and Bolt suggest that—in the governess's mind, at least—Bly House offers similar possibilities for self-transformation. In one sequence of *Helen Walker*, Helen is shown walking alone in the garden, while the uncle (rechristened Edward Goffe) observes on the soundtrack that she is indeed "a charming and sympathetic young lady." She looks upwards and sees a man looking down at her from one of the house's towers. As she does so, McLoughlin cuts to a close-up of a red rose she has dropped on the ground in her excitement. Whereas the governess in the novella admits the figure on the tower "was not the person I had precipitately supposed" (the uncle),[21] *Helen Walker* stresses the opposite: Helen's romantic dreams of Goffe encourage her to believe that he has returned for her.

Bolt's adaptation emphasizes the fact that the governess's romantic desire for a quality existence encourage her to identify Quint with the uncle. Quint himself (Jason Salkey) is made up to look like Colin Firth—both of them have the same ginger mutton-chop whiskers, slightly unkempt hair, and elegant frock coat.[22] However, the governess understands the fact that Quint might not exist; she admits to Mrs. Grose (in a newly written line) that she tends to be "rather easily carried away."

Despite the similarities in terms of plot, it is clear that Bly's "consumer culture" affects Helen Walker and Bolt's governess in very different ways. Helen's fate resembles that of Jane Cubberly and Jenny Gooding in the 1974 and 1992 versions of James's novella—all of them try to set the best behavioral example they can for the children, but are eventually destroyed by the all-pervasive corruption surrounding the house. The two earlier adaptations both advance the neoconservative view that Jane and Jenny's failure stems from their ignorance of "normal" (i.e., nuclear) family life, in which both parents—particularly fathers—should set suitable role models for their children. By contrast, *Helen Walker* initially suggests that any woman—even those who have led sheltered lives—can undertake the responsibility of looking after children, compensating for their lack of experience with boundless enthusiasm.[23] What causes Helen's downfall is her infatuation with the quality of life at Bly, which overstimulates her imagination—the ghosts do not exist except as projections of her narcissistic dreams of self-fulfillment.[24] In one scene, she walks along a corridor, only to be startled by the sound of whimpering from the schoolroom. She opens the door to find Miss Jessel (Elizabeth Morton) crying at a desk and turns around to discover Quint (Christopher Guard) standing in her way. Quint pushes past her and embraces Miss Jessel in a passionate kiss. The sequence ends with a dissolve to a shot of Helen lying in bed moaning just like Miss Jessel; clearly, she is experiencing a sexual fantasy wherein she imagines herself making love to Goffe. Later on, she sees Miles walking alone in the grounds; as she turns back inside the house, she witnesses Quint illuminated by a lurid blue light, beckoning her towards him. This is followed by a dissolve to a medium close-up of Miles sitting up in bed. When she asks whether he has anything to tell her, Miles kisses her passionately. Jack Clayton introduces a similar sequence into *The Innocents* (1962), to draw attention to Miss Giddens's gradual sexual awakening; she has never experienced anything like this before. By contrast, *Helen Walker* suggests that images of Miles, Quint, and Goffe have become so confused in Helen's mind that she imagines Miles as her lover.

The final scene bears witness to Helen's corruption as she quite literally scares Miles to death on the pretext of "saving" him from Quint. The little boy cannot see the ghosts; McLoughlin shows this by intercutting close-ups of Helen and Quint staring fixedly at one another with shots of Miles looking wild-eyed in a desperate attempt to understand why the governess is telling him to speak Quint's name. At length he screams "You devil!!!" at her and collapses into her arms, blood oozing from his nose.[25] McLaughlin subsequently cuts to a shot from Helen's point of view of Quint retreating upstairs: The camera follows him at a distance, pausing at the bedroom door to reveal an empty room save for Miss Jessel playing the Chopin prelude, which throughout the adaptation has been used to signal Quint's (and, by extension, Goffe's) presence at Bly. The entire sequence emphasizes the fact that Helen continues to imagine herself as Miss Jessel, waiting for her lover (Goffe or Quint) to appear.

This reading of *The Turn of the Screw* suggests that Helen's hallucinations represent the imaginative visualizations of someone obsessed with consumer culture, which should prompt us to question whether consumption enables women to determine their own lives. The film shows her independence being transformed into narcissism, which expresses itself through what the media critic Susan J. Douglas has described as "the ability to indulge oneself, pamper oneself, and focus at length on oneself without having to listen to the needy voices of others."[26] Her preoccupation with the life of quality, to the exclusion of everything else, drives Flora to distraction and precipitates Miles's demise.

Although the governess in Bolt's version admits to being equally "carried away" by her experiences at Bly, it is clear that she has greater strength of character than Helen. Despite her initial doubts, she comes to realize that the ghosts are living presences in the house who have turned Flora into a monster and threaten to do the same to Miles. The governess resolves to fight them, partly by "running a tight ship" in the house, and partly by discovering "another turn of the screw of human nature" within herself through prayer. Bolt's idiosyncratic reading of the novella's title suggests that, like Milly Theale in Softley's *Wings of the Dove*, the governess casts herself in a quasi-angelic role, rejecting self-gratification and seeking to redeem others (especially Miles). This is no easy task; at one point, she glances momentarily up at the uncle's portrait hanging in the hallway at Bly, as if realizing that she must extinguish any romantic desires she might have felt for him. Only then will she succeed in delivering Miles "to God"—in other words, save him from further exploitation by the ghosts.

The ending of Bolt's version might be seen as cautiously optimistic, as the governess forces Miles to acknowledge Quint's presence, which enables his spirit to be released from his body and join the angels in heaven. Miles asks "Where?" in a quizzical voice, as if pretending that the ghost still does not exist. He jerks his head around, sees Quint in front of him, utters the line "Peter Quint—you devil!" and dies. The governess does not seem in the least surprised; on the contrary, she appears to offer thanks to God as she cradles his head and looks upwards while the camera pulls backwards to view the two of them from outside the living-room window.

But does a life devoted to helping others really represent a viable alternative for women to the gratifications offered by consumer culture? Annette Kuhn argued as long ago as 1982 that idealistic images of women could be considered oppressive on the grounds that they were important to live up to yet "at the same time unattainable."[27] Stacey's research has revealed that many female filmgoers tried to compensate for this by bridging the gap between the ideal and the real, a practice that involved a considerable degree of active participation. They might not achieve the ideal, but by interpreting what they saw on screen to develop their own subjectivities, they could at least work some way toward achieving their desires. By contrast, the governess believes that to achieve her ideal, she must suppress her desires for quality (personified by the uncle) altogether, in the belief that they are somehow "immoral." She spurns the chance to develop her own subjectivity, placing her trust in God instead. As in *Helen Walker*, Bolt's *Turn of the Screw* denies the female central character the opportunity for self-determination; she can only choose between two roles (angel/monster) created for her by the (male) director.

While seeking to advertise their surface qualities—locations, casts—in the hope of attracting audiences, both adaptations communicate the contradictory message that women in particular should resist such qualities, on the grounds that they might lose the capacity to distinguish right from wrong. Any opportunity they might have to exploit such qualities to develop their own subjectivities is ruthlessly denied. Giddings and Selby argue that the 1990s revealed "the durable change that feminism has wrought in American and British drama productions. There is a whole audience of socially, sexually, and politically enfranchised women whose tastes must be satisfied."[28] Neither version of *The Turn of the Screw* appears to acknowledge such changes; rather, they follow the example of earlier cinematic adaptations of the novella (particularly Rusty Lemorande's 1992 version) by suggesting that any woman who follows her desires represents a threat to the stability of an enduringly patriarchal society.

The Nielsen ratings record that *Helen Walker* attracted an average audience ranging from 9.3 to 9.8 million when first broadcast by CBS on December 3, 1995. NBC's reworking of Hitchcock's *Shadow of a Doubt*, aired at the same time, attracted 13.3 to 14 million viewers. Reviews of the James production are scant; the only comments readily available are to be found on the Internet Movie Database, drawing attention to the "lush location setting" and the cast, "with the incomparable Diana Rigg especially effective as the housekeeper."[29] Bolt's version received its British television premiere on ITV on Boxing Day 1999, and debuted on *Masterpiece Theatre* two months later. Certainly, it was not expected to attract large audiences in Britain, being broadcast opposite the BBC's premiere of Brian DePalma's *Mission Impossible*. And so it proved; the film drew 9.6 million viewers, while the James adaptation attracted exactly half that number.

I contend that both adaptations evoke a world more characteristic of

1950s rather than 1990s television drama, where the woman was asked to be innocent and pure, resisting everything that quality culture has to offer. Julianne Pidduck observes that one of the features of 1990s adaptations—whether on film or television—lies in their capacity to question what she terms (following Henry James) "the house of fiction," as they create spaces in which "identities are shifting, fluid and heterogeneous," while retaining "a startling capacity for innovation and social critique."[30] For these two adaptations at least, the door to experiment, innovation, and social critique within the Jamesian house of fiction has been firmly closed.

Notes

1. Julianne Pidduck, *Contemporary Costume Film* (London: BFI Publishing, 2004), 86.

2. Robert Giddings and Keith Selby, *The Classic Serial on Television and Radio* (Basingstoke: Palgrave, 2001), 83.

3. James Ivory makes much the same point to Robert Emmet Long: "*The Golden Bowl* had a strong cast, and they did a good job . . . there is one dimension of the novel that the television production brings out fully—the dense, oblique psychological atmosphere that was peculiar to the late James." Robert Emmet Long, *James Ivory in Conversation: How Merchant-Ivory Makes Its Movies* (Berkeley: University of California Press, 2005), 245–46.

4. John Caughie, *Television Drama: Realism, Modernism and British Culture* (Cambridge: Cambridge University Press, 2000), 210.

5. I am indebted to Justine Rhodes of Granada for this information.

6. John Hill, *British Cinema in the 80s* (Oxford: Clarendon Press, 1999), 82.

7. Firth's reputation was such that the London *Guardian* reviewer of *Nostromo* (BBC, 1997) described his performance thus: "Mr. Darcy—sorry, Colin Firth—looks great" (quoted in Giddings and Selby, *The Classic Serial on Television and Radio*, 143).

8. Jonathan Freedman, "The Moment of Henry James," in *The Cambridge Companion to Henry James*, ed. Jonathan Freedman (Cambridge: Cambridge University Press, 1998), 8.

9. Aida A. Hozic, "Hollywood Goes on Sale: or, What Do the Violet Eyes of Elizabeth Taylor Have to Do with the 'Cinema of Attractions'?" in *Hollywood Goes Shopping*, ed. David Dessner and Garth S. Jowett (Minneapolis: University of Minnesota Press, 2000), 208.

10. This strategy was characteristic of Hollywood films of the same period; studio executives make no bones about the fact that films are "marketing events" and that their marketing and/or licensing potential determines whether or not they will be made. See Tom Gunning, "The Cinema of Attractions: Early Film, Its Spectator and the Avant-Garde," in *Early Cinema: Space, Frame, Narrative*, ed. Thomas Elsaesser (London: BFI Publishing, 1990), 46–69.

11. Long, *James Ivory in Conversation*, 145.

12. Quoted in Giddings and Selby, *The Classic Serial on Television and Radio*, 106.

13. A prebroadcast article appearing in *TV Key* drew attention to the fact that the actors enjoyed "playing dress up getting into those sets and costumes in the English countryside at an old English manor house." John N. Goudas, "More Than One Day in Valerie Bertinelli's Life," *TV Key*, November 30, 1995, at www.newstimes.com/archive95/dec 0195/tvd.htm (accessed June 24, 2005).

14. Goudas, "More Than One Day."

15. James himself was known to be fond of *Hamlet*—he refers to it in the preface to *The Spoils of Poynton*. Tony Tanner remarked in 1990 that he "would dearly like to see James's *Hamlet*, though I fear it would have turned out to be, literally, interminable." Tony Tanner, "Henry James: 'The Story in It'—and the Story without It" (1997), in *The American Mystery: American Literature from Emerson to DeLillo*, ed. Tony Tanner (Cambridge: Cambridge University Press, 2000), 110).

16. Henry James, *The Turn of the Screw, The Aspern Papers and Other Stories*, ed. Michael Swan (London: Collins, 1963), 321.

17. James, *Turn of the Screw*, 328.

18. James, *Turn of the Screw*, 318.

19. James, *Turn of the Screw*, 318.

20. Jackie Stacey, *Star Gazing: Hollywood Cinema and Female Spectatorship* (London: Routledge, 1994), 200.

21. James, *Turn of the Screw*, 331.

22. The governess in the novella also admits that Quint looks remarkably handsome in the uncle's clothes (James, *Turn of the Screw*, 339).

23. The novella also makes this point at the end when Mrs. Grose admits that the governess's ideas might be right (James, *Turn of the Screw*, 396).

24. Charles Eckert has argued that Hollywood films of the Golden Age between 1920 and 1960 encouraged a similar kind of narcissism by selling products (not only the films themselves but also tie-in merchandise) that could be "bought for their images, their associations, or the psychological gratifications they possessed." Charles Eckert, "The Carole Lombard in Macy's Window," in *Movies and Mass Culture*, ed. John Belton (London: Athlone Press, 1996), 117.

25. Robert Weisbuch has noted this ambiguity in his recent essay on the novella. "James and the Idea of Evil," in *The Cambridge Companion to Henry James*, ED. Jonathan Freedman (Cambridge: Cambridge University Press, 1998), 111.

26. Susan J. Douglas, *Where the Girls Are: Growing Up Female with the Mass Media* (New York: Random House, 1995), 146.

27. Annette Kuhn, *Women's Pictures: Feminism and Cinema* (London: Routledge and Kegan Paul, 1982), 6.

28. Giddings and Selby, *The Classic Serial on Television and Radio*, 119.

29. "Excellent Version of *The Turn of the Screw*," December 23, 1999, at http://uk.imdb .com/title/tt0113271/ (accessed June 23, 2005).

30. Pidduck, *Contemporary Costume Film*, 7–8.

CHAPTER NINETEEN

⟨~⟩

The American (1998)

As with the 1999 *Turn of the Screw*, Paul Unwin's version of *The American* was planned as a coproduction—this time involving the BBC, WGBH Boston, and ALT Films, an American nonprofit production company.[1] The adaptation was conceived as part of a projected nine-part series entitled "Mobil Masterpiece Theatre's American Collection"; other films announced included an adaptation of Willa Cather's *Song of the Lark*, and *Cora Unashamed*, a story by Langston Hughes.[2] The aim of the series, according to ALT's Marian Rees, was to provide quality adaptations involving "our finest American film artists, storytellers and actors—the kind of creative talent the literary material deserves."[3] Although budgets would be modest (roughly $3 million per adaptation), filming would be almost entirely on location, so that each adaptation would be enriched "by really creating the environment in which the story takes place."[4] To broaden the educational appeal of the series, the CPB (Corporation for Public Broadcasting) formed a partnership with the American National Council of Teachers of English to provide a series of online resources focusing in particular on how to teach the adaptations in class, and more generally on the decisions made by writers and/or directors in bringing classic works to the small screen.[5]

The marketability of the series was greatly enhanced by the choice of creative personnel. *The American* starred Matthew Modine, supported by Diana Rigg and Brenda Fricker (whose career on both sides of the Atlantic had blossomed ever since she had won the Best Supporting Actress Oscar for *My Left Foot* [1989]). James's novel had been adapted by the British dramatist Michael Hastings, author of *Tom and Viv* (1994), who had previously collaborated with Michael Winner on *The Nightcomers*. As well as being the creator of the long-running BBC drama *Casualty* (1986–), the director Paul Unwin had extensive experience of the classics, having served as artistic director of the Bristol Old Vic Theater Company before moving into television.

Clearly, this production was conceived along similar lines as WGBH's *Turn of the Screw*, in the sense that it incorporated the elements of the cinema of spectacle—casting, locations, costumes—and was deliberately pitched at consumers—not only general viewers but teachers and students who might subsequently make use of the American Collection website and purchase products relating to the adaptation (videos, DVDs, books). Marian Rees of ALT admitted that "the creative team" involved in *The American* had consulted with teachers in discussions about how individual scenes from the novel were brought to life on film. Educators had been brought "into the process of making these films so that, by the time they come out, they will own them in an educationally rich way."[6]

Even though the adaptation may have been inspired by the logic of consumption, this does not prevent director Paul Unwin from criticizing it.[7] In this chapter, I discuss how he uses a variety of cinematic strategies to suggest that consumption reduces people—particularly women—to commodities, sampled and exchanged at will. Through a series of intercut close-ups, Unwin shows how both Christopher Newman (Modine) and Valentin de Bellegarde (Andrew Scott) control women through their looks by transforming them into objects of spectacle. Alternatively, Unwin repeatedly employs variations of a visual metaphor to suggest that once the two men have selected a partner, they quite literally "consume" her with their bodies. Their range of choice is not restricted to the Parisian world; on several occasions, they stare directly at the camera, as if searching for lovers among the viewers. If James's novel makes much of the contrast between the "Old World" of the Bellegardes and the "New World" of the American (Christopher Newman), Unwin's adaptation suggests there is little to distinguish them. Both depend on the capitalist assumption that women should assume subordinate roles—as lovers, wives, or dutiful daughters—to preserve the stability of a patriarchal society.

However, Unwin shows that neither Claire de Cintré (Aisling O'Sullivan) nor Noémie (Eva Birthistle) conforms to such expectations. Claire not only repudiates Newman at the end of the film (by remaining in the nunnery), but throughout the preceding action she has refused to submit to the controlling power of his gaze. On numerous occasions, she abruptly curtails the conversation by running out of the side of the frame, rendering him quite literally speechless. Peter Bogdanovich also employs this technique in *Daisy Miller* to suggest Daisy's independent spirit; but whereas the earlier film ends with the heroine's death, *The American* suggests that, while Claire remains on the margins of a patriarchal society (by going to a nunnery), she retains the capacity to determine her own destiny. Noémie favors a more direct method of resistance, proving so effective in her courtesan's role that men quite literally need to be protected from her—something that Valentin discovers to his cost as he fights and loses a duel over her. Viewers are encouraged to become creative consumers, to take Claire and Noémie's experiences into account while creating their own spaces for themselves.

Yet clearly this task is not an easy one. Early on in the film, Newman admits that the kind of woman he likes is someone who "knows how to do business," someone acquainted with capitalist logic. As he speaks this line, Unwin cuts to a shot of Noémie in the background, flanked by Newman and Tom Tristram who are both staring at her. While both of them seek to imprison her through their looks, Newman goes a step further by offering to pay her two thousand francs for the painting—so long as he likes it; in other words, placing her under an obligation to finish it to a certain standard. The exploitative nature of the transaction so alarms another artist working nearby that she turns and stares at Newman. None of this occurs in the novel, where Newman admires Noémie for her "Beauty, talent, virtue; she combined everything."[8] What he does not realize at the moment is that she seeks to sell herself rather than the picture.[9]

In the next scene, the two men are shown strolling outside the Louvre; Tristram observes that "What matters is the way you look. First, you gotta get the hang of these clothes"—the characteristically flamboyant Parisian fashions of tailored suits in soft colors and parasols.[10] Unwin cuts to a shot of the two men with Newman staring directly at the camera, followed by a shot of the object of his gaze (Claire de Cintré, accompanied by her brother Henri [Paul Hickey]), and a reverse shot of Newman. In the background, the sound of a solo piano can be heard playing a romantic ballad. The sequence indicates that the phrase "the way you look" not only refers to what the characters wear in public but also implies that the look represents a form of possession, especially from the male point of view. This is underlined soon afterwards when we see him with his back to camera, his cloak almost entirely obscuring Claire as she walks away from him. She has been symbolically "consumed" by his gaze.

A variation of the same sequence appears later on in a newly created ball scene, which does not exist in the novel. Unwin cuts from a medium close-up of Newman's face to a point-of-view shot of Claire arriving; this is followed by a reverse shot of Newman staring open-mouthed at her. As the action unfolds, Newman endeavors once again to possess her—not through a glance but by more direct means. Claire announces her departure by moving to the rear of the frame, her back to camera. Newman enters from the right, turns away from the camera, and places her cloak round her shoulders. Nothing can be seen of her except the back of her head. It is not surprising that she should resist this attempt to "consume" her: "Are all Americans like this, hands here, hands there, hands all over?"[11] Earlier on in the scene, Newman had informed General Packard (Ed Bishop) how he understood that as "money was no longer important . . . I decided to get out" of America and come to Paris.[12] Despite this claim, the capitalist ethos clearly determines his way of thinking: Women are goods, to be sampled at will.

Although originating from the Old World of a Parisian family who considers status more important than money, Valentin treats women in a similar manner. His first meeting with Noémie recalls the scene involving Newman and Noémie at the Louvre; Unwin places her at the center of the frame with Valentin and Newman ogling her, their backs to the camera. Valentin's eyes shadow her every move as she moves towards the camera and exits on the left side of the frame. The novel shows Valentin reacting in much the same way: "He, at all events, was seeing her. . . . He was eventually finding Mademoiselle Noémie extremely interesting; the blue devils had departed, leaving the field clear."[13] In the adaptation, Unwin creates a new scene where the two of them are discovered in bed covered with a yellow counterpane. Valentin lies on top of Noémie, suggesting that he quite literally seeks to "consume" her. This is followed by a close-up of him kissing her left leg and slowly moving up towards her vagina. Noémie's face cannot be seen; for him, she is nothing more than a sex object. The basis of their relationship is well expressed at the end of the scene, as the two of them make love standing up—Valentin, with his back to camera, almost entirely smothers Noémie.

Both men's outlook on life is visually expressed in a sequence where Valentin asks to borrow the spare key to Newman's apartment; in return, he will do everything in his power to arrange a private meeting between Claire and the American. Newman responds, "This is a business proposition between one tradesperson and another." As they speak, we can see nothing in the background except stone statues, gilded portraits, and other bric-a-brac decorating Newman's apartment. Claire represents nothing more than another object—a bargaining tool used to forge a business deal.[14] A similar shot appears in Cellan Jones's *Portrait*, to suggest how Gilbert Osmond views Isabel Archer as a valuable addition to his collection of antiques; she is shown sitting on his sofa, with all of his ornaments (vases, bronze figures) surrounding her, illuminated by candlelight at the rear of the shot.

Neither Newman nor Valentin is satisfied with just one lover; they remain perpetually on the lookout for further conquests. In the ball scene referred to earlier, Newman asks Mrs. Tristram (Alison McKenna), "Who is she?" and Mrs. Tristram replies, "She's been a widow for many years now. We went to the same convent school." In terms of the plot, this exchange refers to Claire, but Unwin shoots the sequence in such a way—with Newman and Mrs. Tristram staring direct to camera—as to suggest that they could be referring to someone in the viewing audience. Valentin reacts in similar fashion during a shot/reverse-shot exchange between Newman and Noémie as Valentin hovers behind Newman and stares directly into the camera. Another character sharing this apparently insatiable desire for more women is the Marquis de Cintré (Philip O'Sullivan), who stares at the camera while insisting to Madame de Bellegarde that he will marry Claire "as she is, perfect and untouched. And she will have everything."[15]

The image of someone staring into the camera lens can be extraordinarily powerful—witness the beginning of Jane Campion's *Portrait of a Lady*, where the young women (who introduce the film by talking about themselves) seek someone to respond in kind to their feelings and emotions. Unwin employs the same type of shot for two reasons: to show how materialism and consumerism foster greed; and to prevent viewers from vicariously admiring the historically accurate sets and costumes. Sarah Cardwell remarks that this technique "offers us to actively involve ourselves in the narrative level, [and] allows a specifically televisual mode of engagement with the text, and the potential development of an alternative relationship with the past depicted."[16] While the late nineteenth-century Parisian society as depicted on screen may certainly possess a certain quality, we are made aware of its tendency to exploit anyone lacking the material and social status to express themselves.[17] Unwin stresses this point in a newly written opening scene taking place in Monsieur de Bellegarde's (T. P. McKenna's) chamber. Red curtains adorn his bed, while lighted candles at the back of the room illuminate the rich cut-glass crystal on the adjoining table. The surroundings may be magnificent, but the characters' behavior leaves a lot to be desired, as Madame de Bellegarde forces her daughter into "a union between two most noble families"—the Bellegardes and the de Cintrés—to prevent public disgrace. At one point, Claire is shown running away from her mother but finds her path blocked by her brother Henri. She whimpers and turns round, and the marquis stands in her way. The camera slowly tracks to the right to show her mother staring impassively at her. Like a caged animal, Claire has no prospect of escaping her fate as she sinks to her knees in a gesture of surrender. In the next scene, Mrs. Bread (Brenda Fricker) is shown at the bedroom door, her hands clasped across her chest in a sign of the cross, as she listens to Claire moaning, "Please, mother, no. No!" Unwin observed in an interview that this sequence portrayed the extraordinarily dark and brooding world of the Bellegardes; how they "lock together, how they damage each other, how they hold each other down."[18] Diana Rigg described Claire as "a trapped bird, if you like, a caged bird, and a very beautiful one," whose family never allowed her any freedom. James "disapproves of how she is expected to behave, under the circumstances, I mean, to him, it's an anathema."[19]

However, as with Daisy Miller in Bogdanovich's film or Kate Croy in Softley's *Wings*, Claire poses a threat to authority even while being forced to accept it—a contradiction deriving from the films' exaggerated portrayal of an ideal society and the reluctance of the female protagonist to meet its demands.[20] Once her first husband has passed away, Claire defies her family by making a conscious effort to pursue new ways of living and seeing. As Newman is about to leave the house, having taken tea with the Bellegardes, she insists that he should stay a little longer and have some cake—even though her mother has already said good-bye to him. The two of them are photographed standing in front of Madame de Bellegarde (who remains seated), implying that they have established some kind of dominance over her.[21] Claire's bid for freedom does not stop there, as she turns away and walks out of the left side of the frame, leaving Newman and her mother staring after her; clearly, she refuses to subject herself to the controlling authority of the male or the maternal gaze. The significance of this gesture is reemphasized a little later when Madame de Bellegarde and Henri leave the room arm in arm and then pause for a moment as if expecting Claire to follow; Unwin cuts to a close-up of her remaining seated. Claire's gradually developing self-belief is also evident when Newman calls at the Bellegardes' house, only to be told by Madame de Bellegarde that the family "are never at home to visitors who arrive unannounced. It is a ridiculous rule and quite out of step with the times." As she speaks, Unwin cuts to a sequence of images shot from Claire's point of view, as Madame de Bellegarde turns away in disgust, while Newman gazes longingly at her. Such moments, as Jackie Byars observes, demonstrate that control of the mise-en-scène has devolved "to the female . . . although . . . frequently the center of attention, she is also frequently the agent of the gaze and, as such, the positive and unabashed expression of feminine desire."[22]

However, Claire is well aware of the ways in which a consumer society seeks to suppress such desires—for example, by representing a financially advantageous marriage as a woman's ultimate goal. This assumption (which permeates James adaptations of the late 1940s such as *The Lost Moment* or *The Heiress*) influences Newman's attempts to woo her, as he believes—quite arbitrarily—that because he has made a lot of money, Claire will naturally consider him an attractive prospect. Byars expresses the belief thus: "American culture was becoming more and more a consumer culture, and increasingly, [the notion of] materialism became more important . . . to strengthen both traditional values and the notion that the American way of life was superior to any other."[23] Claire criticizes Newman for assuming that marriage and family represent "some kind of a natural human journey [for a woman]. It wasn't for me. I couldn't have lived one more night with him [M. de Cintré]. Now you come along. Crash, bang, prairies and wash-tubs. What have you done to me?" While clearly attracted to him, Claire realizes that to marry him represents nothing more than an acceptance of patriarchal authority.

Trapped by the conflicting demands of her family and an overzealous suitor, Claire returns to the convent, a place that (as Mrs. Tristram observes early on in the film) will always be there "if the outside world fails you." As with Isabel Archer in Campion's *Portrait*, Claire gradually begins to understand that female autonomy depends less upon active resistance to patriarchy and more on finding a form of expression that confounds male logic. This is emphasized in a sequence that juxtaposes close-ups of her cutting her red hair with a flashback to her wedding night, where the marquis forces himself upon her against her will. Whereas once she might have accepted a submissive role, she now takes an active decision to render herself unsuitable for masculine consumption, while encouraging the audience to empathize with her suffering. The sense of power that this gives her is suggested through tight close-ups of her expressionless face, as she watches her red hair falling to the ground. Her experiences have rendered her stronger and more selfless than she ever imagined—witness her observation to Newman that although she may no longer be visible to him in body, she will always be with him in spirit: "Even if it is not real to you, allow me that. I can be there, always." She has found a position where she can speak for herself that cannot be accommodated within masculine logic. As she speaks this line, she walks toward the camera with Newman staring at her in the background, and exits out of the right side of the frame. She refuses to be confined, either by the camera or by Newman's all-consuming male gaze.

Noémie Nioche demonstrates a similar ability to enjoy life on her own terms. The first shot of her in the Louvre has her turning her eyes directly at the camera, suggesting that—like Newman and Valentin—she is on the lookout for potential partners both in the art gallery and among the viewing audience. Not surprisingly, she manages to find one—Newman himself. In a later scene, the two of them are shown in bed together with Noémie on top moaning with simulated orgasmic pleasure; clearly, she knows how to give a good time, even if it means putting on an act. Fidelity means as much to her as the men she goes out with—hence her willingness to be seen openly embracing Monsieur Stanislas Kapp (David Heap) in the middle of a horse show, even though she is well aware of Valentin's presence.[24] The fact that this results in a duel disturbs her very little; in a two-shot that concludes the sequence, Noémie is seen standing emotionlessly behind Kapp, suggesting that she has now shifted her loyalty in the belief that it will prove of greater financial benefit to her. As James observes in the novel, Noémie was "immensely tickled" by the whole affair, believing that it would "make her fortune."[25] Her final appearance in the film occurs during Valentin's funeral when she makes an unexpected—and very public—entrance into the church and covers his corpse with kisses. Clearly, she has no respect for protocol; this was supposed to be a family funeral. For those men unfortunate enough to become involved with her, Noémie might be "an odious blot on the face of nature";[26] nonetheless, there is something admirable about the way she exploits the rules that govern her society—that women exist principally as objects of male consumption—to her own advantage. The sheer enjoyment she derives from her performance as a whore resembles that of Moll Flanders (Alex Kingston) in Andrew Davies's 1996 television adaptation, who is so convincing that even the audience can be occasionally duped by her. Sarah Cardwell observes that the pleasure of observing such women "is grounded in our recognition . . . that there is no gender identity behind the expressions of gender: that identity is performatively constituted by the very 'expressions' that are said to be its results. . . . [They force us] to consider the possibility of gender as performance, rejecting biologically essentialist ideals."[27]

The American places its female protagonists in a position of agency that challenges the notion that consumption leads women to be objectified according to the masculine structure of the gaze. Claire de Cintré and Noémie become subjects, rather than objects, of the narrative; their point of view has been privileged. This is emphasized in the final sequence, a montage consisting of Claire looking directly at the camera and speaking the line, "The shutters are down and all the mice are in chains"; Madame de Bellegarde looking morosely into the fire; a shot of Claire lying on a rug looking up at the sky, a pair of white gloves next to her; followed by a wide-angle shot of the convent with Newman's coach driving away toward the camera. Although Claire likens herself to a mouse "in chains," the final shot of her suggests the opposite as she looks up to a new world of possibilities. By contrast, her mother, who perpetually forces her daughter to accept the dictates of the patriarchy, remains imprisoned by a society whose "shutters are down." Compared to other 1990s James adaptations for television (*The Haunting of Helen Walker*, *The Turn of the Screw*), both of which suggest that creative consumption is somehow "dangerous"—particularly for women, *The American* suggests far more possibilities for the construction of femininity, free from any underlying, determining conceptions of sex and/or gender. Such views would most likely have been shared by James himself. Richard Salmon has suggested, with particular reference to *The American Scene* (1907), that James advocated an escape from the "general glare" of public culture—the world of great buildings and magnificent locations that ostentatiously drew attention to themselves (rather like the sets, costumes, and cast in a 1990s television adaptation). Instead, he favored places that could nurture his "ideal of privacy"—something that was "implicitly set against the homogenizing forces of mass culture. From this perspective, the desire for privacy may be viewed not as a desire for pure solipsistic interiority, but a means of tracing marks of individual and cultural difference." This desire applies particularly to women, whose apparent freedom of choice often conceals "a dependence upon the interests of commodity production."[28] Both Claire de Cintré and Noémie, in their different ways, are fully aware of this, and employ different strategies to resist the gender identifications that Parisian society seeks to impose on them. Unwin's *American* has been dismissed by Martin Halliwell as an unsuccessful adaptation that fails to discover "a mode of presentation which replicates the tone of James's novel," preferring instead to deploy "Gothic elements, not only to amplify the psychological drama of the central characters, but also to problematise the past."[29] On the contrary, I would argue that for all the stylistic liberties it takes with the text, Unwin's film pursues a characteristically Jamesian strategy of mounting a critique of mass culture and the extent of an individual's immersion within it.

Notes

1. The acronym stands for "American Literature on Television."

2. Other films subsequently screened in this series include Thornton Wilder's *Our Town* (2003), Eudora Welty's *The Ponder Heart* (2003), Esmeralda Santiago's *Almost a Woman* (2002), and James Agee's *A Death in the Family* (2002).

3. "Mobil Masterpiece Theatre's Collection to Premiere on PBS," press release dated July 14, 1998, at www.cpb.org/programs/pr.php?prn = 163 (accessed June 27, 2005).

4. Karen Everhart Bedford, "Drama Plan Emerging: PBS Looks to Multiple Sources for American Works," *Current*, July 27, 1998, at www.current.org/prog/prog813d.html (accessed June 27, 2005).

5. For a guide to these resources, see Public Broadcasting Service, www.pbs.org/wgbh/masterpiece/americancollection/index.html (accessed June 27, 2005).

6. Bedford, "Drama Plan Emerging."

7. Martin Halliwell likewise observes that *The American* problematizes the past "as purely a site of nostalgic spectacle for the viewer"—even though his argument focuses far more on the film's transcultural elements. He believes that the film's combination of Anglo-American (and Irish) elements (Anglo-American cast, BBC/WGBH funding, shot on location in Dublin) helps to define the film's "transatlantic trajectory." Martin Halliwell, "Transcultural Aesthetics and the Film Adaptations of Henry James," in *Classics in Film and Fiction*, ed. Deborah Cartmell, I. Q. Hunter, Heidi Kaye, and Imelda Whelehan (London: Pluto Press, 2000), 75–79.

8. Henry James, *The American*, ed. William Spengemann (Harmondsworth: Penguin Books, 1986), 38.

9. Carolyn Porter, "Gender and Value in *The American*," in *New Essays on "The American*,*" ed. Martha Banta (Cambridge: Cambridge University Press, 1987), 108.

10. As in Softley's *Wings*, the parasol is used for purely decorative purposes—something that in this adaptation is perceived as characteristic of Parisian society.

11. The novel also makes it clear that Newman views Claire as a valuable object to possess: "All this [education], as I have affirmed, made her seem rare and precious—a very expensive article, as he would have said, and one which a man with an ambition to have everything about him of the best would find it highly agreeable to possess" (James, *The American*, 165).

12. General Packard does not appear as a character in the novel, but is described by Tristram as one of Paris's "clever people" (James, *The American* 56). In the adaptation, Packard thinks that Newman is telling him a funny story; on learning that it is not funny, he advises the younger man to "save your breath." Ed Bishop, the actor playing Packard, had appeared as Caspar Goodwood in James Cellan Jones's *Portrait of a Lady* over three decades earlier.

13. James, *The American*, 197.

14. This scene does not appear in the novel but Valentin expresses similar sentiments as he puts out his hand to Newman and says, "It's a bargain: I accept you; I espouse your

cause. . . . Put yourself into motion, come and see my sister, and be assured of my sympathy!" (James, *The American*, 163).

15. The only reference to this in the novel comes in a conversation between Tristram and Newman: "Oh, she is a widow then?" said Newman. "Are you already afraid? She was married at eighteen by her parents, in the French fashion, to a disagreeable old man. But he had the good taste to die a couple of years afterward, and she is now twenty-five" (James, *The American*, 74).

16. Sarah Cardwell, *Adaptation Revisited: Television and the Classic Novel* (Manchester: Manchester University Press, 2002), 169.

17. The technique was also used in other classic adaptations appearing at the same time, notably Andrew Davies's version of *Moll Flanders* (Granada TV/WGBH Boston, 1996). See Cardwell, *Adaptation Revisited*, 160–85.

18. Caitlin O'Neil, "Adapting the Master" (Interview with Paul Unwin), at www.pbs .org/wgbh/masterpiece/americancollection/adapting.html (accessed June 27, 2005).

19. "A Talk with Diana Rigg," at www.pbs.org/wgbh/masterpiece/americancollection/ american/ei_rigg.html (accessed June 26, 2005.

20. Christine Gledhill, "The Melodramatic Field: An Investigation," in *Home Is Where the Heart Is: Studies in Melodrama and the Woman's Film*, ed. Christine Gledhill (London: British Film Institute, 1987), 6.

21. This strategy was common in Hollywood melodramas of the 1950s. For an example, see Jackie Byars, *All That Hollywood Allows: Re-Reading Gender in 1950s Melodrama* (London: Routledge, 1991), 171–209.

22. Byars, *All That Hollywood Allows*, 178.

23. Byars, *All That Hollywood Allows*, 82.

24. In the novel, this scene is described by Valentin in reported speech, and takes place in the opera house (James, *The American*, 297–300). Unwin's alteration emphasizes the callousness of Parisian society; to all intents and purposes, Noémie is socially no better than the animals on show.

25. James, *The American*, 303.

26. James, *The American*, 431.

27. Cardwell, *Adaptation Revisited*, 176–77.

28. Richard Salmon, *Henry James and the Culture of Publicity* (Cambridge: Cambridge University Press, 1997), 183–84.

29. Halliwell, "Transcultural Aesthetics," 78.

CHAPTER TWENTY

~

Washington Square (1997)

The three major adaptations of the 1990s—*The Portrait*, *Wings*, and Agnieszka Holland's version of *Washington Square*—were all products of the new globalized Hollywood, wherein the major studios had far more opportunities to recoup their expenditure on a film than in the past.[1] There was not only the American market to consider but also the rapidly expanding European and Asian markets.[2] Films could subsequently be rereleased on video and/or DVD, and exhibited on pay-television channels all around the world. Such developments precipitated the growth of niche marketing, with the studios trying to address the needs of filmgoers in different contexts. What might prove interesting to British or European filmgoers might not be so for their American counterparts. In late 1990s Hollywood, the distinction between mainstream and independent cinema—which had been so important two decades earlier when *On a Clear Day* was released—no longer appeared so clear-cut, once Disney had acquired Miramax Films (producers of *Wings*) for $80 million, creating what Justin Wyatt describes as a "major independent" studio.[3] Disney obtained distribution rights to Miramax's library of 200 films, and agreed to finance the development of Miramax's future projects; in return, Miramax retained overall control over their productions, while obtaining greater access to ancillary markets such as video and pay television.

In theory, such developments should have enabled Miramax to create a greater range of experimental and/or noncommercial work for art-house and possibly mainstream distribution. In practice, however, the major independents found themselves somewhat constrained by corporate domination. Despite the fact that films could be marketed to different kinds of audience through cinema, video, and television, most major studios were still reluctant to experiment, preferring instead to commission tried-and-trusted material. In this chapter, I suggest that, like most James adaptations of the previous two decades, *Washington Square* was designed to be visually appealing with its historically accurate sets, costumes, and stellar cast—as Disney (through its subsidiary Hollywood Pictures), in collaboration with the independent Caravan Pictures, sought to repeat the success of Douglas McGrath's *Emma* (1995), which won an Oscar for Best Theme Music. However, I show how the film's director, Agnieszka Holland, manipulates the costume drama form to make a statement about female potential both in nineteenth-century America and in the modern world. Rather than following the example set by Jane Campion in *The Portrait*, however, Holland follows a path pursued by James Ivory in earlier adaptations such as *The Bostonians*, of using "movement images" (for example, the woman at the window) to represent Catherine Sloper's (Jennifer Jason Leigh's) psychological development. Like Olive Chancellor in Ivory's film, Catherine understands the importance of behaving differently as she rejects her suitor, Morris Townsend (Ben Chaplin), and opens her own day-care center in the house that once belonged to her father. Apparently, she has no further need for male company in her new environment, which as Karen Michele Chandler remarks, can be seen to embody "New Age assumptions about healing, individual self-development and nurturing community."[4]

There is little doubt that Disney conceived *Washington Square* as a prestige production, in spite of its comparatively modest budget ($15 million). A television documentary, "On the Set of *Washington Square*," was commissioned for broadcast on cable television. The director, Agnieszka Holland, had attracted considerable critical attention, both in America and her native Poland, for her two films *Angry Harvest* (1985) and *Europa Europa* (1991), both of which had been nominated for Academy Awards as Best Foreign Film. Her first two English-language films, *The Secret Garden* (1993) and *Total Eclipse* (1995), had both been costume dramas. Disney's preproduction notes described the cast for *Washington Square* as an ensemble of great stature, "possessing numerous awards and accolades for dramatic achievement."[5] Jennifer Jason Leigh (Catherine Sloper) had won a New York Critics Circle Award for her role in *Picnic* (1986); her recent film experience included Robert Altman's *Short Cuts* (1993) and *Kansas City* (1996). Just like the television version of *The American*, produced at roughly the same time, the supporting cast contained big-name British actors, who were chosen not only for their abilities but also to increase the production's prestige. Ben Chaplin was cast as Morris on the strength of his role in the Merchant-Ivory–produced costume drama *Feast of July* (1995). Maggie Smith (Aunt Penniman) had starred in Holland's *Secret Garden*, while Albert Finney (Dr. Sloper) had already played a bullying paterfamilias in Bruce Beresford's *Rich in Love* (1992).[6]

In the opening scenes of the film, it seems that Holland has chosen a pictorial, rather than a dramatic, approach to narrative technique. In the novel, James describes Sloper's "handsome, modern, wide-fronted house, with a balcony," set in a square "containing a considerable quantity of inexpensive vegetation, enclosed by a wooden paling." This is a world "which appeared to offer a variety of sources of interest" for its inhabitants.[7] Holland appears to take James at his word by creating considerable "sources of interest." The film opens on a sunlit afternoon with a panorama of the square; it is green and populated by ladies and well-dressed children at play. The camera tracks across the square, and moves along the row of houses opposite until it reaches Dr. Sloper's house. It subsequently enters the house through the parlor window, moving toward the drawing room while focusing on the opulent fixtures and fittings. In a later scene, Sloper's carriage is shown receding into the distance, taking Sloper, Catherine, and Aunt Penniman to the Almonds' house, where a maid is seen closing the front gate and waving after them. The camera dollies to the left to show life in the square—a man and his dog crossing the road, and a governess, parasol in hand, taking a child home. Another governess, pushing a pram, moves towards the camera, while two dray horses pulling a cart enter the square from the right side of the frame. The novel describes *Washington Square* a world of "quiet and . . . genteel retirement" wherein Sloper can lead a "solid and honourable life";[8] Holland's depiction of *Washington Square* is far from quiet, but its emphasis on class distinction (only those in service are shown walking on the street, while the more well-to-do ladies remain on the grass) suggests that the comfortable life of the bourgeoisie derives from the exploitation of the lower orders.[9] However, such sequences also interrupt the flow of the narrative, which might lead one to suspect that Holland employs high production values in order to increase the production's commercial potential—in other words, following the example of Wyler's *Heiress* of selling the lifestyle of late nineteenth-century New York to contemporary audiences. Both the opening scene and the sequence depicting the Slopers' departure for the Almonds' house take place in bright afternoon sunshine that shimmers on their carriage roof and the mane of the white horse pulling it. The scene is ablaze with color, ranging from the creamy-white of the dusty, unmade road to the lush green of the lawns in front of the red brick houses.

As the action unfolds, it becomes clear that Holland employs period detail to show how individuals are shaped by their circumstances.[10] The camera's leisurely progress in the opening scene is interrupted by a scream; suddenly, the camera races through Sloper's house, up the stairs, and into one of the bedrooms. Mrs. Sloper lies dead in childbirth, while her husband stands in a state of emotional turmoil. A maid shows him his newborn daughter; he takes no notice of the child, and instead climbs into bed beside his deceased wife. The sequence prepares us for the story to follow, as Sloper's anguish prevents him from showing any affection for Catherine. In his opinion, Catherine's mere presence caused the death of his wife. This is underlined later on in the film, when Sloper and Catherine are in the Alps, and Sloper refers with almost casual brutality (in Carol Doyle's screenplay) to her mother, who gave her life so that Catherine could inhabit the earth.[11]

A further example of Holland's technique occurs in a sequence immediately following Catherine's return from Europe, as she discovers that human feelings count for nothing in bourgeois New York, despite Aunt Penniman's protestations that she is "too deeply interested in [Catherine's] . . . happiness."[12] James's novel has Catherine returning home and informing her aunt in no uncertain terms of her wish to marry Morris and her unwillingness to continue pleading with her father. Penniman herself is somewhat startled by "the force of the girl's emotion and resolution [that] left her nothing to reply."[13] Holland relocates this scene to the New York harbor, with the camera tracking Catherine and Aunt Penniman from the ship that brings Catherine home through a crowd of tradespeople and their customers. The focus is not on Catherine's change of character but on the parallels between Aunt Penniman's discourse and that of the tradespeople. All of them are obsessed with personal profit, whether emotional or financial. In Aunt Penniman's case, she hopes to bring Catherine and Morris together as soon as possible to fulfill her romantic dreams of a secret marriage, "at which she [Penniman] should officiate as bride's woman or duenna."[14] Clearly, she has no idea of the pain her words might cause. Holland has been inspired by the following passage from the novel:

When they found themselves alone together a certain dryness fell upon the girl's emotion. It came over her with a greater force that Mrs. Penniman had enjoyed a whole year of her lover's society, and it was not a pleasure to her to hear her aunt explain and interpret the young man, speaking of him as if her own knowledge of him were supreme. It was not that Catherine was jealous; but her sense of Mrs. Penniman's *innocent falsity*, which had lain dormant, began to haunt her again.[15] (emphasis added)

The relationship between Catherine's personality and her environment is more directly emphasized in the film's interior scenes. As realized by designer Allan Starski, Dr. Sloper's living room is just what one might expect from someone "fond of the good things of life" with "a dread of vulgarity," as the novel puts it.[16] It is filled with Georgian-style mahogany furniture, with a piano tucked away in one corner. Framed portraits of Sloper's family stare down from red paneled walls. A gilt-edged mirror is placed right opposite the entrance, putting guests on show as soon as they enter. Heavy drapes permit very little daylight to penetrate the room. In this very public space, Catherine remains in the background, apart from those occasions when she is expected to demonstrate her ladylike "accomplishments." As someone accustomed to occupying "a secondary place" in the household,[17] this task can often prove too onerous for her. In one newly created scene, Holland shows the adolescent Catherine (Sara Ruzicka) trying to sing as she is accompanied by her aunt on the piano. Standing in the corner of the living room, encircled by her father, his acquaintances, and their families, she is quite literally imprisoned—which makes her so nervous that she wets herself, much to her father's embarrassment.

The idea of woman's confinement in bourgeois society of the eighteenth and nineteenth centuries has been repeatedly stressed in costume dramas through movement images. In Wyler's *Heiress*, Olivia de Havilland's Catherine looks out of the open window on the night of her intended elopement and wonders whether she will see Washington Square again. Clearly, she has become accustomed to observing life in the square rather than participating in it. When she becomes master of the house at the end of the film, she bolts the door and closes the window curtains, as if to emphasize that she no longer wishes to entertain any thoughts of escape.[18] More recently, Olive Chancellor (Vanessa Redgrave) looks out of the window at Verena Tarrant (Madeleine Potter) in Ivory's *Bostonians*; this may be read as an example of female imprisonment, or more positively as an expression of Olive's desire to challenge the conventions of heterosexual society and discover new possibilities for herself. In Holland's *Washington Square*, the image of Catherine looking out through her bedroom window suggests confinement yet also provides an opportunity for her to act according to her emotions rather than observe social proprieties. As she sees her father coming toward the house, she dashes away from the window, celebrating his arrival at the top of her voice.[19] The camera observes her from the top of the stairs as she rushes to the front door, closely followed by Aunt Penniman. In another scene, the older Catherine throws the window open and leans out, letting her long blonde hair blow in the wind. Holland cuts to a shot of the curtains fluttering in her bedroom, before focusing on Catherine in close-up looking at Morris. She smiles with pleasure before running back indoors. The camera slowly zooms toward her as she kisses the bedroom mirror, strokes it with the back of her hand, and looks up to the heavens in delight. Catherine is certainly indiscreet as she opens the window and calls to Morris in full view of the square. If her father had known about it, he would certainly have forbidden her to see Morris any more. But Holland's point is to stress that love has persuaded Catherine to defy convention and act according to her instincts.[20]

Catherine's emotional progress is further stressed through another redefinition of a movement image—that of the walk. This image fulfills several functions: It provides a means of respite away from the pressures of social convention, it is an opportunity for lovers to get to know another, and it gives matchmakers a chance to further their schemes.[21] In one sequence, Catherine takes a walk across the square, some sheet music under her arm; in the front of the shot, we observe Morris hiding behind a tree, waiting to surprise her. As the camera tracks her movement, Morris suddenly jumps out, giving her a friendly greeting; Catherine jumps back with a scream and drops her music; the two of them rush to pick it up, before it blows away. A carriage is seen crossing left to right at the rear of the frame, with the occupants staring in amazement—clearly, this is not the way people in the square are expected to behave. Catherine rushes across to Morris to thank him but only succeeds in dropping her music once again. The two of them fall to the ground in an ungainly heap. As they scramble to their feet, another carriage crosses the frame right to left. The scene ends with Morris and Catherine dusting themselves off and resuming the walk as best they can. By transforming the walk (an example of a socially respectable ritual) into a scene of pure farce, Holland shows Catherine and Morris developing an almost instantaneous attraction for one another. The very presence of Morris sitting on the ground right next to her provides Catherine with an alternative to patriarchal authority, enabling her to contemplate a future in which she is viewed on her own terms, and not simply as Dr. Sloper's ugly daughter.

Catherine's love affair is brought to a close through another parody of the walk movement image. As Morris walks down an alleyway toward a waiting carriage, on his way to New Orleans, she clings to his arm, begging him not to leave. Holland cuts to a panoramic view of the street; it is pouring with rain as Catherine runs after the carriage, screaming Morris's name.[22] The camera zooms in on her as she collapses exhausted into the muddy street, her eyes full of tears. Holland was criticized in some quarters for coarsening the original novel; one critic asked, "Do we need to see our sad little Catherine lying in the mud after being rejected by her first and only love?"[23] There might be some justification for this; in the novel, the main focus is on Catherine's stoicism, as she listens to Morris telling her not to make a scene or behave violently, as such displays of emotion are "not in [her] character." Catherine complies, as "it was . . . [her] wish that there should be no violence about her save the beating of her heart, which she could not help." It is only when Morris has departed that she "gave herself up to her grief."[24] Holland shows Catherine taking no notice of Morris's requests. Any pretence of respectability has evaporated; at this moment, she does not care whether it is socially acceptable for her to be seen running after her lover, begging him to stay.

What follows in the film is radically different from the novel. Another newly written scene depicts the Sloper family gathering to celebrate the christening of Marian Almond's (Jennifer Garner's) youngest child. Catherine carries the baby out of the living room and sits on the stairs, listening to Marian recalling the days of her youth when "the whole future lay before us." The camera zooms in once again on Catherine rocking the baby to sleep while singing a lullaby. Her future as a governess and child-minder is ensured. In the final moments of the film, she is shown in her own house, playing the piano to an admiring audience of children who sing along with her. She has no further need of male company; in a low-key ending, she proposes that Morris should quit her house for good. The final shot has her sitting at the piano with the child Edith, who gazes at her adoringly. A similar scene appears in Graeme Clifford's *Turn of the Screw* (1989), when the governess (Amy Irving) puts her arm around Flora (Irina Cashen), as the little girl falls asleep clutching her teddy bear. But whereas the governess is eventually forced to submit to Quint's malevolent authority, Catherine Sloper can look forward to a feminist future.[25]

Holland's film depicts Catherine as someone not content with "picking up her morsel of fancy-work," the work of her own plain nature, as the novel suggests,[26] but rather as a youngish woman who has transformed the house of her former powerlessness into a place of nurture for other children, some of whom have been as deprived of love as she once was. While this wish-fulfilling ending is directed at those who have been victims of masculine authority, it has also been judged inappropriate to the sociohistorical context of James's novel. One reviewer remarked that "The film's eagerness to spell everything out in capital letters would probably make James cringe. What he would think about an ending that involves Manhattan's first day-care center and a Marilyn and Alan Bergman song about a piece of string is thankfully beyond imagining."[27]

Yet perhaps James might not cringe as much as Turan assumes; in the late nineteenth century, women on both sides of the Atlantic were challenging patriarchal authority in a variety of reform movements designed to obtain voting rights, improve education, and obtain social equality. The first all-women's suffrage committee was formed in Great Britain in 1865; seven years later, the Prohibition Party became the first national political party in the United States to recognize the right of suffrage for women on its platform. In 1881—a year after the publication of *Washington Square*—Carrie Chapman Catt became an high school principal in Iowa; two years later, she was appointed one of the United States' first female school superintendents, and subsequently devoted herself to women's suffrage. Catherine Sloper's crèche has its historical parallels; having visited Toynbee House in London, Jane Addams cofounded Hull House in Chicago in 1889 to provide practical services and educational opportunities for the poor.

However, I would argue that Holland is less concerned with historical or textual accuracy, and more preoccupied with suggesting new possibilities for women living in the late nineteenth century and in the late 1990s. This is achieved by extending the possibilities of movement images such as the woman at the window or the walk, and through the creation of the new ending. Holland justified her approach in an interview published prior to the film's London opening: "We're in the same situation sociologically and in terms of values as in late Victorian society. . . . In present-day Poland in particular, the obsession with wealth and status is all-consuming."[28]

Holland's argument can be challenged on two counts. While seeking to communicate a feminist message through the film, it might be argued that by preserving the classical narrative form—which sustains the familiar images of woman as natural, realistic, and attractive—her approach was conservative rather than radical. Unlike Jane Campion's *Portrait*, *Washington Square* presents its story in a narrative form that ultimately limits women's options. Secondly, it is clear that the film's analysis of gender, wealth, and status is restricted to bourgeois heterosexual women; it does not even encompass the varieties of femininity that are contained in Unwin's *American*, for instance.

Once again, this may serve to confirm rather than challenge existing what audiences have to come to expect from a late 1990s classical adaptation.

What is certain, however, is that Disney wanted to market *Washington Square* to as wide an audience as possible. They were not entirely happy with the finished film—especially the ending, which they thought was not sufficiently optimistic. Holland revealed that they expected it to be a romantic comedy like Douglas McGrath's *Emma* (1995), which ended well "with marriage and everyone happy."[29] In another publicity interview, published before the American opening, she recalled that "there was a suggestion that we reshoot the ending, but fortunately they [Disney executives] didn't have any specific ideas, and also they weren't very aggressive."[30] Disney marketed *Washington Square* as a love story, where the heroine has to choose between her father and her lover (even though she ends up rejecting both). One of the posters featured Jennifer Jason Leigh and Ben Chaplin locked in a passionate embrace, their eyes fixed on one another. Attention focused mainly on Leigh's face and the white flesh of her left shoulder, bathed in a soft yellow light, with Chaplin's hand stroking her chin. The legend underneath read "She must choose between her father's fortune . . . or the man she loves." *Washington Square* was given a restricted release in the United States, in the hope that favorable reviews and/or audience reaction would enable Disney to transform it into a crossover hit. Unfortunately, it failed at the box office, which according to Holland, rather dampened the studio's enthusiasm for the project: "I think it was somebody's caprice to do the movie. Afterwards, they were very nice, but they seemed indifferent somehow."[31] The film received its British premiere at the National Film Theatre in London, as part of a three-week festival of Henry James films, and was subsequently put on general release in mainstream cinemas. The VHS version of the film in Britain—issued in 1999—was "critically acclaimed" by the National Museum of Photography, Film and Television, but apparently did not sell enough copies to remain on the shelves for long. Nonetheless, the film retains a certain value—if only for the fact that it reveals a characteristically late 1990s preoccupation with female narration, agency, and expression. Its harsh account of the limits and agency and expression for its female protagonist is to some extent mitigated by a virtuoso feminist authorship that boldly alters the ending of the original novel—a move that Julianne Pidduck describes as "part of the pleasure of feminist costume drama . . . [as] autueurist film-makers intervene in formative narratives of gender, sexuality and desire."[32]

Notes

1. Much of the argument in this chapter is based on my article "Rethinking the Costume Drama; Agnieszka Holland's *Washington Square*," *Henry James Review* 24, no. 1 (Winter 2003), 69–82.

2. Five hundred new multiplex screens were built by the Hollywood majors in Britain during the 1980s; there was a similar investment in Japan, which is now the major market for American films outside the United States.

3. Justin Wyatt, "The Formation of the 'Major Independent:' Miramax, New Line and the New Hollywood," in *Contemporary Hollywood Cinema*, ed. Steve Neale and Murray Smith (London: Routledge, 1998), 78.

4. Karen Michele Chandler, "Her Ancient Faculty of Silence: Catherine Sloper's Ways of Being in James's *Washington Square* and Two Film Adaptations," in *Henry James Goes to the Movies*, ed. Susan M. Griffin (Lexington: University Press of Kentucky, 2002), 172.

5. Press book: *Washington Square* (Los Angeles: Hollywood Pictures, 1997), 7.

6. Note also that Sloper was played by a Briton—Ralph Richardson—in Wyler's 1949 version.

7. Henry James, *Washington Square*, ed. Michael Swan (Harmondsworth: Penguin Books, 1963), 16–17.

8. James, *Washington Square*, 16–17.

9. This was apparently Holland's intention, according to the cinematographer Jerzy Zielinski: "We wanted crisp, clean images to communicate a sense of reality." "Zielinski Uses Newest Tools for 1850s Saga," *In Camera* (October 1997): 24.

10. In an interview published after *Washington Square* was released, Holland expressed the belief that it was "about . . . identity, about who you are, whether you are what people expect you to be or how the people see you, if you and your truth are shaped by somebody's expectation or judgement, or if it's possible to find something which is the real you." Gordana P. Crnkovic, "Interview with Agnieszka Holland," *Film Quarterly* 52, no. 2 (1999), 3.

11. Carol Doyle, *Washington Square: A Screenplay* (Los Angeles: Hollywood Pictures, 1997), 73.

12. James, *Washington Square*, 124.

13. James, *Washington Square*, 124.

14. James, *Washington Square*, 76.

15. James, *Washington Square*, 20.

16. James, *Washington Square*, 14.

17. James, *Washington Square*, 11.

18. Julie H. Rivkin, "Prospects of Entertainment: Film Adaptations of *Washington Square*," in *Henry James Goes to the Movies*, ed. Susan M. Griffin (Lexington: University Press of Kentucky, 2002), 156–57.

19. Doyle, *Washington Square: A Screenplay*, 6.

20. The novel has Catherine saying "I don't care who sees us," but she follows it with the phrase "But leave me now" as she begins to tremble again. Clearly, she is very concerned about the consequences of her affair. James, *Washington Square*, 49.

21. See, for example, Simon Langton's BBC/WGBH television version of *Pride and Prejudice* (1995), where Elizabeth Bennet (Jennifer Ehle) is found roaming Darcy's (Colin Firth's) estate; this enables her to "possess" the landscape prior to becoming mistress of it through marriage. The main focus of the walk is on respectability: Bourgeois young women and their suitors should keep themselves and their emotions under control, especially in public.

22. Doyle, *Washington Square: A Screenplay*, 97.

23. Wendy Wilson, "Washington Square," *Rough Cut Reviews*, October 7, 1997, 13.

24. James, *Washington Square*, 142–43.

25. Julianne Pidduck, *Contemporary Costume Film* (London: BFI Publishing, 2004), 68.

26. James, *Washington Square*, 160.

27. Kenneth Turan, "Washington Square: A New Approach to an Old Address," *Los Angeles Times*, October 10, 1997, 14. The song "The Tale of the String" refers to what it takes for "a plain little piece of string" to become "the prettiest music of all." Catherine unsuccessfully tries to sing it as a little girl, when she wets herself.

28. Geoffrey Macnab, "A Harsh Look at Life in the Square," *Independent Eye*, May 8, 1998, 11.

29. Macnab, "A Harsh Look,"11.

30. Amy Taubin, "Squaring Off," *Village Voice*, October 14, 1997, 94.

31. Macnab, "A Harsh Look,"11.

32. Pidduck, *Contemporary Costume Film*, 78–79.

CHAPTER TWENTY-ONE

~

The House by the Cemetery (1981) and The Haunting of Hell House (1999)

Both Lucio Fulci's *The House by the Cemetery* (aka *Quella Villa Accanto al Cimitero*) (1981) and Mitch Marcus's *The Haunting of Hell House* (1999) share a concern with what Freud describes as the *unheimlich*—the uncanny—something that was of particular interest to James himself. As Douglas, the narrator, observes at the beginning of *The Turn of the Screw*, the governess believes that her experiences at Bly House were "beyond anything . . . for general uncanny ugliness, and horror and pain."[1] Both films suggest that the source of such uncanny experiences originates in the house itself, which is represented as an analog of the female body, its erogenous zones transformed into threatening places dominated by a morbid fear of female sexuality. Within its four walls, the principal male characters are quite literally driven to death. This interpretation reverses the plot of *The Turn of the Screw* (where the governess is threatened by Peter Quint), apparently to express the archetypal male fear of being dominated by the "monstrous regiment" of women.

However, I suggest that both films undercut this misogynist viewpoint through the figure of the time traveler and the atmosphere of "strange enchantment" (combining the fantastic and the commonplace) associated with them. In earlier adaptations of similar subject matter—*Berkeley Square, I'll Never Forget You, On a Clear Day*—the male protagonist's encounter with the past enabled him to discover a "high truth" about love's power to transcend time. By contrast, *The House by the Cemetery* and *The Haunting of Hell House* seek to establish a space for the repressed underside of the "normal" (in other words, patriarchal) world to make its appearance, and thereby offer new possibilities for women in a play of fantasy and ritual. Fulci's film has the little girl May Freudstein coming back as a ghost and communicating intuitively, rather than through spoken language. Once the two central female characters of The Haunting of Hell House—Sarah and Lucy—reappear in ghostly form, they quite literally divest themselves of the social obligations imposed on them during their lifetimes as lovers or daughters. For producer Roger Corman, this represented a return to the preoccupations of his cycle of Edgar Allan Poe films, which according to his biographer Beverly Gray had a particular impact on young adolescents of the early 1960s—especially women, who were "quietly struggling with their own emerging sexuality" at a time of profound socioeconomic upheaval in American society.[2]

This chapter concludes by suggesting that both The House by the Cemetery and The Haunting of Hell House were released at a time when the costume drama had carved out a niche for itself in the film industry—not only attracting audiences because of its subject matter but also because of its visual style. With this in mind, both directors approached their material as a quality product, both in terms of subject matter and narrative construction, focusing on character, setting, and location rather than plot development. As Mark Jancovich remarks, adaptations like this (which also include Silence of the Lambs [1991]) seek to distance themselves from most horror films, which are commonly associated with "voyeurism, misogyny and formulaic simplicity." Rather, they seek to advance a feminist viewpoint in an attempt to associate themselves "with legitimate culture through a series of distinctions in which 'horror' is constructed as their own other."[3]

Initially, however, it seems as if The House by the Cemetery and The Haunting of Hell House have been conceived as mainstream horror films—particularly in their interpretation of the Freudian uncanny. In his essay of the same name, Freud identifies several phenomena that might be termed thus—in other words, characterized by "that class of the frightening which leads back to what is known of old and long familiar."[4] They include anything relating to the notion of a double (a cyborg, a twin, a doppelganger), haunted houses (whose association with death and dead bodies stimulates the "uncanny" feeling "in the highest degree,"[5] and castration fears. The horror presented by each of these things relates to the loss of identifiable boundaries—the double explodes the myth that each human being is a discrete entity; castration anxieties are provoked by fear of the collapse of gender distinctions; and the uncanny feeling inspired by a haunted house can be attributed to an inability to separate the known from the unknown. Such fears Freud believes are attributable to the kind of repression that prompts people to establish the distinctions in the first place. Most living human beings have ceased to believe that the dead can appear to them as spirits, except under improbable and remote conditions such as being confined to a haunted (or *unheimlich*) house.[6] As the male has been brought up to believe he is different from the female, this inspires in him a fear of her womb—that "old, and long familiar" place where such distinctions never existed:

> This *unheimlich* place . . . is the entrance to the former Heim (home) of all human beings, to the place where each one of us lived once upon a time and in the beginning. There is a joke saying that "Love is home-sickness"; and whenever a man dreams of a place or a country and says to himself, while he is still dreaming: "this place is familiar to me, I've been here before," we may interpret the place as being his mother's genitals or her body. In this case too, then, the *unheimlich* is what was once *heimisch*, familiar; the prefix "*un*" ("un") is the token of repression.[7]

Here the womb and the haunted house are explicitly identified with one another—both are perceived as places where the boundaries between life and death, man and/or woman, have collapsed, inspiring a fear of the unknown. Many horror films routinely take this argument to its logical (and misogynist) conclusion by linking the haunted house with the figure of the mother. As Barbara Creed remarks, such places invariably conceal "cruel secrets and [have] . . . witnessed terrible deeds, usually committed by family members against each other. . . . The body/house is literally the body of horror, the place of the uncanny."[8] In *The House by the Cemetery*, two of the main characters—Bob Boyle (Giovanni Frezza), a blond-haired child, and his mother, Lucy (Catriona MacColl)—are quite literally sucked back into the womb through the vagina as they desperately try to escape from the monstrous Dr. Freudstein (Giovanni de Nara) up a ladder leading from the cellar to the hallway. While Bob manages to scramble to safety, Lucy's bid for freedom proves fruitless as Freudstein drags her back down the ladder before mutilating her.

Both *The House by the Cemetery* and *The Haunting of Hell House* begin by depicting the haunted house (to use Freud's phrase) as a *heimisch* place—a familiar site offering some kind of refuge from a disordered outside world. *The House by the Cemetery* has the Boyle family moving away from the hurly-burly of New York to a lonely house in New Whitby near Boston, to enable Norman, the head of the household (Paolo Malco), to continue his research into the Freudsteins, the house's previous owners. Norman tells Lucy to "smell that country air" as they arrive. *The Haunting of Hell House* follows its Jamesian source (the early short story "The Ghostly Rental" [1876]) by depicting the house as a place with "no sign of life about it: it looked blank, bare and vacant, and yet . . . it seemed to have a familiar meaning—an audible eloquence."[9] The house appears so familiar and inviting, in fact, that both James Farrow (Andrew Bowen) and his girlfriend, Sarah (Aideen O'Donnell), are shown making passionate love within its walls, Sarah murmuring with pleasure as she does so: "Just us. Alone. The rest of the world be damned."[10]

Sarah's statement turns out to be a savagely ironic, as she dies as a result of an unsuccessful abortion, and subsequently returns as a ghost to torment Farrow. Try as he might, he can neither escape from her nor the house in which the unborn child was conceived. One sequence shows him peering through the locked front gates; on the soundtrack Sarah's voice can be heard whispering, "James!!!" The action continues with a shot/reverse-shot sequence recalling Miss Giddens's first sighting of Quint on the tower at Bly in Clayton's *Innocents*. It begins with a shot from Farrow's point of view of Sarah looking out at him through the windows, followed by a close-up of Farrow's face, and then another point-of-view shot of the windows—only this time Sarah is not there any more. Her voice can be heard once again on the soundtrack, in an echo of the opening scene: "Just us. Alone." The *heimisch* house of the opening scene has now become *unheimlich*, imprisoning Farrow in its clutches. This is underlined in a dream sequence later on, which begins with a shot of Farrow sleeping. The camera tracks past his left shoulder to focus on prison bars with the sea beyond them, suggesting that he has no means of escape. This is followed by a dissolve to a shot of the operating table (where Sarah had her abortion) with blood gushing over the edge, while Sarah's voice is heard once again encouraging Farrow to join her in death: "Alone. Together. Come, James."

The Farrow/Sarah plot works as a counterpoint to the main plot which (following the original story) has a central male character, Ambrose (Michael York), returning every month to the house to collect rent from the ghost of his daughter Lucy (Claudia Christian), who has decided to occupy it. He feels compelled to continue this arrangement in the belief that he was responsible for his daughter's death, as a voice-over at the beginning of the film explains: "The house remains abandoned, left to Ambrose's ghost. Some say he was once in love with this demon, and to this day he still visits this house to pay tribute [to her]." What Ambrose does not realize is that Lucy is not dead at all but merely pretending to be a ghost as part of her overall plan to poison him. Every time he visits the house, he sips a glass of wine in the belief that he must take the offering from Lucy, "whom I so heartlessly rejected when she was alive." However, this wine has been drugged, rendering him less and less capable of distinguishing between dream and reality. Just like Farrow, Ambrose is imprisoned in the *unheimlich* womb of the house, presided over by a female monster, in which the boundaries between life and death, reason and madness, no longer apply: "Each week I feel my soul becoming more poisoned. . . . Practical and rational things mean nothing to me."

The House by the Cemetery begins in much the same way as *The Haunting of Hell House*, with a young woman (Daniela Doria) being discovered putting her blouse back on after having had sex in the house. She searches for her lover but only succeeds in meeting a bloody fate at Freudstein's hands as he drives a knife through the back of her cranium and out through her mouth. In life, Freudstein sought to dissolve the boundaries separating life from death by uncovering the secret of immortality but only succeeded in transforming himself into a zombie, sustaining himself with the blood of his dismembered victims. His house becomes a place where the living are terrorized by the dead—as Norman discovers as he settles down one night to read Freudstein's notes. Suddenly he hears the sound of rustling, looks immediately towards his wife (who is asleep opposite him) and rushes out of the room, as if aware of Freudstein's presence. The sound of childish sobs can be heard on the soundtrack, suggesting that no one—not even little Bob—can escape the zombie's bloodthirsty grasp. Norman rushes wildly around the house and suddenly espies the babysitter Ann (Ania Peroni) trying to force open the door leading to Freudstein's cellar. Fulci intercuts close-ups of Norman's and Ann's eyes, suggesting that both of them have simultaneously discovered the house's terrible secret.

As in Marcus's film, Freudstein's house is likewise ruled by an evil woman—Mary Freudstein, who resembles Hecate, the matron of all witchcraft and all evil—in her long black dress.[11] In one scene, Bob emerges from the cellar and overhears her telling her daughter Mae (Silvia Collatina) to "act like a Freudstein. You know some other guest is surely destined to drop in." She walks toward Bob, takes his hand, and subsequently leads the two children away from the camera. We are left with the uncomfortable feeling that Bob's fate has already been determined—something underlined by the sobs that can be heard on the soundtrack.

Blood is one of the most common images of horror films associated with the *unheimlich* house. As befits a specialist in gore, Fulci's *House by the Ceme-*

tery positively drips with it; one sequence begins with close-ups of Norman's eyes intercut with shots of blood seeping out of Freudstein's coffin. The camera tracks away from the coffin, lingering lovingly on the mutilated body parts in the cellar, then moves towards the table where the doctor performs his experiments. One website congratulated the director for such "outstanding gore effects. . . . Fulci's overkill fuses with [cinematographer Gianetto De] Rossi's artistry resulting in a bloody opulence which is hard to match or make comparisons with."[12] *The Haunting of Hell House* contains a similarly gory scene, when blood gushes out from Sarah's womb as she has her unsuccessful abortion. The image recurs throughout the film as Farrow experiences his nightmarish visions of torment.

So far, it would seem that both films identify the haunted house with the powerful castrating woman/mother as part of a misogynist project to construct "the maternal body as 'abject.'"[13] However, I would suggest that such stereotypes are questioned—chiefly by redefining the figure of the time traveler (a popular character in many James adaptations of the past). In *Berkeley Square* and *I'll Never Forget You*, the time traveler Peter Standish was someone who sought to move back in time in order to discover things about the past as well as to engage in a voyage of self-discovery. Although forced to return to the present at the end, he understood how such "universal truths" as the power of love could transcend time: Even though Helen Pettigrew died of an illness, her passion for him could never die. *On a Clear Day* follows much the same path: The psychiatrist Marc Chabot travels back in time from modern-day New York to eighteenth-century Britain and falls in love with Melinda Tentrees. Only when he returns back to the present does he discover that Melinda's love lives on through Daisy Gamble. By contrast, *The House by the Cemetery* casts the little girl May Freudstein as the time traveler, who can come back from the dead to warn Bob about the dangers lurking in the house, even though she stands at least one hundred meters away from him. Although Fulci has argued in an interview that she may represent nothing more than a figment of Bob's imagination, her role within the film suggests that children—particularly female children—can conjure up a world wherein (as Fulci himself has observed) "everything is possible. . . . Children don't have the same [social and gender] limitations as grown-ups. . . . They have a different wavelength."[14]

Once Sarah becomes a ghost in *The Haunting of Hell House*, she likewise frees herself from social and gender limitations. At one point, she observes on the soundtrack that whereas "James [Farrow], you have thought me dead," she now has the freedom to appear in whatever guise she wishes. In one sequence, she assumes a diabolic form, with a wooden splint wrapped around her, one hand grasping the operating table, while the other hand (tied at the wrist) flaps wildly in the air. On another occasion, she assumes a human form as she runs away from Farrow, dressed in a long black robe. He pursues her but cannot find anything, even though he continually hears her voice intoning "Just us. Alone. Come to me, James, come to me." To taunt him further, she appears in a mirror, her white face contrasting starkly with her black hair, whispering "Promise me." Farrow puts his hand up to the glass, trying to communicate with her, but she melts away. In other James adaptations (e.g., Bogdanovich's *Daisy Miller* or Unwin's *American*), the male character is shown endeavoring to possess the female through the power of the gaze. Sarah's sudden disappearance from Farrow's vision indicates that she possesses the capacity to elude this form of control.

Lucy's domination over her father Ambrose (while pretending to be a ghost) is far more materialistic. *The Haunting of Hell House* follows the original story by showing her forging an agreement by which she will pay a quarterly rent to Ambrose—an installment of which he had just received when he first encounters Farrow.[15] Lucy's ghost is an emblem of the material relationships between desire and possession, having and not having. Only her presence—elusive though it may be—can guarantee Ambrose's financial and even epistemological security. She inserts herself into a financial and domestic economy, at once challenging the male domination of the market and quite literally upsetting the patriarchy.[16]

Throughout his career as a producer and/or director, Corman has been preoccupied with the idea of female emancipation. In his cycle of Poe adaptations in the early 1960s, as Mark Jancovich remarks, Corman represented the dominant females as "positive rather than negative figures"—which perhaps helps to explain why his films were so popular among younger filmgoers (especially the sixteen to twenty-five age group) who were searching for alternatives to established gender roles.[17] *The Haunting of Hell House* represents Corman's attempt to address these questions once again, at a time when feminism and feminist film theory had wrought considerable changes in perception (particularly in James adaptations) of identity and gender construction.

In considering *The House by the Cemetery* and *The Haunting of Hell House*, it must be borne in mind that they were planned as "quality" horror films, focusing attention on character, location, and setting, and employing a pictorial rather than dramatic narrative technique. Jancovich explains that this represented an attempt to create something "offering the pleasures associated with the horror movie—that it will be gripping, terrifying, shocking, and so forth—while also legitimating the film through its distinction from the genre."[18] Fulci acknowledged in an interview that, while *The House by the Cemetery* contained its fair share of gore, the film was conceived as a psychological thriller focusing on character at the expense of the plot, based on Clayton's *Innocents* in the sense that "all that is told may have happened at least in the child's imagination—even his parents' deaths. The spectator may also see the film as a kind of cycle, the events being repetitions of things past."[19] One sequence—directly inspired by *The Innocents* (and *Turn of the Screw*)—begins with a shot of Bob lying in bed and his mother giving him a kiss goodnight. Without warning, he gets up and walks down to Freudstein's lair. The subsequent action unfolds through a series of close-ups of Bob's face, interspersed with point-of-view shots of the table, the ladder leading up to the living room, and the basket full of body parts. Suddenly Bob screams, a pair of cats' eyes is briefly seen, and the little boy runs away calling piteously for his mother. The clear suggestion in this scene is that he has some kind of premonition about what's happening in the cellar; perhaps this is due to some kind of ability to communicate with the dead (like Miles and Flora in *Turn of the Screw*) or maybe—as Fulci suggests—the whole scenario takes place in his imagination.[20] The film incorporates a quotation attributed to James at the end of the film ("Are children monsters, or would monsters be children?") to underline the psychological aspect—even though the phrase does not exist in any of James's works.

The Haunting of Hell House announces its intentions from the start, as the camera tracks Farrow's and Sarah's coach riding on the edge of the cliffs toward the house. In the background, bluish-gray waves crash on to the sandy beach. Marcus cuts to Ambrose's house (actually the Manor House, especially constructed for Corman's studios in Ireland as a location and a commercial hotel), and slowly pans the exterior, concentrating in particular on the verandah and the symmetrical gables. In the background, a narrator sets the scene for what is to come: "Nobody knows the whole story. Some say the lady who lived here died of a broken heart. Others say that the lover murdered her in a violent rage after finding her in bed with another woman." This is followed by a close-up of Farrow telling Sarah that "this [the house] is what I wanted you to see." Marcus repeatedly employs this technique as the camera pans the gray stone buildings and the rain-washed pavements of Farrow's university campus, or tracks its way through the bustling atmosphere of the local market, where teenage pickpockets run in and out of the cramped stalls. The fact that the film has been based on a short story by

Henry James automatically renders it a "quality" product; this is further emphasized by Marcus's pictorial imagination that compensates for any shocking moments. As the publicity for the video box suggests, he sought to transform James's "tale of vengeful spirits and tortured men" into "one of the most *visually rich and stylish* films to be released for years" (emphasis added).[21]

Both *The House by the Cemetery* and *The Haunting of Hell House* are fundamentally "feminine" in structure, in the sense that they place emphasis on character, fashion, and decoration.[22] This, I believe, is a deliberate decision on the directors' part to attract an audience that might not normally attend horror films—particularly women. This was a sound decision; as Brigid Cherry's research into British film-going tastes has revealed, many women are attracted by horror films containing strong or capable female characters. Additionally, they preferred films with "high production values in art direction, set design and costumes. Acting was frequently mentioned as being crucial. . . . The quality of a film was [also] determined by plot and character development."[23] If a horror film contained gory effects, they preferred them to be "over the top" and offset by the "good story with interesting characters. . . . Female viewers appeared not to reject gore or violence *per se* so much as the way the elements were used in the film. . . . More importantly, emotional or psychological responses were frequently deemed important in the enjoyment of a film."[24] In spite of the attention both directors devoted to characterization and psychological development, neither *The House by the Cemetery* nor *The Haunting of Hell House* attracted much response, either from critics or filmgoers. *The House by the Cemetery* has achieved the status of a cult classic among gore fans; mainstream reviewers, on the other hand, have dismissed it as "a primitive picture, with Fulci showing little more than a talent for gruesome knifings."[25] *The Haunting of Hell House* was likened by one reviewer to a television classic adaptation "produced by the BBC. . . . It is a surprisingly sedate and modest effort when compared to the usual films that Corman and Concorde churn out. In fact probably a little too much so. Director Marcus tries earnestly to generate scares but far too often falls on the pedestrian side."[26] As films conceived within the horror genre, they clearly are considered to lack the cultural legitimacy associated with more "classical" literary adaptations—in other words, the kinds of costume dramas that have formed much of the basis of this book. Despite the popularity of big-budget "quality" horror films such as *The Silence of the Lambs* (that seek to distinguish themselves from more popular genres such as the slasher movie,[27] the genre as a whole is still associated with voyeurism, misogyny, and formulaic simplicity. What this chapter has tried to show is that perhaps

The House by the Cemetery and *The Haunting of Hell House* should be revaluated as works that share the concerns of most James adaptations of the 1980s and 1990s. Moreover, it is also clear that by redefining the figure of the time traveler, both films share a characteristically Jamesian concern to offer a different way of looking at things, a way of perceiving beneath their surfaces and discovering a different order of truth and experience. Perhaps this is what encouraged Fulci and Marcus to turn to James in the first place—he offered them the chance to deal with the possible, offering them a greater flexibility and latitude, especially where gender definitions are concerned.

Notes

1. Henry James, *The Turn of the Screw, The Aspern Papers and Other Stories*, ed. Michael Swan (London: Collins, 1963), 316.

2. Beverly Gray, *Roger Corman: An Unauthorized Biography of the Godfather of Indie Film-Making* (Los Angeles: Renaissance Books, 2000), 72.

3. Mark Jancovich, "Genre and the Audience: Genre Classifications and Cultural Distinctions in the Mediation of *The Silence of the Lambs*," in *The Horror Film Reader*, ed. Mark Jancovich (London: Routledge, 2002), 159.

4. Sigmund Freud, "The Uncanny," trans. James Strachey, in *The Standard Edition of the Works of Sigmund Freud*, Vol. 17 (1917–1919) (London: Hogarth Press and the Institute of Psychoanalysis, 1971), 210.

5. Freud, "The Uncanny," 241.

6. Freud, "The Uncanny," 241–43.

7. Freud, "The Uncanny," 245.

8. Barbara Creed, *The Monstrous-Feminine: Film, Feminism, Psychoanalysis* (London: Routledge, 1993), 55.

9. Henry James, "The Ghostly Rental" (1876), in *Eight Uncollected Tales of Henry James*, ed. Edna Kenton (New Brunswick, NJ: Rutgers University Press, 1950), 282–83.

10. Much of the discussion of *The Haunting of Hell House* is based on my article "Corman Revisits the Classics: *The Haunting of Hell House* (1999)," in *Shadows That Stalk: Representations of Fear in American Culture. Proceedings of the 20th Anniversary Conference, 24–25 October 2002*, ed. Bilge Mutluay (Ankara: Hacettepe University / State University of New York at Buffalo, 2003), 177–85.

11. "Origin and History of a Queen of Demosthenes," *New Covenant Church of God*, at www.nccg.org/deliverance/demons01-Hecate.html (accessed August 13, 2005).

12. "The House by the Cemetery," *Lightsfade Reviews*, at www.lightsfade.com/reviews/houseby.htm (accessed March 3, 2005).

13. Sue Thornham, *Passionate Detachments: An Introduction to Feminist Film Theory* (London: Arnold, 1997), 106.

14. Lou Rinaldi, "Lucio Fulci Interview," *Starburst* 4, no. 12 (August 1982), at www.shockingimages.com/fulci/interview2.html (accessed March 3, 2005).

15. James, "Ghostly Rental," 286.

16. Sheri Weinstein, "Possessive Matters in 'The Ghostly Rental,'" *Henry James Review* 21 (2000): 274.

17. Mark Jancovich, *Rational Fears: American Horror in the 1950s* (Manchester: Manchester University Press, 1996), 271, 274.

18. Jancovich, "Genre and the Audience," 156.

19. Rinaldi, "Lucio Fulci Interview."

20. See Stephen Thrower, *Beyond Terror: The Films of Lucio Fulci* (Guildford, UK: FAB Press, 1999).

21. All quotations from the original video box release for "The Haunting of Hell House" (New Horizons, 1999).

22. Lyn Thomas, *Fans, Feminisms and "Quality" Media* (London: Routledge, 2002), 35.

23. Brigid Cherry, "Refusing to Refuse to Look: Female Viewers of the Horror Film," in *The Horror Film Reader*, ed. Mark Jancovich (London: Routledge, 2002), 172.

24. Cherry, "Refusing to Refuse," 173.

25. Gerald Peary, "The House by the Cemetery," *Boston Phoenix*, June 15, 1998, at www.filmvault.com/filmvault/boston/h/housebythecemeter1.html (accessed September 6, 2005).

26. Richard Scheib, "The Haunting of Hell House aka The Ghostly Rental," *SF Horror and Fantasy Film Review*, 2000, www.moria.co.nz/horror/hauntinghellhouse.htm (accessed September 6, 2005).

27. Jancovich, "Genre and the Audience," 16.

CHAPTER TWENTY-TWO

~

Presence of Mind (1999)

The implications of James's religious views—particularly concerning Catholicism—have been exhaustively analyzed by Edwin Sill Fussell in a 1993 book. Although he does not seek to make James a Catholic, he nonetheless insists that the author is preoccupied with religious difference, "no matter if it be phrased as Protestants and Others (Mainly Catholics) or Catholicism and Others (Mainly Protestants)."[1] In *The Turn of the Screw*, for example, the Protestant governess believes that Quint and Miss Jessel are representatives of the Catholic Church who seek to possess and corrupt the children: "[They want them] for the love of all the evil that, in those dreadful days, the pair put into them. And to ply them with that evil still, to keep up the work of demons, is what brings the others back."[2]

The governess adds the apparently innocuous remark that "all roads lead to Rome" with further portentous sayings about "Forbidden ground," namely "the question of the return of the dead in general and of whatever, in especial, might survive, in memory, of the friends the little children had lost."[3] For Fussell, such observations reveal the governess's "vague general sense" that Quint and Miss Jessel are like Catholics, "oppressive and devious and potentially tyrannical (the Inquisition), inciting to the same kind of fear . . . that the country parson's daughter associates with both pre- and post-Reformation catholicity in England, of all places."[4] However, perhaps the governess needs this fear of Catholicism to sustain her Protestant faith: "Protestantism is unavoidably a secondary dependent adversarial communion, a movement upon, or against, or away from, or apart from, a prior communion. . . . What would happen to Protestant Reformism if the Catholic Church should cease to exist?"[5]

Antonio Aloy's film adaptation (1999), originally titled *Celo* and renamed *Presence of Mind* for English-speaking audiences, adapts the novella to focus specifically on Catholicism and its effect on individual people. This chapter shows how the film creates two behavioral extremes: on the one hand, there are those—Miles, Flora, and Mrs. Grose (renamed Mado Remei—for whom the religion has little or no significance, representing little more than a series of outmoded rituals to be performed every Sunday. On the other hand, there are so-called devout Catholics such as the governess's father (a newly created character) who regularly abused his daughter as a child while imposing patriarchal authority over her by forcing her to remain silent about her experiences. As the novella suggests (in the passage quoted above), such people are indeed "oppressive and devious and potentially tyrannical."[6] Despite her unshakeable faith in God, the governess remains scarred for life, haunted by the belief that Miles and Flora might have experienced similar humiliation from Quint (renamed Fosc), Miss Jessel, or the uncle.

Why was the novella altered in this way? I suggest that there were two reasons—first, that this adaptation (unlike any other adaptation covered in this book) was intended primarily for European distribution, being put on general release in Spain in April 2001, after having been shown at film festivals in France (September 1999), Canada (FantAsia Film Festival), and Spain (San Sebastian). Consequently, Aloy reshaped his material to what he perceived as the tastes of an art-house European audience. Secondly, we have to remember that the film's original Spanish title was *Celo*, which translates into English as (1) care, diligence, conscientiousness in the pursuance of one's duties; (2) fervor, enthusiasm; (3) envy, jealousy; and (4) sexual heat in animals.[7] The film explores these several meanings of the word in relation to the novella, focusing in particular on the difficulties of sustaining one's Catholic faith with "care, diligence, and conscientiousness" in an environment dominated by "sexual heat" or "fervor and enthusiasm."

The apathy many people feel towards the Catholic faith is especially evident in a sequence involving the governess (Sadie Frost) and Miles (Nilo Mur), as the governess tries to persuade the little boy to go to confession. Miles fails to see why he should go, on the grounds that he has nothing to confess; the governess responds somewhat lamely by telling him that the experience will do him good. A horse-drawn carriage pulls up nearby with Mado Remei (aka Mrs. Grose) (Lauren Bacall) and Flora (Ella Jones) inside. Miles jumps in, and the three of them leave for church, giggling to each other while the governess remains behind, staring morosely at the ground. In the novella, the governess recalls the churchgoing episode as an occasion when Miles's outfit rendered him so grown-up in appearance "that if he had suddenly struck for freedom I should have had nothing to say." This provides a suitable prelude for the moment when she discovers "something new" about him—his "sudden revelation of a consciousness and a plan."[8] *Presence of Mind* alters the emphasis of the scene to show how going to confession represents little more than a Sunday outing—an opportunity for Miles, his sister, and Mado Remei to dress up and enjoy themselves away from the claustrophobic atmosphere of Bly House. The children's cavalier attitude toward religion is further illustrated in a scene that takes place in the schoolroom. Miles insists that, in purely factual terms, there is no distinction between a ghost and a spirit: The Bible continually refers to the trinity of the Father, Son, and Holy Ghost. The governess disagrees, on the grounds that ghosts do not exist, while the spirit refers to the soul. However, Miles argues—quite logically—that if ghosts do not exist, then why do they appear in the dictionary, smiling at Flora in triumph as he does so. The soul and the spirit mean nothing to him; they are just abstract terms employed in a childish game of semantics.

The children follow the example set by their uncle (Harvey Keitel), who remarks at the beginning of the film that "the [Catholic] notion of redemption through suffering fascinates me though I myself haven't the conviction." He gives the governess a St. Christopher's medal, explaining as he does so that the saint was "the protector of the Christ child—to save oneself by saving innocents." Such high-minded sentiments provide him with an excuse for seduction, as he takes the governess's black-gloved hand and fondles it, staring straight into her eyes as he does so. The uncle's dissolute character is summed up by his costume—a scarlet dressing-grown trimmed with orange and blue—and by his behavior, as he downs a glass of sherry in one gulp before addressing the governess.

The idea that the uncle is somehow responsible for the children's corruption is a familiar one in film adaptations of *The Turn of the Screw*; Graeme Clifford's 1989 version has him simulating sexual congress by threading a rolled-up napkin through a metal ring, while Rusty Lemorande's film, made five years later, transforms him into a drug addict. What renders Aloy's film more intriguing is that Harvey Keitel has been cast in the role—someone more associated with action films (*Taxi Driver, Reservoir Dogs, Pulp Fiction*) than classical adaptations. His persona—both on and off the screen—has always been that of someone firm in his opinions and intolerant of those who dare to contradict him. One journalist interviewing him in April 2005 remarked that, while he remained "thoroughly gracious" on the whole, there were times when she saw "a brief glimpse of a man whom it would be best not to cross."[9] Keitel's presence in the film emphasizes the extent of the uncle's dominance over his family. He might think of himself as aloof with no time for the children, but it is clear that he imposes his will on Bly House and everything that happens therein.[10] It should thus come as no surprise that the children have no conception of why Catholicism should be important as a means of organizing their lives.

The governess experiences even worse treatment at the hands of her father (Jack Taylor), who although only seen in the film's precredit sequence, nonetheless makes his presence felt "as his nightmarish voice assaults the governess through dreams and subliminal visions."[11] One sequence begins with the governess opening a small pocketbook containing a black-and-white photograph of herself standing beside her father's corpse, which had been propped upright especially for the occasion. She moves into her bedroom, takes off her St. Christopher's medal, and slowly undresses, revealing red welts and scars all over her shoulders, hips, and vagina. On the soundtrack, the noise of heavy breathing can be heard. She turns around fearfully (as if expecting someone to catch her unawares) before putting on her nightgown, picking up the photograph once again and staring at it before putting it away in a drawer. While the sequence might be criticized for reducing the governess to a sex object, Aloy emphasizes the fact that what we are witnessing is what the father would have seen, whenever he entered the bedroom uninvited and forced himself on her. Laura Mulvey summed up this technique thus, in her classic essay "Visual Pleasure and Narrative Cinema": "A woman performs within the narrative: the gaze of the spectator and that of the male characters in the film are neatly combined without breaking narrative verisimilitude."[12] The camera assumes a point-of-view role to show how the governess has been physically, mentally, and emotionally assaulted throughout her life.

The effect that this has on the governess's state of mind is further illustrated through a dream sequence comprising images of religion, sex, and corrupted innocence, which begins with two close-ups of the uncle and Fosc (Quint) (Agusti Villaronga). On the soundtrack, the sound of the governess's voice yelling "Don't!!!" can be heard. This is followed by a shot of a white dove flying away, a medium shot of the uncle lifting the winding sheet covering her father's corpse and subsequently kissing the governess, a shot of Miles and Flora, and a close-up of the St. Christopher medal.

Again, this interpretation of *The Turn of the Screw* is a familiar one; the idea that the ghosts are merely projections of the governess's disordered mind can be traced back to Edmund Wilson's famous essay published originally in *Hound and Horn* (1934) and later reprinted in *The Triple Thinkers*, where he remarked that the entire novella was but "a characterization of the govern-ess."[13] Fantasy sequences have become standard in film versions of the novel ever since *The Innocents* (1961), many of them focusing on the governess's state of mind in increasingly sexually explicit detail. Lemorande's 1992 ver-sion includes shots of an exposed nipple, Quint and Miles in bed together, and Flora moving up and down the bed as if a man were lying on top of her. What differentiates *Presence of Mind* from other adaptations is the emphasis on religion; in a later sequence, the governess is shown kneeling in front of the altar during confession. Aloy cuts to a point-of-view shot of Christ on the cross, and cuts back to a two-shot of the governess and Mado Remei crossing themselves. Another point-of-view shot follows, as Christ's body is seen in close-up, covered with red welts. The camera tracks upward toward his face and then cuts back to the governess. Clearly, the Christ figure reminds her of her father—someone who expects godlike devotion from her, but who repays her not with love but with physical and sexual abuse. In a notebook entry for 1895, Henry James observed how he was affected by reli-gious visions, which inspired him to write, "One has never too many—one has never enough. . . . I bow down to Fate, equally in submission and in gratitude. This time it's gratitude; but the form of the gratitude, to be real and adequate, must be large and confident action—splendid and supreme creation."[14] The governess's mind is equally full of visions, but they are not something to be thankful for; they have polluted her life to such an extent that she is incapable of following the path of virtue, in spite of her efforts to rely on her Catholic faith to guide her.

This point is underlined throughout the novella as the governess's opinion of the children rapidly degenerates, even though they have done little to deserve it. At the beginning of the film, they are associated in her mind with images of light and freshness: Flora, "with her hair of gold and her frock of blue" seems like a figure in "a castle of romance inhabited by a rosy sprite."[15] As she becomes more convinced of their alleged corruption by Quint and Miss Jessel, so the light imagery changes, becomes "glaring," and their youth-ful innocence gives way to Miles being described as "an older person" while Flora is characterized as "an old, old woman."[16] By the conclusion of *Presence of Mind*, the governess is beyond redemption as she attempts to rescue Miles from Fosc's/Quint's clutches, while Miles, looking wild-eyed into her face, screams, "Please don't hurt me! Please don't hurt me!" before falling down dead. Aloy then creates a coda that does not exist in the novella, beginning with a panning shot of the toys and dolls in the children's playroom, all of which have been smashed. The governess is discovered cradling a headless doll in her arms, murmuring a little story to herself about a little girl who suffered terribly when a prince carried her off to live in a land of pink sky. The film ends with a two-shot of the governess and Miles walking away from the camera down a corridor into the blackness beyond. Clearly, such images are meant to draw attention to the consequences of the governess's actions— the children have been destroyed, while the governess (once a victim of abuse) becomes the abuser in a sexual fantasy involving Miles.

However, we should not blame the governess for her behavior; Aloy has stressed throughout that perhaps her reactions were inevitable, given her history of childhood abuse. The film mounts a devastating criticism of the Catholic faith by suggesting that it is often misused by those who should set an example to others. This is true not only of the governess's father but the uncle as well. In spite of their antithetical views—the uncle claims to have no understanding of Catholicism, while the father was a minister of the church—both seek to use religion as a means to gratify their lust; by doing so, they create such mental turmoil in the governess and in the children's minds that none of them are capable of looking after themselves. Aloy himself remarked in an interview that he "went a little more with the idea of abuse, and I wanted to not only establish the point of view of the governess. . . . I tried to make everybody seem suspicious; sometimes I'd do it through the governess' eyes . . . but always respecting the mystery and ambiguity."[17]

Such a topic was of particular significance in the late 1990s (and in the present day), when the stability of Catholic churches all over Europe were threatened by reports of child sex abuse. Only recently a report published in Ireland revealed that the entire church system permitted cover-ups allowing known sexual predators to retain their positions and permit free access to young victims. Before 1990, the police were reluctant to investigate such claims because they were fearful of challenging the privileged position of Roman Catholic Church authorities. However, as one report recently claimed, the incidents of child sex abuse had become so widespread by 2002 that Pope John Paul II admitted to being "deeply grieved by the fact that priests and religious have themselves caused such suffering and scandal among the young." Nonetheless, it is still the case that "Tremendous secrecy is still the norm [in the Catholic Church]. . . . Any external peek into how it works is very rare and very valuable."[18] Bearing this in mind, I suggest that one of Aloy's reasons for making the film for a European rather than an Anglo-American audience was to focus attention on such issues and, by doing so, to prevent the Catholic Church from maintaining its veil of secrecy. In a polemical work *The Whole Woman*, which appeared in 1999, Germaine Greer remarked that despite the so-called liberation of women that had taken place in the previous three decades, it was still the case that "Every day we hear of women abused; every day we hear of new kinds of atrocities perpetrated on the minds and bodies of women; yet every day we are told there is nothing left to fight for."[19] *Presence of Mind* proves the truth of this observation, particularly for women brought up in closed societies.

Aloy's film is a fascinating text, particularly when considered in relation to other James adaptations that appeared in the late 1990s. It might not stay particularly close to the original novella, but it nonetheless uses it as a basis to make a statement about gender construction and its relationship to organized religion. Like Paul Unwin's *American* (released two years earlier), it suggests that most men seek to possess women both financially and sexually, and that they are prepared to resort to any strategies to achieve their ends, even if it means abusing their position in society. However, *Presence of Mind* does not propose any alternative behavioral model that might challenge the existing system of patriarchal relations; unlike Claire de Cintré or Noémie, the governess's experiences at the hands of her father (and the uncle) eventually destroy her. Ben Bolt's television version of *The Turn of the Screw*—which also premiered in 1999—has the governess (Jodhi May) offering thanks to God for helping her to cope with the ordeal of redeeming Miles and expelling Quint from Bly. By contrast, *Presence of Mind* suggests that the governess cannot communicate with God in an ostensibly pious society that lets male sexual abuse go unpunished and reduces women to mere sex objects. Another James adaptation—Meg Richman's *Under Heaven*—rewrites *The Wings of the Dove* to project a Gen X view of the world as a place where young people in particular have little faith in established institutions such as the family, government, and/or organized religion. *Presence of Mind* offers a convincing explanation as to why people might feel so disillusioned. Perhaps the only solution is to develop a creed of one's own that repudiates patriarchal authority and/or the regular ritualistic acts associated with the church, and substitutes in its place a creed that enables individuals to define their own relationships to God, and their prospects for future salvation.

Notes

1. Edwin Sill Fussell, *The Catholic Side of Henry James* (Cambridge: Cambridge University Press, 1993), x.

2. Henry James, *The Turn of the Screw, The Aspern Papers and Other Stories*, ed. Michael Swan. London: Collins, 1963, 366.

3. James, *The Turn of the Screw*, 368.

4. Fussell, *The Catholic Side*, 98.

5. Fussell, *The Catholic Side*, 98–99.

6. Rusty Lemorande's 1994 version adopts a similar interpretation, although he omits any suggestion that the governess's father was a member of the church (either Protestant or Catholic).

7. Mike Hodges, "The Screw Turns Again: *Presence of Mind*" *Fangoria* 4 (July 2001): 56.

8. James, *Turn of the Screw*, 372, 375.

9. Sheila Johnston, "Harvey Keitel: No Time to Look Back," *The Independent* (London), April 29, 2005, 14.

10. This is also emphasized in *Presence of Mind* by the fact that he expects a room to be ready for him at a moment's notice, as he promises to visit the children. Eventually he doesn't turn up, pleading "urgent business" in Morocco. Miles remarks, "I knew he wouldn't. He's always too busy," emphasizing the uncle's lack of interest in sustaining an established family life.

11. Hodges, "The Screw Turns Again," 56.

12. Laura Mulvey, "Visual Pleasure," *Visual and Other Pleasures* (London: Macmillan Press, 1989), 27.

13. Edmund Wilson, *The Triple Thinkers* (Harmondsworth: Pelican Books, 1962), 48. Originally published in 1948.

14. Quoted in Susan M. Griffin, "Introduction," *Henry James Review* 22, no. 3 (Fall 2001): 215.

15. James, *Turn of the Screw*, 324.

16. James, *Turn of the Screw*, 381, 390. This aspect of the novella was examined as long ago as the late 1940s by Robert B. Heilman in his essay, "*The Turn of the Screw* as Poem." *Modern Language Notes* (November 1947): 433–45.

17. Hodges, "The Screw Turns Again," 56.

18. Brian Lavery, "Ireland Shaken by Sex Abuse Report," *New York Times*, November 13, 2005, at www.iht.com/articles/2005/11/13/news/ireland.php (accessed November 15, 2005).

19. Germaine Greer, *The Whole Woman* (London: Transworld, 1999), 19.

~

CHAPTER TWENTY-THREE

The Golden Bowl (2001)

The origins of Ivory's *Golden Bowl* are inextricably bound up with other James adaptations that appeared in the late 1990s. After finishing *Howards End* (1992), the then-head of Disney, Jeffrey Katzenberg, asked Merchant-Ivory what they would like to do next. They said *The Portrait of a Lady*, and the production was duly announced in *Time* magazine. Merchant-Ivory secured Glenn Close to play the part of Madame Merle, but eventually gave up on the idea when Jane Campion and Nicole Kidman decided to make their own version of the novel (which eventually appeared in 1996). Merchant-Ivory subsequently thought about *The Wings of the Dove* but eventually backed away when they learned that another film version was about to appear. It was then that they settled on *The Golden Bowl*, which they considered superior to *Wings* on account of the fact that "Its ending was less inconclusive, less a dying fall into sadness. . . . It's something better than that. It's not quite a happy ending, but it's more positive. And it's a very, very good story."[1] The film eventually went ahead with Uma Thurman as the star; she had originally been cast as Kate Croy in the projected production of *Wings of the Dove*, but was eventually replaced by Helena Bonham Carter.

When Ivory's film opened, critical opinion was divided as to its merits. The two contributors to the 2001 collection *Henry James Goes to the Movies* were largely antipathetic towards it; Lee Clark Mitchell criticized the director for converting the "melodramatic" tenor of the novel—"its metaphorical excesses and fantastic hypothetical style"—into a melodramatic plot.[2] Wendy Graham likewise thought that James's work of "critical realism" had been transformed into "heritage cinema"—a fantasy that "organizes a world which is without contradictions because it is without depth, a world wide open and wallowing in the evident."[3] When the film received its U.S. premiere, the *Milwaukee Journal* thought that its structure resembled "a museum-quality reproduction of a time, place and style that is an acquired taste at least;" while the *Laramie Movie-Score* expressed precisely the opposite view by drawing its readers' attention to screenwriter Ruth Prawer Jhabvala's "highly skilled verbal combat" that seemed "reserved almost exclusively for Merchant-Ivory films." Two reviewers expressed their approval in metaphoric terms: "Here, as in many of James's novels, money, possessions, and greed are toxins that can corrode love."[4]

Such comments stem from a fundamental contradiction within the film, which appears to celebrate consumerism (and the capitalist system that supports it), while at the same time criticizing its fundamentally destructive effect on individuals—particularly women. This chapter begins by focusing on the visual style that (in common with most Merchant-Ivory period adaptations) foregrounds the historically accurate costumes and locations.[5] In an interview, Ivory suggested that he had been influenced by the work of John Singer Sargent, as well as a host of other artists "working in England and France in the final decades of the nineteenth century, who specialized in beautiful women. We also collected masses of old photographs of the interiors of very rich Edwardian houses, which were used as a source to guide us in obtaining props and decorating the film's sets."[6] Following the example of *The Europeans* (1979), Ruth Prawer Jhabvala rewrites *The Golden Bowl* to incorporate a series of visual set pieces, designed to show off the director's control of the mise-en-scène. These include a costume ball and a *Ballets Russes*–style dance sequence. The result is a slow-moving film that (in common with the late 1990s versions of *The Turn of the Screw* and *The American*) situates itself squarely within the cinema of attraction, designed to stimulate the pleasures of desire and longing among filmgoers. Even if one lacks the wherewithal to emulate the Ververs' lifestyle, one can still experience a vicarious pleasure in visiting some of the historic buildings where the film was shot (Belvoir Castle and Burghley House).[7] This particular feature of Merchant-Ivory's oeuvre has been regularly exploited in the past by travel guides and coffee-table books, as Andrew Higson suggests, "The pictorial aesthetic adopted by the film-makers, the aesthetics of display . . . is ideal for the display [and promotion] of heritage properties."[8]

The second part of this chapter shows how Ivory seeks to critique the ideology that underpins such visual splendor.[9] This is chiefly done through a series of images demonstrating that characters with social background but no money, such as the prince (Jeremy Northam) and Charlotte Stant (Uma Thurman), are treated like museum exhibits by their respective marriage partners, to be collected and put on public display. In two especially created montage sequences, Ivory shows how most individuals in a capitalist society are denied any freedom of choice—unless they possess sufficient financial muscle to make such choices for themselves.

Many of these issues have been raised in other James adaptations. The use of montage to emphasize the destructive potential of the industrialized world appeared as long ago as 1933 in Frank Lloyd's *Berkeley Square*. James Cellan Jones's *Portrait* repeatedly uses visual metaphors (in one sequence, Isabel sits on a sofa with all of her husband's ornaments—vases, bronze figures—in the background, suggesting that Osmond treats her as just another item in his collection of antiques. In Unwin's version of *The American*, Valentin de Bellegarde is shown in a sex scene endeavoring to "consume" Noémie. What separates Ivory's *Golden Bowl* from earlier adaptations, however, is the fact that none of the characters have the opportunity to improve themselves, either socially or intellectually. In Merchant-Ivory's previous James adaptation—*The Bostonians* (1984)—Olive Chancellor (Vanessa Redgrave) repudiated existing conceptions of femininity and sought to establish a new form of expression. By contrast, Charlotte Stant in *The Golden Bowl* ultimately conforms to American society's expectations of her as a prominent philanthropist's wife, while Maggie (Kate Beckinsale) and the prince (Jeremy Northam) uphold the social standards expected of an upper-middle-class couple, even though they have little or no romantic feelings for one another. Such pessimism is not found in James's novel; for all her apparent readiness to acquiesce to her husband's wishes, it is clear that Charlotte Stant retains her independence of spirit, as she continually frustrates any attempts made by the narrator (or any other character) to find easy explanations for her behavior.[10] Ivory's *Golden Bowl* unequivocally suggests that at least three of the main protagonists no longer possess this capacity to resist; they are pawns in a society devoted to money and the acquisition of possessions.

Perhaps more so than any other recent James adaptation, this *Golden Bowl* seems driven by the materialist ethic. The bulk of the action takes place in portrait-filled rooms with only occasional exterior shots of great houses. Like Adam Verver, Ivory seems preoccupied with putting things on display—paintings by Poussin, Gainsborough, and Tissot, rare Elizabethan gold work, and actors richly dressed in morning coats and evening wear, fancy frocks and fashionable hats, with bejeweled arms and necks. Lee Clark Mitchell remarked cynically that such visual excess reduced James's characters to fashion models participating in a two-hour commercial aimed at an audience "whose affection for such signs of affluent existence is largely unexamined and uncritical."[11] At times, it seems as if the narrative has been deliberately suspended in the interests of visual display—as, for example, in the ball scene taking place at Lancaster House. In the novel James narrates this sequence from Charlotte's perspective as she finds herself the object of more than passing interest from other "ordered revelers," who observe that she has attended the ball with the prince rather than her husband:

> They [the other guests] treated her to much crude contemplation and now and then to a spasm of speech, an offered hand, even in some cases to an unencouraged pause; but she missed no countenance and invited no protection: she fairly liked to be, so long as she might, just as she was—exposed a little to the public, no doubt, in her unaccompanied state, but, even if it were a bit brazen, careless of queer reflexions on the dull polish of London faces, and exposed, since it was a question of exposure, to much more competent recognitions of her own.[12]

This passage suggests Charlotte's reckless nature; although she wants to make her marriage work, she remains passionately in love with the prince—so much so that she is prepared to put her husband's reputation at risk.[13] Ivory's film shifts attention away from the main characters and focuses instead on the ball as a social ritual. One sequence begins with an aerial shot of the guests arriving, followed by a shot of Lady Castledean (Madeleine Potter) greeting two complete strangers as if they were long-lost friends. Two-shots of Charlotte and an uncredited acquaintance are subsequently intercut with medium shots of the guests ascending the stairs to the ballroom. Although Ivory follows the novel by having Fanny Asssingham (Anjelica Huston) inform Charlotte that she is committing a social faux pas by leaving her husband at home,[14] he resituates this scene in the public areas of the ballroom, rather than in a quiet corner "at sight of an empty sofa."[15] This has the effect of distracting attention away from Fanny's words as we watch the colorfully attired guests exchanging small talk in the background.

Invented ball scenes frequently crop up in James adaptations. Sometimes they are used to emphasize the oppressiveness of a patriarchal society that forces young women to dance with as many men as possible in the hope of finding a suitable marriage partner (as in Campion's Portrait). Alternatively, a ball can draw attention to the threatening presence of the male who seeks to consume the female—as in Unwin's American, where Christopher Newman stares fixedly at Claire de Cintré as she makes her first entrance. The ball scene in Ivory's *Golden Bowl* fulfills a thematic function, as it highlights the obsession with appearances that pervades early twentieth-century London society. At one point, Fanny observes to her husband, Bob (James Fox), that while Charlotte and the prince are a handsome couple, perhaps they should not be seen together in society; after all, they are related to one another by marriage. On the other hand, there remains the distinct suspicion that the director is more interested in visual detail for its own sake. Ivory suggested in a postproduction interview that he tried to shoot this scene using anamorphic lenses, which would "slightly blur the background, make it softer in focus than the foreground" and hence focus attention on plot. However, he was also well aware that "our sets, being so overwhelmingly ornate, might be a distraction and take away from the foreground action."[16]

The same criticism might be leveled at the dance sequence taking place at a buffet dinner, which happens immediately after Charlotte and the prince have come back from their visit to Gloucester.[17] In many ways, it recalls the play scene in *Hamlet* as it tells a story of infidelity and revenge (similar to the love triangle between Charlotte, Verver, and the prince) involving a sultan, one of his wives, and a young lover, ending with the sultan killing the lover and the wife committing suicide. Ivory concentrates on the guests whose responses range from disdain to nervous laughter; Mr. Blint (Robin Hart) treats the whole thing as a joke, observing with a nervous giggle to Lady Castledean that the play resembles *Hamlet*. In a world where appearances count for everything, no one dares to step out of line by expressing what he or she *truly* thinks about the performance. Nonetheless, we may also wonder whether Ivory has conceived the entire sequence as an ostentatious display of colorful costumes and half-naked bodies designed to arouse consumerist desires among filmgoers.

Such sequences seem quite at odds with the original novel, which actually includes very little pictorial detail. The only instance where a long descriptive passage occurs is in the Bloomsbury shop where Charlotte and the prince buy a wedding present for Maggie. James explains why in the preface:

> The problem thus was thrilling, for although the small shop [where the bowl was for sale] was but a shop of the mind, of the author's projected world, in which objects are primarily related to each other, and therefore not "taken from" a particular establishment anywhere, only an image distilled and intensified, as it were, from a drop of the essence of such establishments in general, our need . . . prescribed a concrete, independent, vivid existence, the instance that should oblige us by the marvel of an accidental rightness.[18]

The passage itself describes the merchandise, ranging from "miniatures mounted with diamonds" to "a few commemorative medals of neat outline but dull reference" to "carbuncles, each of which had found a home in the ancient sallow satin of some weakly-snapping little box." However, none of the items attracts Charlotte's or the prince's interest: "They looked, the visitors, they touched, they vaguely pretended to consider, but with scepticism, so far as courtesy permitted, in the quality of their attention."[19] This could be taken as an implied rebuke on the narrator's part to anyone—the shopkeeper, Adam Verver, or James Ivory himself—who subscribes to the consumerist fantasy that the display of material possessions alone (including costumes) can satisfy human desires.

However, it soon becomes clear that Ivory is well aware of the dangers of consumerism. The novel describes how the prince chooses to marry Maggie out of a "desire for some new history that should, as far as possible, contradict, and even if need be flatly dishonour, the old [in other words, the prince's past life]."[20] Ivory takes the idea a step further by suggesting that the prince's principal motive for marrying into the Verver family is to obtain financial security; evidently, Fanny did a perfect job in arranging the match for him. However, the prince discovers to his cost that life with Maggie quite literally "consumes" him, forcing him to playing the loyal husband and saying what his wife wants to hear—even if that means suppressing his natural instincts. This is suggested in the film through the repeated use of prison imagery. During the weekend at Matcham, he looks out of the barred window at the other guests squirting soda siphons at one another and observes somewhat wistfully that, while he has endured this marriage for four years, there are occasions when he needs to escape—even for a limited time. At the end of the film, he is shown staring wistfully out of an upper floor window at Charlotte (who is taking a walk in the garden), the shadows of the iron bars across his face as he mechanically tells his wife—in a slightly rewritten version of James's original line—that "she [Charlotte] ought to understand you better. Charlotte hasn't begun to know you."[21]

Charlotte Stant suffers a similar fate, as her husband treats her as little more than another decorative object to add to his collection. Verver's outlook on life is revealed at the beginning of the film in a sequence that begins with an on-screen title referring to the house of Verver, America's first billionaire. The camera pans downwards from the richly gilded ceiling to a marble statue and a potted plant standing next to it, before settling on Verver and the prince looking at a small object—a wedding present from the prince to Verver depicting the prince's ancestor who sailed to America after Columbus but who was fortunate enough to have the continent named after him. The sequence not only emphasizes Verver's passion for putting his treasures on show but suggests that his consumerist mentality renders him insensitive to human endeavor. The great deeds of the prince's ancestor mean nothing to him; it is far more important that he has obtained another valuable trinket for his collection. At one point, Maggie innocently observes that her father keeps a cabinet for his special treasures—many of which have lain there for years. Charlotte is one such treasure, to be shown to anyone fortunate enough to pay him a visit—including the audience. At one point, she climbs the stairs to bed, her slight figure dwarfed by a huge oil painting in the background. The implication is obvious; in Verver's scheme of things, the painting assumes more importance than his wife, being both larger and more visually striking. Charlotte acknowledges this later in the film as she escorts a party of visitors around Verver's house and pauses by one painting—a life-size image of Henry VIII by Hans Holbein—drawing attention to the fact that it dominates all the other pictures in this room. She describes the king's harsh features, which sum up his personality—someone who never let anyone stand in his way, especially his women. Ivory underlines the implications of this speech by cutting to a close-up of Verver looking down impassively at her from an upper floor, as if he were checking that she keeps to the prepared script.[22] Clearly, Charlotte does not experience what the novel describes as a "cheerful submission to duty;"[23] her *joie de vivre* has been extinguished by someone who places more value on a painting that dominates the room and all the people standing in it. Bob Assingham understands her plight; at one point, he observes to Fanny that Charlotte needs the freedom to wander on her own—otherwise, she will remain imprisoned for life in one of Verver's cabinets.

Charlotte's and the prince's futures are well expressed in another newly invented scene at the end of the Lancaster House ball when they are photographed on their own at first, and subsequently together. This moment signals their capitulation to consumer culture; not only have they been "captured" by the camera lens, but their photographic images will subsequently be bought and sold—just like the paintings on Verver's wall.

The consequences of this kind of existence are summed up in two montage sequences—one occurring just after Verver has expressed the desire to begin work in American City, the other at the very end of the film. The first of these begins with a close-up of Charlotte looking at a series of black-and-photos of American City, and is followed by a long sequence of sepia-toned newsreel of actual footage taken in an (unnamed) city in the early 1900s.[24]

This is followed by a tracking shot of an industrial landscape with the sound of a steam locomotive in the background, which dissolves into shots of workers in a steel mill and miners emerging from a pit at the end of their shift. The sequence ends with a shot of a goods train filled with coal, and a further extract from the 1900s newsreel. The structure of this montage recalls Frank Lloyd's *Berkeley Square* (1933), when Helen Pettigrew (Heather Angel) experiences a nightmare vision of factories, war, and destruction in the years separating her own time (1784) from that of her lover, Peter Standish (1928). Such images will also dictate Charlotte Stant's future as an industrialist's wife, spending her time in a "spacious but suspended cage, the home of eternal unrest, of pacings, beatings, shakings all in vain."[25]

The second montage sequence recounts Charlotte's and Verver's voyage across the Atlantic and subsequent arrival in American City. It begins with a sequence of early 1900s newsreel extracts showing an ocean liner and its passengers at sea and subsequently arriving in New York. This is followed by some black-and-white shots of the Ververs' first appearance on American soil; surrounded by photographers, they wave to the crowds as they are driven away. Ivory cuts to some excerpts from local newspapers, welcoming Verver's arrival, followed by a shot of another newspaper—*The Call* ("Devoted to the Interests of the Working People") criticizing him for his wasteful expenditure on art treasures. A third article from the *New York Herald* compliments Charlotte on her intellect as well as her beauty. People expect her to fulfill the beauty queen's role of modeling the latest fashions; brains are not necessary. The sequence ends with another headline from the local American City newspaper announcing the arrival of Verver's treasures, superimposed over a newsreel image of a bustling main street thronged with people, trams, and horse-drawn carriages. The screen gradually fades to black, pausing only to focus on a single cart laden with boxes (most likely belonging to Verver), moving away from the camera. On one level, this montage emphasizes the link between consumerism and the cult of celebrity: The rich will always attract press attention through an ostentatious display of wealth in the form of goods or clothing. On another level, it exposes the realities of Verver's philanthropic enterprise; his obsession with collecting and/or displaying useless art reduces his wife to an object, of no more significance to him than the wooden boxes being slowly transported to his museum.

Interestingly (and perhaps perversely), Ivory himself has insisted that the film's final scenes were intended to be optimistic: The Ververs are treated as celebrities, "almost as world figures. In the open car in which they drive away from the pier, they laugh together at some joke. They are obviously enjoying themselves. . . . Charlotte will become the great figure predicted by the prince. And when Verver dies, she will be rich beyond belief."[26] This may be true, if we assume that Charlotte's main interest in life is money. However, both the novel and the film suggest that this is clearly *not* the case; James tells us that immediately before her departure for America, Charlotte "cleared her acceptance, cleared her impersonal smile, of any betrayal, any slightest value, of consciousness."[27] She adopts her own form of resistance by refusing to disclose her feelings to anyone. Throughout the film, Ivory has suggested that this kind of opposition is futile; Verver sets so little store by his wife's feelings that he probably would not notice whether she had cleared "her impersonal smile . . . of consciousness." All she can do is to play the part of a celebrity who has been both constructed (and simultaneously destroyed) by consumer culture—rather like Lady Castledean, the empty-headed hedonist who takes great pleasure in her adulterous affair with Mr. Blint, secure in the knowledge that her celebrity as one of London's leading hostesses will protect her from scandal. On two occasions, she indulges in a riotous performance of the song "I'm Just a Silly When the Moon Is Full"—a title that aptly expresses her vapid existence. The fact that this role was played by Madeleine Potter is significant; seventeen years earlier, she had played Verena Tarrant in *The Bostonians*—the idealistic fighter for women's rights whose only fault was that she lacked the courage of her convictions. Now she was playing a woman whose life revolved around adultery, fashion, popular music, and gossip. Perhaps Ivory sought to suggest through this piece of casting that women's quest for self-expression in a patriarchal society had ultimately failed.

When the film opened in the United States, one critic berated Ivory for having transformed James's "richly ironic tale" into "a staid, stiff melodrama of heroes, villains, and simple betrayal."[28] I contend that this transformation was deliberate, as the director followed the example set by earlier adaptations of James's novels by showing how human beings were commodified in consumer culture. Whether he was justified in his decision, however, is another matter, as his pessimistic view of humanity—especially his view of women—makes little or no reference to current feminist thinking. In one interview he remarked that, unlike the mid-1980s when *The Bostonians* was released, *The Golden Bowl* (and his later films) appeared at a time when "women's rights . . . and I am speaking of America and Western Europe—[are] mostly taken for granted. It all happened very quickly."[29] As M. Jacqui Alexander and Chandra Talpede Mohanty remark in their introduction to an anthology of feminist writing, obtaining "women's rights" only represents the tip of the iceberg as far as rethinking gender relations is concerned. What needs to be done also is to develop:

(1) A way of thinking about women in similar contexts across the world, in different geographical spaces, rather than as all women across the world; (2) an understanding of a set of unequal relationships among and between peoples, rather than a set of traits . . . premised within a white, Eurocentric, masculine, heterosexist regime; and (3) . . . taking critical, antiracist, anti-capitalist positions that would make feminist solidarity work possible.[30]

It is this apparent complacency on Ivory's part that renders this *Golden Bowl* old-fashioned, especially when compared with other James adaptations that expressed specifically anticapitalist opinions. The film may employ montage to disrupt the flow of the narrative; but unlike Campion's *Portrait*—which uses similar techniques—Ivory's montages reaffirm rather than seek to question established gender relations (dominant male/submissive female). Moreover, he assumes—quite naively, when compared with adaptations such as *Under Heaven*—that human beings can only survive if they accept the roles assigned to them in a capitalist culture. Like the eponymous bowl of the original novel, the film's flaws tended to reduce its value, both in box office and critical terms.[31]

Notes

1. Robert Emmet Long, *James Ivory in Conversation: How Merchant-Ivory Makes Its Movies* (Berkeley: University of California Press, 2005), 152–53.

2. Lee Mitchell, "Based on the Novel by Henry James," in *Henry James Goes to the Movies*, ed. Susan M. Griffin (Lexington: University Press of Kentucky, 2002), 293–94.

3. Wendy Graham, "The Rift in the Loot: Cognitive Dissonance for the Reader of Merchant Ivory's *The Golden Bowl*" in *Henry James Goes to the Movies*, ed. Susan M. Griffin (Lexington: University Press of Kentucky, 2002), 326, 328.

4. "Rotten Tomatoes: The Golden Bowl (2001): Critics Tomatometer," at www.rotten tomatoes.com/m/golden_bowl (accessed October 21, 2005). The *Rotten Tomatoes* site had collected eighty-four reviews of the film from Internet and newspaper sites. Of these, forty-four were positive, while forty were negative.

5. Ivory has likened this technique to "showmanship. You can't be minimalist, you have to give people something. That's why it's larger than life." Daniel S. Moore, "Picture Perfect," *Variety*, October 28, 1996, 62.).

6. James Ivory, "Imagining *The Golden Bowl*," at www.merchantivory.com/golden bowl/ivory.html (accessed October 26, 2005).

7. The fact that this *Golden Bowl* was designed to stimulate the viewer's wish-fulfilling

instincts is also implied in Ivory's observations about the ball scene, shot in Lancaster House, which Ivory found "totally sumptuous. No one had ever filmed there before. We used more than 150 extras for the scene, who were costumed in fancy dress by our costume designer John Bright" ("Imagining *The Golden Bowl*").

8. Andrew Higson, *English Heritage, English Cinema: Costume Drama since 1980* (Oxford: Oxford University Press, 2003), 191.

9. "The film [*Howards End* (1992)] appears quite liberal in its muted critique of capitalism and its social effects. . . . In repeatedly cutting back between the fortunes of the impoverished Basts, on the one hand, and those of the much more worldly and privileged Schlegels and Wilcoxes on the other, the film is able to draw attention to class differences" (Higson, *English Heritage*, 151).

10. This aspect of the novel is also emphasized in Cellan Jones's BBC adaptation.

11. Mitchell, "Based on the Novel," 294.

12. James, *The Golden Bowl*, ed. Patricia Crick (Harmondsworth: Penguin Books, 1987), 214.

13. In Cellan Jones's version of *The Golden Bowl*, Charlotte's behavior is commented on thus by Bob Assingham (Cyril Cusack), talking directly to the camera: "She did want to get married. She did like him [Verver]. She was immensely grateful to him, and perhaps at first she didn't know what was at the back of her mind. In a sense how could she until the situation gradually formed itself in such a way as to reveal it to her. And that was her fault; I don't know; what can you say except that she had once desperately loved Maggie's husband, and she was being thrown more closely together with him than in a sense she ought to have been."

14. James, *Golden Bowl*, 220.

15. James, *Golden Bowl*, 217.

16. Robert Emmet Long, *James Ivory in Conversation: How Merchant-Ivory Makes Its Movies* (Berkeley: University of California Press, 2005), 252.

17. James, *Golden Bowl*, 294–95. Maggie describes the dance as "the Gavrielka" to her father.

18. James, *Golden Bowl*, 25.

19. James, *Golden Bowl*, 115.

20. James, *Golden Bowl*, 52.

21. James, *Golden Bowl*, 565.

22. Wendy Graham remarks quite rightly that the film's identification of Henry VIII with Verver contradicts James's description; this is clearly a move designed to suit the screen persona of Nick Nolte, "who frequently plays professional athletes on the screen, [who] further lifts the onus from Adam by lending him virility, height, and a rugged charm" (Graham, "The Rift in the Loot," 311). Nolte was not Ivory's first choice for the role.

23. James, *Golden Bowl*, 526.

24. Ivory himself indicated in an interview that this was actually "a scene shot in Pitts-

burgh around 1900," which he had "'solarized' ditigally to obtain a more abstract effect, suitable for Charlotte's dream of hell." Long, *James Ivory in Conversation*, 253.

25. James, *Golden Bowl*, 484.

26. Long, *James Ivory in Conversation*, 251.

27. James, *Golden Bowl*, 573.

28. Sean Axmaker, "Henry James Story of Sex and Scheming Turns Musty and Mannered in Ivory's Hands," *Seattle Post-Intelligencer*, May 18, 2001, at http://seattlepi.nwsource .com/movies/23520_goldenq.shtml (accessed November 4, 2005).

29. Long, *James Ivory in Conversation*, 164.

30. M. Jacqui Alexander and Chandra Talpade Mohanty, eds., *Feminist Genealogies, Colonial Legacies, Democratic Futures* (London: Routledge, 1997), ix.

31. The film was made by Miramax in association with the French company TF1. Miramax demanded that the film could only be released with cuts—especially the black-and-white American City montage sequence at the end. Ivory resisted such changes. However, Harvey Weinstein of Miramax threatened to sell the film direct to television and not give it a theatrical release in the United States at all. Eventually, Merchant-Ivory bought the film back from him. It was eventually released by Lion's Gate Films in April 2001, when (according to Ivory) "its [the film's] day had passed. We had to look to its overseas release for any satisfaction—which we got, surprisingly, in England and then in Japan, where it appealed very much to audiences and the press" (Long, *James Ivory in Conversation*, 242–44). The film lost a lot of money; the Internet Movie Database reports that the film's budget was $15 million, and that it had only recouped just over $3 million at the U.S. box office within three months of its release (www.imdb.com/title/tt0200669/business, [accessed October 6, 2005]).

~

Conclusion

In looking at the history of James adaptations over the past seven decades, it is possible to detect some kind of a watershed around the late 1950s and early 1960s. Until that time, the main focus of attention had been on fantasy worlds: the past presented as an alternative to the present in *Berkeley Square* and *I'll Never Forget You*, or the past as a refuge from the present as in *The Lost Moment*. Even a woman's film such as *The Heiress* emerged in the context of a wider incorporation and construction—of women's tastes and interests, which tended towards the romantic and/or fantastic. Patricia Mellencamp observes the centrality of romance and/or fantasy to Hollywood's output, and its profound cultural impact: "[Hollywood] narrative is usually a story of romance, no matter what the genre, director, studio or year. The one-hundred years dominance of this story of the couple coupling has had cumulative significance and, I would argue, major cultural impact."[1]

After the 1960s, there was not only a significant increase in the number of James adaptations, but the subject matter had also changed. Issues of sexuality were more openly discussed—even in a film like *The Innocents* (1962), Miss Giddens (Deborah Kerr) was given the opportunity to acknowledge the presence of powerful instincts within her. Within the next decade, the romance and the fantasy had been superseded by films such as *The Nightcomers*, which incorporated explicit scenes of sadomasochism. At the same time, filmmakers seemed more preoccupied with issues of gender politics—in television adaptations such as *The Portrait of a Lady* and *The Golden Bowl*, and subsequently in films like *The Bostonians*. The past decade or so has witnessed a decline in sexually explicit adaptations (the last one to focus on this was probably Graeme Clifford's *Turn of the Screw*), but issues of gender politics have come to predominate, whether offering new possibilities for men and women (as in *Under Heaven* or *Washington Square*) or delivering some kind of "awful warning" against excessive freedom to determine one's life.

Since the early 1960s, there has also been a greater variety of Jamesian texts to reach the screen. Before then, the only three major works to have received any attention were *Washington Square* (*The Heiress*), *The Turn of the Screw*, and *The Sense of the Past* (*Berkeley Square*). Since then, most of James's major texts have reached the screen in one form or another; J. Sarah Koch's invaluable filmography provides a comprehensive guide, not only including the adaptations covered in this book but also other works that were omitted because no viewing copies were accessible.[2]

As I have tried to suggest, such changes can be attributed to the developments in feminist thinking: The "first wave" of feminism (lasting roughly until the 1960s) fought for and obtained such rights as the right to practice birth control; the "second wave" of feminism brought about further changes—leading to greater equality between the genders and addressing the rights of female minorities, such as lesbian woman; while "third-wave" feminists have more recently proposed that there are many ways to "do" feminism and be a feminist, just as there are many ways to be a man. Amy Schriefer remarks that both men and women in recent years have been "influenced by postmodernism . . . and precipitates the need for create our own identities that acknowledge these identities and multiple positions: 'including more than excluding, exploring more than defining, searching more than arriving.'"[3] What emerges in the most recent James adaptation is a belief in the negotiation and contradiction of differences, allowing for the construction of new gender identities (e.g., a nuclear family without men) that might have been frowned upon in the past.

However, I would argue that the principal reason why Jamesian texts came to be treated in a different way had more to do with sociohistorical changes in the film industry rather than elsewhere. In the Production Code era, a particular conception of gender was prevalent; according to this ideology, the man was perceived as the breadwinner, the protector and guardian of the home, while women (when defined in domestic and familial terms, when occupying domestic and familial roles, or when cast as wives and mothers) represented the height of "civilized" sensibility or virtue. Evidence of this belief can be found in the tenets of the code, with its strictures against adultery and illicit sex, its "scenes of passion," and the requirement that the "sanctity of the institution of marriage" be upheld in Hollywood films.[4] Evidence of this can also be found in the James adaptations of the time, with their emphasis on the romantic, the familial, and the domestic, on women as actual or potential wives—Tina Bordereau in *The Lost Moment*, Catherine Sloper in *The Heiress*, Helen Pettigrew in *I'll Never Forget You*. However, this did not mean that such films could not focus on the contradictions and complexities of women's and men's roles; as Steve Neale remarks, "The Production Code functioned as a framework for negotiation rather than as a mechanically applied or inscribed set of precepts."[5] Nonetheless, the Production Code and its conception of womanhood functioned as an initial point of departure for most women's films. This created a paradox that is clearly evident in *The Lost Moment* and *The Heiress*, as well as in pre–Production Code films such as *Berkeley Square*. On the one hand, both films suggested that such possibilities could only be found in the dream worlds of fantasy and/or romance; on the other hand, the fact that such possibilities had been put forward in the first place suggested that there could be alternatives to marriage, home, and family for those who sought to discover them. As Mellencamp remarks, such stories were something that "many little girls and women believe[d] they must make of their lives."[6]

From the early 1960s onwards, with the gradual decline of and eventual abolition of the Production Code, the conception of gender roles changed. Feminism mounted a series of challenges to the cult of the ideal women; henceforth any adaptations that reinvoked this stereotype would only do so if it sought to challenge feminist thought (for example, Dan Curtis's or Rusty Lemorande's versions of *The Turn of the Screw*). The passing of the Production Code also allowed for different representations of gender and sexuality—particularly in the 1980s and 1990s. The appearance of films such as *The Bostonians*, with its overtly lesbian content, in many ways indicated wider public acceptance of homosexual identities, while several films of the same period—*Under Heaven, The Portrait of a Lady*—indicate a wider conception and construction of "femaleness." New genres emerged—such as the heritage film or costume drama (for example, the three Merchant-Ivory James adaptations) that were specifically feminine in structure, with the emphasis on the domains of fashion and interior decoration, traditionally associated with women and gay men. Such films represented the antithesis of the so-called classical Hollywood cinema with its emphasis on plot and character development.

The break-up of the major studios' monopoly over Hollywood and the parallel growth of independent cinema also encouraged greater experiment; now directors could produce versions of less popular Jamesian texts or provide radical new interpretations of familiar works. *Daisy Miller* and *The Europeans* both appeared in the 1970s; in the subsequent three decades, versions of *The Bostonians, The Portrait, The Wings of the Dove*, and *The Golden Bowl* were also produced. The major studios realized the value of the independent market; hence, they acquired companies of their own to produce low-budget adaptations that could be given limited release at first and (if they proved popular) be subsequently given mainstream distribution. This is what happened, for instance, to Miramax's version of *The Wings of the Dove* (1997). A *New York Times* article in 1996 noted the fact that during the late 1990s there appeared to be a major James revival in the cinema, following in the footsteps of the Austen revival in the middle of the decade. This was attributed to many things—the need for "movies for educated grown-ups;" the fact that James's works have "a dark eroticism which is quite suppressed;" or perhaps that the films were produced at a time when gay and gender studies enjoyed considerable popularity in higher education institutions.[7] Such issues were further explored in the two anthologies of essays on James films—*Henry James on Stage and Screen* and *Henry James Goes to the Movies*—that appeared in 2000 and 2002 respectively.[8] While these issues are undoubtedly important, it is still my contention that the origins of the James revival of the 1990s could be found in the favorable conditions of production at the time—for example, the fact that major studios were willing to make major investments in "independent" productions (such as Disney, through its subsidiaries Hollywood Pictures and Miramax, the makers of *Washington Square* and *Wings of the Dove*, respectively).

In the past, most television adaptations of James were exempt from the restrictions—both cinematic and financial—that affected their cinematic counterparts. Broadcasting organizations such as the BBC or PBS could produce what they liked, in the secure knowledge that ratings and/or commercial considerations were considered less important than educating and/or informing audiences. Hence, James Cellan Jones could produce intriguing versions of *The Portrait of a Lady* and *The Golden Bowl*, which (unlike the Hollywood films of the Production Code period) were securely located in reality rather than fantasy—in other words, communicating a strong sense of the historical period. In recent years, however, the ethics of the market has also influenced television productions; structurally speaking, Paul Unwin's *American* resembles other costume dramas of the period produced for the cinema, in the sense that it is feminine in structure, with the emphasis on visual display. Such resemblances enable many television productions to obtain a cinema release before they are broadcast; to date, this has not been the case with any James adaptations, but was certainly the case with Roger Michell's version of Jane Austen's *Persuasion* (1995).

Nonetheless, what has emerged from this survey is that despite changing conditions of production, most James adaptations tend to fall into two categories. On the one hand, there are those that seek to challenge existing conventions of gender and/or sexuality, and offer new possibilities for self-expression for men and women alike. On the other hand, there are others that take a neoconservative view of Jamesian material by reasserting the importance of marriage, home, and family while suggesting that anyone who seeks to challenge this status quo will inevitably be destroyed or destroy themselves. Such views are common to recent films (*The Wings of the Dove*), as well as earlier films such as *The Nightcomers* or *The Turn of the Screw* (1974). This distinction, I would suggest, can be partly attributed to the texts themselves, which invite a variety of interpretations. This is especially evident in a work like *The Bostonians*, which, as Michael Davitt Bell remarks, is a work notable for "a pronounced instability of judgemental location: we can find him [the narrator] at different times and occasionally at the same time, both supporting and abusing almost all the characters and positions in the novel."⁹ *The Golden Bowl* might be seen as calling into question "the very institution of marriage itself, which James seems otherwise to be affirming (and which "first-wave" critics of the novel assumed he endorsed). . . . The result is that she [Maggie Verver] is now both greatly praised or else greatly damned by James critics."¹⁰ Perhaps one should approach James's novels in terms of competing plots—competing past and present plots, competing masculine and feminine plots, and competing heterosexual and homosexual plots—which may help to explain why "James can be interpreted as either antifeminist or, more broadly anti-ideological (or anti-*idee fixe*). . . . The critical dispute ranges quite literally from James as enlightened compatriot to women, ahead of his time, to James as downright hostile misogynist."¹¹

Yet perhaps there is another reason why directors have interpreted James either as an "enlightened compatriot" to women or "hostile misogynist." Ann Douglas's seminal work *The Feminization of American Culture* (1977) argued that the values prevalent in contemporary American culture could be traced back to Victorian times. As religion lost its hold on the public mind, so clergymen and educated women, powerless and insignificant in the male-dominated industrial society of the mid-nineteenth century, bonded together to exert a profound effect on the only areas still open to their influence—arts and literature. The values they created—for example, the passive or self-sacrificing heroine—permeated the popular literature of the day and continue to influence modern popular culture. Henry James himself was profoundly affected by this movement; Douglas described him as

the great feminine novelist of a feminine age of letters; certainly he was preoccupied with the sexual identity of the novel and the novelist. From the start of his
literary career in the 1860s, he had insisted to the reading public, and himself, that
fiction, the traditional province of women, be accorded all the seriousness of history, the customary province of men."[12]

At the same time, many men and women were becoming deeply concerned about the feminization of American culture and the closing of the
frontier (both metaphorical and physical) that it suggested. James himself
stresses this point in *The Bostonians* through the central character Basil
Ransom:

> The whole generation is womanized; the masculine tone is passing out of the world;
> it's a feminine, nervous, hysterical, chattering, canting age, an age of hollow
> phrases and false delicacy and exaggerated solicitudes and coddled sensibilities,
> which, if we don't look out, will usher in the reign of mediocrity, of the feeblest
> and flattest and most pretentious that has ever been. The masculine character, the
> ability to dare and endure, to know and yet not fear reality, to look the world in
> the face and take it for what it is . . . this is what I want to preserve, or rather . . .
> recover; and I must tell you that I don't in the least care what becomes of you
> ladies while I make the attempt![13]

Muscular Christianity became popular in clerical circles; in the educational arena, there were movements to limit the number of women who
could become grade-school teachers or enter higher education. Social Dar-
winism with its emphasis on the right of the strong to triumph over the weak
dominated social and political theory. Naturalism, with its emphasis on brute
instinct and natural force, influenced novelists such as Frank Norris. He
believed in a new masculine fiction with less attention to style and more to
action and adventure. "Who cares for fine style! Tell your yarn and let your
style go to the devil. We don't want literature, we want life," Norris bellowed.
The impulse for manly fiction must come far from "the studios of the aes-
thetes, the velvet jackets and the uncut hair, far from the sexless creatures
who cultivate their little art of writing as the fancier cultivates his orchids,"
and lead one into "a world of Working Men, crude of speech, swift of action,
strong of passion, straight to the heart of a new life, on the borders of a new
time, and there only will you learn to know the stuff of which must come
the American fiction of the future."[14]

These conflicting traditions persist to this day; as Michael Kimmel
remarks, the response of many men to the changes wrought by feminism or

by the emergence of alternative structures of the family and/or sexuality has ranged from "the angry resistance of men's rights groups to the defensive retreat to the cosmic archetypes of the mythopoets—exactly the responses of most American men to these challenges for the past 150 years."[15] Hollywood films such as *Dances with Wolves* (1992) reminded us that the western frontier is still the quintessential mythic site for demonstrating manhood, while films such as *Fatal Attraction* (1990), *Basic Instinct* (1991), and *Disclosure* (1994) showed the man taking revenge against the independent woman who dared to invade his territory. Those who propagated alternative behavioral models still appeared in some ways to be reinforcing male power. Dustin Hoffman's films *Kramer vs. Kramer* (1979) and *Tootsie* (1982) both suggested that men could be not only better mothers than women but also better women than women. The new man still emerged at the expense of women; he was not new enough for a truly egalitarian relationship with an equally strong woman.

More significantly, I would argue that it is this conflict between masculine and feminine values that underlies the ways in which film directors have responded to James's texts. This applies as much to adaptations made in the United States as in the United Kingdom (the majority of which were made with American money or at least designed with American filmgoers in mind). Many directors adopted a Social Darwinist view by showing brute force and natural strength triumphing over generosity and compassion. This is certainly the case with those versions of *The Turn of the Screw* that show the governess's destruction at Quint's hands—*The Nightcomers*, Dan Curtis's 1974 version, or Rusty Lemorande's 1992 update—as well as Peter Bogdanovich's *Daisy Miller*. Other films put forward a viewpoint that appears to limit female potential or depict it as potentially destructive, such as Softley's *Wings*. Ivory's *Europeans* seeks to demonstrate the dangers of women adopting the ideology of the oppressor in order to make themselves heard—as, for instance, in the portrayal of Baroness Eugenia, who tries to act like a man and feminize her suitors, but ends up alone and rejected. It is only those films that seek to propose alternative methods of self-expression—for males and females alike—that do not involve oppression and allow the powerless and insignificant to make themselves heard, that represent a genuine alternative to the dominant masculine tradition in American culture. This is why works such as Cellan Jones's *Golden Bowl* or Campion's *Portrait*, whose central characters adopt forms of behavior that are consciously inexplicable in reasonable, logical (masculine) terms, constitute such important milestones in the canon of James adaptations. Even films like *Under Heaven*, with its emphasis on alternative structures of the family—in which no men are involved—or Unwin's *American*, where the female central characters gain the power to determine their respective destinies, show the powerless emerging triumphant over those who would seek to oppress them. Ann Douglas remarks that perhaps one of the things that many nineteenth-century novelists— especially those writing in the latter part of the century, when the reaction against the feminization of the culture was taking place—could not conceive was a society based on "sexual equality, a non-oppressive economic system, [and] an honest culture."[16] It is a credit to many filmmakers of the modern period that they have successfully created imaginative worlds determined by such principles, even while there are others who would seek to repudiate them.

Notes

1. Quoted in Alison Butler, *Women's Cinema: The Contested Screen* (London: Wallflower Press, 2002), 29.

2. J. Sarah Koch, "A Henry James Filmography," in *Henry James Goes to the Movies*, ed. Susan M. Griffin (Lexington: University Press of Kentucky, 2002), 335–57.

3. Amy Schriefer, "Translating Third Wave Theory into Third Wave Activism," *Laughing Medusa: An Online Literary Journal of Women's Studies*, 2002, at www.gwu.edu/ ~medusa/thirdwave.html (accessed December 7, 2005).

4. "A Code to Govern the Making of Motion and Talking Pictures: The Reasons Supporting It and the Resolution for Uniform Interpretation" (Hollywood: Motion Picture Producers and Distributors of America, 1934), 6.

5. Steve Neale, *Genre and Hollywood*, (London: Routledge, 2000), 195.

6. Butler, *Women's Cinema*, 29.

7. Dinitia Smith, "Hollywood Trains Its Lights on a Master of Shadow" *New York Times*, October 30, 1996, A6.

8. John R. Bradley, ed., *Henry James on Stage and Screen* (London: Palgrave, 2000); Susan M. Griffin, ed., *Henry James Goes to the Movies* (Lexington: University Press of Kentucky, 2002).

9. Michael Davitt Bell, *The Problem of American Realism: Studies in the Cultural History of an Idea* (Chicago: University of Chicago Press, 1993), 91.

10. Richard A. Hocks, "Recanonizing the Multiple Canons of Henry James," *American Realism and the Canon*, ed. Tom Quirk and Gary Scharnhorst (Newark: University of Delaware Press, 1994, 164–65).

11. Hocks, "Recanonizing the Multiple Canons," 160.

12. Ann Douglas, *The Feminization of American Culture* (New York: Anchor Books, 1988), 260.

13. Henry James, *The Bostonians*, ed. Charles B. Anderson (Harmondsworth: Penguin Classics, 1986), 327.

14. Quoted in Michael Kimmel, *Manhood in America: A Cultural History* (New York: Free Press, 1996), 144–45.

15. Kimmel, *Manhood in America*, 330.

16. Douglas, *The Feminization of American Culture*, 329.

Bibliography

"About the Production: Iain Softley and Hossein Amini Approach the Novel." In Press book: *The Wings of the Dove*. London: Miramax Films / Renaissance Dove, 1997.

Adair, Gilbert. "The Ivory Tower: *The Bostonians*." *Sight and Sound* 55, no. 4 (Autumn 1984): 621.

Alexander, M. Jacqui, and Chandra Talpade Mohanty. *Feminist Genealogies, Colonial Legacies, Democratic Futures*. London: Routledge, 1997.

Amini, Hossein. "Adapting *The Wings of the Dove*." *Scenario* 3, no. 3 (1997): 49–51, 199, 201.

———. *Henry James' The Wings of the Dove—A Screenplay*. London: Methuen Film, 1998.

———. "*The Wings of the Dove*: Screenplay." *Scenario* 3, no. 3 (1997): 7–46.

Andreas, Carol. *Sex and Caste in America*. Englewood Cliffs, NJ: Prentice-Hall, 1971.

Andrews, Nigel. "The Nightcomers." *Monthly Film Bulletin* (May 1972): 99.

Anesko, Michael. "The Consciousness on the Cutting Room Floor: Jane Campion's *The Portrait of a Lady*." In *Henry James on Stage and Screen*, edited by John R. Bradley, 177–90. London: Palgrave, 2000.

———. *Henry James and the Profession of Authorship*. Oxford: Oxford University Press, 1986.

Arce, Hector. *The Secret Life of Tyrone Power*. New York: Bantam Books, 1979.

Archibald, William. *The Innocents*. New York: Random House, 1950.

Archibald, William, and Truman Capote. "The Innocents." Unpublished film script, 1961.

Armstrong, Michael. "Some Like It Chilled." *Films and Filming* (February 1971): 28.

Atkinson, Brooks. "The Innocents: A Ghost Story from Henry James' *The Turn of the Screw*." *New York Times*, February 2, 1950.

———. "The Theatre 1947." *New York Times*, October 5, 1947, sec. 2.

———. "The Theatre 1950." *New York Times*, February 12, 1950, sec. 2.

Axmaker, Sean. "Henry James Story of Sex and Scheming Turns Musty and Mannered in Ivory's Hands." *Seattle Post-Intelligencer*, May 18, 2001. http://seattlepi.nwsource.com/movies/23520_goldenq.shtml (accessed November 4, 2005).

Baker, Roy. *The Director's Cut: A Memoir of 60 Years in Films*. Richmond, Surrey: Reynolds and Hearn, 2000.

Balderston, John L. *Berkeley Square: A Play in Three Acts.* New York: Macmillan, 1929.

Bamigboye, Baz. "De Niro and Uma Put Love Tryst before a Film Date." *Daily Mail* (London), March 4, 1994.

Barber, Lynn. "You Know, I'm Not Everybody's Cup of Tea!" *The Observer* (London), June 15, 2001.

Barrett, Eric. "Have They Done Any Better?" *Picturegoer* (December 13, 1951): 13.

Basinger, Jeanine. *A Woman's View: How Hollywood Spoke to Women 1930–1960.* New York: Alfred A. Knopf, 1993.

Baxter, John. *The Hollywood Exiles.* London: Macdonald and Jane's, 1976.

Bayley, John. "Introduction." In Henry James, *The Wings of the Dove*, 7–31. Harmondsworth: Penguin Books, 1986.

Bedford, Karen Everhart. "Drama Plan Emerging: PBS Looks to Multiple Sources for American Works," *Current*, July 27, 1998. www.current.org/prog/prog813d.html (accessed June 27, 2005).

"Behind the Scenes of '*Somewhere in Time*.'" *American Cinematographer* (July 1980): 669.

Beidler, Peter G. *Ghosts, Demons and Henry James: The Turn of the Screw at the Turn of the Century.* Columbia: University of Missouri Press, 1989.

Belafonte, Dennis, and Alvin H. Marill. *The Films of Tyrone Power.* Secaucus, NJ: Citadel Press, 1979.

Bell, Michael Davitt. *The Problem of American Realism: Studies in the Cultural History of an Idea.* Chicago: University of Chicago Press, 1993.

Bentley, Nancy. "Conscious Observation of a Lovely Woman: Jane Campion's *Portrait* in Film." *Henry James Review* 18 (1997): 174–79.

Bergman, Andrew. *We're in the Money: Depression America and Its Films.* New York: Harper Colophon Books, 1971.

Bergson, Philip. "Feeling the Quality." *What's On* (London), September 27, 1984.

Bernstein, Matthew. *Walter Wanger: Hollywood Independent.* Minneapolis: University of Minnesota Press, 1994.

Berry, Neil. "Enduring Ephemera: James Cellan Jones, Henry James and the BBC." In *Henry James on Stage and Screen*, edited by John R. Bradley, 119–27. Basingstoke: Palgrave, 2000.

Besas, Peter. "The Turn of the Screw." *Variety*, November 2, 1992.

Bewley, Marius. *The Complex Fate: Hawthorne, Henry James and Some Other American Writers.* New York: Gordian Press, 1967.

Biography of Susan Hayward. Los Angeles: Paramount Pictures Press Release, 1943.

Birdsall, Eric. "Interpreting Henry James: Bogdanovich's *Daisy Miller*." *Literature Film Quarterly* 22, no. 4 (1994): 272–78.

Blackmur, R. P. "In the Country of the Blue." *Kenyon Review* 5, no. 4 (Autumn 1943): 690–97.

Bousquet, Marc. "Cultural Capitalism and the 'James Formation.'" In *Henry James Goes to the Movies*, edited by Susan M. Griffin, 210–40. Lexington: University Press of Kentucky, 2002.

Bradbury, Nicola. "Filming James." *Essays in Criticism* 29, no. 4 (October 1979): 293–301.

Bradley, John R., ed. *Henry James on Stage and Screen.* London: Palgrave, 2002.

Braun, Eric. *Deborah Kerr.* London: W. H. Allen, 1977.

Brosnan, John. "Somewhere in Time." *Starburst* 1, no. 7 (1981): 16–17.

Brown, Geoff. "Nasty Bugs but Nastier People." *The Times* (London), January 1, 1998.

Buckley, Leonard. "The Golden Bowl." *The Times* (London), May 5, 1972.

Butler, Alison. *Women's Cinema: The Contested Screen*. London: Wallflower Press, 2002.

Butler, Ivan. *Horror in the Cinema*. 3rd ed. Cranbury, NJ: A. S. Barnes, 1979.

Byars, Jackie. *All That Hollywood Allows: Re-Reading Gender in 1950s Melodrama*. London: Routledge, 1991.

"Call Yourself a Scientist!—*The Turn of the Screw* (1992)." http://twtd.bluemountains.net.au/Rick/liz_ts.htm (accessed January 25, 2004).

Calta, Louis. "The Innocents." *New York Times*, April 21, 1959.

Cardwell, Sarah. *Adaptation Revisited: Television and the Classic Novel*. Manchester: Manchester University Press, 2002.

Carlson, Jerry. "*Washington Square* and *The Heiress*: Comparing Artistic Forms." In *The Classic American Novel and the Movies*, edited by Gerald Peary and Roger Shatzkin, 86–110. New York: Frederick Unger, 1977.

Caughie, John. *Television Drama: Realism, Modernism and British Culture*. Cambridge: Cambridge University Press, 2000.

Chandler, Karen Michele. "Agency and Social Constraint in Jane Campion's *The Portrait of a Lady*." *Henry James Review* 18 (1997): 191–93.

———. "Her Ancient Faculty of Silence: Catherine Sloper's Ways of Being in James's *Washington Square* and Two Film Adaptations." In *Henry James Goes to the Movies*, edited by Susan M. Griffin, 170–90. Lexington: University Press of Kentucky, 2002.

Chase, Donald. "Clayton's *The Innocents*." *Film Comment* 34, no. 1 (January/February 1998): 56–73.

Cherry, Brigid. "Refusing to Refuse to Look: Female Viewers of the Horror Film." In *The Horror Film Reader*, edited by Mark Jancovich, 169–79. London: Routledge, 2002.

Cheshire, Ellen. *The Pocket Essential: Jane Campion*. Harpenden, UK: Pocket Essentials, 2000.

Chopin, Kate. *The Awakening*. New York: Bantam Books, 1982.

Ciment, Michel. "Voyage to Discover Herself." In *Jane Campion Interviews*, edited by Virginia Wright Wexman, 178–85. Jackson: University Press of Mississippi, 1999.

Clayton, Jack. "Accepting the Challenge." *Films and Filming* (December 1961): 7.

A Code to Govern the Making of Motion and Talking Pictures: The Reasons Supporting It and the Resolution for Uniform Interpretation. Hollywood: Motion Picture Producers and Distributors of America, 1934.

Coleman, John. "Amusette." *New Statesman* (London), December 1, 1961.

Collier, Lionel. "The Greatest Romance of the Year." *Picturegoer* (November 11, 1933): 14.

———. "On the Screens Now." *Picturegoer* (April 7, 1934): 26.

Considine, Shaun. *Bette and Joan: The Divine Feud*. London: Century Hutchinson, 1989.

Cook, Jim. "On a Clear Day You Can See Forever." *Movie* 24 (February 1977): 61–62.

Cooke, Alistair. *A Decade of Masterpiece Theatre: Masterpieces*. New York: Alfred A. Knopf, 1981.

Coupland, Douglas. *Generation X: Tales for an Accelerated Culture*. New York: St. Martin's Press, 1991.

Creed, Barbara. *The Monstrous-Feminine: Film, Feminism, Psychoanalysis*. London: Routledge, 1993.

Critchley, Julian. "Divorce as a Holiday Theme." *The Times* (London), June 3, 1968.

Crnkovic, Gordana P. "Interview with Agnieszka Holland." *Film Quarterly* 52, no. 2 (1999): 2–9.

Cross, David. "Framing the 'Sketch': Bogdanovich's *Daisy Miller*." In *Henry James on Stage and Screen*, edited by John R. Bradley, 127–43. London: Palgrave, 2000.

Deutsch, Helene. *The Psychology of Women*. 2 vols. New York: Grune & Stratton, 1944–45.

Doane, Mary Ann. *The Desire to Desire: The Woman's Film of the 1940s*. Basingstoke: Macmillan Press, 1988.

Douglas, Ann. *The Feminization of American Culture*. New York: Anchor Books, 1988.

Douglas, Susan J. *Where the Girls Are: Growing Up Female with the Mass Media*. New York: Random House, 1995.

Doyle, Carol. *Washington Square: A Screenplay*. Los Angeles: Hollywood Pictures, 1997.

Eaton, Mark. "Henry James Films as Middle-Brow Culture." In *Henry James on Stage and Screen*, edited by John R. Bradley, 157–77. London: Palgrave, 2000.

Eckert, Charles. "The Carole Lombard in Macy's Window." In *Movies and Mass Culture*, edited by John Belton, 95–119. London: Athlone Press, 1996.

Ellis, John. *Visible Fictions: Cinema: Television: Video*. London: Routledge, 1982.

Engleman, Ralph. *Public Radio and Television in America: A Political History*. London: Sage, 1996.

"Excellent Version of *The Turn of the Screw*." December 23, 1999. http://uk.imdb.com/ title/tt0113271 (accessed June 23, 2005).

Facts and Figures about Public Broadcasting in America. Washington, DC: Corporation for Public Broadcasting, 1991.

Felman, Shoshana. "Turning the Screw of Interpretation." In *Literature and Psychoanalysis: The Question of Reading: Otherwise*, edited by Shoshana Felman, 94–208. Baltimore: Johns Hopkins University Press, 1977.

Ferguson, Ken. "A Tribute to a Great Actress." *Films and Filming* (April 1970): 24–25.

Fleck, David John. "On a Clear Day . . . Lucid Fantasies." *Cinéfantastique* 3 (Winter 1978): 47–54.

Fluck, Winfried. "Power Relations in the Novels of James: The 'Liberal' and the 'Radical' Version." In *Enacting History in Henry James: Narrative, Power and Ethics*, edited by Gert Buelens, 15–37. Cambridge: Cambridge University Press, 1997.

Foss, Chris. "Female Innocence as Other in *The Portrait of a Lady* and *What Maisie Knew*: Reassessing the Feminist Recuperation of Henry James." *Essays in Literature*, September 22, 1995. www.highbeam.com/library/doc3.asp?DOCID = 1P1:28616278&refid = ip_almanac_hf&ctrlInfo = Round9d%3AProd2%3ATYF%3AContinue (accessed January 31, 2004).

Fox, Jordan R. "Somewhere in Time with Jeannot Szwarc." *Cinéfantastique* 10, no. 4 (Spring 1981): 14–19.

Freedman, Jonathan. "The Moment of Henry James." In *The Cambridge Companion to Henry James*, edited by Jonathan Freedman, 1–21. Cambridge: Cambridge University Press, 1998.

―――. *Professions of Taste: Henry James, British Aestheticism and Commodity Culture.* Stanford, CA: Stanford University Press, 1990.

Freeland, Cynthia A. "Feminist Frameworks for Horror Films." In *Post-Theory: Reconstructing Film Studies,* edited by David Bordwell and Noel Carroll, 195–219. Madison: University of Wisconsin Press, 1996.

French, Philip. "Somewhere in Time." *The Observer,* January 4, 1981.

Freud, Sigmund. "A Child Is Being Beaten" (1919). In *Sexuality and the Psychology of Love,* edited by Philip Rieff, 114–38. New York: Collier Books, 1963.

―――. "The Uncanny." In *The Standard Edition of the Works of Sigmund Freud,* vol. 17 (1917–19), translated by James Strachey, 219–56. London: Hogarth Press / Institute of Psychoanalysis, 1971. (Original edition 1955.)

Friedan, Betty. *The Feminine Mystique.* Harmondsworth: Penguin Books, 1965.

Frischkorn, Craig. "Frank Lloyd's *Berkeley Square* (1933): Re-adapting Henry James's *The Sense of the Past." Literature Film Quarterly* 28, no. 1 (2000): 3–9.

Fussell, Edwin Sill. *The Catholic Side of Henry James.* Cambridge: Cambridge University Press, 1993.

Gaines, Jane. "Women and Representation." In *Issues in Feminist Film,* edited by Patricia Erens, 75–92. Bloomington: Indiana University Press, 1990.

Garnett, Tay. "William Wyler." In *Directing: Learn from the Masters,* edited by Anthony Slide. Lanham MD: Scarecrow Press, 1996.

Gelder, Ken. "Jane Campion and the Limits of Literary Cinema." In *Adaptation: From Text to Screen, Screen to Text,* edited by Deborah Cartmell and Imelda Whelehan, 157–71. London: Routledge, 1998.

Gentile, Mary C. *Film Feminisms: Theory and Practice.* Westport, CT: Greenwood Press, 1985.

Gibbs, Wolcott. "Black Magic and Bundling." *New Yorker,* February 11, 1950.

Gibson, Susie. "The Terror of Representation: The Difficulty of Filming the Novels of Henry James." *Metro Magazine* 117 (1998): 42–49.

Giddings, Robert, and Keith Selby. *The Classic Serial on Television and Radio.* Basingstoke: Palgrave, 2001.

Gilbert, Sandra M., and Susan Gubar. "Infection in the Sentence: The Woman Writer and the Anxiety of Authorship (1979)." In *Feminisms: An Anthology of Literary Theory and Criticism,* edited by Robyn R. Warhol and Diane Price Herndl, 21–33. New Brunswick, NJ: Rutgers University Press, 1997.

Gilliatt, Penelope. "The Innocents." *The Observer* (London), November 26, 1961.

Gledhill, Christine. "Between Melodrama and Realism." In *Hollywood Narrative: The Paradigm Wars,* edited by Jane Gaines, 129–69. Durham: Duke University Press, 1992.

―――. "The Melodramatic Field: An Investigation. *Home Is Where the Heart Is: Studies in Melodrama and the Woman's Film,* edited by Christine Gledhill. London: British Film Institute, 1987.

Goetz, Ruth, and Augustus Goetz. *The Heiress: A Play.* London: Samuel French, 1979.

Goudas, John N. "More Than One Day in Valerie Bertinelli's Life." *TV Key,* November 30, 1995. www.newstimes.com/archive95/dec0195/tvd.htm (accessed June 7, 2003).

Graham, Wendy. *Henry James' Thwarted Love.* Stanford, CA: Stanford University Press, 1999.

―――. "The Rift in the Loot: Cognitive Dissonance for the Reader of Merchant Ivory's

The Golden Bowl." In Henry James Goes to the Movies, edited by Susan M. Griffin, 303–30. Lexington: University Press of Kentucky, 2002.

Gray, Beverly. Roger Corman: An Unauthorized Biography of the Godfather of Indie Film-Making. Los Angeles: Renaissance Books, 2000.

Greer, Germaine. The Whole Woman. London: Transworld, 1999.

Griffin, Susan M., ed. Henry James Goes to the Movies. Lexington: University Press of Kentucky, 2002.

———. "Introduction." Henry James Review 22, no. 3 (Fall 2001): 215–16.

Groombridge, Brian. Television and the People: A Programme for Democratic Reform. Harmondsworth: Penguin Books, 1972.

Gunn, Hartford. "Public Television Program Financing: A Proposal for the PBS Station Program Cooperative (SPC)." Educational Broadcasting Review, October 1972. www.current.org/pbpb/documents/spc72.html (accessed November 25, 2005).

Gunning, Tom. "The Cinema of Attractions: Early Film, Its Spectator and the Avant-Garde." In Early Cinema: Space, Frame, Narrative, edited by Thomas Elsaesser, 46–69. London: BFI Publishing, 1990.

Halliwell, Martin. "Transcultural Aesthetics and the Film Adaptations of Henry James." In Classics in Film and Fiction, edited by Deborah Cartmell, I. Q Hunter, Heidi Kaye, and Imelda Whelehan, 68–97. London: Pluto Press.

Hansberry, Karen Burroughs. "Susan Hayward." In Femme Noir: Bad Girls of Film, 247–55. Jefferson, NC: McFarland, 1998.

Haralson, Eric. Henry James and Queer Modernity. Cambridge: Cambridge University Press, 2003.

Harding, Bill. The Films of Michael Winner. London: Frederick Muller, 1978.

Harris, Thomas J. Bogdanovich's Picture Shows. Metuchen, NJ: Scarecrow Press, 1990.

Hasted, Nick. "The Wings of the Dove." The Independent (London), January 2, 1998.

Hastings, Michael. The Nightcomers: A Screenplay. London: Scimitar Films, 1971.

———. The Nightcomers—A Speculation. London: Pan Books, 1973.

Havill, Adrian. Man of Steel: The Career and Courage of Christopher Reeve. London: Headline Book, 1996.

Hawthorne, Nathaniel. "The Custom House: Introductory Sketch." In The Scarlet Letter, 2–34. Harmondsworth: Penguin Books, 1994.

Hedges, Elaine R. "Afterword." In The Yellow Wallpaper, by Charlotte Perkins Gilman, 50–55. New York: Feminist Press, 1973.

Heilbrun, Carolyn G. Towards a Recognition of Androgyny. New York: Harper and Row, 1973.

Heilman, Robert B. "'The Turn of the Screw as Poem." Modern Language Notes (November 1947): 433–45.

Herman, Jan. A Talent for Trouble: The Life of Hollywood's Most Acclaimed Director, William Wyler. New York: G. P. Putnam's Sons, 1996.

Higham, Charles. Olivia and Joan: A Biography of Olivia de Havilland and Joan Fontaine. Sevenoaks, Kent: New English Library, 1984.

Higson, Andrew. Dissolving Views: Key Writings on British Cinema. London: Cassell, 1996.

———. English Heritage, English Cinema: Costume Drama since 1980. Oxford: Oxford University Press, 2003.

———. "Re-presenting the National Past: Nostalgia and Pastiche in the Heritage Film."

In *Fires Were Started*, edited by Lester Friedman, 93–110. Minneapolis: University of Minnesota Press, 1993.

Hill, John. *British Cinema in the 80s*. Oxford: Clarendon Press, 1999.

Himmelstein, Hal. *Television Myth and the American Mind*. 2nd ed. Westport, CT: Praeger, 1994.

Hipsky, Martin A. "Why Does America Watch Merchant-Ivory Movies?" *Journal of Popular Film and Television* 22, no. 3 (Fall 1994): 79–106.

Hirsh, Allen. "The Europeans: Henry James, James Ivory, and that Nice Mr. Emerson," *Literature Film Quarterly* 11, no. 2 (1983): 112–18.

Hocks, Richard A. "Recanonizing the Multiple Canons of Henry James." In *American Realism and the Canon*, edited by Tom Quirk and Gary Scharnhorst, 146–70. Newark: University of Delaware Press, 1994.

Hodges, Mike. "The Screw Turns Again: *Presence of Mind*." *Fangoria* 4 (July 2001): 55–58.

Holtz, Geoffrey T. *Welcome to the Jungle: The Why behind Generation X*. New York: St. Martins Griffin, 1995.

Horne, Philip. "The James Gang." *Sight and Sound* (January 1998): 12–19.

———. "Varieties of Cinematic Experience." In *Henry James on Stage and Screen*, edited by John R. Bradley, 35–56. London: Palgrave, 2000.

Horner, Harry. "Designing *The Heiress*." *Hollywood Quarterly* 5, no. 1 (Autumn 1950): 2.

"The House by the Cemetery." *Lightsfade Reviews*. www.lightsfade.com/reviews/houseby.htm (accessed March 3, 2005).

"House in the Square." *Variety*, October 12, 1951.

———. *Variety*, December 11, 1951.

Houston, Penelope. "The Bostonians on Location." *Sight and Sound* 53, no. 1 (Winter 1984): 2–3.

Howard, Leslie Ruth. *A Quite Remarkable Father*. London: Longmans Green, 1959.

Hozic, Aida A. "Hollywood Goes on Sale: or, What Do the Violet Eyes of Elizabeth Taylor Have to Do with the 'Cinema of Attractions'?" In *Hollywood Goes Shopping*, edited by David Dessner and Garth S. Jowett, 205–22. Minneapolis: University of Minnesota Press, 2000.

Hutchings, Peter. *Hammer and Beyond: The British Horror Film*. Manchester: Manchester University Press, 2000.

Ian, Marcia. "How to Do Things with Words: Making Language Immaterial in *The Wings of the Dove*." In *Henry James on Stage and Screen*, edited by John R. Bradley, 212–40. London: Palgrave, 2000.

Irigaray, Luce. "Women-amongst-Themselves: Creating a Woman-to-Woman Sociality." In *The Irigaray Reader*, edited by Margaret Whitford, 190–97. Oxford: Basil Blackwell, 1991.

Ivory, James. "Imagining *The Golden Bowl*." www.merchantivory.com/goldenbowl/ivory.html (accessed October 26, 2005).

———. "The Trouble with Olive: Divine Madness in Massachusetts." *Sight and Sound* 54, no. 2 (Spring 1985): 95–100.

Izzo, Donatello. *Portraying the Lady: Technologies of Gender in the Short Stories of Henry James*. Lincoln: University of Nebraska Press, 2001.

James, Henry. *The American*, edited by William Spengemann. Harmondsworth: Penguin Books, 1986.

――――. *The American Novels and Stories of Henry James.* Vol. 1, edited by F. O. Matthiessen. New York: Alfred A. Knopf, 1947.

――――. *The Aspern Papers and The Turn of the Screw*, edited by Anthony Curtis. Harmondsworth: Penguin Classics, 1986.

――――. *The Bostonians*, edited by Charles B. Anderson. Harmondsworth: Penguin Classics, 1986.

――――. *The Complete Notebooks*, edited by Leon Edel and Lyall H. Powers. New York: Oxford University Press, 1987.

――――. *Eight Uncollected Tales of Henry James*, edited by Edna Kenton. New Brunswick, NJ: Rutgers University Press, 1950.

――――. *The Europeans.* Harmondsworth: Penguin Books, 1964.

――――. *The Golden Bowl*, edited by Patricia Crick. Harmondsworth: Penguin Books, 1987.

――――. *The Jolly Corner and Other Tales*, edited by Roger Gard. Harmondsworth: Penguin Books, 1990.

――――. *Letters, 1875–1883.* 2 vols., edited by Leon Edel. Cambridge, MA: Belknap Press of Harvard University Press, 1975.

――――. *A Life in Letters*, edited by Philip Horne. Harmondsworth: Penguin Books, 2000.

――――. *The Portrait of a Lady.* Harmondsworth: Penguin Books, 1979.

――――. *Selected Short Stories*, edited by Michael Swan. Harmondsworth: Penguin Books, 1963.

――――. *The Sense of the Past.* London: W. Collins, n.d.

――――. *The Turn of the Screw, The Aspern Papers and Other Stories*, edited by Michael Swan. London: Collins, 1963.

――――. *Washington Square*, edited by Michael Swan. Harmondsworth: Penguin Books, 1963.

――――. *The Wings of the Dove*, edited by John Bayley with notes by Patricia Crick. Harmondsworth: Penguin Books, 1986.

Jancovich, Mark. "Genre and the Audience: Genre Classifications and Cultural Distinctions in the Mediation of *The Silence of the Lambs.*" In *The Horror Film Reader*, edited by Mark Jancovich, 151–63. London: Routledge, 2002.

――――. *Rational Fears: American Horror in the 1950s.* Manchester: Manchester University Press, 1996.

Johnston, Sheila. "Harvey Keitel: No Time to Look Back." *Independent* (London), April 29, 2005.

Jones, Alan. "Turn of the Screw." *Shivers: The Global Magazine of Horror*, no. 6 (March 1993): 19–21.

Jones, Laura. *The Portrait of a Lady: The Screenplay Based on the Novel by Henry James.* Harmondsworth: Penguin Books, 1997.

Kaye, Heidi, and Imelda Whelehan. *Classics in Film and Fiction.* London: Pluto Press, 2000.

Kellner, Douglas. "Hollywood and Society," 1996. www.gseis.ucla.edu/courses/ed253a/Mckellner/HOLSOC.html (accessed December 15, 2003).

Kimmel, Michael. *Manhood in America: A Cultural History.* New York: Free Press, 1996.

King, Geoff. *New Hollywood Cinema: An Introduction.* London: I. B. Tauris, 2002.

Klinger, Barbara. *Melodrama and Meaning: History, Culture and the Films of Douglas Sirk.* Bloomington: Indiana University Press, 1994.

Kobal, John. *Gotta Sing Gotta Dance: A Pictorial History of Film Musicals.* London: Hamlyn, 1971.

Koch, J. Sarah. "A Henry James Filmography." In *Henry James Goes to the Movies,* edited by Susan M. Griffin, 335–57. Lexington: University Press of Kentucky, 2002.

Kuhn, Annette. *Women's Pictures: Feminism and Cinema.* London: Routledge and Kegan Paul, 1982.

L. H. C. "The Heiress." *Today's Cinema* (London) 6062 (August 18, 1950): 9.

Landis, Judson J., and Mary G. Landis. *Building a Successful Marriage.* New York: Prentice-Hall, 1948.

Lasky, Jesse. *I Blow My Own Horn.* London: Victor Gollancz, 1957.

Lauritza, Monica. *Jane Austen's Emma on Television: A Study of a BBC Classic Serial.* Göteborg: Acta Universitatis Gothoburgensis, 1981.

Lavery, Brian. "Ireland Shaken by Sex Abuse Report." *New York Times,* November 13, 2005. www.iht.com/articles/2005/11/13/news/ireland.php (accessed November 15, 2005).

Leavis, F. R. *The Great Tradition.* Harmondsworth: Peregrine Books, 1983. (Original edition, 1948.)

Leff, Leonard J. *Hitchcock and Selznick: The Rich and Strange Collaboration of Alfred Hitchcock and David O. Selznick in Hollywood.* Berkeley: University of California Press, 1987.

Lidz, Franz, and Steve Rushin. "How to Tell a Bad Movie from a Truly Bad Movie." *New York Times,* August 5, 2001.

Long, Robert Emmet. *The Films of Merchant Ivory.* New York: Harry N. Abrams, 1997.

———. *James Ivory in Conversation: How Merchant-Ivory Makes Its Movies.* Berkeley: University of California Press, 2005.

"The Lost Moment." *Monthly Film Bulletin* 16, no. 182 (February 1949): 25.

"The Lost Moment: Spotlight Reviews." www.amazon.com/exec/obidos/tg/detail/-/63002 08664/qid = 1134593736/sr = 8–2/ref = sr_8_xs_ap_i2_xg127/103–5655956–4230241? v = glance&s = video&n = 507846 (accessed December 14, 2005).

Lundberg, Ferdinand, and Maryna Farnham. *Modern Woman: The Lost Sex.* New York: Grosset & Dunlap / Universal Library, 1947.

Lustig, T. J. *Henry James and the Ghostly.* Cambridge: Cambridge University Press, 1994.

Madsen, Axel. *William Wyler: The Authorized Biography.* New York: Thomas Y. Crowell, 1973.

Mankofsky, Isodore. "Filming in the Time Warp of Two Different Eras." *American Cinematographer* (July 1980): 683, 686.

Matthiessen, F. O. "Introduction." In *The American Novels and Stories of Henry James,* by Henry James. New York: Alfred A.Knopf, 1947.

———. *Henry James: The Major Phase.* London: Oxford University Press, 1944.

May, Elaine Tyler. *Homeward Bound: American Families in the Cold War Era.* New York: Basic Books, 1988.

Mazzella, Anthony J. "The Story . . . Held Us: *The Turn of the Screw* from Henry James to Jack Clayton." In *Henry James Goes to the Movies,* edited by Susan M. Griffin, 11–34. Lexington: University Press of Kentucky, 2002.

MacDougall, Ranald. "I'll Never Forget You." Unpublished script No. 53493. Los Angeles: Twentieth Century-Fox Film, 1951.

Macnab, Geoffrey. "A Harsh Look at Life in the Square." *Independent Eye* (May 8, 1998): 10–11.

Mayne, Judith. *Cinema and Spectatorship.* London: Routledge, 1993.

McClelland, Doug. *The Complete Life Story of Susan Hayward, Immortal Screen Star.* New York: Pinnacle Books, 1973.

McCormack, Peggy. "Reexamining Bogdanovich's *Daisy Miller.*" In *Henry James Goes to the Movies,* edited by Susan M. Griffin, 34–60. Lexington: University Press of Kentucky, 2002.

McDonald, Paul. "Reconceptualising Stardom." In *Stars,* edited by Richard Dyer, 175–201. London: BFI Publishing, 1998.

McRobbie, Angela. *Feminism and Youth Culture.* London: Macmillan Press, 1991.

McWhirter, David. "In the 'Other House' of Fiction: Writing, Authority and Femininity in *The Turn of the Screw.*" In *New Essays on Daisy Miller and The Turn of the Screw,* edited by Vivian R. Pollak, 121–49. Cambridge: Cambridge University Press, 1993.

"Memories of Susan Hayward." www.geocities.com/audrey_64063/mythoughtsonsusan.html (accessed July 16, 2002).

Miller, Laura. Review of Douglas Coupland, *Girlfriend in a Coma. New York Times,* April 12, 1998, sec. 7.

Milne, Tom. "Retrospective: 'The Lost Moment.'" *Monthly Film Bulletin,* no. 593 (January 1983): 170–71.

Mitchell, Lee Clark. "Based on the Novel by Henry James." In *Henry James Goes to the Movies,* edited by Susan M. Griffin, 297–321. Lexington: University Press of Kentucky, 2002.

"Mobil Masterpiece Theatre's Collection to Premiere on PBS." Press release, July 14, 1998. www.cpb.org/programs/pr.php?prn = 163 (accessed June 27, 2005).

Modleski, Tania. *The Women Who Knew Too Much: Hitchcock and Feminist Film Theory.* London: Methuen, 1988.

Moore, Daniel S. "Picture Perfect" *Variety,* October 28, 1996.

Muir, John Kenneth. *Terror Television: American Series 1970–1999.* Jefferson, NC: McFarland, 1999.

Mulvey, Laura. *Visual and Other Pleasures.* London: Macmillan Press, 1989.

Murphy, Kathleen. "Jane Campion's Shining: Portrait of a Director." *Film Comment* 36, no. 5 (1996): 29–33.

Nadel, Alan. "Ambassadors from an Imaginary 'Elsewhere': Cinematic Convention and the Jamesian Sensibility." In *Henry James Goes to the Movies,* edited by Susan M. Griffin, 193–210. Lexington: University Press of Kentucky, 2002.

Neale, Steve. *Genre and Hollywood.* London: Routledge, 2000.

Nicholls, Mark. "She Who Gets Slapped: Jane Campion's *Portrait of a Lady.*" *Metro* 111 (August 1997): 43–47.

Niebuhr, Reinhold. "Our Country and Our Culture." *Partisan Review* 29, no. 3 (May–June 1952): 300–302.

"The Nightcomers." *Film Facts* (April 1972): 84–86.

"Nightmare Classics: *The Turn of the Screw.*" Los Angeles: Viacom, 1989.

O'Neil, Caitlin. "Adapting the Master" (Interview with Paul Unwin). www.pbs.org/wgbh/masterpiece/americancollection/adapting.html (accessed June 27, 2005).

"Origin and History of a Queen of Demosthenes." www.nccg.org/deliverance/demons01-Hecate.html (accessed August 13, 2005).

Orr, John. "Introduction: Proust, the Movie." In Cinema and Fiction 1950–90: New Modes of Adapting, edited by John Orr and Colin Nicholson. Edinburgh: Edinburgh University Press, 1992.

Orr, John, and Colin Nicholson. Cinema and Fiction 1950–90: New Modes of Adapting. Edinburgh: Edinburgh University Press, 1992.

Palmer, James W. "Cinematic Ambiguity: James's The Turn of the Screw and Clayton's The Innocents." Literature Film Quarterly 5 (1977): 198–214.

Parish, James Robert, and Don E. Starke. The Swashbucklers. New Rochelle, NY: Arlington House, 1976.

Peary, Gerald. "The House by the Cemetery." Boston Phoenix, June 15, 1998. www.filmvault.com/filmvault/boston/h/housebythecemeter1.html (accessed September 6, 2005).

Person, Leland, S. Henry James and the Suspense of Masculinity. Philadelphia: University of Pennsylvania Press, 2003.

———. "Still Me(n): Superman Meets The Bostonians." In Henry James Goes to the Movies, edited by Susan M. Griffin, 99–127. Lexington: University Press of Kentucky, 2002.

Petley, Julian. English Gothic: A History of Horror in Cinema. Richmond, Surrey: Reynolds and Hearn, 2000.

Pidduck, Julianne. Contemporary Costume Film. London: BFI Publishing, 2004.

———. "Of Windows and Country Walks: Frames of Space and Movement in 1990s Austen Adaptations." Screen 39, no. 4 (Winter 1998): 381–400.

Pirie, David. A Heritage of Horror: The English Gothic Cinema 1946–72. London: Gordon Fraser, 1973.

Poirier, Richard. The Comic Sense of Henry James: A Study of the Early Novels. New York: Oxford University Press, 1960.

Poole, Adrian. Henry James. Hemel Hempstead: Harvester Wheatsheaf, 1991.

Porter, Carolyn. "Gender and Value in The American." In New Essays on The American, edited by Martha Banta, 95–112. Cambridge: Cambridge University Press, 1987.

Powers, James. "Koch Produced, Minnelli Helmed." Hollywood Reporter, June 17, 1970.

Press book: Berkeley Square. Los Angeles: Fox Film Corporation, 1933.

Press book: Daisy Miller. Los Angeles: Paramount Pictures Corporation, 1974.

Press book: The Heiress. Los Angeles: Paramount Pictures Corporation, 1949.

Press book: The Lost Moment. Los Angeles: Universal International Pictures, 1947.

Press book: Washington Square. Los Angeles: Hollywood Pictures, 1997.

Press book: The Wings of the Dove. Los Angeles: Miramax Films / Renaissance Dove, 1997.

Production Notes: Somewhere in Time. Los Angeles: Universal City, 1980.

Production Notes: The Portrait of a Lady. Beverly Hills, CA: Gramercy Pictures, 1996.

Program Notes, National Film Theatre Season: Merchant Ivory at Twenty-One. London: National Film Theatre, 1982.

Public Broadcasting Service. www.pbs.org/wgbh/masterpiece/americancollection/index.html (accessed June 27, 2005).

Putt, S. Gorley. A Reader's Guide to Henry James. Ithaca, NY: Cornell University Press, 1966.

Raw, Laurence. "Corman Revisits the Classics: *The Haunting of Hell House* (1999)." In *Shadows That Stalk: Representations of Fear in American Culture. Proceedings of the 20th Anniversary Conference, 24–25 October 2002*, edited by Bilge Mutluay, 177–85. Ankara: Hacettepe University / State University of New York at Buffalo, 2003.

———. "Hollywoodizing Henry James: Jack Clayton's *The Innocents* (1961)." *Henry James Review* 25, no. 1 (March 2004): 36–61.

———. "Horrific Henry James: Michael Winner's *The Nightcomers* (1971)." *Literature Film Quarterly* 31, no. 3 (2003): 193–99.

———. "James Cellan Jones's View of Female Potential in *The Portrait of a Lady* (1968) and *The Golden Bowl* (1972)." *Henry James E-Journal* no. 7. September 2003. www2 .newpaltz.edu/~hathawar/ejourn7.html (accessed November 6, 2005).

———. "Making Meaning: Publicizing Iain Softley's *The Wings of the Dove* (1997)." *Literature Film Quarterly* 32, no. 3 (2004): 175–81.

———. "Observing Femininity: Peter Bogdanovich's *Daisy Miller*." *Henry James E-Journal*, no. 4. 2001. www.newpaltz.edu/~hathaway/ejourn4.htm (accessed January 22, 2003).

———. "Preserving Henry James' *Sense of the Past: On a Clear Day You Can See Forever* (1970) and *Somewhere in Time* (1980)." *Interactions* 13, no. 1 (Spring 2004): 81–91.

———. "Reconstructing Henry James: *The Heiress*." *Literature Film Quarterly* 30, no. 4 (2002): 243–49.

———. "Rethinking the Costume Drama; Agnieszka Holland's *Washington Square*." *Henry James Review* 24, no. 1 (Winter 2003): 69–82.

Rebello, Stephen. "Jack Clayton's *The Innocents*." *Cinéfantastique* 13, no. 3 (Autumn 1983): 13–17.

Recchia, Edward. "An Eye for an I—Adapting Henry James's *The Turn of the Screw* to the Screen." *Literature Film Quarterly* 15 (1987): 28–35.

Rinaldi, Lou. "Lucio Fulci Interview." *Starburst* 4, no. 12, August 1982. www.shockingi-mages.com/fulci/interview2.html (accessed March 3, 2005).

Ritchie, Karen. *Marketing to Generation X*. New York: Lexington Books, 1995.

Rivkin, Julie H. "Prospects of Entertainment: Film Adaptations of *Washington Square*." In *Henry James Goes to the Movies*, edited by Susan M. Griffin, 147–67. Lexington: University Press of Kentucky, 2002.

Rosen, Marjorie. *Popcorn Venus: Women and Their Sexuality in the New Film*. London: Davis-Poynter, 1975.

"Rotten Tomatoes: The Golden Bowl: Critics Tomatometer." 2001. www.rottentoma toes.com/m/golden_bowl (accessed October 21, 2005).

Rowbotham, Sheila. *Woman's Consciousness, Man's World*. Harmondsworth: Penguin Books, 1973.

Rowe, John Carlos. "For Mature Audiences: Sex, Gender and Recent Film Adaptations of Henry James's Fiction." In *Henry James on Stage and Screen*, edited by John R. Bradley, 190–212. London: Palgrave, 2000.

Rushkoff, Douglas. *The GenX Reader*. New York: Ballantine Books, 1994.

Sadoff, Dianne F. "Hallucinations of Intimacy: The Henry James Films." In *Henry James Goes to the Movies*, edited by Susan M. Griffin, 254–81. Lexington: University Press of Kentucky, 2002.

Said, Edward. *Culture and Imperialism*. New York: Alfred A. Knopf, 1994.

Salmon, Richard. *Henry James and the Culture of Publicity*. Cambridge: Cambridge University Press, 1997.

Savoy, Eric. "The Queer Subject of 'The Jolly Corner.'" *Henry James Review* 20, no. 1 (Winter 1999): 1–21.

Scheib, Richard. "The Haunting of Hell House aka the Ghostly Rental." *SF Horror and Fantasy Film Review*. 2000. www.moria.co.nz/horror/hauntinghellhouse.htm (accessed September 6, 2005).

Schriefer, Amy. "Translating Third Wave Theory into Third Wave Activism." *Laughing Medusa: An Online Literary Journal of Women's Studies*. 2002. www.gwu.edu/~medusa/thirdwave.html (accessed December 7, 2005).

Selznick, David O. *Memo from David O. Selznick*, edited by Rudy Behlmer. New York: Modern Library, 2000.

"Selznick Gets Rights to 'Wings of the Dove.'" *New York Times*, October 25, 1944.

"Seven Questions with Iain Softley, the Director of 'The Wings of the Dove.'" 1997. www.indiewire.com/people/int_Softley_Iain_971120.html (accessed September 30, 2005).

Shields, John C. "*Daisy Miller*: Bogdanovich's Film and James's Nouvelle." *Literature Film Quarterly* 11, no. 2 (1983): 105–11.

Shindler, Colin. *Hollywood in Crisis: Cinema and American Society 1929–1939*. London: Routledge, 1996.

Shipman, David. *Marlon Brando*. London: Sphere Books, 1989.

Shubik, Irene. "Drama." In *The New Priesthood: British Television Today*, edited by Joan Bakewell and Nicholas Garnham, 87–98. London: Allen Lane/Penguin Press, 1970.

Shulgasser, Barbara. "Under Heaven: Bad Copy of 'Wings of the Dove.'" *San Francisco Examiner*, June 26, 1998. www.sfgate.com/cgi-bin/article.cgi?f=/e/a/1998/06/26/WEEKEND3821.dtl (accessed December 24, 2005).

Simon, John. "Jacobin—not Jacobite (1974)." *Reverse Angle: A Decade of American Films*, 153–55. New York: Crown, 1981.

Sindelar, Dave. "Berkeley Square" (1933). *Scifilm Musings*, October 3, 2002. www.scifilm.org/musings2/musing421.html (accessed September 7, 2005).

Sinyard, Neil. "Historian of Fine Consciousness: Henry James and the Cinema." In *Filming Literature: The Art of Screen Adaptation*, edited by Neil Sinyard, 26–40. London: Croom Helm, 1986.

———. *Jack Clayton*. Manchester: Manchester University Press, 2000.

———. "Pearl of Ambiguity: *The Innocents*." *Jack Clayton*. Manchester: Manchester University Press, 2000.

Skinner, Margo. "Michael Winner Directs Brando in 'The Nightcomers.'" *Hollywood Reporter*, October 14, 1971.

Slide, Anthony. *Directing: Learn from the Masters*. Lanham, MD: Scarecrow Press, 1996.

Smith, Dinitia. "Hollywood Trains Its Lights on a Master of Shadow." *New York Times*, October 30, 1996.

Solanas, Valerie. *S.C.U.M.: Society for Cutting Up Men Manifesto*. New York: Olympia Press, 1968.

Solomon, Aubrey. *Twentieth Century Fox: A Corporate Financial History*. Metuchen, NJ: Scarecrow Press, 1988.

Solomon, Barbara H. "Introduction." *Herland and Selected Stories by Charlotte Perkins Gilman*, xi–xxxi. New York: Signet Classics, 1992.

Sorensen, Sue. "'Damnable Feminization': The Merchant Ivory Film Adaptation of *The Bostonians.*" *Literature Film Quarterly* 25, no. 3 (Autumn 1997): 231–35.

Spigel, Lynn. *Make Room for TV: Television and the Family Ideal in Postwar America.* Chicago: University of Chicago Press, 1992.

Stacey, Jackie. "Feminine Fascinations: Forms of Identification in Star-Audience Relations." In *Stardom: Industry of Desire*, edited by Christine Gledhill, 146–75. London: Routledge, 1991.

———. *Star Gazing: Hollywood Cinema and Female Spectatorship.* London: Routledge, 1994.

Stam, Robert. "Introduction: The Theory and Practice of Adaptation." In *Literature and Film: A Guide to the Theory and Practice of Adaptation*, edited by Robert Stam and Alessandra Raengo, 1–59. Malden, MA: Blackwell, 2005.

———. "The Minnelli Magic." *Literature through Film: Realism, Magic and the Art of Adaptation*, 165–75. Malden, MA: Blackwell, 2005.

Stein, Ruthe. "Under Heaven: Love Triangle Focuses on Fatal Patient." *San Francisco Chronicle*, June 26, 1998. www.sfgate.com/cgi-bin/article.cgi?f = /c/a/1998/06/26/DD54053.DTL (accessed December 24, 2005).

Stern, Daniel. "An Ambitious New Series Brings the American Short Story to TV." *New York Times*, April 3, 1977.

Stevens, Hugh. "Queer Henry *In the Cage.*" In *The Cambridge Companion to Henry James*, edited by Jonathan Freedman, 120–39. Cambridge: Cambridge University Press, 1998.

Sutton, Shaun. *The Largest Theatre in the World: Thirty Years of Television Drama.* London: British Broadcasting Corporation, 1982.

Swaab, Peter. "The End of Embroidery: From *Washington Square* to *The Heiress.*" In *Henry James on Stage and Screen*, edited by John R. Bradley, 56–72. Basingstoke: Palgrave, 2000.

"A Talk with Diana Rigg." www.pbs.org/wgbh/masterpiece/americancollection/american/ei_rigg.html (accessed June 26, 2005).

Tambling, Jeremy. *Henry James.* Basingstoke: Macmillan Press, 2000.

Tanner, Tony. "Henry James: 'The Story in It'—and the Story without It." In *The American Mystery: American Literature from Emerson to DeLillo*, edited by Tony Tanner, 104–21. Cambridge: Cambridge University Press, 2000.

Tarlach, Gemma. "Out: 10 Years after Cobain, Can Grunge Speak to Spirit of a Generation?" *Milwaukee Journal Sentinel*, April 8, 2004.

Taubin, Amy. "Squaring Off." *Village Voice*, October 14, 1997.

Taylor, Paul. "The Lost Moment." *Time Out* (June 27–July 3, 1980): 50.

"This Week's General Releases." *Picture Show* 30, no. 780 (April 14, 1934): 21.

Thomas, Lyn. *Fans, Feminisms and "Quality" Media.* London: Routledge, 2002.

Thompson, Kristin. *Storytelling in the New Hollywood: Understanding Classical Narrative Technique.* Cambridge, MA: Harvard University Press, 1999.

Thornham, Sue. *Passionate Detachments: An Introduction to Feminist Film Theory.* London: Arnold, 1997.

Thrower, Stephen. *Beyond Terror: The Films of Lucio Fulci.* Guildford, UK: FAB Press, 1999.

Tittley, Mark. "Generation X Papers: The Postmodern Generation." www.tomorrowto-day.biz/generations/xpaper1005.htm (accessed October 2, 2005).

Turan, Kenneth. "Washington Square: A New Approach to an Old Address." *Los Angeles Times*, October 10, 1997.

"The Turn of the Screw." *Los Angeles Herald-Examiner*, April 22, 1974.

"The Turn of the Screw." *Video Business*, May 23, 1983.

Turner, Adrian, "Interview with William Wyler." *Films and Filming* 325 (October 1981): 14–16.

Universal News: Somewhere in Time. Los Angeles: Universal City, 1980.

Wagner, Rob. "The Movies: *Berkeley Square*." *Rob Wagner's Script*, November 25, 1933: 8.

Wald, Jerry. "This Is Why We'll Film James Joyce." *Films and Filming* (September 1958): 9, 30.

Wallace, Leonard. "Star-Spangled Weddings." *Picturegoer* (December 9, 1950): 10.

Waller, Gregory A. "Made-for-Television Horror Films." *American Horrors: Essays on the Modern Horror Film*, edited by Gregory A. Waller, 145–61. Urbana: University of Illinois Press, 1987.

Walton, Priscilla L. "Jane and James Go to the Movies: Post Colonial Portraits of a Lady." *Henry James Review* 18 (1997): 187–90.

Weiler, A. H. "Zodiac Couples Adds to Spate of Sex Films," *New York Times*, June 18, 1970.

Weinstein, Sheri. "Possessive Matters in the Ghostly Rental." *Henry James Review* 21 (2000): 270–78.

Weisbuch, Robert. "Henry James and the Idea of Evil." In *The Cambridge Companion to Henry James*, edited by Jonathan Freedman, 102–20. Cambridge: Cambridge University Press, 1998.

———. "Winterbourne and the Doom of Manhood in *Daisy Miller*." In *New Essays on Daisy Miller and The Turn of the Screw*, edited by Vivian R. Pollak, 65–89. Cambridge: Cambridge University Press, 1993.

Wendell, Susan. "Women and Disability." In *Encyclopedia of Feminist Theories*, edited by Lorraine Code, 136–39. London: Routledge, 2000.

"Where Could I Meet Other Screenwriters" (Interview with Ruth Prawer Jhabvala). *Sight and Sound* 48, no. 1 (Winter 1979): 18–20.

Williams, Linda. "Film Bodies: Gender, Genre and Excess." In *Feminist Film Theory: A Reader*, edited by Sue Thornham, 267–80. Edinburgh: Edinburgh University Press, 1999.

———. *Critical Desire: Psychoanalysis and the Literary Text*. London: Edward Arnold, 1995.

Williams, Richard. "Sex and Sensibility." *The Guardian*, January 2, 1998, sec. 2.

Williamson, Tom. "The History of the Men's Movement." *Men Freeing Men: Exploding the Myth of the Traditional Male*, edited by Francis Baumli. Jersey City, NJ: New Atlantis Press, 1985. www.amazoncastle.com/feminism/menhist.shtml (accessed November 27, 2005).

Wilson, Edmund. *The Triple Thinkers*. Harmondsworth: Pelican Books, 1962. (Original edition, 1948).

Wilson, Val. "Black and White and Shades of Grey: Ambiguity in *The Innocents*." In

Henry James on Stage and Screen, edited by John R. Bradley, 103–18. Basingstoke: Palgrave, 2000.

Wilson, Wendy. "*Washington Square*." *Rough Cut Reviews* (October 7, 1997):13.

Wiseman, Thomas. "Mr. Power Dismounts." *Evening Standard* (London), July 20, 1956.

———. "Susan Hayward Gives Me the Recipe for Her Marriage." *Evening Standard* (London), February 26, 1956, 7.

Wlaschin, Ken. "Liberated Women," *Films and Filming* (November 1971): 27.

Wolf, Matt. "In Time for Uncle Oscar." *The Times* (London), December 22, 1997.

Wood, Robin. "Images and Women." In *Hollywood from Vietnam to Reagan*, edited by Robin Wood, 202–21. New York: Columbia University Press, 1986.

———. *The Wings of the Dove*. London: BFI Publishing, 1999.

Wood, Thomas. "If You Knew Susie." *Picturegoer* (December 29, 1951): 8.

Woodward, Kathryn. *Identity and Difference*. London: Sage, 1997.

Wyatt, Justin. "The Formation of the 'Major Independent': Miramax, New Line and the New Hollywood." In *Contemporary Hollywood Cinema*, edited by Steve Neale and Murray Smith, 74–87. London: Routledge 1998.

Zaller, Robert. "*The Bostonians* and *Swann in Love:* A Note on the New Misogyny." *Film and History* 15, no. 4 (December 1985): 91–92.

Zielinski, Jerzy. "Zielinski Uses Newest Tools for 1850s Saga." *In Camera* (October 1997): 24.

Index

About the Author

Laurence Raw was educated at the Universities of Exeter and Sussex, U.K. He began his academic career at Bilkent University (Ankara, Turkey) and subsequently worked with the British Council for seven years. Since 1999, he has taught in the Department of American Culture and Literature, Baskent University, Ankara, Turkey. He has also taught at the Bosphorus University, Istanbul, and Ege University in Izmir.

His major publications include *Changing Class Attitudes* (1994) and *The Country and the City* (1997), plus a series of co-edited volumes in the Ege University Cultural Studies series, including *Crossing the Boundaries* (1997), *The Culture of History: The History of Culture* (1998), *Dialogue and Difference* (2000), and *New Cultural Perspectives in the New Millennium* (2001). He has also published extensively on adaptation in *Literature Film Quarterly* and the *Henry James Review*.